OXFORD READINGS IN SOCIO-LEGAL STUDIES

Family Law

OXFORD READINGS IN SOCIO-LEGAL STUDIES

Forthcoming titles in this series

Family Law

EDITED BY

John Eekelaar and Mavis Maclean

OXFORD UNIVERSITY PRESS
1994

Oxford University Press, Walton Street, Oxford OX2 6DP

Oxford New York
Athens Auckland Bangkok Bombay
Calcutta Cape Town Dar es Salaam Delhi
Florence Hong Kong Istanbul Karachi
Kuala Lumpur Madras Madrid Melbourne
Mexico City Nairobi Paris Singapore
Taipei Tokyo Toronto
and associated companies in
Berlin Ibadan

Oxford is a trade mark of Oxford University Press

Published in the United States
by Oxford University Press Inc., New York

British Library Cataloguing in Publication Data
Data available

Library of Congress Cataloging in Publication Data
A reader on family law / edited by John Eekelaar and Mavis Maclean.
(Oxford readings in socio-legal Studies)
Includes bibliographical references.
1. Domestic relations.   2. Family policy.
I. Eekelaar, John.   II. Maclean, Mavis.   III. Series.
K670.A58R43   1994   346.01'5—dc20   [342.615]   94–36045
ISBN 0–19–876364–6
ISBN 0–19–876363–8 (pbk.)

Set by Hope Services (Abingdon) Ltd.
Printed in Great Britain
on acid-free paper by
Bookcraft Ltd.
Midsomer Norton, Avon

Contents

Part Three: Professions and procedures
....

Introduction

Preliminary remarks

What is the socio-legal approach?

Socio-legal study in Britain has tended to be strongly associated with empirical studies of 'law in action' and indeed much of the impetus for 'socio-legal' work has come from a desire to know 'what actually happens' in the application of law. But socio-legal studies implies much more than assembling empirical information about how legal institutions work or describing what lawyers or other actors say that they do. The way in which such knowledge is sought, how it is interpreted, and the use to which it is put occur within a wider set of values and objectives.

Research has also been driven by a variety of forces, often associated with the sources of funding, and this has inevitably led to a diversification of such values and objectives. One important strand links socio-legal study to social policy research. Within this tradition socio-legal study complements an established body of research which examines the impact of (primarily) state policies on various forms of social organization. The research is frequently used to feed back into policy formation. Another strand associates socio-legal study more closely with sociological research. In his review of the state of the sociology of law in Britain, Roger Cotterell (1990: 779) observed that taking a sociological perspective on law involved understanding law in terms of social theory so that 'legal theory is to be seen as a particular branch or application of social theory'. If socio-legal study is regarded in this way, its value will be viewed in the light of its contribution to understanding the nature of social organization.

We see socio-legal study as related to all these strands and as having important contributions to make to each. But, while researchers have found that it has provided valuable input into social and even economic theory, it also has a significant role in the development of *legal* theory. Just as legal theory has been enriched by drawing upon philosophy and political theory, so it has also gained by insights from socio-legal study.

But it is a two-way process. Because socio-legal study focuses on the intersection between the legal and the social, it needs to draw on broader legal theory to explain what might constitute the 'legal' and on social theory to understand the 'social'. Socio-legal study does not stipulate which of these theories needs to be used. For example, socio-legal writers may use a number of conceptions (in the sense of 'background theories') of law. They may find 'positivist' theories attractive. These accept the existence of law as being a *fact*, irrespective of its values, whether the fact takes the form of an intellectually coherent body of norms, whose existence depends on an institutional body of persons accepting its legitimacy as a 'juristic presupposition',[1] or of a special kind of relationship between norms (propositions of law) and actual (empirically observable) social facts.[2] Or they may prefer what Simmonds (1993) has termed more 'maximalist' perceptions of law (such as natural law, feminist, critical, or Marxist theory), which incorporate strong assumptions as to its functions and purposes into the notion of law itself.

Some conception[3] of law is necessary, but the relative eclecticism is possible because socio-legal study imposes the unifying discipline of observing the way in which law works through those who believe themselves to be acting out the law. In doing this, the actors are engaged in a complex interpretive process, comprising at least their own perception of the law, their own role, and its impact on others. This is not merely a crude question of the extent to which the will (whatever that may be) of a lawmaker is successfully imposed. It is a question of relating how the form and content of the law (as may be found in statements of law in legal textbooks), which are matters for intellectual comprehension and interpretation, move beyond such *intellectual* existence into social reality. And it is more even than that, for, inasmuch as social reality feeds back into the form and content of law, who is to say that social reality is not a source of law? These are some of the main theoretical questions raised by socio-legal study.

The design of this reader

The idea that socio-legal study has a particularly important part to play in understanding modern family law lies behind our selection of readings. We begin (Reading 1.1) with demographic information describing contemporary family behaviour and setting it in a political context, so as to provide a factual starting-point. The data are British, but the trends towards an ageing society, towards more women with children being in paid but intermittent employment, and towards high divorce rates are common to developed economies throughout the world. In Reading 1.2 we look at what may be termed 'pre-legal' or 'informal and negotiable' obligations between family members. Having laid down a baseline of information about the social world in which family law operates, we go on in Chapter 2 (Readings 2.1 and 2.2) to consider two contributions to theoretical frameworks underlying analysis of the role of the law in family matters. Further reflections on theoretical matters are also offered later in this Introduction, and these should be considered together with those readings.

Having introduced readers to these empirical and theoretical issues, the following chapters cover specific areas of family law. Chapter 3 (Readings 3.1 and 3.2) deals with relationships between adults, reflecting on the legal and social implications of marriage and parenthood. This leads naturally (Chapter 4) to issues concerning children, particularly their financial support and the effects of parental separation. The problems underlying the readings in Chapters 3 and 4 are primarily those which occur when adjustments are made between families and new family forms emerge. Chapter 5, however, concentrates primarily on problems experienced by individuals (adults or children) *within* families and the role of the law in dealing with them. The general concerns about legal processes in family matters (especially those raised in Reading 5.3) are explored more fully in the final chapter.

We should emphasize that these readings are intended primarily to raise fundamental issues rather than to provide a comprehensive set of legal or other data for any one jurisdiction: hence the inclusion of American material and material published some years ago but which addresses the legal–social interaction in a stimulating way. We should have liked to range more widely but have been restrained by space. We should note, though, that, in the United States, some Eastern European countries, and Ireland, abortion and adoption are key issues. (For a comparative account see Glendon 1987; on the United States, see Dworkin 1993; on Ireland, see Charleton 1992; on Eastern Europe, see Fuszara 1991 and Kwak 1994.) African countries are struggling with apparent conflicts between 'traditional' values and internationalized norms of family behaviour (Armstrong *et al.* 1993) and with the problems of family breakdown amidst poverty (Burman 1992). We have also omitted issues relating to the elderly (Cretney *et al.* 1991; Eekelaar and Pearl 1989; Maclean, Eaton, and Eekelaar 1992), the implications for family law of a pluralistic society containing a variety of ethnic groups and chosen lifestyles (Poulter 1986, 1987; Ghandhi and MacNamee 1991; Henson 1993), and the social and moral problems increasingly being raised by new medical reproductive technologies (Lee and Morgan 1989; Eekelaar and Sarcevic

1993). This is not because we think them unimportant. We would expect, however, that the present readings will provide the student with a basis upon which to explore these further areas with a sharpened critical awareness.

The empirical base

Since the socio-legal approach draws heavily on social data, it is necessary to give a brief overview of the contribution which empirical research has made to our present state of knowledge before embarking on theoretical discussion.

Studies particularly related to divorce/separation issues

Empirical studies relevant to family law are drawn from a number of social science disciplines. *Demographic* studies draw on large-scale statistical sources, like census data, or national surveys, such as the General Household Survey in the United Kingdom, which are carefully constructed to avoid sampling bias. These can provide the kind of information set out in Reading 1.1. Some of it, such as fertility patterns and the age structure of the population, is not specifically related to law, though it has implications for legal and social policy. Other data, such as statistics of marriage and divorce (which are legal events), concern legal matters directly. Demographers have been able to achieve very refined information linking social data to legal matters, usually by supplementing national demographic statistics with large samples of court documents. For example, John Haskey has shown that there are sharp differences in liability to divorce between different occupational and social groups— couples where the husband was in the armed forces, unemployed, or on an unskilled occupation were in the highest risk groups (Haskey 1984)— and that couples who cohabited before marriage were more likely to divorce than those who did not (Haskey 1992). He has also explored the effects of legislative changes on the demographic characteristics of divorcing parties (Haskey 1986*a*) and the relation between the grounds for divorce and the social and demographic features of divorcing couples (Haskey 1986*b*).

Kathleen Kiernan and Valerie Estaugh (1993) have used data from the General Household Surveys to compile important information on people who cohabit without marrying. Although this remains a minority practice in Great Britain (compared with Denmark and Sweden), it has grown substantially during the 1980s: from 5 per cent of 20–24-year-old women and 3 per cent of 25–34-year-old women in 1979 to 13 per cent and 8 per cent, respectively, in 1989. Most cohabitants still seem to marry when they have a child: in 1989 only one in four of never-married cohabitants had ever had a child. But they also found that cohabiting couples with children tended to be concentrated in lower socio-economic groups than married people with children. This was not the case for those without children. A study comparing mothers who are married with unmarried, cohabiting mothers shows similar results (McRae 1993).

Sociologists of the family use a variety of techniques to gather data. A major source is interviews with samples of respondents. The researchers must be careful to identify and acknowledge any special characteristics of the sample, especially if the sample is small or if there has been a high rate of refusal to take part. In such a case, it is important to know whether the non-participants have any special characteristics. Researchers must also ensure that questions are put to different respondents consistently and that the respondents understand the questions in the same way as the researchers. This type of research need not aim to produce a miniaturized picture of the whole of society (assuming that this is even conceivable), but an insight into social processes. The researcher should always be cautious about the extent to which findings can be generalized to a wider group. Similar findings in other related studies could provide some support to their generalizability. All researchers and their readers must also guard against assuming that the association of factors proves a causal relationship between them. A common example is found in attempts to ascertain the causes of divorce. To show that divorce is more prevalent among some socio-economic groups than among others does not prove that social status in itself contributes to divorce. Perhaps people in certain social classes marry younger; we would then need to see whether divorce is the more common, the younger people are when they marry. This is indeed the case, but then there are other relevant factors: pre-marital conception seems to have a powerful effect, especially when coupled with youth (Murphy 1985). Yet again, perhaps the causes are to be sought in quite different social forces, as explained below.

The first important empirical studies of the family of a socio-legal nature occurred in the United States in the 1950s and arose out of growing interest in the phenomenon of divorce as an apparent sign of social disorganization. In the earliest major study by William Goode (1956), 425 divorced mothers in urban Detroit were interviewed in the winter of 1948. Goode did not see divorce as a sign of pathology (i.e. the malfunctioning of the social system), but as an institutional mechanism for dealing with strain. At that time he concluded it had not been fully accepted in American culture. Yet, in the 1990s, Frank Furstenberg and Andrew Cherlin (1991: 4) and Goode himself (1992: 13) could describe divorce as being part of the American 'marriage *system*'. Goode (1982, 1992) proposed an explanation of divorce at the *macro* level (that is, one which accounts for it in terms of a society's social structure), in the form of an *industrialization* theory. This identifies the increasing extent to which the population is engaged in jobs where the worker deals independently with an external source (unlike cooperative family undertakings, such as peasant agriculture), rewards are provided on an individual basis, ignoring the family circumstances of the worker, and pay is given to the worker to spend as he or she chooses. All this can weaken family stability and lead to increased divorce where it was formerly low. But in other societies, such as Malaysia and Japan (where divorce rates fell from previously high rates), different social forces were at work. Goode concludes that some societies (like ours) may experience a 'stable, high divorce-rate system'. Such a system may function reasonably well if members of broken families can be reabsorbed into a support system, such as where women remarry (as used to be common in the United States) or where care of the children is taken over by the extended family, as in African societies, a practice revealed in interviews with separated women in Zimbabwe by Alice Armstrong (1994) and Fareda Banda (1993).

Unfortunately, as Goode (1992) observes, most societies are failing to make the divorce system 'work'. This has been shown by empirical studies in many countries. Lenore Weitzman (1985) in the United States and ourselves in the United Kingdom (Eekelaar and Maclean 1986) were simultaneously collecting data in the early 1980s. Weitzman's research was based on interviews carried out in 1978 with 114 divorced men and 114 divorced women in Los Angeles county in the year following their divorce. She found that the standard of living of divorced women with children in the household dropped by 73 per cent in the first year after divorce, whereas that of former husbands rose by 42 per cent. Of course, the findings apply only to that part of California. They were also limited to the period immediately following the divorce. We used a different sampling methodology. We contacted people who had divorced between 1971 (when the reformed divorce law took effect) and 1981 through a national quota sample such as is used by marketing and polling organizations. The sample was therefore much more likely to mirror the national picture of people who had been divorced for some years, but must be viewed within the limitations of its size (184 women and 92 men were interviewed). One of the major findings was that, while there was little difference in the economic position of divorced men and women from childless marriages, it was very different where there had been children. In the latter case, only 18 per cent of women living alone with dependent children were above the official 'poverty' line, compared with 46 per cent of the men who had dependent children at the time of divorce. While this showed a large gulf between the position of men after divorce and that of women who were left with the children, our data also showed that, while a small proportion of men could probably afford to pay much more to their former partners, many would find it difficult because they were either unemployed or had repartnered and had taken on additional responsibilities.

Other American research has used different methodologies. *Cohort* studies (also referred to as *longitudinal* studies) select a representative group of people at a particular moment, and follow them over time. The US Panel Study of Income Dynamics (PSID) created a panel in 1968, and data from those who divorced at the same time as Weitzman's sample showed only a 9–13 per cent decline in the women's economic status and a 13 per cent increase for men (Hoffman and Duncan 1988). Some of the differences between these and Weitzman's figures may be due to differences in the samples (the panel studies included separated, but not divorced women, who suffer less of a drop in income, and were wider in scope) but seem mostly to be a function of different measures of economic status (Sorenson 1992). Nevertheless, while it may be difficult to pinpoint the *degree* of divergence between the economic position of men and women (with children) after divorce, its existence is not in doubt. It has been found again in a recent study in the United States (Maccoby and Mnookin 1992, ch. 10), in a range of studies from the Australian Institute of Family Studies (Harrison, MacDonald, and Weston 1987), from Germany (Willenbacher and Voegeli 1988), and from Canada (Stewart 1991), and even in African societies (Burman 1992; Banda 1993).

The reasons for the disparity are clear. Men's earning capacity is seldom detrimentally affected by marriage. In the case of women, the economist Heather Joshi (1985) calculated that to have two children costs the average British mother the equivalent of ten years' salary, as she is likely to take four years out of paid work, spend three years in part-time work, and lose the prospects of promotion. These are referred to as 'opportunity' costs. The calculation excludes loss or impairment of pension entitlements and the direct costs of bring up children. Of course, so long as the mother continues to share in the economic resources of her partner, these losses and costs may be invisible (or, at least, they are compensated for). But, if the couple part, the disparity strikes home.

It has not proved easy to agree on how compensation should be calculated. We once suggested that the proper measure was to attempt to close the gap by trying to ensure that the former caregiver (usually the mother) could maintain a standard of living as close as possible to the 'norm' for a 'couple' family of the occupational status of the major earner, at that time of their lives, and that the necessary resources to achieve this should be extracted from the major earner if (he) was living at a higher standard (Eekelaar and Maclean 1986: 146–7). We saw this as being justified in order to redress the unequal risks of joint parenting. In the United States, Ira Ellman (1989) has proposed that, apart from career damage due to child care, only damage that was 'financially rational' (in the sense that it increased the overall economic status of the couple) should be compensated, while Thomas Oldham (1992, 1993) makes a suggestion similar to ours: that a form of income-sharing should be devised in the case of marriages which produced children. The issue is taken up by Kate Funder (Reading 3.2), who advances another possible solution. In the absence of a clear lead by Parliament, Eekelaar has attempted to discover whether divorce court registrars (now called district judges) operate a favoured 'model' for dealing with post-divorce finances. Through semi-structured interviews with a large number of them, he found that they inclined to an 'individualistic model' which, at the end of a marriage, sought to 'restore the individual's investment in a joint enterprise and to compensate each individual for damage caused by the failure of the enterprise' (Eekelaar 1991: 88).

Information on the possible effects of divorce on children was first provided in studies by *child psychologists*. These tended to show an association between children's experience of family disruption and disturbed or delinquent behaviour (Rutter 1972). But studies by psychologists are usually based on groups of subjects who have already identified themselves by reason of their disturbed behaviour and it is difficult, if not impossible, to know how much, if any, of the behaviour is attributable to the experience of divorce (Emery 1988, ch. 3). This is a major limitation of two highly publicized books co-authored by the San Francisco psychologist Judith Wallerstein, which showed a good deal of emotional disturbance in children who had experienced divorce and who had sought treatment (Wallerstein and Kelly 1980; Wallerstein and Blakeslee 1989). Many of the parents were themselves already quite disturbed.[4]

More instructive is a small cohort study by psychologists in Berkeley,

California, of two sets of (ordinary) nursery schoolchildren, which followed the children up to the age of 14. It showed that the children from families which eventually divorced had begun to show signs of disturbance *before* the divorce (Block, Block, and Gjerde 1986). This could indicate that parental conflict, even in intact families, has adverse effects on children. This is quite consistent with finding behavioural problems with children of divorced families, where such conflict is likely to be aggravated, but suggests that the problem lies in the conflict, not in the divorce (which might even *diminish* the conflict). Large cohort studies, such as the British Child Development Study, which collected information on *all* children born in a particular week in 1946, and again in 1958, and the United States National Survey of Children (based on a random sample of children born in 1976), have confirmed this (Cherlin *et al.* 1991). These issues are pursued further by Martin Richards in Reading 4.2.

Apart from the question of interpersonal relationships, divorce creates 'structural' problems related to economic disadvantage, educational disruption, and severence of family relationships. The longitudinal studies suggest that these can cause long-term disadvantage to children of divorced families. Richards (Reading 4.2) discusses this too. How far it is possible to paper over these structural cleavages by, for example, maintaining the parental roles of both parents after divorce, is problematic. Legal policy tends to encourage the idea of co-parenting after divorce: in England and Wales the Children Act 1989 ensured that joint parental responsibility survived divorce. But extensive research by Eleanor Maccoby and Robert Mnookin (1992) of over one thousand families which divorced in California in the mid-1980s, at a time when that state encouraged co-parenting after divorce, reveals that this arrangement remains quite rare. Although at a point three years after the divorce the researchers found that most children retained *some* contact with the outside parent (over 80 per cent of children had seen that parent during the previous six months), regular visits to an outside father had declined from 76 per cent to 60 per cent. They also found that, while on divorce 15 per cent of families set up 'dual residence', this declined by nearly one-half over three years; moreover, even where the child was living in dual residence, the mothers tended to be more involved in day-to-day caring. Interestingly, absent fathers tended to believe that they were much more involved with the children than they were thought to be by the mothers. Research evidence about the exercise of fatherhood is usefully collected in Lewis and O'Brien (1987).

Less information has been obtained directly from children themselves.

Researchers in London interviewed one hundred volunteers, contacted by advertisement, who had experienced divorce when they were children (Walczak and Burns 1984). These respondents selected themselves. Ann Mitchell's sample of fifty children taken from Scottish divorce files is probably more representative. Her research also has the value of comparing the children's experiences with those of their parents, and shows a high degree of failure by parents to appreciate their children's feelings (Mitchell 1985).

These studies need to be supplemented by studies of the emerging new family forms, especially step-families. Evidence from the UK National Child Development Study suggests that the problems of step-children are not significantly greater than those of other children (Ferri 1984), but clear, detailed evidence is lacking,[5] and the process of step-parenting raises complex interrelational issues (Dimmock 1992). Detailed studies exist on specific procedures, such as step-parent adoption,[6] and on adoption generally. However, more research is needed on the interactive effects of cross-family relationships, such as their possible connection with the higher divorce rate in second marriages.

Physical protection of family members

We have concentrated on issues related to emerging forms of family behaviour because there is little consensus about what is happening or how to evaluate it. Where physical violence is concerned, the picture may seem a little clearer. This may be an illusion, because, as has been forcefully pointed out, particularly by Michael Freeman (1984), patriarchal ideology may legitimize, and hence mask, family violence. The history of the 'marital rape exemption' in English law is a clear example (O'Donovan 1993, ch. 1). Nevertheless, from the point of view of the formal content of the law today, the exercise of physical violence within marriage, or in any domestic relationship, is a criminal offence.

The difficulties occur in relation to the extent of social penetration within the 'private' domain of the family. It has been estimated, on the basis of interviews with 161 divorced men and 237 divorced women, that violence has occurred in somewhere between 30 and 40 per cent of divorces in the United Kingdom (Borkowski, Murch, and Walker 1983). The issue of the public–private distinction is examined by Ruth Gavison in Reading 2.1 and later in this Introduction. Small-scale studies have tracked the experiences of women who have been subjected to domestic violence (Dobash and Dobash 1980; Pahl 1985; Davis, Cretney, and Collins 1994). The many dilemmas facing these women are reflected in the debate over whether the civil or criminal law is the appropriate response, and, particularly, whether 'pro-arrest' and 'no drop' policies are desirable. Such policies reflect a wish to overcome forcibly the public–private divide by instigating an automatic public response to domestic violence. But the price is paid in loss of control by the woman over her own domestic life, a vivid illustration of the conflicts identified by Gavison. The issues are explored in Reading 5.1.

Much empirical work has been carried out in the area of child care, and we cannot in this Introduction provide a detailed account of it. But it has had a very strong influence on policy. One of the most important studies was that by Jane Rowe and Lydia Lambert in the early 1970s of nearly three thousand children in the care of local authorities or voluntary agencies. This found that social workers considered that over one-fifth of the children 'needed' a substitute home and that 'if a pre-school or primary school age child has been in care for as long as six months, his chances of returning to his parents are slim' (Rowe and Lambert 1973). This led directly to provisions in the Children Act 1975 which enhanced state interventive powers to sever the parental relationship in order to facilitate the placement of children in substitute homes. Yet, within a few years the tide turned, and a series of studies conducted in the 1980s preceded the radical realignment of state powers under the Children Act 1989.

This research reveals some of the problems which may be caused by possible values held by researchers. Research conducted, or sponsored, by groups which have a particular value-commitment must always be regarded cautiously. Perhaps the fact that Rowe and Lambert's study was conducted by the Association of British Adoption Agencies built in a bias towards emphasizing the advantages of severing parental links in favour of secure substitute homes. The fact that the questionnaire provided to social workers was headed 'Study of Children in Need of Substitute Families' may have suggested the desirability of this solution to the social workers, on whose opinions the findings were substantially based. Fox Harding regards this as an illustration of the 'state paternalist' perspective of child care (Fox Harding 1991: 77; see also Reading 5.2).

Disquiet over social work practices in the late 1970s generated by pressure groups resulted in a number of research projects funded by the Department of Health and Social Security and the Economic and Social Research Council.[7] Two of the most influential (Packman 1986; Millham *et al.* 1986) also relied heavily on interviews with social workers, but this time incorporated interviews with parents and followed groups of children over time. The consequence was to cast a sharper light on areas of difference between social workers and parents, especially (as one would expect) where intervention was coercive, and, in particular, on the difficulties some parents experienced in maintaining contact with their children who were in care. This was not always because of active opposition by social workers. It might be because of what Spencer Millham and his colleagues call 'non-specific' restrictions, inherent in the separation, or because of the families' circumstances (Fox Harding 1991: 125). Nevertheless, the government highlighted the evidence showing that parents who had been the subjects of legal interventions felt insufficient effort had been made to achieve their cooperation[8] and so partnership and participation became central policies initiated by the Children Act 1989 (Parton 1991).

Robert Dingwall and his colleagues employed an *ethnographic* technique (Dingwall, Eekelaar, and Murray 1983). Its origins lie in anthropology and it involves the researcher shadowing the research subjects, observing their actions, and noting their words as closely as possible. This makes it possible to appreciate more clearly what people do rather than what they report to an interviewer. It is a particularly valuable way of recording interactive processes, such as the dynamics of group meetings. Their research focused on how medical and other workers identified cases of child abuse (which often involved placing a certain *interpretation* on equivocal events) and how decisions to intervene coercively (or not) were reached, especially in a multi-professional context. By observing health visitors making their visits and case conferences reaching their decisions, the researchers concluded that social workers operated a 'rule of optimism' which reinforced institutional pressures *against* intervention by inclining to interpret parental behaviour *in favour* of parents, giving them credit for loving their children and making allowances for social and cultural differences. Legal intervention was triggered if the parents were considered incorrigible or if the matter went beyond social services' control. It is thus perhaps not surprising that later research found that parents who were subjected to legal intervention reported poor relationships with social services, for it was the fact that relationships were poor which probably led to the intervention. How far legal and managerial attempts to promote partnership will succeed remains a matter for further research (Thoburn 1991).

Processes and professionals

Much empirical work in family law has examined court procedures and practices of professionals (usually lawyers). An important set of studies of divorce procedures has been carried out by Mervyn Murch and Gwynn Davis and their colleagues at Bristol. Two such studies were published in *Grounds for Divorce* (Davis and Murch 1988). The first excluded 'contested' cases and involved studying nearly three thousand divorce files and interviewing 396 people, drawn from four courts; the second was confined to 'contested' cases and involved studying files, observing some court processes, and interviewing a little over one hundred people. In concentrating on the views reported by the adult 'clients' of the system, the research gives a strong 'consumer-oriented' view of the procedures and the researchers' conclusions were very influential on the Law Commission's proposals for a new divorce procedure.[9] This type of work has led Murch and Hooper to make inquiries of professionals involved in family issues which come into the court system and, as a result, to expose the wide variety of professional 'domains' which constitute a 'matrix' in what they deem to be an 'emerging family justice system' (Murch and Hooper 1993). In Reading 5.3, however, Michael King and Judith Trowell are sceptical about the ability of the law to respond to children's 'needs' as perceived by psychologists. Legal processes have inherent limitations in dealing with children's development and relationships. Yet, for reasons considered later, it may be impossible to avoid them.

Our understanding of the role of professionals can also be advanced by ethnographic methods. As explained above, this usually involves direct observation of the subjects under investigation, as was done in the leading American study (Sarat and Felstiner 1986). But, where observation has not been possible, researchers have used secondary sources, such as clients' files (Ingleby 1992), or a mixture of methods (scrutiny of files, observation of mediation, client interviews) (Davis 1988). These studies have exploded the image of divorce lawyers as generators of *litigation*. Although the American lawyers were more contentious, the overriding strategy is to achieve *settlement* through *negotiation*. Richard Ingleby (Reading 6.1) also stresses the importance of the lawyer in providing advice and in assisting the client in dealings with third parties.

This evidence is important in evaluating the respective roles of (non-lawyer) mediation (in the United Kingdom usually referred to as 'conciliation') and lawyer-based negotiation. Again, Dingwall (Reading 6.3) has used ethnographic techniques: in this case, audio recordings of conciliation sessions, to which he has applied conversational analysis. The research is designed to reveal the dynamics of a three-party encounter. Wider evaluations of the 'effects' of mediation/conciliation are reported by Lee Teitelbaum and Laura DuPaix in Reading 6.2. A large research project was conducted at the University of Newcastle, primarily for the purpose of advising government as to whether conciliation was likely to be 'cost-effective' (University of Newcastle 1989). The Unit found no evidence that inserting conciliation into the machinery would save overall costs, but, since it did not ascertain whether doing so was likely to reduce overall judicial activity, its methodology probably precluded it from being able to decide the issue (Eekelaar 1991: 159–63). Maccoby and Mnookin (1992) seem to demonstrate that compulsory court-based mediation has reduced court-contested custody cases in California. There is other American evidence to this effect (see Emery 1988: 134) and the same may be true with regard to 'in-court' conciliation schemes in England and Wales. However, court-based conciliation, especially if compulsory, may be very different from conciliation/mediation practised by voluntary bodies. (For an excellent discussion, see Roberts (1993). The view, taken by King, that at root legal procedures are inappropriate for dealing with family troubles may have an appeal to governments anxious about public expenditure, and, indeed, government proposals made in 1993 indicate that this is so. These effectively seek to replace publicly funded legal services providing for the management of people's divorces by subsidized mediation, which is believed to be cheaper, and to avert court action as far as possible (Lord Chancellor's Department 1993).

Having given a brief survey of some of the main sources of empirical knowledge relevant to family law, we turn to a discussion of some theoretical and policy issues.

Theoretical and policy issues

Application and non-application of law: public and private

We will not consider recent feminist writings such as those of Catherine MacKinnon (1989), Carol Pateman (1988), and Susan Moller Okin (1989), important as they are, since these provide background political theory, like the legal theories referred to earlier. More directly relevant to socio-legal study is what feminism has said about the relation between the legal and the social. The debate has often centred on the so-called public–private dichotomy.[10] Olsen (1985), for example, argues that the distinction between intervention and non-intervention in family life is incoherent. She asks whether to abolish divorce would be to intervene or not to intervene; whether not regulating the exercise of parental power (for example, through the absence of a law against corporal punishment) is a form of intervention or not, since the result is to enhance parental power.

'The state', she writes, 'is not accused of intervening in the family when it forces children to live with their parents or when it prohibits doctors from treating minors without parents' knowledge and approval' (Olsen 1985: 853).

Yet the precise nature of the feminist critique is not always clear and the importance of this debate to the relation between the legal and the social is such that we have included Gavison's searching critique of the possible claims that are being made (Reading 2.1). For example, it may be that Olsen's analysis overlooks a distinction between intervention and *intrusion*. To return home a runaway child might not be thought of as intervention, but may reasonably be considered less *intrusive* than billeting social workers in the home to prevent her departure. The values at stake may not be best elucidated by assertions, or denials, of a generalized public–private dichotomy.[11]

Legal and social rules

We do not see law as a monolithic enterprise constantly seeking to impose a predetermined vision on society, whether by intervention or otherwise. True, it may often, indeed usually, have that character when it is the product of the modern state or judiciary. But socio-legal study may reveal that legal rules or practices can also emerge, often in the interaction between legal practitioners, other professionals, and clients, as *problem-solving* devices, designed to maintain social equilibrium.[12] This is especially noticeable in the relatively wide discretionary basis for settling matrimonial disputes. So socio-legal study can show that, in the exercise of this discretion, judges and practitioners *in fact* develop practices which determine the outcome of cases (Eekelaar 1991). As Ingleby observes: 'the strength of informally created norms is such that they can even override apparently inflexible law' (Reading 6.1; see also Jackson and Washoff 1993). Similarly, values of child-welfare professionals have affected the way in which courts decide disputes over children.[13]

We can observe the relation between social practice and law in Finch's exploration of various possible bases for family obligations (Reading 1.2). In the pivotal distinction between 'behavioural regularities' and 'normative rules' Finch notes how people may derive a sense of obligation ('ought') from social practice ('is'). Finch describes the 'is' as including the presence of *approbation* or *disapprobation*. But, according to the classic account by H. L. A. Hart (1961), approbation—or, at least, disapprobation (the 'internal point of view')—distinguishes social rules from 'regularities' of conduct ('habits'). However, Finch's concerns, unlike Hart's, are not with an analysis of rules, but with the sources of action of family members: are they derived from social rules, from internal constraints ('inner morality'), or from law? Finch offers no firm answer to this question, observing that her main point is 'to indicate that they raise important empirical questions'. Her own study shows, however, that a complex set of norms ('social rules') exists alongside, and perhaps in contradiction to, the 'law'.

What might seem scarcely beyond doubt, though, is the *prescriptivity* of 'family law' itself. It seems to be telling people what they should do. But reality is more complex. Difficulty lies in interpreting *what* is being prescribed and how far *law* is doing the prescribing rather than merely providing the facilities for giving effect to the prescriptions of (non-legal) social rules (Eekelaar 1987). Feminist writers, such as Smart, have stressed how marriage law has been a vehicle for the implementation of the ideology of patriarchy (Reading 2.2; see also Smart 1984: 143–5). But, while it has been that, it has also been much more. Katherine O'Donovan writes: 'Explanations for state intervention to control marriage can be summarised as stemming from the interests of patriarchy, of the Church and of the State.'[14] This is revealed in Stephen Parker's illuminating study of the relation between legal and 'informal' marriages. He observes that, prior to the Marriage Act 1757, which imposed rigorous formal requirements for entering legal marriage, many *de facto* cohabitations were treated as marriage so that the man was a husband 'and obliged to maintain his wife and children. It was not only the community that gained control in this way. The knowledge that a marriage would be locally implied from the fact of pregnancy gave power to women who were concerned that the man might desert them' (Parker 1990: 19). This prescriptive character of marriage law is part of the universal propensity of human cultural behaviour to regulate reproduction. Although people are always transgressing, anthropological literature maps the vast universe of prescriptivity in marriage customs, ascription of parenthood, and discharge of marital and parental obligations.

Shifts in prescriptive content

We cannot of course describe all that here. However, we must draw attention to a major shift in the *public* (and, therefore, the legal) content of the prescriptivity of family law which occurred when, after a considerable struggle,[15] no-fault divorce was introduced in 1971.[16] Legal policy and, we suspect, legal theorists have yet to appreciate the profound significance of this event, which Smart (Reading 2.2) describes as the ending

of the 'punitive obsession'. A fault-based divorce law was a logical consequence of a particular view of marriage as imposing *legal* obligations and,
accordingly, of divorce as a form of relief available to an innocent party
for a wrong suffered. Once no-fault divorce is accepted, the legal basis for
obligations deriving solely from marriage is undermined.[17] And it soon
followed, in England, Scotland, and elsewhere, that independent grounds
needed to be found for the imposition on one party to a former marriage
of a legal obligation to support the other after divorce. The logical conclusion that marriage might be an 'unnecessary legal concept' is raised by
Eric Clive in Reading 3.1.

The move to no-fault divorce coincided with (and, indeed, may have
been intimately connected with) the culmination of the long process by
which the availability of divorce *at all* slowly spread from the privileged
aristocracy to virtually the entire population.[18] Of course, just as some
people deliberately evaded the reach of marriage law, as Parker (1990)
describes, many of those whose economic circumstances denied them
the opportunity of divorce simply separated (Gibson 1993). For them, the
prescriptivity of marriage meant nothing because they had no effective
means for applying its norms. There was, in effect, a vast underclass left
to regulate themselves according to whatever extra-legal social mores
prevailed.

One of the principal objects of the 1971 reform was to bring these people
within the ambit of the law. But the very Act which gathered them in also
virtually deprived marriage law of its prescriptive content. Thus, at the
moment when marriage all but ceased to be legally binding, it did so for
everyone. One effect of this can be seen in the great rise in divorce since that
date (Reading 1.1), though we would not attribute the rise in the instability
of marriage solely to that event. But it also required a realignment of family
law itself. In his theorization of the 'new' family law, Parker (1990) argues
that its 'form' can be explained through the tension caused by the clash
between the 'ideal' of the 'traditional' two-parent family (where the husband is the main earner), promoted initially by post-war family policy and
latterly by consumer images of family life, and social reality as revealed in
Reading 1.1. He observes (1990: 140–3) that the two major functions of the
new family law are to promote 'state policies on women and the family by
preserving the kernel of the traditional model' and to try to 'contain' the
support obligation within this fragmenting unit in order to protect public
funds. Writing in 1982, Smart (Reading 2.2) sees family law as moving away
from supporting male domination, while still retaining a 'traditional' image
of women as protectors of children and dependent on male breadwinners.

Our emphasis, however, would be different. The first 'function' mentioned by Parker is supported primarily by reference to the non-application of law in certain family contexts (for example, a husband has no obligation to reveal his earnings or assets to his wife; the support obligation is largely non-enforceable while a married couple live together), by some remarks by Lord Denning, and by the fact that remedies usually tend to be extended to unmarried cohabitees only if they 'behave like married people'. This view has received powerful support, especially in the context of accounting for domestic violence (Freeman 1984; Freeman and Lyon 1983). The remnants of some 'traditional' model can indeed be found in this way. But they seem too weak to be described as amounting to a 'major function' of modern family law, especially as the most significant legal site for upholding that model, the image of marriage reflected in a fault-based divorce law, has been removed.[19] Furthermore, it is often very difficult to know whether the 'law' (in the form of judges' utterances or parliamentary policy) is attempting to impose behavioural patterns or mainly reacting to community norms and assumptions.[20] We recall the point made earlier that law may arise partly as a means of maintaining stability where tensions arise in social behaviour.

Readers will make their own assessments of this issue. We would wish, however, to develop the second 'major function' identified by Parker, which relates to the 'dependency' issue raised by Smart. The state clearly has a direct interest in the functioning of the family as a means of distribution of resources to children and (where they have no, or insufficient, independent income) their carers. Failure of that system has immediate impact on the community. It has always been at times when such failures have been perceived as constituting a serious threat to the community that the law has intervened, attempting to force families to behave as ideology says they should.[21] But, as we have seen, 'marriage' ideology has broken down. It has therefore been necessary to construct, somewhat hurriedly, a new one: we see this in the assertion in the Children Act 1989 and the Child Support Act 1991 of the 'responsibilities' of parenthood, especially in financial matters. (See further Reading 4.1 and Maclean and Eekelaar 1993.)

It may be thought that this is just another way of re-establishing the 'traditional' family, especially as the measures seem to be directed primarily against men, the traditional breadwinners. But a closer examination shows very significant changes. First, marriage is irrelevant. Secondly, the terms of these schemes are rigidly gender-neutral. They are designed to fit any configuration of child care and working practice that the parents care to establish. Thirdly, the obligations arise irrespective either of the rights and wrongs between the adults or of whether the man intended to father a child.[22] Fourthly, any new legal obligations that the liable parent may subsequently acquire through marriage or remarriage are subordinated to the parental obligation, which is a sharp downgrading of the dominance of traditional marriage, and any 'social' obligations towards step-children are ignored. Fifthly, the obligations persist only as long as the children are minors. If any further obligation to support the former carer is to arise, its basis has to be found elsewhere.

This strategy is far from being a mere replication of the traditional prescriptions of marriage. Nor does it conform to the prediction by Smart in Reading 2.2 that a new form of 'extended family', giving rise to obligations arising from the fact of living in a particular household structure, might be emerging. It may even be wondered what the *prescriptive* content is. It is doubtful whether it can be represented as being designed to keep families together or as underwriting any particular household structure. It might instead be seen as a means of *managing* resource distribution to dependants by regulating financial flows across households in such a way as to minimize the costs to the community. This characterization gains force in looking at the way in which the British and Australian child-support schemes in particular attempt to quantify the money to be paid by using precise formulaic methods, applied by administrative tribunals. Put crudely, this perspective sees the state as saying that people may organize their domestic lives as they like, but making clear what the price tag will be. Whether the price strikes the right balance between individual and collective responsibility is central to Krause's critique (Reading 4.1).

Conflicts and containment

This is far from being the only, or even the major, consequence of the breakdown of the prescriptiveness of marriage. Parker (1990: 157) notices that 'the concept of marriage as a legal status was displaced by discussion about the family and attention focused on mothers rather than wives. These shifts brought with them changing notions of justice which were not dependent on legal marriage.' Elsewhere (Parker 1992) he argues that, during the course of this century, family law has moved from being justified primarily in terms of rights and duties to a utilitarian justification which depends on a balancing of interests, including the public interest. It would seem that these shifts in notions of justice are part of the process.

However, the same changes could equally be explained in terms of a wider vision of people's rights (Eekelaar 1994a). Nineteenth-century family law emphasized the rights of the husband and of the father and the duties of the wife and children. True, morality dictated that the husband/father should act with their welfare in mind, but the legal structure of the relationship left the man wide scope to decide what was in the interests of their welfare. The breakdown in the dominant position of the husband/father's rights has led to increased attention being paid to wives' rights, the rights of unmarried cohabitees (or even vulnerable people threatened by someone with whom they have not 'cohabited'),[23] and, of course, the rights of children. Whichever analysis is adopted reflects preferences regarding a wider explanatory framework, and does not affect Parker's observations that these interests (or rights) needed reconciliation. Much modern family law consists of a search for principles for such reconciliation, and there is a possibility that human rights principles (for example, as found in the European Convention on Human Rights and the UN Convention on the Rights of the Child) may play a growing part in that reconciliation.

Many of the readings in this collection are about the strains put upon decision-making frameworks developed in earlier days by the emergence of the recognition given to new sets of interests. Richards (Reading 4.2) explains how children's interests are now more broadly conceived than hitherto, and those of absent parents and other family kin are more readily given weight. In order to see the visible results of this broadening, one has only to view the potential legal line-up in modern child protection proceedings, where lawyers for the child, the social services, the parents, the guardian *ad litem*, and possibly other family members may be found presenting their viewpoint to the court. Inevitably, the larger the scope of the interests recognized, the greater the potential for conflict: witness the conflict, noted by Krause in Reading 4.1, between the absent parent's desire for independence and the claims of (his) new family, on the one hand, and the interests of the children he is no longer living with and those of his former spouse, on the other.

We do not wish to attempt a summary of these developments. We do, however, wish to underline the problems that they have posed for dispute-solving mechanisms (traditionally, lawyers and courts). We have already observed that King and Trowell (Reading 5.3) suggest that legal mechanisms, and the discourse of legal entitlements, are inappropriate to finding solutions to the 'needs' of children caught up in these conflicts. Teitelbaum and DuPaix (Reading 6.2) show that similar arguments are made in favour of mediation. It is clear that, if the 'law' is viewed primarily through its outworks of lawyers' offices, court premises, and enforcement officers, it appears as a crude engine, especially where the conflicts involve heavy adult emotion and vulnerable childhood psychologies. The collapse of the court-based divorce law testifies to this. There is widespread feeling that there must be a better way.

Yet the very fact that the range of interests affected by family issues is now seen to extend more widely than hitherto has enhanced the role of the law. To leave decision-making to welfare professionals is inconsistent with a process which *assures* the open weighing of the variety of interests involved. Fox Harding's assessment of child-care policy (Reading 5.2) mentions the role that interest groups and ideological shifts had on the formation of the Children Act 1989. Although some objectives were achieved through changes in practice only (such as the attendance of parents at case conferences), many could not have been effected without legal intervention. Parton and Martin (1989) have noted that the tendency to 'disaggregate the interests of individual family members' has led to greater 'legalism' in family issues. In Reading 6.3 Dingwall and Greatbatch go further in showing how 'legalistic' construction of three-party encounters, whether in court or in mediation, may be necessary to protect the interests of participants.

Ironically, it is also true that increased sensitivity to the interests of individual family members leads to more intrusive intervention, as in the case of child sexual abuse. The only way this can be tolerated within current political ideology is by sanctioning such intervention through elaborate procedural devices, which provide some *legitimation* for intrusion. According to Parton (1992), the same wish to limit state intrusions underlies the policy of the Children Act 1989 to restrict interventions to particularly 'dangerous' situations. The consequence may be that social policy towards children will focus almost exclusively on ensuring that social services comply with the approved management regimes of potentially high-risk cases rather than assist the wider population of children who are not (yet) so seriously threatened.

It may be contended that, while legal machinery may be necessary to give effect to the increasingly wide sweep of recognition of adult interests, this is not necessary, or may even be counter-productive, in the case of children. But how are their 'needs' perceived? How are they to be reconciled with what we care to recognize as the interests of relevant adults? Child psychology is itself vulnerable to normative values within society,[24] though these values, too, might be influenced by theories developed within psychotherapeutic traditions. The balance that is struck between adults' interests, the perceived wishes of children, and claims by welfare professionals and, indeed, by the legal system can itself be characterized as a matter of law. But full account must be taken of the worries of King and Trowell (Reading 5.3) concerning the limitations of the legal *process* in responding to children's needs. One possible response, which courts may be making, is to move towards modes of decision-making in matters concerning children which are less final and which aim to position children in environments—if necessary, under the guidance of welfare professionals—in which they are afforded greater opportunity to influence the longer-term outcome for themselves, a process Eekelaar (1994b) has termed 'dynamic self-determinism'. As we see it, the solutions adopted inevitably reflect perceptions of the 'entitlements' of individuals. We return, therefore, to the complex interaction between legal categorization and socio-cultural practice, which at the beginning of this Introduction we saw as the subject-matter of socio-legal study.

Notes

1. As in Kelsen's 'pure theory of law': see Paulson (1992: 311–32); Raz (1979: ch. 6).
2. Such theories are sometimes described as 'social' or 'sources' theses: see Waluchow (1989), who holds that it does not undermine an empirical, positivist theory of law to maintain that morality can be included as a possible source of law.
3. See Dworkin (1986: 94). Dworkin's use of 'conception of law' seems to mean much the same as 'theory of law'.
4. See Furstenberg and Cherlin (1991: 130) for a sharp criticism of any claim that the sample could in any sense be described as 'normal'.
5. For a summary of existing evidence, see Furstenberg and Cherlin (1991: 134).
6. e.g. Masson, Norbury, and Chatterton (1983).
7. Parton (1991: ch. 2) gives an excellent account of these events.
8. 'The evidence from research was that taking compulsory powers not only failed to achieve better planning and security but was often counter-productive. Family ties were more difficult to maintain after court orders and relationships between parents and social workers were often damaged. Packman (1986) and the Dartington research team found parents distressed, disgruntled, even outraged by compulsion. Parents felt they had no say in the decisions that had been made, that matters had been taken out of their hands and they were now unable to influence social workers' plans for their children' (Department of Health 1991: 39–40).
9. See Davis and Murch (1988: 156); Law Commission (1990).
10. The literature is vast. The more accessible English material relevant to family law is in O'Donovan (1985) and Freeman (1985).

11. See Eekelaar (1989).
12. The 'spontaneous' nature of this kind of law is a feature of the 'evolutionary' theory of law proposed by F. A. Hayek: see Ratnapala (1993).
13. For a general criticism of this process, on the grounds that it subverts legal values and the interests of adults, see Fineman (1988).
14. O'Donovan (1985: 44). For a study of the role of the early Church, see Goody (1983).
15. For a full history of western divorce law, see Phillips (1988) and Stone (1990).
16. Divorce Reform Act 1969. Traces of 'fault' remain in the letter of the divorce law. But, as a practical matter, fault is no longer an issue in the question whether and to which spouse divorce should be granted.
17. This is fully discussed in Eekelaar (1991).
18. The story is vividly told in Gibson (1993).
19. Note that the 'marital rape' exemption which Freeman considered to be a significant element in the patriarchal ideology was removed by the House of Lords in R. v. R. [1991] 4 All ER 481.
20. For example, it was only in 1993, two years after wives' earnings began to be taxed separately from those of their husbands, that market research organizations abandoned classifying a household's class according to the occupation of the 'head of the household', who was always taken to be the 'man': see *The Independent* (31 Mar. 1993).
21. See Meulders-Klein and Eekelaar (1988: i. 87–92).
22. It might be observed that, ultimately, the mother has control over whether the child should be born: see Meulders-Klein (1990).
23. See the Law Commission's recommendation that people within a defined group, which includes close relatives, persons engaged to be married, and persons who have 'had a sexual relationship with each other (whether or not including sexual intercourse)', should be given certain remedies against molestation: Law Commission (1993).
24. See Dingwall and Eekelaar (1986).

Bibliography

ARMSTRONG, ALICE (1994), 'School and Sadza: Custody and the Best Interests of the Child in Zimbabwe' 8 *International Journal of Law and the Family* 151.
—— CHALOKA BEYANI, CHUMA HIMONGA, JANET KABEBERI-MACHARIA, ATHALIAH MOLOKOMME, WELSHMAN NCUBE, THANDABANTU NHLAPO, BART RWEZAURA, and JULIE STEWART (1993), 'Uncovering Reality: Excavating Women's Rights in African Family Law' 7 *International Journal of Law and the Family* 314.
BANDA, FAREDA (1993), 'Women and Law in Zimbabwe: Access to Justice on Divorce', D.Phil. Thesis, University of Oxford.
BLOCK, JEANNE H., JACK BLOCK, and PER F. GJERDE (1986), 'The Personality of Children Prior to Divorce' 57 *Child Development* 827.

24   *Introduction*

44444454

BORKOWSKI, MARGARET, MERVYN MURCH, and VAL WALKER (1983), *Marital Violence: The Community Response* (Tavistock).

BURMAN, SANDRA (1992), 'First-World Solutions for Third-World Problems', in Lenore J. Weitzman and Mavis Maclean (eds.), *Economic Consequences of Divorce: The International Perspective* (Oxford University Press).

CHARLETON, PETER (1992), 'Judicial Discretion on Abortion: The Irish Perspective' 6 *International Journal of Law and the Family* 349.

CHERLIN, ANDREW J., FRANK F. FURSTENBERG, JR., P. LINDSAY CHASE-LANSDALE, KATHLEEN E. KIERNAN, PHILIP K. ROBINS, DONNA RUANE MORRISON, and JULIEN O. TEITLER (1991), 'Longitudinal Studies of Effects of Divorce on Children in Great Britain and the United States' 252 *Science* 1386.

COTTERRELL, ROGER B. M. (1990), 'Sociology of Law in Britain: Its Present Prospects', in V. Ferrari (ed.), *Developing Sociology of Law: A Worldwide Documentary Inquiry* (International Sociological Association Research Committee, Milan).

CRETNEY, S., G. DAVIS, R. KERRIDGE, and A. BORKOWSKI (1991), *Enduring Powers of Attorney: A Report to the Lord Chancellor* (Lord Chancellor's Department, London).

DAVIS, GWYNN (1988), *Partisans and Mediators* (Oxford University Press).

—— and MERVYN MURCH (1988), *Grounds for Divorce* (Oxford University Press).

—— S. CRETNEY, and J. COLLINS (1994), *Simple Quarrels* (Oxford University Press).

Department of Health (1991), *Patterns and Outcomes in Child Placement* (HMSO).

DIMMOCK, B. (ed.) (1992), *A Step in Both Directions: The Impact of the Children Act 1989* (National Step-Family Association, London).

DINGWALL, ROBERT, and JOHN EEKELAAR (1986), 'Judgements of Solomon: Psychology and Family Law', in Martin Richards and Paul Light (eds.), *Children of Social Worlds* (Polity Press).

—— —— and TOPSY MURRAY (1983), *The Protection of Children: State Intervention and Family Life* (Blackwell).

DOBASH, R. E., and R. P. DOBASH (1980), *Violence against Wives* (Open Books).

DWORKIN, RONALD (1986), *Law's Empire* (Fontana).

—— (1993), *Life's Dominion* (Harper Collins).

EEKELAAR, JOHN (1987), 'Family Law and Social Control', in J. Eekelaar and J. Bell (eds.), *Oxford Essays in Jurisprudence (Third Series)* (Oxford University Press).

—— (1989), 'What Is Critical Family Law?' 105 *Law Quarterly Review* 244.

—— (1991), *Regulating Divorce* (Oxford University Press).

—— (1994a), 'Families and Children: From Welfarism to Rights', in C. McCrudden and G. Chambers (eds.), *Individual Rights and the Law in Britain* (Clarendon Press, Oxford).

—— (1994b), 'The Interests of the Child and the Child's Wishes: The Role of Dynamic Self-Determinism' 8 *International Journal of Law and the Family* 42.

—— and MAVIS MACLEAN (1986), *Maintenance after Divorce* (Oxford University Press).

—— and DAVID PEARL (eds.) (1989), *An Ageing World: Dilemmas and Challenges for Law and Social Policy* (Oxford University Press & Nihon Kajo).

—— and PETAR SARCEVIC (eds.) (1993), *Parenthood in Modern Society: Legal and Social Issues for the Twenty-First Century* (Martinus Nijhoff).

ELLMAN, IRA M. (1989), 'The Theory of Alimony' 77 *California Law Review* 1.

EMERY, ROBERT E. (1988), *Marriage, Divorce and Children's Adjustment* (Sage).

FERRI, ELSA (1984), *Stepchildren: A National Study* (Nfer-Nelson).

FINEMAN, MARTHA (1988), 'Dominant Discourse, Professional Language and Legal Change in Child Custody Decision-Making' 101 *Harvard Law Review* 727.

FOX HARDING, LORRAINE (1991), *Perspectives in Child Care Policy* (Longman).

FREEMAN, MICHAEL D. (1984), 'Legal Ideologies, Patriarchal Precedents, and Domestic Violence', in M. D. A. Freeman (ed.), *State, Law and the Family: Critical Perspectives* (Tavistock).

—— (1985), 'Towards a Critical Theory of Family Law' *Current Legal Problems* 153.

—— and C. M. LYON (1983), *Cohabitation without Marriage: An Essay in Law and Social Policy* (Gower Press).

FURSTENBURG, FRANK F., and ANDREW J. CHERLIN (1991), *Divided Families* (Harvard University Press).

FUSZARA, M. (1991), 'Will the Abortion Issue Give Birth to Feminism in Poland?', in M. Maclean and D. Groves (eds.), *Women's Issues in Social Policy* (Routledge).

GHANDHI, P. R., and E. MACNAMEE, 'The Family in UK Law and the International Covenant on Civil and Political Rights 1966' 5 *International Journal of Law and the Family* 104.

GIBSON, COLIN (1993), *Dissolving Wedlock* (Routledge).

GLENDON, MARY ANN (1987), *Abortion and Divorce in Western Law: American Failures, European Challenges* (Harvard University Press).

GOODE, WILLIAM J. (1956), *Women in Divorce* (Free Press).

—— (1982), *The Family* (2nd edn., Englewood Cliffs).

—— (1992), 'World Changes in Divorce Patterns', in Lenore J. Weitzman and Mavis Maclean, *Economic Consequences of Divorce: The International Perspective* (Oxford University Press).,

GOODY, JACK (1983), *The Development of the Family and Marriage in Europe* (Cambridge University Press).

HARRISON, MARGARET, PETER MACDONALD, and RUTH WESTON (1987), 'Payment of Child Maintenance in Australia: The Current Position, Research Findings and Reform Proposals' 1 *International Journal of Law and the Family* 92.

HART, H. L. A. (1961), *The Concept of Law* (Clarendon Press).

HASKEY, JOHN (1984), 'Social Class and Socio-economic Differentials in Divorce in England and Wales' 38 *Population Studies* 419.

—— (1986a), 'Recent Trends in Divorce in England and Wales: The Effects of Legislative Changes' 44 *Population Trends* 9.

—— (1986b), 'Grounds for Divorce in England and Wales: A Social and Demographic Analysis' 18 *Journal of Biosocial Science* 127.

HASKEY, JOHN (1992), 'Pre-marital Cohabitation and the Probability of Subsequent Divorce: Analyses Using New Data from the General Household Survey', *Population Trends* (Summer 1992), 10.

HENSON, DEBORAH M. (1993), 'A Comparative Analysis of Same-Sex Partnership Protections: Recommendations for American Reform' 7 *International Journal of Law and the Family* 282.

HOFFMAN, S. D., and G. J. DUNCAN (1988), 'What Are the Economic Consequences of Divorce?' 25 *Demography* 641.

INGLEBY, RICHARD (1992), *Solicitors and Divorce* (Oxford University Press).

JACKSON, EMILY, and FRAN WASHOFF, with MAVIS MACLEAN and REBECCA EMERSON DOBASH (1993), 'Financial Support on Divorce: The Right Mixture of Rules and Discretion?' 7 *International Journal of Law and the Family* 230.

JOSHI, HEATHER (1985), *Motherhood and Employment*, Department of Employment Occasional Paper no. 34 (Office of Population, Censuses and Surveys, London).

KIERNAN, KATHLEEN R., and VALERIE ESTAUGH (1993), *Cohabitation, Extra-marital Childbearing and Social Policy* (Joseph Rowntree Foundation).

KWAK, A. (1994), 'Children's Rights and Adoption', in M. Maclean and J. Kurczewski, *Families, Politics, and the Law* (Oxford University Press).

Law Commission (1990), *Family Law: The Ground for Divorce*, Law Com. no. 192 (HMSO).

—— (1993), *Family Law: Domestic Violence and Occupation of the Family Home*, Law Com. no. 207 (HMSO).

LEE, ROBERT, and DEREK MORGAN (eds.) (1989), *Birthrights: Law and Ethics at the Beginnings of Life* (Routledge).

LEWIS, CHARLIE, and MARGARET O'BRIEN (eds.) (1987), *Reassessing Fatherhood: New Observations on Fathers and the Modern Family* (Sage).

Lord Chancellor's Department (1993), *Looking to the Future: Mediation and the Ground for Divorce. A Consultation Paper* (Cmnd. 2424).

MACCOBY, ELEANOR E., and ROBERT H. MNOOKIN (1992), *Dividing the Child: Social and Legal Dilemmas of Custody* (Harvard University Press).

MACKINNON, CATHERINE (1989), *Toward a Feminist Theory of the State* (Harvard University Press).

MACLEAN, MAVIS, and JOHN EEKELAAR (1993), 'Child Support: The British Solution' 7 *International Journal of Law and the Family* 205.

—— G. EATON, and J. EEKELAAR (1992), 'Old and at Home' *Journal of Social Welfare and Family Law* 297.

MASSON, J., D. NORBURY, and S. CHATTERTON (1983), *Mine, Yours or Ours? A Study of Step-parent Adoption* (HMSO).

McRAE, SUSAN (1993), *Cohabiting Mothers: Changing Marriage and Motherhood?* (Policy Studies Institute).

MEULDERS-KLEIN, M.-T. (1990), 'The Position of the Father in European Legislation' 4 *International Journal of Law and the Family* 131.

—— and J. EEKELAAR (eds.) (1988), *Family, State and Individual Economic Security* (Story Scientia).

MILLHAM, SPENCER, ROGER BULLOCK, KENNETH HOSIE, and MARTIN HAAK (1986), *Lost in Care: The Problems of Maintaining Links between Children in Care and their Families* (Gower).

MITCHELL, ANN (1985), *Children in the Middle: Living through Divorce* (Tavistock).

MURCH, M., and D. HOOPER (1993), *The Family Justice System* (Family Law).

MURPHY, M. J. (1985), 'Demographic and Socio-economic Influences on Recent British Marital Breakdown Patterns' 39 *Population Studies* 441.

O'DONOVAN, KATHERINE (1985), *Sexual Divisions in Law* (Weidenfeld & Nicolson).

—— (1993), *Family Law Matters* (Pluto Press).

OKIN, SUSAN MOLLER (1989), *Justice, Gender and the Family* (Basic Books).

OLDHAM, THOMAS J. (1992), 'Putting Asunder in the 1990s' 80 *California Law Review* 1091.

—— (1993), 'The Economic Consequences of Divorce in the United States', in A. Bainham and D. Pearl (eds.), *Frontiers of Family Law* (Chancery Law Publishing).

OLSEN, FRANCES E. (1985), 'The Myth of State Intervention in the Family' *Michigan University Journal of Law Reform* 835.

PACKMAN, JEAN, with JOHN RANDALL and NICOLA JACQUES (1986), *Who Needs Care? Social Work Decisions about Children* (Blackwell).

PAHL, JAN (ed.) (1985), *Private Violence and Public Policy: The Needs of Battered Women and the Response of the Public Services* (Routledge).

PARKER, STEPHEN (1990), *Informal Marriage, Cohabitation and the Law 1750–1989* (Macmillan).

—— (1992), 'Rights and Utility in Anglo-Australian Family Law' 55 *Modern Law Review* 311.

PARTON, NIGEL (1991), *Governing the Family* (Macmillan).

—— (1992), 'The Contemporary Politics of Child Protection', *Journal of Social Welfare and Family Law* 100.

—— and NORMA MARTIN (1989), 'Public Inquiries, Legalism and Child Care in England and Wales' 3 *International Journal of Law and the Family* 21.

PATEMAN, CAROL (1988), *The Sexual Contract* (Polity Press).

PAULSON, STANLEY L. (1992), 'The Neo-Kantian Dimension of Kelsen's Pure Theory of Law' 12 *Oxford Journal of Legal Studies* 311.

PHILLIPS, RODRICK (1988), *Putting Asunder: Divorce in Western Society* (Cambridge University Press).

POULTER, SEBASTIAN (1986), *English Law and Ethnic Minority Customs* (Butterworths).

—— (1987), 'Ethnic Minority Customs, English Law and Human Rights' 36 *International and Comparative Law Quarterly* 589.

RATNAPALA, SURI (1993), 'The *Trident Case* and the Evolutionary Theory of F. A. Hayek' 13 *Oxford Journal of Legal Studies* 201.

RAZ, JOSEPH (1979), *The Authority of Law* (Oxford University Press).

ROBERTS, SIMON (1993), 'Alternative Dispute Resolution and Civil Justice: An Unresolved Relationship' 56 *Modern Law Review* 452.

ROWE, JANE, and LYDIA LAMBERT (1973), *Children who Wait* (Association of British Adoption Agencies).

RUTTER, M. (1972), *Maternal Deprivation Reassessed* (Penguin Books).

SARAT, H., and W. L. F. FELSTINER (1986), 'Law and Strategy in the Divorce Lawyers' Office' 20 *Law and Society Review* 93.

SIMMONDS, N. E. (1993), 'Bringing the Outside In' 13 *Oxford Journal of Legal Studies* 147.

SMART, CAROL (1984), *The Ties that Bind* (Routledge).

SORENSON, ANNEMETTE (1992), 'Estimating the Economic Consequences of Separation and Divorce: A Cautionary Tale from the United States', in Lenore J. Weitzman and Mavis Maclean, *Economic Consequences of Divorce: The International Perspective* (Oxford University Press).

STEWART, DANA G. (1991), 'Single Custodial Females and their Families: Housing and Coping Strategies after Divorce' 5 *International Journal of Law and the Family* 296.

STONE, LAWRENCE (1990), *The Road to Divorce: England 1530–1987* (Oxford University Press).

THOBURN, JUNE (1991), 'The Children Act 1989: Balancing Child Welfare with the Concept of Partnership with Parents' *Journal of Social Welfare and Family Law* 331.

University of Newcastle (1989), *Report to the Lord Chancellor on the Costs and Effectiveness of Conciliation in England and Wales* (University of Newcastle upon Tyne).

WALCZAK, Y., and S. BURNS (1984), *Divorce: The Child's Point of View* (Harper & Row).

WALLERSTEIN, JUDITH S., and SANDRA BLAKESLEE (1989), *Second Chances: Men, Women and Children a Decade after Divorce* (Bantam Press).

—— and JOAN KELLY (1980), *Surviving the Breakup* (Grant McIntyre).

WALUCHOW, W. J. (1989), 'The Weak Social Thesis' 9 *Oxford Journal of Legal Studies* 23.

WEITZMAN, LENORE J. (1985), *The Divorce Revolution: The Unexpected Social and Economic Consequences for Women and Children in America* (Free Press).

WILLENBACHER, B., and W. VOEGELI (1988), 'Multiple Disadvantages of Single-Parent Families in the Federal Republic of Germany', in M.-T. Meulders-Klein and J. Eekelaar (eds.), *Family, State and Individual Economic Security* (Story Scientia).

Part one

....

The social and conceptual context

1. Changing family structures and family behaviour

1.1 The family way

A. COOTE, H. HARMAN, H. HEWITT

There is no doubt that the structure of family life is changing. The trends which indicate long-term change became especially marked during the 1970s, continued through the 1980s, and as yet show little sign of slackening. The same broad changes are taking place in all Western European countries; however, some changes are more marked in the UK than elsewhere.

Changes in the UK have been well documented in a recent publication by the Family Policy Studies Centre. Summarizing their findings, the authors Kiernan and Wicks observe that 'the 1980s may have been a watershed in which some traditional features of family life were challenged'. What follows is drawn from their work and that of others; it refers to the UK except where specified.

Marriage

More people marry later

Between 1971 and 1987, the median age at which people marry for the first time rose from 21.4 to 23.3 (women and 23.4 to 25.3 (men). In the same period, the proportion of women getting married in their teens fell from 31 per cent to 13 per cent. The proportion of people married by the age of 30 fell from 93 per cent to 79 per cent (women) and from 84 per cent to 57 per cent (men).[1]

Fewer people marry

Between 1970 and 1987, the marriage rate per 1,000 of the total population fell from 7.5 to 7.0.[2] The proportion of people married by the age of

50 fell between 1971 and 1987 from 96 per cent to 83 per cent (women) and 93 per cent to 79 per cent (men).[3]

Divorce

More people are getting divorced

The number of divorces per 1,000 existing marriages has more than doubled—from 4.7 in 1970 to 12.6 in 1987. The UK increase (7.9) is greater than in any other EC country. Belgium, Denmark, France, and Netherlands come next, with between 5.1 and 5.4 divorces per 1,000 marriages.[4]

Most divorces are initiated by women

In 1988, 73 per cent of divorce proceedings were started by women. Of those women granted divorces in 1988, the majority had cited their husband's 'unreasonable behaviour' as the reason why they wanted to end the marriage. Men most frequently cited their wife's 'adultery'.[5]

Cohabitation

More people cohabit

Between 1981 and 1987, the proportion of single women cohabiting increased from 8 per cent to 17 per cent. 'Nowadays', say Kiernan and Wicks, 'it is virtually a majority practice to cohabit before marrying. Among women marrying for the first time in 1987, 48 per cent had cohabited prior to marriage, compared with 7 per cent of women marrying at the beginning of the 1970s. Around 7 out of 10 second marriages are now preceded by a period of cohabitation.[6]

Cohabitation after divorce lasts longer

People cohabiting prior to remarriage do so for longer (the median time has risen from 28 months in 1979 to 34 months in 1987).[7]

Remarriage

More marriages involve at least one divorced partner

While the proportion of marriages where both partners are getting married for the first time is falling, from 79 per cent in 1971 to 64 per cent in 1987, marriages involving at least one divorced partner are on the increase, from 21 per cent in 1971 to 36 per cent in 1987.[8]

However, the remarriage rate among divorced people is falling

The drop in remarriage rates is noticeable in all age groups, but especially so among younger people. For example, between 1971 and 1987, the annual rate of remarriage per 1,000 divorced women fell from 364 to 151 in the 25–9 age group and from 141 to 70 in the 35 to 44 age group. The equivalent figures for men show a drop from 503 to 156 (25–9 age group) and from 254 to 98 (35–44 age group). Kiernan and Wicks suggest: 'Part of the explanation . . . is likely to be that not only have divorced people continued to cohabit extensively but they have also been cohabiting for longer periods.'[9]

Remarriages are more likely to end in divorce than first marriages

The reasons are uncertain, but material from the US suggests that risks increase with the complexity of the re-formed families.[10] 'For example, couples in which only one of the parties has been previously married and where there are no step-children have the lowest risk, whilst those marriages where both husband and wife are remarrying and both have children from previous marriages have the highest risk.[11]

Lone parenthood

More women are bringing up children on their own

Between 1971 and 1987, lone parents as a proportion of all families with dependent children rose from 8 per cent to 14 per cent. Nine out of 10 of lone parents are women—and that figure has hardly changed since 1971.[12] The UK, with Denmark, has one of the highest proportions of lone parents in the EC, although it is not significantly higher than many others. Germany and France have 12–13 per cent lone parents as a proportion of all families with children; Belgium, Luxembourg, and Netherlands, 10–12 per cent; Spain, Ireland, Italy, and Portugal, 5–10 per cent; Greece under 5 per cent.[13]

The biggest increase in lone parents is accounted for by divorced and single mothers

Between 1971 and 1988, among all families with dependent children, the proportion of lone divorced mothers has risen from 2 per cent to 6 per cent; the proportion of lone single mothers has risen from 1 per cent to 5 per cent. The proportion of widowed single mothers has dropped from 2 per cent to 1 per cent.[14]

There are more lone parents in inner cities

In 1981, the last year for which accurate UK data is available, the national average for the proportion of one parent families was 14 per cent. This compares with 26.6 per cent for Inner London, 19.9 per cent for Liverpool, 18.8 per cent for Birmingham and 20.4 per cent for Glasgow.[15]

General characteristics of lone parents in the EC

The degree of information about lone parents varies from one country to another, but in her recent study of lone parents in the European Community, Jo Roll concludes that the following generalizations are possible:

• The overwhelming majority are women.
• The unmarried category is the smallest.
• The largest consists of divorced/separated people.
• Very few are aged under 25.
• They have fewer children than couples do. Most have only one child.
• Their children are on average older than those in two-parent families.
• Most live on their own.
• Over half leave the 'lone parent state' within 5 years.[16]

Childbirth

Women are having fewer children

Between 1970 and 1987 the number of children per woman dropped from 2.44 to 1.82. In every other EC country, except Belgium, Denmark, and Luxembourg, the decrease was greater.[17]

Women are starting their families later

The average age of a woman having her first child rose from 23.9 in 1970 to 26.4 in 1987. (These figures relate to first marriages only. For all first births, regardless of legitimacy, it is estimated that the woman's age has risen from 24.5 in 1980 to 25.0 in 1987.) The same is happening in all EC countries, other than Greece and Portugal.[18]

Births outside marriage are rising

The proportion of all births which take place outside marriage has risen from 8 per cent in 1970 to 21 per cent in 1986. The trend is more pronounced in Sweden, Denmark, France, and Norway; it is less pronounced in West Germany, the Netherlands, and Ireland.[19]

More women remain childless

According to Kiernan and Wicks, there are 'indications that recent generations of women nearing the end of their reproductive span, those born
in the late 1940s and early 1950s, are more likely to be childless than their
predecessors born in the late 1930s and the rest of the 1940s'.[20]

Children in families

More children born outside marriage are registered by both parents

The proportion of these children who are jointly registered has risen
from 49 per cent in 1975 to 68 per cent in 1987. Of the joint registrations
made in 1987, 7 out of 10 were made by parents living at the same
address.[21]

The great majority of children live with both their natural parents

In 1985, 80 per cent of children under 16 were living with both natural
parents (78 per cent with married parents, 2 per cent with cohabiting parents.) The other 20 per cent were living as follows:

- 10 per cent with lone mother.
- 7 per cent with natural mother married to 'stepfather' (this may include
  some natural fathers who have married the mother since the birth).
- 2 per cent with natural mother cohabiting with 'stepfather'.
- 2 per cent elsewhere (eg. lone father, adoptive or foster parents, relatives, special home, or school).[22]

More children live with a 'stepfather'

In 1979, 84 per cent of children under 16 were living with both natural
parents. The drop to 80 per cent in 1985 is mainly accounted for by the
increase—from 4 to 7 per cent—of children living with natural mother
married to a 'stepfather'.[23]

Changes are more marked for the 0–4 age group

Between 1979 and 1985, the proportion of children in this age group living with both natural parents fell from 90 to 84 per cent. The biggest
change here was in the proportion living with lone mother—up from 7 to
10 per cent.[24]

Children are more likely to experience diverse family settings

It is now increasingly likely that children will experience more than one family setting as they pass through childhood—as a result of changes brought about, for example, by divorce, absence of one parent (usually the father), lone parenthood, cohabitation, remarriage, arrival of half-siblings, etc.[25]

Elderly people

There are more people over 65

The proportion of the population aged 65 and over has risen from 10.9 per cent in 1951 to 13.2 per cent in 1971 and 15.6 per cent in 1987. This represents an increase of more than 2 million people aged 65-plus since 1951. The proportion is expected to level out over the next decade, with 15.6 per cent (nine million individuals) in 2001, but to rise steeply after that, to 16.1 per cent in 2011 and 19.2 per cent (11.5 million) in 2027.[26]

There are more people over 75

The 75-plus age group, as a proportion of the population as a whole, has risen from 4.7 per cent in 1971 to 6.7 per cent in 1987. The proportion is expected to rise to 7.5 per cent (more than 4 million individuals) by 2001 and 8.9 per cent (more than 5 million) in 2027. The 85-plus age group has risen from 0.86 per cent of the population in 1971 to 1.30 in 1987; it is expected to be 2 per cent (more than 1 million individuals) in 2001 and 2.20 per cent (nearly 1.5 million) in 2027. Kiernan and Wicks observe: 'Ageing has implications for the family as a whole . . . more children today grow up in extended families, with several grandparents alive, and, often, some great-grandparents. Extended families seldom live together in Britain, but the interaction between members of the modern extended family is likely to be important.'[27]

Most elderly women live alone or with relatives other than their husband

Of men aged 65-plus, 73 per cent are married; 17 per cent are widowed, 3 per cent are divorced/separated; 6 per cent are single. For women, the picture is very different—because they live longer and tend to marry men older than themselves. Fifty per cent of women aged 65-plus are widowed; 37 per cent are married, 3 per cent divorced/separated, and 10 per cent single. Among all women aged 80 and over who are living in private households, 12 per cent live with their husband; 61 per cent live alone, and 26 per cent with children or other relatives. (One per cent live with non-relatives.)[28]

Work and the family

More married women go out to work

The proportion of married women going out to work has doubled— from 30 per cent in 1951 to 60 per cent in 1987. Almost all the increase has been in part-time employment. In more than half of all couples with dependent children, both partners are in paid employment.[29]

Lone mothers are less likely to go out to work

Comparing mothers with children of all ages, 42 per cent of lone mothers were in paid employment in 1984/6, compared with 52 per cent of married women.[30] The difference is much greater among mothers with children under 5: 17 per cent of lone mothers went out to work in 1985 (7 per cent full-time, 10 per cent part-time), compared with 29 per cent of all mothers with children under 5 (8 per cent full-time, 21 per cent part-time).[31] In 1987, 27 per cent of lone mothers had earnings as their main source of income, compared with 86 per cent of two-parent families.[32]

Fewer mothers of under-fives are employed in UK than in other EC countries

Only in the Netherlands and Ireland do fewer mothers with children under 5 go out to work (full or part-time). In Belgium, Denmark, and France, more than half are in employment; in West Germany, Greece, Italy, and Luxembourg, one-third or more. This compares with 29 per cent in the UK. The most striking difference is among those working full-time: 8 per cent of mothers of under-fives in the UK, compared with 25–45 per cent in Belgium, Denmark, Greece, France, Italy, and Luxembourg.

Among lone mothers of children under 5 who work full-time the difference is even more marked: 7 per cent in the UK compared with 27 per cent in West Germany, 44–9 per cent in France, Belgium, and Italy, and 50 per cent in Denmark.[33]

Most fathers work full-time

Among fathers of children under 5, 83 per cent work full-time, compared with 8 per cent of mothers. The UK figure is low for the EC: apart from

Ireland (79 per cent) and Netherlands (85 per cent) more than 90 per cent of all fathers with children under 5 are in full-time employment in other EC countries.[34]

Women do most of the unpaid work at home

Between 1983 and 1987 (where comparative figures are available), there was a very small increase in the numbers of households where domestic tasks were done mainly by men or shared equally with women. However, in most households, most tasks were still done mainly by women.[35] There is more sharing of household tasks where women work full-time, but very little difference between women who are not in paid employment and those who work part-time.[35]

When it comes to looking after children, women do almost all of the work. The proportion of two-parent families where men play a part in looking after sick children *decreased* between 1983 and 1987; so did the proportion where men played a part in 'teaching children discipline'.[37] Kiernan and Wicks report:

One survey measured the time spent looking after children aged under 5. It found that mothers put in a massive 87 per cent of the 50 or so hours a week involved. Although fathers are involved with child care, this is mainly with its more enjoyable and less demanding aspects—such as play and outings—while mothers are more involved with routine, repetitive daily tasks such as feeding, dressing, and bathing.[38]

Child care facilities

Few children have access to child care facilities

In England there are only 28,951 local authority day nursery places for three million children under 5,[39] and only some 320 out-of-school care facilities for a primary school population of 4.2 million.[40] A survey of working women conducted on behalf of the Department of Employment and the Training Agency found that only 198 women out of 1.1 million surveyed had children in creches provided by employers.[41]

In October 1989, the Department of Education wrote to all schools urging them to make their premises available after school for use by child care schemes. The Kids' Club Network, which specializes in out-of-school care, was contacted by 300 schools responding to the government's circular. However, a follow-up survey by KCN found that only 7 out of the 300 had decided to go ahead and establish out-of-school clubs.[42]

The UK compares poorly with other EC countries

Only 2 per cent of children under 3 are in publicly funded child care services. This compares with 44 per cent in Denmark, 20–5 per cent in France and Belgium, 5 per cent in Italy, and 4 per cent in Portugal. Only the Netherlands, Luxembourg, and Ireland provide fewer places for this age-group than the UK. (There are no figures for Spain.)

For children over 2 and under primary school-age (3–4 year olds), the UK provides publicly funded child care service for 44 per cent of this group. Compulsory schooling starts earlier in the UK than in some other EC countries, so direct comparisons cannot be made. In Belgium, West Germany, Spain, France, Ireland, Italy, and Portugal, primary school starts at 6. In Belgium and France, 95 per cent of children aged 3–5 are in 'pre-primary schooling' or other publicly funded facilities; in Italy, 88 per cent; in Spain, 66 per cent; in West Germany, 60 per cent; in Ireland, 52 per cent, and in Portugal, 25 per cent.[43]

Ethnic differences

There are considerable differences in family structure and household composition between different ethnic groups—especially between families of Afro-Caribbean and Asian origin. It can be misleading, therefore, to make a simple comparison between white and ethnic minority families.

Compared with either white or Afro-Caribbean ethnic groups, Indian, Pakistani, and Bangladeshi groups tend to have larger households and larger families, with more dependent children per family and more families per household. The mean number of dependent children per family is 2.1 (where the family head is Indian), 2.9 (Pakistani), and 3.3 (Bangladeshi), compared with 1.8 (West Indian/Guyanese and white) and 2.0 (African). These Asian groups also have a much smaller proportion of lone parent families (between 8 and 9 per cent, compared with 11 per cent of white families and 18 per cent of all ethnic minority groups)

Compared with either white or Asian ethnic groups, Afro-Caribbean groups have a higher preponderance of lone parent families: 42 per cent of all West Indian/Guyanese families and 24 per cent of all African families. They also have more families with a female head: 37 per cent of all West Indian/Guyanese and 20 per cent of African families, compared with 9 per cent of white and 15 per cent of all ethnic minority families.[44]

Public attitudes

Opinion surveys suggest that there is a gap between what people think ought to happen in families and what is increasingly happening in real life. However, signs of changing attitudes among younger age groups suggest that over time, if people carry their attitudes with them as they grow older, the gap may decrease.

Divorce

Forty per cent of the population surveyed for the 1987 British Social Attitudes report[45] felt that divorce should be made more difficult; only 27 per cent disagreed. Men were more in favour than women of a relaxation of divorce laws.[46] Older people, especially women, were less in favour of more relaxed divorce laws.[47] People living together were the least likely to favour making divorce more difficult.

Parenthood

In the same survey, 78 per cent of respondents agreed with the statement: 'To grow up happily, children need a home with both their own father and mother.' Younger people (aged 18–34), especially younger women, agreed less strongly, as did the more highly educated, those divorced or separated, and cohabitees.[48]

Women at work

Attitudes towards the idea of a woman working outside the home vary according to the age of her children.[49] Most people believed that in families with children under school age, the mother should remain at home. But for families with older children, most people support the notion of a 'compromise' arrangement whereby women work part of the time outside the home.[50] These views may reflect low expectations of finding workable solutions to the problem of child care. Younger people, especially 18–24 year olds, were less committed to traditional working arrangements (where father works full time and mother stays at home); thirty-six per cent supported the idea of the mother of a child under five having a job; only 10 per cent thought she should stay at home.[51]

Child care and domestic work

Men's actual role in child care contrasts sharply with what people think *ought* to happen: 51 per cent of those questioned thought the task of looking after sick children ought to be shared equally between women and men, compared with 30 per cent who reported that they did share it equally; 67 per cent reported that it was done mainly by women. On the question of 'teaching children discipline', 82 per cent said it should be shared equally and only 67 per cent reported that it was; 19 per cent said it was done mainly by women and 13 per cent said it was done mainly by men.[52]

When it comes to other household work, there is also a striking contrast between what actually happens and what people say *should* happen. For instance, 45 per cent said the task of preparing an evening meal should be shared equally and only 17 per cent reported that it was; 77 per cent reported that it was done mainly by women. Fifty-four per cent said household cleaning should be shared equally; 23 per cent reported that it was; 72 per cent said it was done mainly by women.[53]

As we noted earlier, there has been a very slight increase during the 1980s in the numbers of men taking part in household tasks; we can perhaps anticipate a narrowing of the gap between expectation and reality in the coming decades.

Future trends

The trends we have observed in the second half of the 20th century are expected to continue well into the 21st century.

It has been predicted that, by the 21st century:

- More people will never marry.
- More couples will cohabit instead of marrying.
- More children will be born to cohabiting couples.
- Between one-third and two-fifths of new marriages will end in divorce.
- Fewer people will remarry.
- More children will live in lone-parent families.
- More children will live with a step-parent.
- There will be more elderly people, looked after at home by their relatives.[54]

That families are changing is beyond dispute. How are we to interpret these changes? First, we look back at the historical context and then examine the reasons why people make certain personal choices today.

Historical perspective

Families have always been subject to change. It has been common throughout history for children to experience diverse forms of family life and to be looked after by people other than their natural parents. The characteristics of family and community life, and the way in which they change over time are highly complex. Here we can offer no more than the briefest summary.

Historians have observed that in pre-industrial society the village as a whole, rather than the family, was the significant social group: people lived in close proximity to each other, with relatives close at hand. In strictly statistical terms, individual peasant families may have resembled the modern 'nuclear' family,[55] but they depended day-to-day on a much broader web of relationships. Children were not the centre of family life, as they often are today, and it was not unusual for them to be left to fend for themselves while their parents worked in the fields. Meanwhile, in aristocratic households, children were commonly placed in the hands of servants from the moment they came into the world and were given little attention by their mothers or fathers. Babies were breastfed by nurses and children often formed their first attachment with someone other than a natural parent. The word 'family' in the 17th century was used to describe a household made up of kin group and servants: 'his family were himself and his wife and daughters, two mayds and a man' (1631).[56]

It has remained the practice of better-off families to delegate childcare. Wetnursing may be a thing of the past, but the nanny is still a regular feature of upper- and middle-class family life, regardless of the mother's employment status. The measure of surrogate care experienced by a child would appear to increase roughly in line with the size of the family fortune (witness the royal grandchildren). Margaret Thatcher was called to the bar when her twins were less than two years old and worked full-time throughout their childhood, commuting from Orpington to London and leaving them with a nanny.[57] There is certainly nothing new about mothers combining parenthood and paid employment. In many communities, especially working-class ones, women have regularly done so.

If the problems associated with modern family life are set in an historical perspective, it can be seen that other problems have receded. The changes brought about by industrialization, urbanization, and war were more traumatic for families than the changes we are witnessing now. For example, when the process of industrialization drew peasants off the land

and into the factories, families found their lives dramatically transformed. Wages were low, working hours long (14–17 hours a day), living conditions appalling. Children worked in mines and mills with their parents. Babies were often breastfed by undernourished, exhausted, and preoccupied mothers and raised by the street not the family. In all social groups, it was more common 100 years ago than it is today for women to die in childbirth and, on average, men and women died younger—so that children were at greater risk of being orphaned. More children died before reaching adulthood; few received anything other than rudimentary education; many were not educated at all.

We should not, however, underestimate the significance of the changes we are living through today. What is changing, slowly, is the correlation between the ideal and the norm: between how people think family life ought to be lived, and how people are actually living. What used to be a fairly strong correlation is growing weaker. The change is as much about the character of relationships within families as about the size and structure of family units.

For more than a century and a half, a particular model of family life has been dominant. It is, essentially, the model of the middle-class Victorian family: the private, self-contained unit, with breadwinning father married to non-employed, caring mother and two or more children. It has never been universal. However, it has exerted a forceful influence as an *ideal*. The origins of its influence can be traced to Victorian philanthropy: in the interests of reforming the working classes and saving them from the iniquities forced upon them by industrialization, the well-meaning middle classes set about teaching temperance and respectability—a package including a system of values about family life which emphasized maternal care, domesticity, and privacy. Gradually, over many decades, the middle-class model spread into working-class communities. By the 1950s, it had become conventional for a working-class woman to be isolated at home, with her children as her prime concern and the centre of her attention, while her husband went out to earn a living for them all. The family was seen as a refuge, a 'haven in a heartless world'.[58]

As we suggest in the previous section, most people still think this is (approximately) the best way for family life to be lived; however, the conventional model of the mid-century is now becoming *atypical*—and for sound reasons.

Family structures are linked with economic patterns. The 'Victorian' family model reflected the social conditions and the dominant culture of a newly-industrialized society. We are now experiencing a major shift away from a manufacturing to a service-based economy, from industry characterized by mass-production and the fragmentation of skills, to a new phase dominated by information technology and flexible specialization. It is to be expected that such long-term changes in the character of the economy are accompanied by changes in the character of the family.

We would not suggest, however, that economic conditions *determine* family structure. The process is a great deal more complex. The post-war welfare state (which itself reflected the industrial and social patterns of the mid-century) contributed to changes in family life—not least by socializing health care and housing and making free education available to all. The growth in consumerism, a vital factor in the post-war economic boom, played its part in shaping family life; as did the automation of domestic appliances, the declining birth rate, and the rapid expansion of higher education in the 1960s. All of these developments, which were related to economic factors, influenced the role of women and contributed to the development of the modern women's movement, a cultural revolution whose influence spread far beyond its direct participants.[58] The changing expectations of women have been a significant factor in the shifting landscape of family life during the latter part of the 20th century. So has the development of Britain as a multi-ethnic society.

In the last decade, the policies of the Conservative government have made their mark on family life. Housing, child care, family planning, and the incomes of poorer families have all felt the impact of the Conservatives' economic policies. Rising interest rates have hit mortgages and one in ten families accepted as homeless by local authorities now cite mortgage repossession as the cause; 126,000 were accepted as homeless in 1989 compared with 53,000 in 1978.[60] Local authorities, forced to reduce spending, have had little alternative but to cut back or abandon non-statutory services: these include nurseries and after-school care. Meanwhile, pressures on Health Service spending have led some District Health Authorities to reduce family planning services. Fiscal policies have hit families with children: the overall tax burden of a family of four on average income has increased from 23.6 per cent of income in 1979 to 25.6 per cent in 1990.[61] Child benefit, widely accepted as being one of the most efficient ways of helping children, has been frozen, so that it is now worth £1.35 per week less than if would have been, had it kept pace with prices. Income tax cuts and benefit changes have meant that during the 1980s, the richest 10 per cent of families have gained about £40 per week per family, while the poorest 50 per cent of families have lost around £8.50 per week.[62]

Women no longer spend most of their adult lives bearing and rearing children; it is rare for the period devoted to full-time child care to be more than 18 years and far more common for it to be between six and eight years. Changes in expectations and life styles, as well as in the costs of living, have meant that most families need two incomes to get by. As more men fail to provide for their children, it is becoming increasingly clear to women that financial dependence is not a safe option. Most women want to work, use their abilities, enjoy a measure of independence, and earn a living. Meanwhile, they are increasingly in demand as paid workers. When all this is taken into account, it comes as no surprise to find that the traditional, Victorian model of family life is becoming a minority pursuit.

Personal choices

Within this context of economic, social, and cultural developments, how are personal choices made? Why do people decide to get divorced? Or live together without getting married? Or bring up children on their own?

Divorce

As we noted earlier, nearly three-quarters of divorce proceedings are instigated by women.[63] Most commonly, they claim that their marriage has broken down irretrievably because of their husband's 'unreasonable behaviour'. The reason most frequently cited by men suing for divorce is the wife's adultery.[64] It would be unwise to assume that this reflects the real reasons for marriages breaking down, since getting a divorce involves meeting legal criteria. However, it does suggest that women and men experience the down-side of marriage in different ways.

As the nature of marriage has changed (from social institution to private relationship) couples have placed more emphasis upon the personal qualities of their partners—they now look for companionship, communication, and sexual compatibility.[65] The transition from culturally prescribed roles to negotiated roles is bound to cause tension—both to individuals and to the institution of marriage.

A successful marriage, according to the 1987 British Social Attitudes report,[67] is seen to be sustained above all by good personal relations between spouses, rather than by such things as a comfortable lifestyle or having children. People were asked which factors they considered to be 'very important to a successful marriage'. Top of the list came 'faithfulness' (86 per cent rated it very important), 'mutual respect and appreciation; (77 per cent), 'understanding and tolerance' (69 per cent). Material factors were said to be much less important: 'adequate income' was rated very important by 34 per cent, 'good housing' by 33 per cent, and 'having children' by 31 per cent. (Attitudes seem to have changed since 1952, when a Gallup Poll found that 'a regular/adequate income' was ranked alongside 'mutual respect and appreciation' and 'understanding and tolerance' as being the most important factors for a successful marriage.)[68]

Divorce is more often felt to be justified when personal relations are poor, than when material conditions change for the worse. When people were asked what reasons were sufficient for divorce, 'consistent unfaithfulness' came top of the list (cited by 94 per cent), followed by 'violence' (92 per cent), and 'ceasing to love the other' (75 per cent). These factors came well ahead of 'can't have children' (7 per cent) and 'financially broke' (4 per cent).[69]

There are variations across the population. Those in non-manual work, those with better qualifications, and young people tend to attach less importance to 'adequate income' and 'good housing' than those in manual work and those with few or no qualifications.[70] Older people are more likely to say that material circumstances affect the security of the marriage.

Certainly, most women instigating divorce are effectively choosing to be much less well off than they would be in marriage. This would seem to support the finding that material conditions are relatively unimportant. There is none the less evidence that, for some groups in the population, intolerable pressures may be placed on their partnership because of poor housing and low income.[71] Unemployment can have a devastating effect on marriage.[72] One study concluded that unemployment causes a 70 per cent increase in the likelihood of marriage break-up the following year.[73] A Northern Ireland survey[74] found that around three-quarters of those interviewed reported unemployment having a negative effect on domestic relations, and only 4 couples (out of 343 surveyed) felt that unemployment had brought them together.

The reality of marriage may not live up to new expectations for many people—particularly women, for whom the status and roles traditionally conferred by wedlock may be becoming less important than the need to develop at a personal level. More women are joining the workforce and this trend is expected to continue.[75] There are considerable stresses in trying to balance the competing demands of work and home-life. And while women's lives are changing, there is little evidence, as we have seen, that men's lives are undergoing compatible changes.

Cohabitation

The decision to cohabit is sometimes made because couples are not in a position to marry—they may already be married to someone else.[76] Indeed much cohabitation is temporary, often leading to marriage. Some people may decide consciously not to marry. According to Relate (previously known as the Marriage Guidance Council) this may be because they want to avoid the roles they see as being part of marriage, or because they do not want to incorporate a religious or bureaucratic component into their relationship.[77] At the same time, legally and fiscally there are fewer and fewer distinctions between cohabitation and marriage. People may more easily decide that the formal act of marriage is not relevant to their relationship. It does not follow that these who decide to cohabit are less committed to the relationship than those who decide to marry. Indeed, it would be fair to say that relatively little is known about cohabitation. There are, as yet, no data from longitudinal studies of cohabitation, which could form the basis for a comparison with marriage.

Lone parenthood

As we have seen, nine out of ten single parents in the UK are women. For the majority, the decision to become a single parent is inextricably linked with the decision to end a marriage. For a few (8 per cent) their fate is determined by the death of a spouse. But nearly one in four has never married. Did they set out with the intention of going it alone?

Beatrix Campbell has written eloquently about the conditions of young women in northern British towns and cities, hit hard by unemployment in the early 1980s.

unemployed girls who've never experienced economic independence are doing the only thing they can—having babies, either getting married or not, but often staying with their mam and dad and, quite soon, getting a council house. They never consider an abortion, often don't use contraception. They want kids. Of course they do. There isn't anything else. Being a mother has a certain status after all, it makes you a grown up person . . . Faced with the alternatives of the dole, or the angry aggravation of the streets, motherhood brings a sense of belonging. More important, it offers a transition from immaturity made permanent by poverty, to a state of maturity.[78]

Many of these young mothers got council homes and were glad of it, Campbell reported, but their new independence meant trading the over-crowded and emotionally fraught conditions of their parents' home for some of the worst housing in the country.

They are lonely and they are poor. Though if you're young and poor the surest guarantee of a council house is parenthood, it is only because the housing cata-clysm of the fifties and sixties produced cold, camp deserts that no one else wants to live on.[79]

What is clear from Campbell's account is that it is not council housing poli-cies which 'cause' young women to have babies on their own, but their lack of opportunity to do anything else. If there is any structural cause, it is the organization of society which leaves girls from poor, working-class backgrounds at 16 with no qualifications, no training, no prospects of any employment which might bring them a sense of worth, security, or auton-omy—in short, no way of gaining entry into the adult world.

These conclusions seem to be supported by a 1989 survey by One Parent Families,[80] conducted among young single mothers. None of those surveyed had thought of pregnancy or motherhood as a passport to guaranteed housing or income. Indeed, the notion of anyone getting pregnant out of deliberate intent to jump the housing queue seemed to strike them as improbable if not foolish. Very few of the women they interviewed had 'set out' to become pregnant: their pregnancies were largely unplanned; very few intended to become single parents and had initially seen themselves as part of a couple—until their partners saw it differently.

There are undoubtedly some women who decide that they have suffi-cient financial and other resources, and determine to bring up a child by themselves. There are no figures available, but One Parent Families esti-mates[81] that these women are a very small percentage of the total num-ber of single mothers. It is unlikely that many of these (predominantly middle-class) mothers would apply for council housing.

The social consequences of change

The 'breakdown of traditional family life' has been blamed for a range of social problems: for the failure of young people to 'achieve' at school or at work, for the growth of juvenile delinquency, violence, and crime, for child sexual abuse and—more grandly—for the general disintegration of the 'social fabric'.

As we have noted, some commentators have marked out for special concern the declining role of the breadwinning, 'natural' father, and the increasing preponderance of lone mothers. What is implied is, firstly, that the father-figure in the traditional family is the key to social stability and cohesion and, secondly, that women alone are inadequate parents. The concern about suffering caused to children by the loss of a natural parents is of course quite proper, but it must be placed in context. By focusing attention on what happens in families where the father is absent, we ought not to overlook what can happen in families where the father is present. For example, most domestic violence and child sexual abuse is perpetrated by married men against their own wives and children.[82] In addition, the great majority (84 per cent) of adults convicted of criminal offences are male; and men account for an even higher proportion (91 per cent) of those convicted of violent crimes.[83] Many of these male convicted criminals are married men and it is undoubtedly the case that many boys learn to be violent and/or criminal by following the example of their own fathers. It is extremely rare for women to commit violent crimes, or to abuse their children sexually.[84] Moreover, as we have noted, women do almost all the work involved in bringing up their children, whether or not they are living with the children's father; this has remained unchanged for generations.

It cannot therefore be assumed that men are bound to be an asset to family life, or that the presence of fathers in families is necessarily a means to social harmony and cohesion. However, as is often the case, there are grains of truth stuck in the teeth of misguided assumptions. These can be prised out if approached from a different angle: what needs to be considered is not the role of fathers and mothers, as such, but the impact of change on children.

It is beyond the scope of this report to investigate every possible consequence of the changing patterns of family life. We have chosen to focus upon three main areas:

a How divorce affects the development of children, in particular the nature of the link between divorce and relative 'under-achievement'.

• How children are affected by being brought up mainly by a single parent, in particular how lone parenthood might be linked with relative 'under-achievement' or with 'anti-social' behaviour.

• How remarriage affects children, particularly the relationship between remarriage and the incidence of child sexual abuse.

Divorce

There is evidence from longitudinal research[85] that children whose parents had divorced before they reached 15 had a lower level of attainment in later life, than those whose parents remained married, or who lost a parent through death. Their lack of self-esteem, which contributed to their relatively low attainment, was shown to be connected with feelings of being left by the parent who ceased to live with them after the marriage ended. The evidence needs to be treated cautiously, since these divorces took place well before divorce generally became more commonplace and therefore, conceivable, less stigmatizing. However, similar findings emerged from another study of younger children, carried out by the Child Care Development Group at the University of Cambridge.

It was worse to lose contact with a parent through divorce than through death, for a number of reasons. For one thing, the child was a lot more likely to feel deliberately abandoned; secondly, the remaining parent was less likely to convey positive feelings about the absent parent. Thirdly, the child was more likely to lose contact with grandparents and other relatives on the absent parent's side of the family.

However, what counted most for the children was not the divorce itself, but the quality of their separate relationships with each of their parents. This, according to the research is far more important for the child than the quality of the relationship *between* the parents—except in cases where children are drawn into the parents' quarrel and deployed as a 'pawn in the game' by one party against the other.

In their book *Divorce Matters*,[86] Burgoyne *et al.* observe that the distress of children following divorce is, as a rule, relatively short-lived, subsiding gradually after a 'matter of months or a year': 'The time this takes depends very much on what happens after the divorce and the quality of the children's relationship with *both* parents. Broadly speaking, the better their relationship with their parents, the less marked the distress will b and the shorter the duration.'

They confirm that it is better for children to maintain contact with both parents, even when there is continuing conflict between parents.

Children in such situations seem better off than those who have completely lost contact with the non-custodial parent—usually, of course, the father. While conflict is upsetting for children, its effects are partially separable from those arising from the loss of the parent.

It appears that, within two years of their parents' divorce, more than one-third of children have no contact with the non-custodial parent.[87] Clearly,

it is of enormous value for children to have a positive and enduring relationship with both parents—father and mother. Would it therefore benefit children if divorce were made more difficult to obtain? Here, we must
recognize that few couples undertake lightly the decision to divorce.
There is far more evidence of people enduring prolonged misery within
marriage, trying to 'make it work', or believing it is their 'lot', than there
is evidence of couples springing fecklessly apart.

it is common for partners to go on believing that their life together is quite normal and tolerable until a chance discussion casts their difficulties in a different
light . . . As a result many women, and perhaps some men, continue to tolerate
even violent physical abuse, partly because there may be no alternative, but also
because they believe it to be an inevitable aspect of marriage.[88]

We have seen that most divorce suits are brought by women and most
women cite 'unreasonable behaviour' as their reason. It is worth noting
that considerable numbers of women get divorced to escape their husband's violence. A 1989 survey of 1,000 married women found that 28
per cent said they had been hit by their husbands[89] and Women's Aid,
the network of refuges for battered women, estimate that the 25,000
women who pass through their doors in a year represent the 'tip of the
iceberg'.[90]

There are some circumstances where breaking off contact with one
parent is less harmful for the child than continuing the contact, in particular where the parent has been violent or sexually abusive towards the
child. Where this is not the case, however, the evidence suggests that the
child's development is far less likely to be damaged if contact is maintained with the non-custodial parent. It is this contact, rather than the
ease or difficulty with which couples can divorce, which ought to concern policy-makers.

Lone parenthood

There is little evidence to support the assertion (increasingly common of
late) that lone parenthood—or one motherhood—is *itself* a direct cause of
under-achievement of children, juvenile delinquency, crime, or general
social disintegration. Many studies point specifically to the similarities
rather than the differences between children from one and two parent
families. For example, one which compared children from 'broken' and
'intact' homes, measuring self-concept, attitudes towards the family and
peer relationships, observed that: '. . . the most meaningful outcome of
the study was the finding of many similarities and few differences

between children whose fathers had been absent for two or more years and children whose father was living in their homes'.[91]

The Study Commission on the Family has commented on the difficulty of drawing conclusions from research, as so much of it is based on children 'already identified as "maladjusted"'.

Bias can be introduced into an analysis of the links between family circumstances and delinquency which is based on children in care and custody. Children from family backgrounds which are considered 'abnormal' may be more likely to be taken into custody than children from 'normal' homes even when similar offences are involved.[92]

There are, however, two major factors which, though not inevitably linked with lone parenthood, are often associated with it—and may cause problems.

1. *Changing relationships*   As with those whose parents divorce, children in lone-parent families may experience trauma, loss, and insecurity, which may have a detrimental effect on their development. It is usually better for such children if the absent parent is known to them, and maintains a loving, affirming relationship. However, if that doesn't happen, it is possible—and common—for children to form attachments with other adults who care for them, which are of great value. The 'key issues' according to the Study Commission on the Family, are 'the quality of parent/child relationships and the degree of insecurity experienced'. The Commission points out that 'many children in "intact" homes suffer from family insecurity and emotional deprivation, whilst many children from "broken" homes lead happy, normal lives'.[93] Michael Rutter has stressed the overriding importance of bonds formed by children: '. . . love, the development of bonds, a stable but not necessarily unbroken relationship and stimulating interaction are all necessary qualities'.[94]

If a parent is absence, 'the detrimental effect . . . will be alleviated to a greater or lesser extent depending on the quality of substitute care and the presence or lack of other adults or children with whom the child has formed an attachment'.[95] This point is underlined by the British Medical Association in its evidence to the Finer Committee on One Parent Families: '. . . in practice, it would seem that there are compensatory mechanisms which allow children to be as emotionally healthy in one parent families as in two parent families'.[96]

We may conclude that if there are no such mechanisms at work in the life of a child in a lone parent family, that child is less likely to develop its full potential, than are other children in one- or two-parent families. What is important, it seems to us, is to recognize that suffering can occur; to avoid confusing the general category to which a child's family belongs with those aspects of a child's experience which can bring about feelings of trauma, loss, and insecurity; and to understand the mechanisms which can alleviate potential harm.

2. Poverty   There is ample evidence that lone parenthood is associated with poverty. In her study of lone parents in the EC, Jo Roll concludes that 'lone parent families are more vulnerable to poverty and low income than two-parent families': 'Lone fathers are better off than lone mothers and, among lone mothers, widows are generally better off than unmarried or divorced mothers.'[97]

Those with paid jobs were better off than those without, although the evidence suggested that even those in employment had 'living standards very close to subsistence levels'. Lone parents, Roll observes, are not a homogeneous group. 'A divorced mother in her late 30s, working full-time, with a university education and who has only briefly (or never) left the labour force is in a very different position from a young divorced mother, with little education and a child below school age, struggling to balance child care and a part time job.'[98]

Nevertheless, on average, lone parents fare worse than two-parent families. Comparing lone with two-parent families, Roll found that in the UK, 30 per cent had a car compared with 85 per cent of two-parent families, 66 per cent had central heating, compared with 82 per cent, and 64 per cent had a telephone, compared with 88 per cent. Most strikingly, 29 per cent owned their homes, compared with 67 per cent of two-parent families. Lone parents were more likely to live in high-rise blocks or subsidized housing in parts of town away from the houses of two-parent families.[99] Lone parents are concentrated in the lower income groups, and these groups, according to a recent government report, are getting poorer. The report shows that between 1979 and 1987, incomes for the average rose by nearly a quarter—23.1 per cent—while those for the bottom 10 per cent, after allowing for housing costs, increased by on 0.1 per cent.[100]

While it is possible to show differences between children of lone-parent and two-parent families, in terms of their emotional and educational development, the weight of evidence suggests that these differences are due to the different material circumstances of the families in question. For example, a follow-up study of one of the national cohorts of children found that educational disadvantage among illegitimate children could be 'largely explained by socio-economic status rather than birth status'.[101] The Inner London Educational Authority's evidence to the Finer Committee concluded that: '. . . educationally, the difficulties of children from one-parent families are not on the whole peculiar to these children, but are common to children from low income groups'.[102]

A longitudinal study of boys in six London schools found a strong association between marital separation and delinquency but 'when matched for income or for parental criminality or for family size there was no clearly significant difference between delinquents and non-delinquents in the incidence of such separations'.[103] This was borne out by more recent findings in the United States which showed that: '. . . once the effect of family income was allowed for, there was no longer a tendency for delinquents guilty of more serious offences to come from incomplete (*sic*) parental homes'.[104]

What we learn, in summary, is that lone parenthood is often linked with material deprivation. We also learn that material deprivation is often linked with such problems as juvenile delinquency and educational under-achievement. To argue that lone parenthood is therefore a *cause* of delinquency or under-achievement is an affront to reason—not unlike shooting the messenger.

Remarriage

It is more common now than it was in the post-war decades to find people voicing concern about the effects of remarriage on children. As Burgoyne *et al.* point out, child psychology suffered in the past from an over-emphasis on the mother–child relationship:

Fathers, if mentioned at all in the influential books of twenty years ago, were seen as emotional and financial supports for mothers rather than having any important direct role in the lives of children. Maternal deprivation was seen as the central problem. Provided mother was around, the child's social needs were seen as being met.[105]

Remarriage, according to this view, was desirable because it provided continuing support for the mother; she gained a new breadwinner, the child a new family.

More recent research suggests that remarriage can have positive and negative effects. On the positive side, it can bring better material conditions if the new parent is in paid employment, without heavy financial commitments to a previous family. This could also be true where a lone parent entered a first marriage or cohabiting union.

On the negative side, remarriage may exacerbate difficulties already experienced by a child adjusting to the loss of one parent. For example, the step-parent may be presented as a replacement for the absent parent; his arrival (it is usually a step-father) may curtail contact with the absent father; or the new marriage may involve rewriting of history so that the previous marriage comes to be regarded as a 'bad dream'.[106] In some circumstances, children with step-parents might face more difficulties than those who remain in lone-parent families.[107]

More dramatically, it has been claimed that children living in reconstituted families are more vulnerable to sexual abuse than those living with both natural parents.

Andreas Gledhill and 'others' who wrote the Centre for Policy Studies document, *Who Cares?*,[108] rely on data from the NSPCC about children placed on the Society's 'at risk' register between 1983 and 1987. Of those registered because of sexual abuse (CSA), 37 per cent lived with two natural parents, 20 per cent with their natural mother alone, and 33 per cent with their natural mother and a father substitute. These data should be treated with caution, as the NSPCC deals only with those children considered 'at risk'; children who are not in conventional families tend to be drawn more readily to the attention of organizations such as the NSPCC. However, the NSPCC data are largely supported by the US sociologist Diana Russell, who interviewed a random sample of 930 adult women about childhood experience of sexual abuse.[109]

Russell reports: 'by far the majority of incest perpetrators in our survey who were parents or parent figures were biological fathers (60 per cent), with stepfathers constituting the next largest group (33 per cent)'. She goes on to observe that 'many more daughters are accessible to biological fathers than stepfathers' and therefore the proportion of abuse by stepfathers is far greater. Altogether, 749 of the respondents had lived with a biological or adoptive father for most of the time before they were 14; of these, 18 reported incestuous abuse during that time (2.4 per cent). By comparison, 29 respondents had lived for most of the time with a stepfather, of whom 10 reported abuse (34.5 per cent). Russell also found a more serious level of abuse by step-fathers: of those reporting abuse by biological fathers, 26 per cent reported 'very serious sexual abuse' compared with 47 per cent for abuse by step, adoptive, or foster fathers; but it should be noted that at this level of analysis, the actual numbers were very small (7 and 8 respectively).

Russell offers two explanations for the prevalance and seriousness of abuse by step-fathers: the absence of the incest taboo, and the possible absence of the kind of bonding which commonly occurs between biological fathers and their daughters.

The implications are alarming: if divorce is on the increase, more children are likely to spend part of their childhood living with a man who is not their natural father. Are we to conclude that hindering divorce would help to curb child sexual abuse?

There is a danger, in focusing upon the rate of abuse among stepfathers, of losing sight of the whole picture. It is worth recalling Diana Russell's finding that biological fathers account for most child sexual abuse (out of a total of 45 abusing parent figures, 27 were biological fathers). It is also worth noting that, of all those children known to the NSPCC who have experienced 'non-accidental injury', the largest proportion live with both natural parents (41 per cent, compared with 21 per cent living with their natural mother alone and 28 per cent living with their natural mother and a father substitute).[110]

Many women divorce to escape from the abusive behaviour of their husbands: as we have already noted, most divorce suits are brought by women and the most common ground on which they sue for divorce is 'unreasonable behaviour'. In short, it cannot be assumed that marriage is a passport to safety for women or children. Divorce in many cases will be a better means of protection than staying in an unsatisfactory marriage.

As far as remarriage is concerned, caution is clearly in order. Russell suggests that women should be 'more careful in their evaluation of prospective men friends, lovers, or marriage partners'; they should be watchful, avoid placing their daughters in vulnerable situations and 'work even harder to establish a relationship of trust between themselves and their daughters'. 'Then, if the daughters feel any discomfort about the way their stepfathers relate to them, they are more likely to confide in their mothers about it.'[111]

Russell reports several cases in her survey where women who had been sexually abused by a step-father, believed that these men had married their mothers especially in order to have access to the daughters. This appear, she says, 'to be a definite strategy employed by some pedophiles, and the more women who know about it the less effective a strategy it may become'. A study of convicted offenders bears this out.[112]

We need to know why men sexually abuse children. Gledhill and 'others' blame one-parent families: 'Even the best one parent families are unlikely to impart to a child the skills which a child learns when brought up by both natural parents. In particular, this deficiency manifests itself in violent conduct such as child abuse.'[113]

Their source is Patricia Morgan who claims that 'any rise in the number of boys without close ties to males with socially acceptable standards of behaviour (e.g. fathers) . . . is virtually guaranteed to generate a brutalised and violent masculine style'.[114] This does not appear to tally with the findings of the Study Commission on the Family, which reports that 'father-absent-boys may be less masculine'.[115] Nor does it take account of the fact that many boys observe or experience the violent and brutal behaviour of their own fathers, and learn accordingly how to be men.

More significant is the evidence that a high proportion of sexually abusive fathers had divorced parents.[116] The implication is that boys whose parents divorce may be more likely to become child abusers in later life. However, it is not the divorce itself which creates the problem, but the opportunity (or lack of it) for a young male to mature psychologically—to learn to distinguish fantasy from reality, and to understand and respect the separate identity of others. What counts, whether or not a boy's parents have divorced or he has been raised in a one-parent family, is the quality of his relationships, during his childhood, with his natural parents and with any other parent figure with whom he forms a close bond. A positive, secure relationship with a step-parent can help a child to mature psychologically; a negative, insecure relationship with a natural parent can hinder that process.[117]

What is of paramount importance, if children are to be protected, is that mothers should be able to judge *from a position of strength* whether or not to introduce a step-father into their families. That means knowing about the risks they may be running and being free to make alternative choices. A vital factor here is the material deprivation suffered by so many lone parent families. Single mothers who are trapped in poverty and desperate to find a way of providing for their children may be less likely to weigh the dangers of sexual abuse against the possible material advantages of remarriage.

It should be stressed here that it is not only in reconstituted families that the strength of the mother can be a vital factor in protecting children from sexual abuse. The same is true within marriage or cohabiting unions, where fathers abuse their own children. Women are more likely to be deterred from taking action against their husbands or cohabitees if they feel themselves to be heavily dependent—either financially or emotionally—upon them.

The impact of change on children

Summarizing this section on the social consequences of change, it is possible to make some very broad generalizations about the impact of change on children.

- Two factors of considerable importance to the development of a child are the quality of the child's relationship with its parents (including its natural parents and other parent-figures with whom it forms a close bond); and the material circumstances in which the child grows up.
- Underlying trends in the patterns of family life (outlined above) suggest that more children are—and will be—vulnerable to the possible adverse effects of change.
- Changing family circumstances increase the chances of a child experiencing disruption and insecurity; they do not inevitably cause it.
- Children who grow up in a loving and secure relationship with their natural parent(s) and/or non-biological parent(s) are less likely than children who do not (all other things being equal), to experience difficulties as they grow up.
- Positive and secure bonds formed with non-biological parent figures can compensate for the loss or absence of natural parents.
- Children who live in better-off families are less likely than children in poor families to experience difficulties as they grow up.
- Children who live in one-parent families are more likely to suffer from material deprivation, but less likely to suffer relational difficulties than those who live in reconstituted families.

Notes

1. K. Kiernan, and M. Wicks, *Family change and future policy* (Family Policy Studies Centre, June 1990), pp. 6–7.
2. Eurostat: Demographic Statistics, 1988, Table VI, quoted in J. Roll, *Lone Parents in the European Community* (Family Policy Studies Centre, 1989).
3. Kiernan and Wicks, op. cit., p. 7.
4. J. Roll, *Lone Parent Families in the European Community* (Family Policy Studies Centre, 1989).
5. *Social Trends*, 20 (HMSO, 1990).
6. Kiernan and Wicks, op. cit., pp. 8–9.
7. Ibid.
8. Ibid., p. 9.
9. Ibid., p. 9.

10. Haskey, J., 1988, 'Trends in marriage and divorce and cohort analyses of the proportions of marriages ending in divorce', *Population Trends* No. 54 (HMSO). Quoted in Kiernan and Wicks, op. cit., p. 15.
11. L. K. White and A. Booth, 1985, 'The quality and stability of remarriages: the role of stepchildren', *American Sociological Review*, vol. 50, no. 5. Quoted in Kiernan and Wicks, op. cit., p. 16.
12. Kiernan and Wicks, op. cit., p. 13.
13. J. Roll, op. cit.
14. Kiernan and Wicks, op. cit., p. 14.
15. Kiernan and Wicks, op. cit., p. 14.
16. J. Roll, op. cit.
17. Eurostat: Demographic Statistics 1988, Table VI and Tables 10, column 10, quoted in J. Roll, op. cit. (1970 figure refers to Great Britain, 1987 to UK).
18. Eurostat: Demographic Statistics 1988, Table 8, Col. 9, quoted in J. Roll, op. cit.
19. Kiernan and Wicks, op. cit., p. 10.
20. C. Shaw, 'Recent Trends in family size and family building', *Population Trends*, No. 58 (HMSO, 1989), quoted in Kiernan and Wicks, op. cit., p. 11.
21. Kiernan and Wicks, op. cit., p. 11.
22. L. Clarke, *Children's Changing Circumstances: Recent Trends and Future Prospects*, Table 6 (Centre for Population Studies Research paper 89–4, December 1989). (Percentage figures rounded up, accounting for discrepancy of 1% in total.)
23. Ibid.
24. Ibid., Table 5.
25. Kiernan and Wicks, op. cit., p. 17.
26. Ibid., pp. 20–21.
27. Ibid., p. 22.
28. Ibid.
29. Ibid., p. 26.
30. Ibid., p. 27.
31. Eurostat: Labour Force Survey 1985: special analysis carried out by the EC Statistical Office at the request of Peter Moss, Thomas Coram Research Unit, for the European Childcare Network. Quoted in J. Roll, op. cit.
32. Kiernan and Wicks, op. cit., p. 28.
33. Eurostat: Labour Force Survey, 1985, op. cit., quoted in J. Roll, op. cit.
34. Ibid.
35. *Social Trends*, 1990, Table 2.9 (HMSO).
36. Kiernan and Wicks, op. cit., p. 29.
37. *Social Trends*, 1990, op. cit.
38. Kiernan and Wicks, op. cit., pp. 29–30.
39. Thomas Coram Research Unit. *Under fives services provision and usage*, February 1990; OPCS Monitor PPI 89/1.
40. J. Dawson, *A patchwork of provision—Kids Clubs today* (Kids Club Network, 1990).

41. *The Independent*, 9.4.90. 'Firms failing to provide child care'.
42. Kids Club Network, *Back to the Drawing Board: School-based Childcare* (KCN, 1990).
43. P. Moss, *Childcare and Equal Opportunity*, Consolidated Report to the European Commission, European Childcare Network, April 1988. Quoted in J. Roll, op. cit.
44. J. Haskey, 'Families and households of the ethnic minority and White populations of Great Britain', *Population Trends*, Autumn 1989.
45. S. Ashford, 'Family Matters', *British Social Attitudes*, 1987 Report. Jowell *et al.*, *Social and Community Planning Research*, 1987.
46. Ibid., pp. 122–3; p. 143. 31% men and 23% women disagreed or disagreed strongly with the statement: 'Divorce in Britain should be made more difficult to obtain than it is now.'
47. Ibid., pp. 122–3; p. 143. For example, 34% of men aged 18–44 disagreed or disagreed strongly, compared with 18% of women over 55.
48. Ibid., pp. 134–5.
49. Ibid., pp. 128–9; p. 145.
50. Ibid., p. 128. 60% of those surveyed for the 1987 British Social Attitudes report thought that women should work part-time if children were in their early teens.
51. Ibid., p. 129.
52. *Social Trends*, 1990, table 2.9. op. cit.
53. Ibid.
54. Kiernan and Wicks, op. cit., p. 43.
55. P. Laslett and R. Wall (eds), *Household and Family in Past Time* (New York, 1972).
56. J. Finch, *Family Obligations and Social Change* (Polity Press and Basil Blackwell, 1989), ch. 2. See also R. Williams, *Keywords* (Flamingo Press, 1983), p. 131.
57. N. Wapshott and G. Brock, *Thatcher* (Futura, 1983), p. 62.
58. Young and Willmott, *Family and Kinship in East London* (Penguin, 1957).
59. A. Coote and B. Campbell, *Sweet Freedom* (Basil Blackwell, 1987).
60. National Audit Office, *Homelessness: A Report by the Comptroller and Auditor General* (HMSO, August 1990).
61. *Hansard*, 4.4.90, cc. 605–6.
62. J. Hills, *Changing Tax* (Child Poverty Action Group, 1988), p. 13.
63. 73% of divorce proceedings in 1988 were started by women. Government Statistical Service. *Social Trends* 20 (HMSO, 1990).
64. *Social Trends 1990*, op. cit.
65. C. Clulow, 'Marriage in the 1990s', *Sexual and Marital Therapy*, vol. 5, no. 1 (1990).
66. D. Hannan, *Traditional Families?* (Economic and Social Research Institute, Dublin, 1977). Rapoport *et al.* (eds), *Families in Britain* (Routledge and Kegan Paul, London, 1982). Both quoted in S. Harding, 'Interim report: The chang-

ing family', in Jowell *et al.* (eds.), *British Social Attitudes—special international report* (Social and Community Planning Research, 1989).

67. S. Ashford, 'Family Matters', in Jowell *et al.* (eds.), *British Social Attitudes, the 1987 Report* (Social and Community Planning Research, 1987).

68. R. J. Wybrow, *Britain Speaks Out*. A social history as seen through the Gallup data (MacMillan), p. 33.

69. S. Ashford, op. cit.

70. Ibid., pp. 124–5.

71. Ibid.

72. J. Mattinson *et al.*, *Work, Love and Marriage*. Tavistock Institute of Marital Studies (Duckworth, 1988).

73. R. Lampard, *An examination of the relationship between marital dissolution and unemployment*. ESRC Social Change and Economic Life Initiative, Working Paper 17, (May, 1990).

74. E. Evason, *On the edge. A study of poverty and long term unemployment in Northern Ireland* (1989).

75. *Social Trends 20* (HMSO, 1990).

76. *Social Trends 19* (HMSO, 1989), p. 42.

77. Relate (Marriage Guidance), personal communication.

78. B. Campbell, *Wigan Pier Revisited* (Virago, 1984), pp. 63–5.

79. Ibid., p. 67.

80. E. Clark, *Young single mothers today: a qualitative study of housing and support needs* (National Council for One Parent Families, Summer 1989).

81. Personal communication.

82. Cleveland Refuge and Aid for Women and Children, *Private Violence: Public Shame*, 1984; 1988. Survey of women who sought refuge to escape domestic violence between January 1977 and June 1982 (total: 393) showed that 74.6% were married, compared with 20.4% cohabiting; 2.8% single, and 2.2% separated; these findings are supported by unpublished figures supplied to London Women's Aid by the Metropolitan Police. See also, D. E. H. Russell, 'The Prevalence and Seriousness of Incestuous Abuse: Stepfathers vs. Biological Fathers', in *Child Abuse and Neglect*, vol. 8, pp. 15–22 (1984).

83. *Criminal Statistics, 1988* (HMSO).

84. 3.5% of women convicted of criminal offences were convicted for crimes of violence, *Criminal Statistics 1988*, op. cit; D. E. H. Russell, op. cit., found that 2% of parent–child incest perpetrators were mothers.

85. M. MacLean, and M. Wadsworth (1988), 'Children's Life Chances and Parental Divorce' in *International Journal of Law and the Family*, vol. 2, pp. 155–66.

86. J. Burgoyne, R. Ormrod, and M. Richards, *Divorce Matters* (Penguin, 1987), p. 127.

87. J. Bradshaw and J. Millar, *Lone Parent Families in the UK*, Final report to the Department of Social Security, May 1990 (unpublished).

88. J. Burgoyne *et al.*, op. cit., p. 93.

89. *World In Action* (Granada TV), quoted in *The Independent*, 1 August 1990.
90. Quoted in *The Independent*, 1 August 1990.
91. M. M. Thomas, 'Children with Absent Fathers', *Journal of Marriage and the Family*, 30. 1, p. 89. Quoted in Popay *et al.*, *Parents, Children and Public Policy* (Study Commission on the Family, 1983).
92. Popay *et al.*, 1983, op. cit.
93. Popay *et al.*, op. cit., p. 32.
94. M. Rutter, *Maternal Deprivation Reassessed* (Penguin, 1972), p. 21.
95. Popay *et al.*, op. cit., p. 31.
96. Quoted in Popay *et al.*, op. cit., p. 32.
97. J. Roll, *Lone Parent Families in the European Community* (Family Policy Studies Centre, 1989).
98. Ibid.
99. Ibid.
100. *Households Below Average Income: A Statistical Analysis 1981–87* (HMSO, July 1990). (1979 figures included in the appendix of this report; comparison with 1987 supplied by the Institute for Fiscal Studies to *The Independent*, 25 July 1990.)
101. Quoted in Popay *et al.*, op. cit., p. 35.
102. Ibid.
103. Ibid.
104. Ibid.
105. Burgoyne *et al.* op. cit., p. 132.
106. Ibid., p. 135.
107. J. W. B. Douglas, *Broken families and child behaviour*, Journal of the Royal College of Physicians, 4 (1970), p. 203.
108. A. Gledhill and Others, *Who Cares?* (Centre for Policy Studies, Policy Study No. 111, 1989).
109. D. E. H. Russell, 'The Prevalence and Seriousness of Incestuous Abuse: Stepfathers vs. Biological Fathers', in *Child Abuse and Neglect*, vol. 8, pp. 15–22 (1984).
110. M. de Young, *The Sexual Victimisation of Children* (1982), p. 11.
111. D. E. H. Russell, op. cit.
112. J. R. Conte *et al.*, *What sexual offenders tell us about prevention: preliminary findings*, paper presented to the Third National Family Violence Conference, Durham, New Hampshire, July 1987.
113. Gledhill and others, op. cit., p. 13.
114. P. Morgan, 'Feminist Attempts to Sack Father: a case of Unfair Dismissal?' in D. Anderson, D. and G. Dawson (eds.) *Family Portraits* (Social Affairs Unit, 1986), pp. 52–3.
115. Popay *et al.*, op. cit., p. 30.
116. M. de Young, op. cit., p. 11.
117. M. Rutter, op. cit.

1.2 The proper thing to do

JANET FINCH

Introduction

In this chapter I switch the focus of discussion away from the social contexts of family support and onto individual human beings, attempting to work out their relationships with their own relatives. The emphasis is less on patterns of support which occur in practice (although this discussion must always be grounded in concrete examples) and more upon the underlying 'sense of obligation'. In what sense can we say that any practical and material support which we give to our relatives in the contemporary British context is grounded in feelings of duty, obligation, or responsibility? More generally, what place should we accord to morality in understanding family relationships?

I shall argue that we need a subtle and complex view of how individuals operate in their own social worlds if we wish to understand how duty and obligation work within families. The idea that people recognize easily what their responsibilities are, and that most then simply carry them out, is certainly too crude. Even in societies where rights and responsibilities seem more clear-cut than in contemporary Britain, the reality is not like that. It is useful perhaps to consider an example from such a society to illustrate the complexities which we have to handle. In her discussion of ethnographic data from Tunisia Cuisenier discusses the issue of inheritance and in particular the custom that women do not actually claim their share, although they are entitled to inherit along with their brothers under Islamic law. When they make such claims customarily this is regarded as scandalous, although brothers have no right to deny them in law. Cuisenier cites the account of one of her informants who discusses this:

It isn't that we do our sisters out of their rights. God has given them their share and it's unlawful to refuse them. It's out of solidarity that a girl marries and goes to live with her husband; she will be sheltered from need and will stop being dependent on her family when she becomes dependent on her husband. It's quite right she should give up the idea of doing her brothers out of their share and so making them a bit poorer. (Cuisenier, 1976, p. 142)

What does this example tell us about rights and duties within families? First, it shows that legal rights and obligations are not the same thing as the moral obligations in practice: brothers have the legal obligation to share inheritance with their sisters, but they think it wrong that they should be expected to do so in reality. Obligations can look quite unambiguous to an outsider but in practice there can be considerable room for manœuvre. Second, people do not operate in a vacuum when they think about obligations and duties within their own families; they make an assessment of what would be the proper thing to do by considering the social and economic circumstances of the individuals involved. In the above example, whether you really should have to share your inheritance with your sister depends on her circumstances and yours: a woman who can be presumed to have an alternative form of support cannot really expect to deprive her brothers, whatever the law says. We see people using ideas about justice and fairness which are related to the life circumstances of each family member, and which operate independently of legally codified rights and duties. Third, it follows from this that it is perfectly proper to take your own interests into account when considering your responsibilities to your relatives; although in the Tunisian example it looks as if it is fine for men to act in a self-interested way but less fine for women. This brings us to the fourth point: the gender divisions seem to be a crucial element here, as in so many other aspects of family life. Rights, duties, and obligations work differently for women and men in practice, and this is considered to be quite proper: a woman who tries to contravene this will be regarded as acting scandalously.

Although the details of this case clearly are rather different from the British context, it is useful to consider such an example as a way of reflecting upon the questions which we should be asking about our own more familiar arrangements. Even in a situation where rights and duties seem more fixed, we see that they are open to considerable negotiation in practice and that the outcome of those negotiations will be an interplay between, on the one hand, ideas about moral obligations derived from the wider culture, and, on the other hand, very personal assessments about the circumstances of one's own relatives.

In this chapter I shall explore the question of how obligations and duties towards one's relatives operate in the British context. I shall look at the issue from two different angles which complement rather than contradict each other. I shall suggest that there are two different ways of looking at family obligations—as normative guidelines and as negotiated commitments—which together present a rounded picture of how people act towards their relatives in practice. The idea that family obligations can be understood as normative guidelines, the subject of this chapter, focuses mainly on how the content of obligations is defined.

The idea of normative guidelines

I have previously made extensive use of words like duty, obligation, and responsibility to refer to those features of family relationships which I wish to explore. My choice of words is deliberate and reflects the language commonly used in everyday life—if not always the actual words, then certainly the ideas to which they refer. They are words which refer to a moral component in relationships and imply that what people actually do is governed quite significantly by beliefs about 'the proper thing to do'.

This is the place to explore more fully the meaning of such ideas. Although much of this chapter will be concerned with the actual content of the underlying principles upon which family obligations are based, I shall begin with a more abstract consideration of the words and the concepts which we need to develop this kind of discussion. The questions which I shall pose include: Can we say that there are moral rules which direct people towards the proper or correct way to treat their relatives? Is there a consensus about what constitutes correct behaviour? Can we explain people's actions towards their relatives by saying that they are following these moral rules? What is a 'moral' rule? Is 'rule' the best word anyway; would 'norms' or 'guidelines' be better?

In developing this discussion I shall draw upon a range of debates in philosophy and social science which consider questions about how far human actions can be seen as stemming from moral considerations, and whether these are produced by forces internal or external to the individual. Such complex issues merit more extensive treatment than I can give them here. They go to the heart of certain central questions which social theorists have tried to resolve, about how far human beings can be seen as taking autonomous, independent actions and how far we are constrained by social forces. As Philip Abrams put it in his discussion of the common ground between history and sociology,

[The problem] is easily and endlessly formulated but, it seems, stupefyingly difficult to resolve. People make their own history—but only under definite circumstances and conditions; we act through a world of rules which our own action creates, breaks and renews—we are creators of rules, the rules are our own creations; we make our own world—the world confronts us as an implacable and autonomous system of social facts. The variations of the theme are innumerable. (Abrams, 1982, p. xiv)

One of the most influential formulations of this issue in recent years is Giddens's discussion of the relationship between social structure and human agency. In that discussion, he accords a central place to norms and obligations in social life, which he sees as necessarily built into all human interactions. The social order, which facilitates human interaction, is built upon normative concepts: in a given set of circumstances some people have legitimate rights, others have obligations, and so on. But that social order has to be 'sustained and reproduced in the flow of social encounters' (Giddens, 1979, p. 86). Where people act purposefully and strategically in their encounters with others—for example if I try to ensure that my brother sees the financial support of our parents as his responsibility rather than mine—this represents, in Giddens's terms, an attempt to 'mobilize obligations' through the responses of other people. I am drawing on my understanding of the legitimate social order, and thereby helping to reproduce it, but in terms of direct consequences for myself I am making specific claims about which rights and obligations are going to be recognized in this particular situation.

I make no claims to advance these theoretical debates at a general level. But I find them helpful in suggesting ways in which we can understand how family obligations operate in reality. I shall draw on them in the course of this chapter and the next. To begin this discussion of the concepts of duty, obligation and responsibility in families I shall consider a number of contrasts which are built into relevant debates, under five headings.

Describing and prescribing

The first set of contrasts need not detain us too long because the point is fairly straightforward, although it is important to make it explicit. The contrasts here are:

Behavioural regularities vs Normative rules
Is vs Ought.

The central issue to which these contrasts refer concerns how we interpret observed behaviour. If we observe as a matter of fact that most people do try to give assistance to their aged parents, should we conclude therefore that there is an underlying moral rule which prescribes that such assistance should be given? Put like that, it is obvious that observing a 'behavioural regularity' does not necessarily imply a 'normative rule'.

There are other possible explanations of why people might assist their parents, for example that they do it because they hope to inherit goods or property when the parents die. In effect, I have been using this distinction between behavioural regularities and normative rules when I have talked about actual patterns of support on the one hand and the 'sense of obligation' on the other. It is actually quite easy to fall into this particular trap of confusing the two in empirical research on family relationships, since it is usually rather difficult to get information directly about the underlying normative rules (if they exist), and in the absence of such information it is tempting for researchers to take the evidence of observed behavioural regularities to imply that certain normative rules do exist (Schneider, 1968, p. 6).

In moral philosophy similar issues are dealt with by developing the distinction between 'is' and 'ought' and through debates about whether 'ought' can ever be derived from 'is'. These debates as such need not be considered here. Understanding the 'ought' component in family obligations is not a matter of what is possible in terms of logical arguments, but whether in practice people do derive prescriptions about what 'ought' to happen from their observations about what generally does happen. Put like that, the matter is quite complex since one of the grounds upon which people justify their own actions is that they are only doing (or not doing) the same as most other people. Although probably most people would accept that a particular action is not *necessarily* right or wrong just because everyone does it, the fact that it is commonplace does change the nature of an individual moral decision about whether or not to do it.

The fact that people do sometimes derive 'ought' from 'is' in practice can be seen by considering the kind of decision faced by a daughter who has elderly and infirm parents and also a full-time job. In such circumstances it is known that many women consider giving up their jobs, and some decide to do so. If a woman does give up her job to care for her parents she will receive public endorsement for having acted appropriately, although the same would not necessarily apply to a son who made such a decision (Finch and Groves, 1980; Groves and Finch, 1983). Women who wish to stay in employment are vulnerable to pressure on the grounds that many other women do give up their jobs, it is the common response to parental need, therefore it is what a particular individual ought to do. Examples of women who have experienced such pressures can be found in Lewis and Meredith's study of daughters who have cared for their mothers. One said that she was 'adamant' about not giving up her job and thought that she was 'completely justified in standing my ground' when under pressure to do so, indicating by the strength of her language that she did find it difficult to resist the expectation that this is a reasonable thing to do. Another interviewee challenged the assumption that this is the kind of sacrifice which should be made by women rather than men.

My brother suggested to me. He suggested I give up my on. I said, why don't you give up your job? (Lewis and Meredith, 1988, p. 78)

Although not articulated directly by the interviewees in this example one can see that the dilemma posed derives partly from the conflational 'is' and 'ought'. Because many women *do* give up their jobs to care for a parent, it becomes easier for brothers, social workers, and whoever else makes an intervention in a particular case, to say that a particular woman *should* do so. Possibly in a logical sense 'ought' cannot be derived from 'is', but in reality people act as if there is *some* relationship between the two. The question of what precisely is that relationship in a given set of circumstances is one of the many interesting empirical questions which one can ask about family obligations in practice.

The scope of normative guidelines

The contrasts which I shall deal with here are an overlapping set which derive in the first instance from moral philosophy:

Absolute vs Relative
Abstract vs Concrete
Universal vs Situational.

The point here is really about the scope of normative rules or guidelines, and whether they can be said to apply equally in all circumstances. Would I be willing to allow my 25-year-old son to live rent-free in my house if he did not have a job? Only if he was trying hard to get a job? Would it matter to me how he lost his previous job? Or would I feel that children should be able to rely on their parents when they need to whatever other circumstances obtain? Again, I am less interested in the detail of philosophical debates than in using the contrasting concepts to help develop our understanding of how people perceive the nature of normative rules in practice. Do people espouse certain clear and absolute rules which they would consider it wrong to breach in any circumstances? (Whether in practice they do sometimes breach them is a separate issue to which I shall return.) Do people think about family obligations in terms of abstract principles, or alternatively as concrete rules about particular relationships? Do people consider that there are certain rules which apply to everyone in all circumstances, or that the right thing to do has to be worked out separately in each situation?

Empirical studies of family relationships do not give clear answers to these questions, since different writers interpret their findings in different ways. One strand of thought can be illustrated by work which derives from social psychology, in the tradition represented by Argyle and Handerson (1985). They review empirical material on family relationships taken from a number of different societies and use it to itemize 'rules' of relationships. They see the obligation to help kin as a strong example of such rules, and say that there are certain basic rules which seem to apply cross-culturally: you should be prepared to help kin when they need it, beyond the assistance that you would give to friends or neighbours; you should be prepared particularly to help your own children and your parents. Although in fact much of the data which they consider concerns what I have called behavioural regularities other than normative prescriptions, Argyle and Henderson offer an interpretation which sees certain rules of kin relationships as widely (perhaps universally) applicable, and not depending upon the details of a particular situation. A similar line of reasoning, although with quite different intellectual foundations, can be found in the work of those socio-biologists who argue that the foundations of kin support are genetic and therefore universal.

A contrasting approach can be found in the work of Douglas on the meaning and use of social rules. His view is that moral rules in social life are relative not absolute, and that the meaning of those rules can be understood only in relation to situations where they are put to use. Although he does not deny that people do understand moral rules in an abstract as well as a 'situated' sense, he argues that philosophers of all traditions have rather missed the point by analysing moral rules solely in terms of abstract generalizations. The point that they miss is that people's experience of moral rules in practice is essentially problematic: we regularly disagree with each other—perhaps even with ourselves—about the right thing to do in particular circumstances; we find it difficult in practice to work out what is the moral or ethical intent of someone else's statement or action (Douglas, 1971, pp. 135-9). This problematic nature of moral rules is an unavoidable and a necessary part of human societies for two reasons. First, the whole point about moral responsibility is that it must be possible for a person to take several different courses of action: for a decision to be a *moral* one, it has to be problematic. Second, the concrete situations in which decisions are located are themselves complex and changing, so decisions about the proper course of action cannot be pre-programmed (ibid. pp. 167-9).

One does not have to agree with the detail of Douglas's position to accept the force of his argument that, when we look at how moral rules operate in practice, we are struck by the importance of situation and context in understanding why particular rules or norms operate when they do. Philosophers in fact are not blind to these distinctions in quite the way that Douglas implies. There is a well established contrast in moral philosophy between 'autonomous' morality (which concerns matters of principle which are universal and generalizable) and 'social' morality which derives from the way that people live their lives. A key feature of the latter is that a particular action may not be considered wrong in itself, but becomes wrong because of the consequences which it has in particular circumstances (Baier, 1970).

The principal use of these debates in developing an understanding of family obligations and responsibilities, is to raise certain questions which require an empirical answer: How far do people treat moral issues in their family relationships as matters which have to be worked out in particular situations, rather than matters of generalizable principle? Are there any guidelines at all which are regarded as matters of general principle and not subject to pressures of circumstance?

The source of the guidelines

The main contrasts here are:

Individual morality vs Social morality
Internal constraints vs External constraints

There is an obvious contrast in ideas about the source of moral rules which, to put it simplistically, is: Does each individual make up the rules for her/himself, or do we simply follow the rules imposed upon us within the society in which we live? Put like that, it seems obvious that there are elements of both the individual and the social in the way that people's moral actions should be understood.

That conclusion perhaps is more obvious to a sociologist interested in what happens in practice than to a moral philosopher, especially one concerned with the long-standing debates about reasoning and rationality as the basis for moral actions. Halsey, commenting as a sociologist upon that tradition, argues that although reasoning plays some part the values which an individual adheres to cannot be understood solely in those terms. Custom, convention, and upbringing are other key elements, so that 'most people, for most of the time, take morals as given from their social surroundings' (Halsey, 1985, p. 7). Whilst Halsey is careful to point out that he does not imply any particular theory of social causation by this observation, the issues raised here do relate to the very long-standing debate in social science about how far individuals can be said to internalize social rules, and under what circumstances they can reject them—the issues which I referred to at the beginning of this chapter, quoting from Abrams and from Giddens.

Again, the main point which I want to take from these debates is not to argue conclusively for a particular theoretical position, but to indicate that they raise important empirical questions. In this case it can be expressed in the form: In practice do people go along with socially accepted moral rules in family relationships? In what circumstances do people want to derive their own guidelines on some other basis, such as rationality? When and where do conflicts arise between these two elements in morality, and how are they dealt with? I considered these questions earlier, in relation to the impact of the law and public policies on the ways in which people think about their own family responsibilities. However, these are not the only source of the 'social' element in morality.

It is important also to link these questions to another: in practice how far do people perceive that clear moral rules exist which are socially derived? I shall return to this issue later, but it is worth noting here that we do have evidence to suggest that people may not always have a clear idea of what is the socially approved moral position in many circumstances, or they may feel that different rules apply to different groups in society (say, different social classes). Bott, in her discussion of the norms of family life based upon intensive study of 20 couples, suggests that there are very few items which would count as what she calls 'norms of common consent', that is, prescriptive statements upon which most of her respondents do in fact agree. But there are many circumstances in which people's ideas about 'social norms' influence what they do. Her use of the term social norms refers here to items about which people *think* that there is agreement among the relevant social group. This does not mean that agreement *does* exist necessarily: often in fact it does not (Bott, 1957, p. 197). So when we ask questions about how far people's actions are shaped by considerations of socially approved morality, we need to understand what a particular individual actually perceives that morality to be—which may not be the same thing as a normative consensus on a particular matter which could be demonstrated empirically.

Application of the guidelines

The next set of contrasts to which I refer concerns the application of rules or guidelines for conduct. I raise them here in a preliminary way because questions of how the rules get applied affect our understanding of what we mean when we talk about moral rules, norms or guidelines. The contrasts which I shall consider are:

Beliefs vs Actions
Rules vs Guidelines.

The idea of moral norms or rules encompasses both beliefs in an abstract sense and actions which are based on those beliefs. The relationship between beliefs and actions is particularly important if one is interested in how family obligations and duties operate in practice, and that relationship is not necessarily straightforward.

There are a number of reasons for this, the most important of which is that we need to select and apply relevant rules in any given situation. For example, relationships between siblings in adult life seem to operate on the basis of reciprocity: when support is given, it must be repaid in a fairly obvious way. Suppose that I have a relationship with my sister where we have each given the other various types of assistance over the years. One day she arrives on my doorstep saying that she has been made homeless through non-payment of rent. Does the principle of reciprocity operate straightforwardly here, so that I offer her a temporary home whatever disruption it causes? Do I only offer it if I have plenty of space in the house? Do I have to consider how other members of my household will feel about it? Would it make a difference if she had been made homeless for a different reason, let us say, walking out on a violent marriage? In this example, the principle of reciprocity is only one of the possible guidelines for my action, and I need to decide whether it is the appropriate one in *this* set of circumstances. Moral philosophers commonly recognize that there is an important difference between endorsing or justifying a particular moral rule in general terms, and justifying a particular action based upon that rule (Rawls, 1967; Wallace and Walker, 1970; Warnock, 1971). We are not necessarily talking here about inconsistency between principles and practice: it is perfectly possible to agree with a rule in general terms, but believe that it is not relevant to particular circumstances, or to believe that it does not apply to myself for particular reasons. In addition there is the possibility that several different rules, all of which I endorse in general terms, could apply potentially to a given situation although each of them suggests a different line of action. Empirical evidence about family life suggests that situations do arise where people need to select relevant rules, sometimes where different rules conflict with each other.

The most obvious examples of conflicting rules concern situations where a person feels torn between their responsibilities to one person and equally pressing responsibilities to someone else. For example, one of the interviewees in Lewis and Meredith's study spoke very directly about the emotional difficulties she experienced in 'having to choose between one kind of duty and another kind of duty', in her case between her duty to her mother who needed full-time care, and her duty to her children who needed the income from her employment. Although on one level she wants to insist that the children should take precedence, it is clear also that she finds the conflicts very difficult to handle,

Someone said I should have given up my job and looked after my mother . . . I said, well I have three young children and if I give up work my children would miss a lot . . . [I had to] choose between one kind of duty and another kind of duty. That was very difficult. I had to choose to let her go [into a home]. (Lewis and Meredith, 1988, p. 78)

This is just one example which could be replicated across a number of studies.

I shall return to this issue of selecting and applying moral rules later and I shall argue that it is central to understanding how family obligations operate in practice. I have mentioned these matters briefly here because they help us to sort out what we mean by 'rules' of morality. The considerations which I have elaborated above should, I think, lead us to reject the use of the word rules in a strong sense—that is, meaning clear and specific prescriptions for action, which remove the element of individual judgement from a situation by specifying in advance what is going to be done (Warnock, 1971, p. 65). The idea of rules in this sense is probably applicable, if at all, to a very restricted range of circumstances in family life; although in relation to any empirical example it is worth asking the question: are there *any* situations in which the honouring of family obligations can be understood as simply rule-following behaviour in this strong sense?

More promising in terms of its analytical potential is a weaker use of the concept of rules, which can be highlighted by the distinction between rule-governed and rule-guided behaviour. This is a distinction which derives from, for example, the writing of Douglas (1971) and has been usefully applied to family relationships by Sarah Cunningham-Burley (1985) in her work on grandparenthood. She wishes to retain the word 'rules' to denote that external constraints are important in a person's negotiation of the role of grandparent, but she argues that actions are rule-guided rather than rule-governed, because people elaborate and apply their own understanding of the appropriate behaviour for grand-parents in concrete circumstances.

If the notion of moral rules is to be used in relation to family obliga-tions, I suggest that it is usually most appropriate to use it in this weaker sense, in which actions are seen to be 'guided' by rules, but not 'gov-erned' by them. It could be argued that the use of the word rules is not really appropriate, if people in practice have to take an active part in actu-ally working out what to do in specific situations. Indeed, I think that there is a case for suggesting that the concept of 'norms' is more appro-priate than rules, in that it refers by implication to behaviour which is expected, but not required in quite the same sense that a rule requires compliance. Also the concept of norms places the issue firmly in the realm of moral values and beliefs. Alternatively, it could be suggested that, since behaviour for the most part is rule-guided not rule-governed, the rather weaker concept of 'guidelines' for action might be appropriate, making more explicit the idea that people do have a good deal of flexibil-ity about how these guidelines are applied. In fact my own preference is for the use of the term 'normative guidelines', and that preference is strengthened by a consideration of the type of guidelines which operate in the sphere of family obligations.

What type of guidelines are they?

In this final set of contrasts, and building upon the preceding discussion, I shall consider the nature of the rules or guidelines about family obliga-tions, especially the question: What kind of advice or prescriptions are contained in these guidelines? The contrasts with which I am working are:

Rules vs Principles
General advice vs Detailed prescriptions
Hierarchy of priorities vs Parallel sets of values.

I have already noted, for example on the basis of Bott's (1957) work, that in family life there appear to be very few issues upon which there is a clear consensus at a general level about the right thing to do. It follows from this that there are few guidelines of the type which give detailed specifications for appropriate action. This conclusion is borne out in the empirical work of Firth, Hubert, and Forge on middle-class family relationships where they show that the concepts of duty and responsibility are very important in the way that people understand their own family relationships. However, as they put it, whilst there are general standards of conduct which apply to kin relationships, there are no rules about putting into effect these notions of responsibility, so that an individual has to make choices about how to respond when a relative needs specific assistance (Firth, Hubert, and Forge, 1970, pp. 451–2). A more recent empirical illustration of the lack of detailed guidelines for appropriate action can be found in the work of Allatt and Yeandle (1986) on the family relationships of young people who are unemployed. They argue that a central guiding principle upon which parents in these families operate is the idea of 'fairness', a principle which is deeply embedded in family life, but which needs to be brought to the surface and re-interpreted to suit the particular circumstances. In particular, parents regularly had to reconsider questions of how much money should be taken from and given to a young employed member of the household, so that the situation could be demonstrated as complying with the principle of fairness to all parties.

The general point I would take from these empirical examples is that the nature of the advice available to an individual in these guidelines about family relationships and responsibilities remains at the most general level, and in no sense does it give detailed specifications for action. Further, the guidelines seem to be less to do with specifying what actual actions are right or wrong, and more concerned with giving criteria which can be used to work out what would be right or wrong in particular circumstances.

This second—and very important—point can be developed further by introducing the work of some feminist writers who have considered the differences between women and men in the way they handle moral claims upon them. From the perspective of a moral philosopher, Noddings has argued that women do not approach moral problems in the same way as men: they do not order priorities hierarchically and they do not discuss such issues in terms of abstract principle. Rather, when faced with a moral dilemma, women tend to ask for more information about the situation and see it as a concrete problem to be resolved, not as an abstract dilemma to be settled by reasoning. Noddings is careful to point out that she is not suggesting that women are unable to arrange principles hierarchically or to derive logical conclusions, but that 'they see this process as peripheral to or even irrelevant to moral conduct'

(Noddings, 1984, p. 96). Drawing rather similar conclusions, but arriving at them via her empirical work as a social psychologist, Carol Gilligan (1982) has argued that women's approach to morality is different from men's and specifically that the idea of moral 'rules' really does not work for women. Women's morality, she argues, is situationally and contextually based and they are much less likely than men to fall back upon moral rules of a generalizable and abstract kind. When faced with moral dilemmas in which there are conflicting claims or considerations, men and boys tend to respond by developing a set of rules which will secure a just or fair outcome, and this often entails prioritizing claims. Women and girls, by contrast, will try to resolve the situation in such a way that no one gets hurt, if necessary themselves making a sacrifice rather than expecting that of other people.

The question of whether men's and women's morality in fact does differ in these ways is a question which requires further empirical work and I shall pursue that later in this chapter. I raise the distinction here, however, to highlight the general point that the nature of the advice contained in guidelines for moral action is such that it leaves room for women and men to take quite different messages from it, and to make use of the guidelines in quite different ways. The feminist philosopher Jean Grimshaw who builds upon the work of Noddings and Gilligan, makes a useful distinction between rules and principles which, in my view, considerably advances the argument at this point. In her usage, a 'rule' is a guideline for conduct which eliminates, or at least minimizes, the need for reflection and judgement in particular situations; whereas a 'principle' specifically invites reflection rather than blocking it. Principles, she suggests, are best expressed in the form 'Consider . . .' (the effect which your actions will have upon other people; whether other people's needs should outweigh your own etc.). In her view, the contribution of Noddings and Gilligan would be assisted by making this distinction (Grimshaw, 1986, p. 207).

It seems to me that this distinction between rules and principles is very useful and applies much more generally than to the question of gender differences. In using the concept of 'normative guidelines' I wish to imply hereafter that guidelines should be understood as principles rather than as rules. This definition supports other lines of argument which I have been developing in this discussion. Warnock, for example, suggests that acting upon moral beliefs is not a case of accepting moral rules, but more of 'recognizing or accepting some range or variety of reasons for judging' the appropriate course of action (Warnock, 1971, p. 70). Douglas, who comes from quite a different intellectual tradition, none the less reaches rather similar conclusions when he writes, 'social rules are the criteria that normal members of the society are expected to make use of in deciding what to do in any situation for which they are seen as relevant' (Douglas, 1971, p. 141),

To summarize, this perspective suggests that we might expect to find that the principles reflected in normative guidelines about family obligations have the following characteristics: general rather than detailed; concerned with criteria for judgement rather than specifications for action. In other words, it makes sense of available empirical data to say that these guidelines are concerned with *how you work out* the proper thing to do in given circumstances, rather than *specifying what* you should do. It is important to have further research which tests this analysis systematically.

Normative guidelines for family obligations

In the second part of this chapter, I move on to consider what the normative guidelines for working out obligations to kin actually are. I shall be building upon the preceding discussion about the nature of such guidelines and how they operate. I have chosen to focus here upon five normative guidelines which I consider the most important ones in relation to family obligations, on the basis of existing evidence.

The principle of selection: (i) who is this person?

In deciding whether to offer assistance to a particular person, or in working out whether I can expect that person to offer assistance to me, a prime consideration is my relationship with him or her, in both senses of that word. On the one hand, there is the question of where we each stand in a genealogical sense; on the other hand, there is the question of how well or badly we get along on a personal level. This distinction between the structural and the personal relationships—of course intimately intertwined in practice—is a longstanding one in social science even if it is not used as much as it should be in contemporary writing on the family, as Bulmer (1985) has suggested. I shall argue that my 'relationship' to other people, in both senses, underscores some of the most important normative guidelines for support between kin. I begin in this section with the structured elements of relationships, arguing that the principle of selection operates, so that my obligation to give support to a relative is stronger or weaker, depending upon that person's position in my kin network. When faced with a concrete decision about whether to give assistance, the first question to be asked is: who is this person?

The necessity for making this kind of selection flows from the fact that the rules of British kinship are 'permissive' not 'obligatory' (Allan, 1979), which means that an individual is obliged to select which shall be honoured. However, the selection should not be wholly open and idiosyncratic. There are guidelines for working out whose claims are strong and whose weaker. The clearest empirical support for this idea in recently produced work comes from Qureshi's study of the family care of elderly people, where the data demonstrate a 'hierarchy of obligations' (Qureshi and Simons, 1987; Ungerson, 1987).

Most of the existing empirical evidence does not give such clear guidance on the prioritizing of claims as does this work. There is a problem common to many studies in this field, in that an insufficiently clear distinction is made between 'is' and 'ought', so that much of the evidence is actually about what happens in practice rather than the moral question of what ought to happen. In so far as any hierarchical priorities are established clearly, they usually focus upon the nuclear rather than the extended family. That is, one's spouse and immature children always 'count' as the closest circle of family between whom assistance should be shared (Firth, Hubert, and Forge, 1970). These are the relationships which are not my specific concern in this book, but they are an essential part of the total picture when one is considering the broader issues of obligations to kin and how they are prioritized.

Genealogical principles   I have previously reviewed much of the evidence necessary to answer questions about how the principles of selection operate. I suggested that in the context of the white majority in Britain, kin relationships can be seen as a series of concentric circles, of which the outermost circle is not relevant for a kin support discussion since it contains relatives with whom one has no contact, although their existence is known of, and usually their names. Some obligations seem to be acknowledged in respect of kin in the two other circles, with obligations to people who fall in the inner circles being more extensive than to those in the outer. The identity of kin falling into these inner and outer circles cannot be predicted solely on the basis of genealogical relationship, but apparently people always count their spouses and children as part of this 'close family' and most people count their parents. It is quite common to include grandchildren, but less common to count grandparents as close kin (Bott, 1957; Firth, Hubert, and Forge, 1970; Morgan, 1975). The situation of various ethnic minority groups living in Britain is different, with a greater likelihood that more people will be included in the inner circle, extending quite often to cousins and in-laws.

So far as evidence on the dominant culture of the white majority is concerned, there seem to be various principles of selection which have the effect of designating the relatives to whom one has the strongest obligations. First, there is the principle that one's own kin are favoured over one's spouse's, despite the fact that this kinship system is bilateral in the sense that married couples recognize the relatives of both *as* kin. But when it comes to matters of duty, with the exception of the spouse themselves, obligations seem to operate most strongly in relation to one's own direct kin, both ascendent and descendent (Argyle and Henderson, 1985, p. 223). Assistance may be given to the close relatives of one's spouse, but there is some evidence that this is seen as helping your spouse to meet his or her own obligation. After the death of a spouse people feel a less clear sense of obligation to the spouse's kin (Firth, Hubert, and Forge, 1970, pp. 95–111). The second underlying principle of selection is that lineal links are stronger than lateral ones (La Fontaine, 1985, p. 54). Most obviously this means that duties towards one's parents and children are much stronger than towards brothers and sisters. Although quite a lot of assistance passes between brothers and sisters in practice (especially between sisters), there is not the same underlying sense of obligation as occurs in assistance between parents and children (Argyle and Henderson, 1985, p. 220). The third principle which one can see in operation is that lineal ties of obligation apply particularly to one generation in each direction, but much more ambiguously thereafter. There may be an obligation to keep in contact across three or four generations, but less of a clear obligation to give assistance (Bott, 1957; Schneider, 1968).

Finally, there is the principle that people in the same genealogical position should be treated similarly. The best example probably is siblings, so that most obviously in the case of inheritance, there is an expectation that all children will be treated 'alike'. This idea is of early nineteenth-century origin and grew to serve the growing entrepreneurial classes. The early, aristocratic tradition was to favour one child, typically the eldest son, over the rest. It may be that fragments of this can still be traced in British kin relationships, but for the most part the idea of equivalent treatment for people in equivalent positions seems to hold good. However, there sometimes is room for ambiguity about whether two positions are indeed equivalent, for example whether grandchildren should acknowledge equivalent obligations to their maternal and parental grandparents.

Remarriage and the introduction of step relationships into a kin network also can produce ambiguities about whether the step-relative counts as equivalent to the corresponding blood relationship.

Collectively these principles seem to define which genealogical relationships imply the stronger obligations and which the weaker, although they are principles which leave room for competing obligations even within the inner circle of close kin. Where such conflicts occur there seems to be a tendency to favour the marriage relationship and the descendent generation (that is, spouses and children) but there are no clear-cut rules and these are situations which commonly are treated as tricky to resolve. I shall draw an empirical example of such a situation from Mansfield and Collard's (1988) study of the early years of marriage. It is an example which concerns the anxieties of a young wife that her husband was continuing to give his own mother a considerable amount of emotional and moral support in a way which he had done before their marriage. She was especially worried about the way her husband had been used as his mother's sole support during the time when she thought that an unmarried daughter was pregnant, an anxiety which she had not mentioned to her own husband. The way in which the interviewee talks about this makes it clear that she found the situation very difficult to handle, that it was very difficult to tell her husband that he should *not* be supportive to his mother, but none the less she felt a conflict of interest with her mother-in-law which should have been resolved in her own favour:

We had an argument about it—that was when I sort of had a go at him, saying that his mother would have to learn to—she would have to go to his father, you know, she couldn't keep coming to Keith all the time. (Mansfield and Collard, 1988, p. 96)

In this case, although there is an expectation on one level that the parent has less strong claims to support once their child is married, it is also clear that making such principles stick within the inner circle of kin is not a straightforward matter.

It is also important to note that boundaries are not fixed and it is quite possible for people who normally would be regarded as distant to get redefined as close kin. The effect is to create stronger mutual obligations than one would predict just from their genealogical positions. There are two particular circumstances in which this commonly arises, one of which is the sharing of households. Evidence from recent studies of the care of elderly people suggest that they expect to, and do in practice, turn in the first instance to other members of their household when they need practical support (Wenger, 1984; Qureshi and Simons, 1987).

The other situation in which more distant kin get drawn into the inner circle is through a process of substitution. Again, the evidence for this comes mainly from studies of elderly people. Where they have never had children, for example, or where their children have already died or perhaps have emigrated, there seems to be a tendency for close bonds, involving obligations to provide assistance, to be formed with more distant kin such as nephews or nieces who, as it were, take the place of a child (Allan, 1983; Wenger, 1984). In such situations it may not be obvious to an outsider why, for example, one particular niece has taken on a great level of responsibility for an elderly aunt than have others although there is some evidence that this may be a consequence of their respective positions in the kin network as a whole. Firth, Hubert, and Forge (1970, p. 390) give the example of one of their interviewees who felt some responsibility for her mother's sister, because when her own parents had been alive they had been close and had taken some responsibility for the management of the aunt's affairs. Once her parents were dead, the niece felt that she 'inherited' that responsibility. In this kind of example, it seems that a commitment to give support is really explained by the existence of a third person, who forms the genealogical link between the two parties. Assistance is given 'for the sake of' or 'in the place of' that third party, in a rather similar way to the support which passes between in-laws.

Gender as a cross-cutting principle   In this discussion about principles of selection my emphasis has been upon genealogical relationships. But there is also the issue of gender, which appears to cut across the other principles. So, for example, we need to modify the observation that the parent–child relationship forms the clearest case of family duty, by distinguishing between sons and daughters, and between mothers and fathers. The precise form which 'duty' takes in these cases will also vary with ethnicity.

The question which I am concerned with here is not so much about patterns of kin support in practice, but whether it can be said that women have a clearer, or a different, sense of obligation towards their relatives than do men. This theme comes across strongly in Ungerson's study of a small number of women and men who were caring for an infirm relative. In a discussion entitled 'Men's love, women's duty' she argues that the distinction between love and duty is the key distinguishing characteristic between men and women, when they explain the reasons why they are providing personal care for a relative. Whilst women sometimes talked about love and affection as well as duty, 'the word "duty" never crossed the lips of any of the men'. The women meanwhile quite often spoke in terms like 'one has a responsibility to one's family' or 'you have a duty to help your relatives' (Ungerson, 1987, pp. 91–4). This kind of evidence supports Graham's (1985) observation that a sense of responsibility forms the 'central motif' of women's accounts of caring for their relatives.

Ungerson's work is relatively unusual in that she makes visible these questions about obligation and duty, and treats them separately from support which is actually given. In many other studies there are problems about using the data in a discussion about responsibilities and duties, because the fact that support passes is taken to mean that a sense of oblig-ation is present. In other words, there is a tendency to derive 'ought' from 'is' in an inappropriate way. However, Ungerson's study is on a very small scale and clearly there is a need to test out her analysis on a larger population. More generally, we lack up-to-date studies of the kind needed to answer the questions raised in this section. Contemporary research is needed to answer questions such as: Do the principles of selec-tion which I have outlined still hold? What variations have resulted from Britain's having become a multi-racial society? Are there really strong gender divisions in the ways in which the selection principles operate? How do those vary within ethnicity, and possibly with other characteris-tics such as social class, or employment status? Research capable of answering such questions would have to be designed in such a way that answers about principles of responsibility and obligation are not simply 'read off' from examples of support.

The principle of selection: (ii) how do I get on with this person?

At a commonsense level the quality of the relationship between two people is an obvious criterion for selection. The idea that anyone would give significant social or practical support to someone for whom they had hostile—or even neutral—feelings seems inherently implausible. It proba-bly strikes us as unremarkable if people say that 'getting on well' with an infirm person provided their motivation for offering personal care, as did some of the interviewees in Ungerson's (1987) study.

On the other hand, if there are normative guidelines about giving sup-port to relatives, and especially if there are 'rules' about such matters, then the whole point about them is that the decision is to some extent removed from the feelings involved in an individual case. The role played by the quality of the relationship in the question of selecting whom to support is likely to be quite complex and implies consideration of two issues: Does the quality of a relationship override the principles of selec- tion which are derived from genealogical relationships? If it does not override those principles, does it at least modify them? A different way of expressing the same issues would be: Are there guidelines about *how* you should take the quality of the relationship into account when deciding whether to offer support to a relative, or in working out whether it is appropriate to accept support from them?

I shall begin this discussion by drawing a distinction between feeling close to someone and giving the practical support. Stated in this way, it is obvious that the two do not necessarily go together, although in practice many studies of kin relationships have treated them as if they did, espe- cially studies like Young and Willmott's (1957) which have emphasized mother–daughter relationships as the main channels of practical assis- tance within families. However, more recent studies which have tried to distinguish between the two have found that relationships in which a great deal of practical support is being given are sometimes characterized by emotional closeness and warmth, but sometimes not. For example, Cornwell's study, in the same area of London as Young and Willmott's but two decades later, found that 'Some relationships are based upon shared skills and practical activities and that is all; others involved some degree of emotional intimacy and the mothers and daughters are each other's confidante; still others are based simply on family loyalty and a sense of duty' (Cornwell, 1984, p. 112).

In the rather different context of a study of the carers of elderly people in Sheffield, Qureshi (1986) found that although 72 per cent of carers said that they felt emotionally close to the person for whom they were pro- viding personal care, the rest did not. Qureshi concluded that levels of 'liking' had little effect upon whether a person was or was not giving practical support, especially to a parent. Lewis and Meredith, in their study of daughters who had cared for their mothers, felt that feelings of affection and duty were usually present together, and indeed that their interviewees held these feelings 'in delicate balance' (Lewis and Meredith, 1988, p. 28). Conclusions about the comparative unimportance of emotional closeness are borne out by studies of people not necessarily involved currently in practical support, especially the work of O'Connor and Brown (1984) on women's close relationships. This study shows that levels of intimate confiding to other people are not necessarily related to on-going practical dependency.

From this kind of evidence, it seems that the quality of the relationship, especially between parents and children, plays a relatively small part in determining whether support actually is given. However, (following the principle that 'ought' should not be derived from 'is') there is a separate question about whether the quality of the relationship is something which should be taken into account in defining who is obligations to whom. One possible interpretation of the data on parent–child relationships is that on the whole the normative prescription to give assistance is so strong between parents and children, that the quality of the relationship is not allowed to override it. Unfortunately most of these studies do not separate out the normative element in a way which would make one confident in drawing that conclusion. We still lack the systematic evidence which would tell us just how poor the parent–child relationship has to be before the usual normative guidelines cease to operate; or conversely whether a particularly good parent–child relationship means that assistance should be offered beyond the normal 'call of duty'.

The same problem arises with support passing between other relatives, although because there is more variation in these it is a little easier to pick up hints about how normative guidelines may operate. I think that one can make a case for the quality of the relationship operating as a 'defining in' criterion; so that, although normally one might not be expected to give extensive practical support to an aunt or a sister, if your relationship with her is particularly close and warm, then you should be prepared to give that support and she has the right to expect it. For example, the evidence reviewed by Argyle and Henderson (1985) on relationships between siblings suggests that these do not demonstrate the same strength of obligation as in parent–child relationships, but that this can develop if there is a close relationship between a particular pair of siblings. Conversely, if someone has a rather poor relationship on a personal level with a particular brother or sister, there seems to be nothing like the same kind of pressure as one finds with parents and children to overlook personal dislikes and to give them assistance if they need it. Examples of this can be found in the study by Firth, Hubert, and Forge of middle-class kinship. They cite several instances where relationships between siblings had become difficult after disputes over inheritance from their parents, and where little contact had been retained. In one such case, an informant told the researchers that he felt his own brothers and sisters had mostly behaved very badly and that he would be very reluctant to either give or ask for assistance from them, apart from one brother of whom he was particularly fond (Firth, Hubert and Forge, 1970, p. 376).

To take this argument one step further, I would suggest that the quality of a personal relationship between two individuals may operate at a normative level so that a good relationship 'defines in' that person to a structure of obligations, but a poor relationship does not necessarily 'define out'. This latter point applies to parent–child relationships with particular force, but the 'defining in' process may operate there also. A study in the United States by Hoyt and Babchuk (1983) brings out this point rather well. They studied a sample of 800 adults and asked questions about close and confiding relationships within families. They found that people are highly selective, even within the close kin group, about those with whom they are especially intimate, and although adult children (where they exist) are a popular choice as confidants, most people singled out *certain* adult children but not others. On the basis of this evidence (and indeed of commonsense observation), we can conclude that even parent–child relationships vary in their degree of warmth and intimacy. So any tendency to 'define in', that is to strengthen ties of obligation on the basis of good quality relationships, probably applies to parents and children as well as to other kin relationships.

At the most general level, therefore, I would conclude that the quality of a relationship between two individuals does not determine the strength of obligation to provide support in any simple way. The clearest statement of this particular normative guideline is in the form: 'You should be especially willing to assist people to whom you feel close'. But the opposite is not implied where relationships are of poorer quality. In those circumstances, the normative rules based upon genealogical relationships would seem still to apply, although we really know little about how far this has to be pushed before the quality of the relationship becomes the most significant normative consideration.

Reciprocity, exchange, and mutual aid

The concept of reciprocity has been an important one which historians have used to understand the dynamic of aid passing between members of a kin group. Along with the concepts of duty and obligation, the idea of reciprocity is associated distinctively with family relationships in many people's minds, and some writers take the view that it has considerable explanatory power (Morgan, 1975, p. 81; Bulmer, 1987, p. 161–2). It can be argued that it underlies certain other principles which operate in family life, such as fairness (Allatt and Yeandle, 1986).

Studies of family relationships sometimes fail to see its significance because they focus upon issues like 'dependency' which imply one-way support, whereas it is possible to demonstrate that even elderly people who are themselves receiving significant support from family members often are also giving assistance as well (Wenger, 1984). The importance of reciprocity is indicated by Pahl's study of household work strategies, based in the Isle of Sheppey. In discussing 'informal' labour (which could be paid or unpaid, but which is outside the formal economy) he shows that such exchanges between kin, neighbours, and friends happen most frequently where people are able to reciprocate in some way, and he notes that typically people claim they do more for others than they receive in return, indicating 'the general concern of people not to appear too dependent on others' (Pahl, R. E., 1984, p. 250).

The idea that the giving of goods and services ought to be a two-way process in families is the central one which I shall discuss in this section. I shall consider how far this provides a normative guideline for use in particular circumstances. I shall introduce this by referring to three overlapping but not identical terms: reciprocity, exchange, and mutual aid. Of the three, mutual aid is a term perhaps best used purely descriptively, to indicate that in practice the flows of aid in families are in several directions. Especially if one takes a fairly long-term perspective, it would be difficult to say that certain individuals are net givers and others net gainers overall. I shall not review the empirical evidence which supports that conclusion here. My main concern here is more with explanations of *why* aid in families is mutual, what is the basis of that aid, and how far we can say that the principle that aid 'should' be mutual is a central normative guideline in family life.

Social exchange   In this context, the concepts of exchange and reciprocity offer rather different ways of understanding the basis of mutual aid. In my view the concept of exchange is the less satisfactory of the two, for both empirical and theoretical reasons. The basis idea of exchange is a simple one, implying that people assist others and get something back in return, although it is often difficult for a researcher to identify what is actually being exchanged. One problem is that exchanges of help take many different forms and some of them may be subtle and indirect (Sussman, 1965). Similar problems are created by the fact that people may not necessarily be able to say whether a particular object or service which they give to a relative counts as part of an on-going pattern of exchange or not. In his study of three-generation American families, Hill draws an important distinction between exchanges, gifts, and loans, and demonstrates that people categorize their actions between these three differently in different situations (Hill, 1970, p. 69). A researcher still may wish to treat gifts and loans as part of an exchange, but then the rules which govern these particular types of exchange need to be elicited.

A further empirical problem, which also leads us into more theoretical considerations, is that exchanges can be of different types, and are not necessarily of equal value, as the concept of 'exchange' implies. Thus at the very least we have to be able to identify different types of exchange, along some kind of continuum of equal and unequal benefits. Gouldner, in his classic discussion of the norm of reciprocity, argues that most exchanges are in fact unequal in terms of their value, but that there is some normative pressure to create an equivalence if not equality. As he puts it, there should at least be 'tit for tat' even if there is not 'tat for tat' (Gouldner, 1973, p. 244).

Attractive though this argument is, it may apply with less force to family relationships than to other situations of social exchange, since one of the key features of these relationships is that there is less likelihood—or even possibility—that people will end the relationships if the terms of the exchange are unsatisfactory. As Argyle and Henderson (1984) have pointed out, social exchange theory seems rather an inadequate basis for understanding social relationships where, as a matter of empirical observation, people do seem to stay in some relationships even when they are not getting much out of them.

There also is the question of whether a person's economic or social circumstances change the nature of the exchange in which they are involved. For example, does a person who has a low-paid job, in a kin group where the others are economically secure, get different terms of exchange? Or does that person get excluded from certain types of kin exchanges (or even from all such exchanges) because their capacity to pay back is at a level lower than the rest? Evidence about the relationship between kin and support class position suggests that people probably are not cut out completely in such circumstances, certainly not from exchanges of practical support. That conclusion is supported by the evidence of Goldthorpe and his colleagues (1980) on men who have been socially mobile. In families where men's class position (measured by their occupation) has risen above that of their parents, this seems to have little effect on the likelihood that they will turn to kin for practical support. Economic support may well be different, however. Studies of men who are unemployed suggest that some worry about becoming 'too dependent' on relatives, especially on parents, and this could be interpreted as being unable to sustain their own position in patterns of exchange. On the other hand, unemployed people do make great efforts to reciprocate and examples have been quoted elsewhere of various types of support— economic as well as practical—being given by the unemployed to their relatives. The evidence is inconclusive, therefore, on this question of whether a person's economic or class position changes the nature of exchanges with their kin. It seems fairly clear that disparities in social and economic position do not cause kin exchanges to cease in any simple way. However, possibly they may change the terms under which those exchanges are conducted. That conclusion must be tentative for lack of systematic evidence. The main point which I want to make here is that the concept of exchange seems insufficiently subtle to deal with these issues.

Essentially the argument against exchange theory as a way of under-standing the basis of mutual aid in families is that it is too simple to cap-ture the complexities of the flow of aid, especially over long periods of time, because it implies that people exchange equivalent goods in pairs. This does not mean that it has *no* relevance; indeed it may be very appro-priate to understanding certain kinds of short-run exchanges, which is precisely the way in which Anderson (1971) used it to interpret his histor-ical data on family relationships (see Bulmer, 1987, pp. 165–8, for an elab-oration of this point).

Reciprocity   The concept of reciprocity, it seems to me, is a more useful one, but to exploit its potential we have to understand it in quite a subtle way. The particular development of the concept of reciprocity which I find most useful in understanding family support comes from the work of anthropologists, who make the perspective of time, and flows of assis-tance over time, central to their analysis. Levi-Strauss (1969), in his discus-sion of the structures of kinship, develops the idea of 'cycles' of reciprocity which involve a number of people and which give shape to exchanges over a long period of time. The concept of cycles of reciprocity has been developed and applied mainly by anthropologists who were studying soci-eties other than Britain. But a good deal of the British literature on kin support could be reinterpreted in these terms. An example would be Grieco's (1987) work on the use of kin networks to gain employment. She shows that, when one person gets a job through the sponsorship of a rela-tive, this creates a strong obligation to reciprocate by giving equivalent assistance to other members of the kin network. The importance of this can be seen in the way that it underscores a whole system of chain migra-tion linked with employment, which provides us with a good illustration of the practical consequences of cycles of reciprocity in the British context. Grieco is clear that the basis of the obligation to reciprocate is membership of the kin group where one has been a beneficiary, and that this overrides a number of other considerations, including personal preferences. She cites three cases of people who gave a home to a relative, whom they did not particularly like, because they felt that this was part of the pattern of reciprocity in which they were involved (pp. 88–9).

Sahlins developed a similar idea by drawing an important distinction between 'balanced' and 'generalized' reciprocity. Balanced reciprocity entails direct exchange, where the balance is created by returning the equivalent of the thing received, without delay. Generalized reciprocity, however, does not imply immediate or equivalent reciprocation, and indeed there may be *no* specific expectation of a counter-gift. A gift may eventually be reciprocated, but there is no specific expectation as to when, where and how. Situations of generalized reciprocity can tolerate a one-way flow over a long period of time, whereas balanced reciprocity requires a two-way flow over a fairly short time-scale (Sahlins, 1965, p. 147–8).

Putting together these ideas, it seems to me that we have a model particularly useful to understanding support within families, where it is embedded within relationships which, by their very nature, tend to last a very long time. It is a model in which some support may be reciprocated over the short-term in a way which looks like an equivalent exchange; but other types of support may not be seen as part of such a system at all, or may create an expectation that the giver will eventually get something back in some other time and place as yet unspecified, and possibly from a third party. On this basis, we can generate some very interesting empirical questions about the normative basis of reciprocity in families: Under what conditions do people feel a pressure to reciprocate in the short term? Are there particular relationships which will tolerate a one-way flow over a long period of time, and what kind of pressure is there for eventual reciprocation? In family relationships, do people operate with an expectation that there may never be direct reciprocation, but that they will eventually 'be repaid' for their generosity by receiving support from someone else?

When we distinguish in this way between observed patterns of mutual aid and the normative basis of reciprocity as it applies within families, it is actually difficult to answer these empirical questions for lack of data which make that specific distinction. Existing evidence points to a possible conclusion that genealogical distance is a key factor in whether there is pressure for short-term reciprocity, with husband–wife and parent–child relationships being those most likely to be able to tolerate a one-way flow for quite long periods (Allan, 1983). One can argue that the normative expectations of obligation and duty built into these relationships (which I explored earlier in this chapter) makes generalized reciprocity possible in ways which would not apply to most other relationships, with a generalized duty to support one's parents, for example, acting as some kind of guarantee that reciprocal assistance will be provided at some stage in the future.

At the same time, it is possible to argue that a structure of generalized reciprocity, once established, has the effect of strengthening the relationships within which it is embedded. This case is argued by Gouldner, who refers to the norm of reciprocity acting as 'a kind of all-purpose moral cement', because in the time lag between one part of the exchange and the other there is a period of indebtedness, in which both parties have a disincentive to break off the relationship or let it deteriorate. Also the knowledge that one is locked into a relationship (or set of relationships) in which there is a commitment to give support acts as a kind of insurance policy for the future. Especially if the normative pressure to reciprocate is diffuse and generalized, Gouldner argues, pressure can be applied 'to countless ad hoc transactions, thus providing a flexible moral sanction for transactions which might not otherwise be regulated by specific status obligations' (Gouldner, 1973, p. 249).

Calculations and balance sheets   It seems to me that these are important insights into the ways in which norms of reciprocity operate within family relationships, and that they give rise to a further series of questions about how people actually use the model of reciprocity in daily life. I will consider that issue through the concepts of calculations and balance sheets. The basic issue is expressed in the following questions: How do people calculate their own and other people's position in structures of reciprocal support? Is the idea of a 'balance sheet' appropriate? How frequently does that balance sheet get revised and on what criteria?

Again, it is difficult to answer these questions on the basis of existing evidence, not least because it is very difficult to get access empirically to the kind of calculations which people may make in part unconsciously (Leira, 1983). Firth, Hubert, and Forge (1970, p. 449) suggest that everyone keeps a 'mental ledger' of services and gifts exchanged between kin, but that these are mostly concerned with what they term 'petty services': visiting, exchanging Christmas cards, giving a lift in the car. The more substantial types of support come into a different category. Bulmer (1987) regards the idea of a lifetime balance sheet as an appropriate way of conceptualizing the nature of social care within families especially, but he does not attempt to provide empirical evidence which would support that. Gouldner (1973) has produced an interesting argument that the kind of calculations which people make about long-term reciprocity depend very much on the past conduct of the people concerned, drawing a distinction between conduct (the basis of the norm of reciprocity) and a person's social status (the basis of duties or obligations). On this argument, a person's credit or debit is calculated mainly in terms of their moral worth, based on judgements about how they have behaved in the past.

I am attracted to both these ideas, but they do require empirical confirmation. We need to know what kind of balance sheet people actually keep, and how far the conduct of their relatives (good or bad) towards themselves or other people alters their calculations about where each person stands in the long-term structure of reciprocity. The kind of questions which I have in mind are: If my father is violent towards me, does that absolve me from any pressure to reciprocate, whatever else he may have done for me in the past? Or does it mean that I am not completely absolved, but I only have to do the minimum? If he is violent not to me but to my sister, does that absolve me as well as her? I use the case of violence to bring out the point in a clear-cut way, but of course there are very many less dramatic examples which could be used to illustrate the same issue. Indeed the question of *what* actions might count is itself an empirical question. There is also a question about whether women and men calculate such matters differently, which seems very likely given the evidence I have already cited about gender differences in evaluating moral claims.

In concluding this discussion of reciprocity as a normative guideline in family relationships, I suggest that it should be regarded as a principle which is separate from the principles of selection, but linked to them. Building mainly upon Gouldner's work, I would suggest that the question 'What has this person done, for me and for other people, in the past?' gets set alongside the question 'Who is this person?' when people are working out whether they ought to give assistance to a particular relative. It means that the guidelines about what should be given and to whom are less fixed in advance of concrete situations than they might appear if one considers solely obligations to particular people. Conversely, the norm of reciprocity helps to fill out the guidelines based upon obligation to particular people: the latter may tell you *whom* you should assist, but the principles embodied in reciprocity help you to decide *what* you should do or give.

The balance between dependence and independence

Family relationships provide the setting for some of the most obvious and extreme situations where one human being is dependent upon another for basic comforts and survival. Physical dependence characterizes the family relationships of the very young, and those who are severely incapacitated. Economic dependence again applies to young people and in a very large measure to women. On a descriptive level, we might wish to say that dependence of one person upon another—not always mutual or symmetrical—is a prime characteristic of family life. However, at a normative level the picture is more complex. Available evidence suggests strongly that it is seen as desirable and proper for family relationships to demonstrate a balance between dependence and independence in relation to the support which kin give to each other. This balance can be seen as part of a broader normative expectation that there should be a combination of intimacy and distance in kin relationships, especially those outside the nuclear family unit which are my particular concern here.

This desired balance between dependence and independence obviously links quite closely with the norm of reciprocity which I considered above. The norm of reciprocity implies that it is desirable for all people to give to others as well as to receive from them. The capacity to give to others is seen by some writers, most influentially in the work of Titmuss, as an essential part of human social life (Titmuss, 1970; Arrow, 1975). The implication of this line of reasoning for family relationships is that a state of affairs where one person is dependent upon another, unless perhaps it lasts for a very short time, is inherently undesirable. Rather than relationships of dependency strengthening family ties, they may actually weaken them because people's concept of the proper balance has been violated; conversely, where that balance is achieved, kin relationships are likely to be stronger (Anderson, 1977; Pinker, 1979, p. 13).

The particular balance of dependence and independence which is regarded as proper and desirable in exchanges between kin has been characterized by Litwak as 'partial aid'. Writing mainly about the United States, he argues that in an industrialized and democratic society, people expect to receive only part of the services which they need from kin, and the rest from formal organizations. Since this is the expectation, no family member is in a position to provide the entire service needed, and therefore no one can 'ask for complete subservience' from a relative, although people do sometimes overstep the mark and fail adequately to respect this norm of partial aid (Litwak, 1965, p. 310). This analysis potentially is a fruitful one, and I shall try to develop it in the context of data available about contemporary British society.

Young adults and their parents   The most obvious empirical examples of how this normative guideline applies concern relationships between generations. First, in the case of young people I have already noted that it has become less common in the twentieth century for young people to share their parents' home after marriage, except in the case of some people with minority ethnic backgrounds. That particular form of dependence seems to be not only uncommon in practice, but also is regarded as normatively undesirable, at least for the white majority. For example, in Bott's study, where the data were collected in the 1950s, she was able to demonstrate that one of the few norms of family life upon which most people were agreed, is that each elementary family unit should be financially independent of relatives and have its own dwelling (Bott, 1957, p. 197). Interesting confirmation that this expectation still applies is to be found in McKee and Bell's study of households affected by male unemployment. In discussing the support received by such households from other kind, McKee argues that, in effect, the proper balance between dependence and independence was preserved through sustaining the position of the unemployed person in patterns of reciprocal exchange. Although gifts from kin (especially parents) were welcomed on one level, at the same time, 'Unemployed households were not always in a position of receiving or depending upon others for resources but sought actively to reciprocate in kind. Unemployed households fought against dependency and against the stereotype of "always being on the receiving end"' (McKee, 1987, p. 115).

The clear message that, once married, young people should be independent of their parents in terms of housing and finance, does not mean that they are expected to cut themselves off completely from their parents after marriage—far from it. It appears that the desired relationship is a very subtle blend of dependence and independence which people often regard as quite difficult to accomplish successfully, although they have a fairly clear idea of what they are aiming for. Diana Leonard Barker (1972) in her study of young people in South Wales in the early 1970s, has produced some very valuable data about how young people's relationships with their parents change in anticipation of marriage and after the event.

The picture which she paints is of parents, especially mothers, working very hard to produce the desired balance through a process of 'spoiling and keeping close'. Whilst encouraging their children to become independent in various ways in the period before they left the parental home, mothers also 'spoiled' them with gifts and services. The effect was to 'keep them close' in emotional and practical terms when they had moved into the more independent state characterized by marriage and a separate home.

These data now are somewhat out of date, and there is a real lack of equivalent studies which would enable us to see how the desired blend of dependence and independence for young people has changed in the circumstances of the 1980s, and what are the processes by which it is achieved. One important exception is the study reported by Allatt and Yeandle (1986) of young unemployed people, where it is clear that parents find it difficult to construct the 'proper' forms of financial support for their young adult children, when at one and the same time those children are significantly dependent upon their parents for economic support, yet at a stage in their lives when it is felt that they 'ought' to be achieving a measure of responsible independence. It seems that the idea of an appropriate balance of dependence and independence is still highly relevant.

Older people and their children   The second illustration of the idea of a 'proper balance' concerns elderly people. Of course it is quite incorrect to assume that elderly people are necessarily dependent upon their families or anyone else just because they are old. As Wenger (1984; 1986) has demonstrated forcefully, many people even in the over-80 age groups are competent and able to live independently, even if they have some physical impairment. None the less, extreme old age in particular is a time popularly associated with greater dependence upon one's relatives, and at a normative level there appear to be some very strong expectations about what the desired balance should be. In particular, it is the norm of *inde*-pendence which comes across most strongly in contemporary work, with the present generation of elderly people strongly valuing their autonomy (Wenger, 1984).

Sixsmith (1986) has provided some very interesting data which underline the importance of retaining one's 'own home' as both a symbolic and a practical expression of this autonomy. His data show that the strong value which elderly people place upon independence is partly a matter of freedom and lack of control (you can do what you like, no one else tells you what to do) and partly a matter of not putting oneself in a situation where further reciprocal obligations are created which possibly cannot be fulfilled. Sixsmith reports that the phrase 'you are not beholden to anyone' was commonly used by older people when talking about why they valued their independence, and it seems to me that this is very revealing. It suggests that the acceptance of support (whether from a relative or from another source) could have the effect of disturbing the desired balance of dependence and independence, by putting the elderly person in a client status which they would be in no position to counteract through the giving of equivalent gifts. This is not to suggest that *no* support can be accepted from relatives, far from it. But older people seem concerned to ensure that any support given can be defined as part of an on-going pattern of *mutual* aid, rather than as assistance which places them in a position of dependency.

The argument about achieving the proper balance, and not being put in a situation where you are defined as dependent upon others, does make sense in relation to the evidence about flows of support between generations. Since there seems to be an expectation that older generations will give support to younger, and that people in the ascendent generation will continue to be net givers throughout their lifetimes, it is a particularly sensitive issue for older people to be in a position of dependency. This whole line of argument of course could be tested empirically and one might expect to find that people who have more resources which they can give to relatives, especially through the medium of inheritance, would be less worries about 'becoming beholden'. If that is the case, it implies that the possibilities for achieving the desired balance vary according to a person's social class and economic position: older people in comfortable economic circumstances are more restricted, partly because they may need to rely on relatives less anyway (being in a position to purchase domestic nursing support) and partly because when relatives do help, that assistance can be reciprocated in some form.

References

ABRAMS, P. (1982), *Historical Sociology* (London: Open Books).
ALLAN, G. (1979), *A Sociology of Friendship and Kinship* (London: Allen and Unwin)
ALLAN, G. (1983), 'Informal networks of care: issues raised by Barclay' (*British Journal of Social Work*, 13, 417–33).
ALLATT, P. and YEANDLE, S. (1986), 'It's not fair, is it? Young unemployment, family relations, and the social contract'. In S. Allen, A. Watson, K. Purcell, and S. Wood (eds.), *The Experience of Unemployment* (London: Macmillan).

ANDERSON, M. (1971), *Family Structure in Nineteenth Century Lancashire* (Cambridge: Cambridge University Press).

ANDERSON, M. (1977), 'The impact on the family relationships of the elderly of changes since Victorian times in governmental income-maintenance provision'. In E. Shanas and M. B. Sussman (eds.), *Family Bureaucracy and the Elderly* (Durham, N.C.: Duke University Press).

ARGYLE, M. and HENDERSON, M. (1985), *The Anatomy of Relationships* (Harmondsworth: Penguin).

ARROW, K. J. (1975), 'Gifts and Exchanges'. In E. S. Phelps (ed.), *Altruism, Morality and Economic Theory* (New York: Russell Sage Foundation).

BAIER, K. (1970), 'The moral point of view'. In G. Wallace and A. D. M. Walker (eds.), *The Definition of Morality* (London: Methuen).

BARKER, D. L. (1972), 'Young people and their homes: spoiling and "keeping close" in a South Wales town' (*Sociological Review*, 20, 4, 569–90).

BOTT, E. (1975), *The Family and Social Network* (London: Tavistock).

BULMER, M. (1987), *The Social Basis of Community Care* (London: Allen and Unwin).

CORNWELL, J. (1984), *Hard Earned Lives: Accounts of Health and Illness from East London* (London: Tavistock).

CUISENIER, J. (1976), 'The domestic cycle in the traditional family organisation in Tunisia'. In J. G. Peristiany (ed.), *Mediterranean Family Structures* (Cambridge: Cambridge University Press).

CUNNINGHAM-BURLEY, S. (1985), 'Constructing grandparenthood: anticipating appropriate action' (*Sociology*, 19, 3, 421–36).

DOUGLAS, J. (1971), *American Social Order* (New York: Free Press).

FINCH, J. and GROVES, D. (1980), 'Community care and the family: a case for equal opportunities?' (*Journal of Social Policy*, 9, 4, pp. 487–514).

FIRTH, R., HUBERT, J., and FORGE, A. (1970), *Families and their Relatives* (London: Routledge and Kegan Paul).

GILLIGAN, C. (1982), *In A Different Voice: Psychological Theory and Women's Development* (Cambridge, Mass: Harvard University Press).

GOLDTHORPE, J., LLEWELLYN, C., and PAYNE, C. (1980), *Social Class in Modern Britain* (Oxford: Clarendon Press).

GOULDNER, A. W. (1973), *For Sociology: Renewal and Critique in Sociology Today* (London: Allen Lane).

GRIECO, M. (1987), *Keeping It In The Family: Social Networks and Employment Change* (London: Tavistock).

GRIMSHAW, J. (1986), *Feminist Philosophers: Women's Perspectives on Philosophical Traditions* (Brighton: Harvester).

GROVES, D., and FINCH, J. (1983), 'Natural selection: perspectives on entitlement to the Invalid Care Allowance'. In J. Finch and D. Groves (eds), *A Labour of Love: Women, Work and Caring* (London: Routledge and Kegan Paul).

HALSEY, A. H. (1985), 'On methods and morals'. In M. Abrams, D. Gerrard, and N. Timms (eds.), *Values and Social Change in Britain* (London: Macmillan).

HILL, R. (1970), *Family Development in Three Generations* (Cambridge, Mass: Schenkman).

HOYT, D. R., and BABCHUK, N. (1983), 'Adult kinship towards networks: the selective formation of intimate ties with kin' (*Social Forces*, 62, 1, 84–101).

LA FONTAINE, J. S. (1985), 'Anthropological perspectives on the family and social change' (*Quarterly Journal of Social Affairs*, 1, 1, 29–60).

LEIRA, A. (1983), 'Women's work strategies: an analysis of the organisation of everyday life in an urban neighbourhood'. In A. Leira (d.), *Work and Womanhood: Norwegian Studies* (Oslo, Norway: Institute For Social Research).

LEVI-STRAUSS. C. (1969), *The Elementary Structure of Kinship* (Boston: Beacon Press).

LEWIS, J. and MEREDITH, B. (1988), *Daughters Who Care* (London: Routledge).

LITWAK, E. (1965), 'Extended kin relations in a democratic industrial society'. In E. Shanas and G. Streib (eds.), *Social Structure and the Family: Generational Relations* (New York: Prentice Hall).

McKEE, L. (1987), 'Households during unemployment: the resourcefulness of the unemployed'. In J. Brannen and G. Wilson (eds.), *Give and Take in Families* (London: Allen and Unwin).

MANSFIELD, P. and COLLARD, J. (1988), *The Beginning of the Rest of Your Life? A Portrait of Newly-Wed Marriage* (London: Macmillan).

MORGAN, D. H. J. (1975), *Social Theory and the Family* (London: Routledge and Kegan Paul).

NODDINGS, N. (1984), *Caring: A Feminine Approach to Ethics and Moral Education* (Berkeley: University of California Press).

O'CONNOR, P. and BROWN, G. W. (1984), 'Supportive relationships: fact or fancy?' (*Journal of Social and Personal Relationships*, 1, 159–75).

PAHL, R. E. (1984), *Divisions of Labour* (Oxford: Basil Blackwell).

PINKER, R. (1979), *The Idea of Welfare* (London: Heinemann).

QURESHI, H. (1986), 'Responses to dependency: reciprocity, affect and power in family relationships'. In C. Phillipson, M. Bernard and P. Strang (eds.), *Dependency and Interdependency in Old Age* (London: Croom Helm).

QURESHI, H. and SIMONS, K. (1987), 'Resources within families: caring for elderly people'. In J. Brannen and G. Wilson (eds.), *Give and Take in Families* (London: Allen and Unwin).

RAWLS, J. (1967), 'Two concepts of rules'. In P. Foot (ed.), *Theories of Ethics* (Oxford: Oxford University Press).

SAHLINS, M. (1965), 'On the sociology of primitive exchange'. In M. Branton (ed.), *The Relevance of Models in Social Anthropology* (London: Tavistock).

SCHNEIDER, D. M. (1968), *American Kinship: A Cultural Account* (Englewood Cliffs: Prentice-Hall).

SUSSMAN, M. (1965), 'Relationships of adult children and their parents in the United States'. In E. Shanas and G. Streib (eds.), *Social Structure and the Family* (Englewood Cliffs: Prentice-Hall).

TITMUSS, R. (1970), *The Gift Relationship* (London: Allen and Unwin).

UNGERSON, C. (1987), *Policy is Personal: Sex, Gender and Informal Care* (London: Tavistock).

WALLACE, G. and WALKER, A. D. M. (1970), Introduction. In G. Wallace and A. D. M. Walker, *The Definition of Morality* (London: Methuen).

WARNOCK, G. J. (1971), *The Object of Morality* (London: Methuen).

WENGER, G. C. (1984), *The Supportive Network* (London: Allen and Unwin).

YOUNG, M. and WILLMOTT, P. (1957), *Family and Kinship in East London* (London: Routledge and Kegan Paul).

2. Conceptual frameworks

2.1. Feminism and the public/private distinction

RUTH GAVISON*

It has become fashionable to expand the list of villains in social, political, and legal thought. The list now includes not only criminals and malfeasors of all sorts, but also theoretical perspectives and complex human practices such as language and science. In this paper I want to examine, in some detail, the identification of one such villain: the 'public/private distinction'. Although my main purpose is to discuss the specific feminist challenge to this distinction, feminists have not been the only critics of this distinction,[1] nor have feminists limited their criticism to this distinction alone.[2] For these reasons, my focus on the feminist challenge to the public/private distinction should be relevant and useful to those posing broader challenges to distinctions and vocabularies.

Different claims concerning the relationship between public and private realms are central to feminist theory as a whole.[3] But only some of these claims voice positions that may be interpreted as challenges to the *distinction* itself, rather than challenges to social arrangements dubbed 'private' or 'public'. One powerful, and representative, challenge to the distinction is that presented by Catharine MacKinnon:

For women the measure of the intimacy has been the measure of the oppression. This is why feminism has had to explode the private. This is why feminism has seen the personal as the political. The private is public for those for whom the personal is political. In this sense, for women there is no private, either normatively or empirically. . . . To confront the fact that women have no privacy is to confront the intimate degradation of women as the public order. The doctrinal

* I presented versions of this paper at Boalt Hall, USC, and the West-Coast Fem-Crits, and learned a lot from the discussions. Special thanks go to Bruce Ackerman, Scott Altman, Dick Craswell, Denhy Curtis, Meir Dan-Cohn, Alon Harel, Barbara Herman, David Heyd, Chris Littleton, Dan Ortiz, Tom Morawetz, Judi Resnik, Ferdy Schoeman, Mike Shapiro, and Kathleen Sullivan.

choice of privacy in the abortion context thus reaffirms and reinforces what the feminist critique of sexuality criticizes: the public/private split.[4]

To assess such calls for the abolition of the public/private distinction, we must do at least three things: explore the meaning of the challenge; ask whether we accept the descriptive and normative judgments implicit in the challenge; and analyse the utility of the distinction as a conceptual tool.

In Part I, I discuss the differences between internal and external criticisms of distinctions. Internal challenges are criticisms of specific uses of terms like 'public' and 'private' or of specific arrangements designated by these labels. External challenges invite us to abolish or delegitimate such distinctions altogether. Feminist analyses of the public/private distinction include both internal challenges, which most feminists accept, and external challenges, which some feminists endorse and other criticize or reject.

In Part II, I examine one factor which makes this particular distinction so difficult to challenge externally: that the terms 'private' and 'public' assume a variety of meanings, with differing normative implications, within the relevant literature. Understanding and assessing both the contexts in which the distinction is used as well as the external criticisms of the distinction requires close attention to these differences.

Finally, in Part III, I seek to explain the grounds for the feminist challenges to the public/private distinction, both external and internal. I will conclude by reconstructing and evaluating those arguments fundamental to the external challenge.

The feminist challenge to the public/private distinction is both insightful and important. When the external elements of this challenge become too sweeping, however, they become misleading and counterproductive and may actually facilitate the devaluation of important aspects of human life that are currently identified as 'private' and 'personal'. Thus, studying the feminist criticisms of the public/private distinction reveals both the strengths and the weaknesses of the fashionable practice of leveling profound critiques at the linguistic and epistemological underpinnings of political positions.

I.   External and internal challenges

Intelligible discussion about endorsing or rejecting distinctions rests on presuppositions about reality, perception, thought, and language. As a result of these varying descriptive or normative assumptions, challenges to distinctions may represent many different types of statements. First, the challenger may argue that there is *no difference* between the things which are thus distinguished, or that if there is a difference, it is not an important one. This challenger may concede that many people *believe* that there is a real difference, and that the language reflects this belief. Such challengers will seek to expose the false belief by attacking both the steps that led to it and the linguistic structures which facilitate the assumption. This challenge thus addresses both the best way to analyse and construct reality and the ways in which language may help us to see (or to obscure) reality.

Other challengers, however, do not fault distinctions for obscuring reality. Instead, their complaint comprises a complex normative argument: The distinction itself plays a part in creating or perpetuating injustice, in reaching or justifying bad decisions, and in paralysing the forces needed for reform.

Here we must distinguish between two types of complex normative arguments. The first kind of argument, an internal challenge to a distinction, asserts that negative effects emerge from the particular way in which the distinction has been drawn. According to the internal challenge, the distinction leads to society's mistaken belief that distinctions between realms, such as the public and the private, are givens of social life, rather than human determinations which can and should be assessed according to human values. Beyond this general criticisms, however, this challenge acknowledges that the distinction can be used in beneficial ways. The second challenge, an external criticism, claims that there is no useful, helpful, or valid way to draw the distinction. In an important sense, only external challenges really challenge the distinction itself, rather than particular political arrangements sometimes called 'private' or 'public'.

An external criticism of the public/private distinction may appeal to individuals in different ways. Naturally, those who believe that there is no important difference between private and public will favor external challenges to the distinction.[5] Others may be attracted to a external challenge if they believe that our social structure is so pervaded by misleading and dangerous uses of the terms that the only path to clear thought and to just solutions is through delegitimating the distinction.[6] For these challengers, questions other than those relating to the existence of differences may be relevant to assessing the value of the distinction. One such question is whether it is desirable to maintain the difference or to invoke it to justify special treatment.[7] Those who think that the difference is either inevitable or desirable will be much more likely to advocate the continued existence of the linguistic framework than those who think that the difference is undesirable, or that its invocation or justification wrongly presents it as inevitable.

In any event, a discussion of a distinction and its challenges presupposes a need to distinguish between answers to questions of reality and desirability on the one hand, and questions of linguistic and conceptual choice on the other.[8] For example, the claim that women are responsible for most of the child-rearing in society is a description which can and should be assessed independently of the choice of whether to label the women's realm as 'private'. Similarly, whether this division of labour is desirable can and should be assessed independently of the linguistic/conceptual choice. Nevertheless, one's position on either of the latter questions may be affected by answers given to the former in complex ways.

II. Public and private

Since the primary function of distinctions is to highlight differences, a good question with which to begin is whether there are differences between public and private, and, if so, whether such differences are important. A look at the huge social science and humanities literature invoking the distinction quickly reveals that the alleged differences are of many types. This variety of alleged differences arises because the terms 'private' and 'public' occur in various senses, which are distinct though interrelated, and because these terms typically have both descriptive and normative meanings which, if not carefully distinguished, can lead to confusion or equivocation. A term used descriptively in a premise, for example, often acquires a different normative sense when used to yield a conclusion.

To gain a sense of the breadth of the external challenge to the public/private distinction, it is important to recall the many usages of these terms in various discourses. Although a comprehensive account of such usages is beyond the scope of this article, a representative sample can be used to illustrate the pervasive and heterogeneous invocations of the distinction. To avoid repetition, this brief survey will not cover feminist literature.

One important invocation of the public/private distinction separates realms of life. Here, a distinction is drawn between the political realm (involving decisions which concern the welfare of all) and the realms of family and market (involving decisions to promote private interests). The distinction may then be used in various ways. It may be used descriptively, such as to explain that in the United States private interests are valued more than political ones. The distinction may also facilitate evaluations, such as the assessment of the relative costs and benefits of the tendency of individuals to 'mind their own business'.[9]

Another version of the public/private distinction arises in popular discussions of 'privatization' related to political economy. Here, discussion centres on problems of managing and financing business enterprises and the distribution of products. Questions also arise concerning how society should treat 'public goods' and whether the private sector can provide such goods.[10]

We can examine a different form of the public/private distinction in the context of the debate regarding public and private moralities and the limits of enforcing morality.[11] This discussion also addresses the 'dirty hands' problems, questioning whether people should have different moral obligations when they are acting within their public roles as opposed to acting as a private individual.[12]

To return to the legal context, a distinction between private and public has been invoked to explain the validity of legal systems. For example, one of H. L. A. Hart's widely endorsed insights is that the normativeness of legal systems is based, at least in part, on the attitudes of individuals toward the law, with a difference between private individuals and public officials.[13] While private individuals must usually conform, for whatever reason, in order for the legal system to exist, public officials must actually accept the standards as binding.[14]

A. Senses of public/private

From the preceding examples, we see that the public/private distinction can be invoked in many contexts, for many purposes, and in many different senses.[15] The following groups of senses in which the public/private distinction is invoked should serve as a useful guide to our discussion.

1. *Accessible/inaccessible* A central sense of the public/private distinction concerns accessibility in the form of being known or observed. The private is that which is unknown and unobserved; the public is that which is known or observed, or at least is capable of being known or observed, because it occurs in a public place.

It is important to note that being known and being observed are also distinct ideas. For example, although observation is one way to acquire certain information about a subject, this information may also be available through other means, such as voluntary disclosure. Additionally, unlike mere knowledge, observation may have secondary effects such as inhibition and distinction.[16] Of the many definitions of privacy that seek to use the terms 'public' and 'private' exclusively for concerns of accessibility, some focus on knowledge and information,[17] while others focus on physical access and observability.[18]

2. Freedom/interference   Another central sense of the public/private distinction contrasts freedom with interference. Here, the 'private' is the 'free,' the sphere in which others do not interfere. The 'public' will acquire a different meaning depending on the source of the interference. For example, when we talk about legal prohibitions or other forms of state regulation, we shall talk of the 'political'.[19] In other contexts, such as discussing the powers of 'free' markets or of social conventions and expectations, we shall talk of the 'social'.

3. Individuals/society (groups)   Finally, the public/private distinction can highlight differences between individuals and various sorts of groups or collectives. The distinction here is a matter of degree, with small, voluntary groups existing somewhere in between—labelled 'private' when compared to larger, more anonymous 'publics', but 'public' when compared to distinct individuals.

Within the category of the individual, it becomes useful to draw some subdivisions. We can distinguish three concepts, all of which are identified as especially private in some contexts: that which is intimate, that which may be related to an individual's self-identity or personhood, and that which is self-regarding, affecting only the individual (or his close and voluntary associates). Though these senses of the individual are distinct, they are also interrelated. While some aspects relevant to one's identity are not intimate, such as one's religious or political commitments or one's career, other aspects, including sexual orientation and the choice of partners and life styles, are. Similarly, some self-regarding decisions are neither intimate nor related to self-identity.

We might also want to differentiate between that which pertains only to individuals' lives, and that which presupposes some social and political structures. Public officials and public offices are a good example of the second category, for they presuppose a system of norms essential for the existence of groups.

4. Complex meanings   Finally, all these senses may combine to create cluster-meanings. We find such meaning in the idea of 'private life', signifying that part of life which is often unknown and inaccessible, at least to the public at large. People often view the 'private life' as a realm entitled to noninterference and freedom from accountability due to its basic self-regarding nature, connection to the intimate, and importance to one's self-identity and welfare. 'Private life' is often perceived to be free in fact, governed only by the free consent of the adults whose lives are concerned. To 'private life' belong the 'personal' aspects of one's life, especially those related to domestic arrangements.

Another complex cluster of meanings centres on matters which are thought to be 'in the public interest'. This broad classification may signify matters about which the public is in fact interested, or matters about which it should be concerned.[20] The normative sense of public concern may be related to the fact that these matters have direct or indirect effects on the public welfare, or that these are matters which the public constructs or regulates through its norms and culture. This normative claim may mean that the public should seek to know about such matters, that it should seek to make them visible, or that it should seek to change them, perhaps even through deliberate social and political processes. This discussion illustrates how the complex senses of 'public' or 'private' build on the different senses of these terms noted above, as well as on their movement along the descriptive-normative spectrum discussed below.

B. Descriptive and normative

The descriptive-normative spectrum, along which many of these public/private senses travel, has many points. At the extreme descriptive end of the spectrum, we find questions which pertain only to 'brute facts': Is this piece of information *in fact* known? Was this incident *in fact* observed? Was this conduct *really* governed solely by the person's wishes? At the other extreme, we find questions which call for full-fledged normative judgements: All things considered, *should* this fact be published and made accessible to the public? *Should* this behaviour be regulated by the law? Between these extremes we find usages of the terms which are partly descriptive and partly normative. Although such usages describe situations, the situations presuppose or depend upon normative elements. Because the connections between descriptions and normative conclusions are often condensed into single uses of a term, these usages have hybrid senses.

The presumptive entitlement is a good illustration of the hybrid creature. Consider, for example, the parts of our bodies which we label 'private parts'. This label suggests that most of us typically keep these parts inaccessible and covered, and that this is the result of social norms which require that such parts should be inaccessible. This complex social fact, reflecting both norms and practices conforming to the norms, provides a reason for entitling these parts to remain private in the full normative sense: No one should be permitted to expose them or publicize them or interfere with them against our wishes. Thus, the same single ascription of privateness performs many functions on the descriptive-normative spectrum, including a presumptive entitlement that this privateness should be protected.

As mentioned above, the presumptive entitlement is sometimes regarded as conclusive, so that the same single ascription can function as a description or as a fully-fledged normative conclusion. However, even if the reason supporting the presumptive entitlement is fully normative, it may be defeated by other reasons which are applicable to the situation. For example, there may be a criminal practice of hiding drugs in one's private parts precisely because of those parts' presumptive entitlement to noninterference. It may therefore be justifiable to conduct a forced search in such places if there is reason to think the entitlement has been abused.[21] The normative conclusion that follows is that, all things considered, this conduct should not be private (free), despite the presumptive entitlement to noninterference raised by the privacy (intimacy) of one's 'private' parts. This does not change the fact that these parts are private in the intimate sense, and that this usage is not purely descriptive.

Another descriptive-normative complexity arises when the resolution of a normative question requires attention to elements which may be facts in one sense and contested states of affairs in another. Actual consent, for example, might be a requirement for making something private (presumptively entitled to be free from interference). In an important sense, the existence of such actual consent is a question of fact. We may be reluctant, however, to accept such 'facts' as sufficient to create the presumption of noninterference if we believe that there is an undesirable systemic constraint compelling the adoption of particular preferences.

A 'public place' is another in-between entity. Often, 'public place' evokes conventional, social, or legal norms which make the place accessible to all. In other words, we contrast the notion of 'private property', with its normative exclusionary structure, with 'public places'. Labelling a place (or a thing) as 'public' is a description, from which the normative conclusion that it should be made accessible follows.

Debate about an ascription based on social norms may include challenges to these norms. In addition to questioning the overall normative conclusion, we may also argue about whether something that is considered private (presumptively entitled to noninterference) *should* be seen that way. This fact lends additional complexity to argumentative moves that invoke the distinction and senses of private and public.

This issue should be distinguished, however, from a different source of complexity discussed above: the labelling of things as 'private' or 'public' based on the existence of some normative structures. Consequently, the adequacy of the labelling may change with changes in these normative structures. For example, what is considered private (intimate) has changed considerably over the most recent decades of Western civilization. These changes affect the adequacy of labelling something as 'intimate', but not the structure of the way in which this adequacy is determined.

C. *Distinctness and interrelatedness*

It should be obvious that the various senses of public and private are distinct. Someone can watch us without interfering with us (a peeping Tom, for example), thus limiting our privacy (inaccessibility) but not our privacy (freedom). And privacy (inaccessibility) may actually enhance our privacy (freedom) by permitting us, unobserved by potential enforces, to act in ways which may violate social norms.[22]

Use of the same term, such as privacy, in different contexts often hides the significance of the normative-descriptive dimensions and is likely to cause confusion. We may want our intimate activities to be inaccessible to others; calling them 'private' invites others to respect these wishes. None the less, others do not always respect such wishes, and the activities may become accessible after all. Similarly, we may want our private (intimate) activities to remain private (free-from-interference). We emphasize this claim by stressing the activities' private nature. None the less, this desire may not be honoured, and it may be considered legitimate for the law to prohibit such conduct.[23]

The cluster meanings of public/private show how these distinct senses can be interrelated. We saw that certain features of situations, such as their intimacy, centrality to self-identity, or self-regardingness can create presumptive entitlements to inaccessibility and noninterference. It may well be, for example, that a person cannot attain full self-identity without having some intimacy, and that intimacy, in turn, may require some inaccessibility. On the other hand, the attainment of full personhood may require public participation, public affirmation of some commitments or relationships, or some forms of accountability. On the societal level, perhaps harms cannot be socially or politically redressable unless they are perceived to be important enough to be subject to public scrutiny.

Against this background, the task facing critics of the public/private distinction looks formidable. The alleged differences between public and private are so numerous, so fundamental, and so pervasive that it is hard to imagine a challenger denying their existence with the simple claim that there is no difference. However, invocation of the rich vocabulary can justify many arguments challenging the distinction. This richness may support powerful internal challenges to the particular ways in which the public/private lines have been drawn and conclusions about them have been reached, and the external argument that, on balance, the usage is undesirable.

III. Feminist challenges

On the surface, many feminist challenges to the public/private distinction appear to be external, denying that any difference exists. The challenges, however, actually document the ways in which the real and pervasive differences between private and public affect the welfare of women in our society. As a result, many feminists advocate changing existing social and political structures in order to eliminate the difference between private and public in some contexts and to downplay its importance in others. Above all, such feminists urge that the distinction should not be invoked as a justification for different treatment in either legal or social realms. In this way, feminist arguments can be internal challenges, invoking the distinction and using it as a central tool of description and evaluation.

Refuting the desirability of the difference and its implications lend support to the denial of difference but alters somewhat the nature of the claim: The challenge serves to facilitate sympathetic consideration of different social arrangements, rather than to deny existing (or even useful) differences. These provocative denials of difference should therefore be interpreted, at least in part, as invitations to look anew at our world, to see how much of it is constructed, unjustified, and based on prejudices and myths. These claims should be characterized as external claims only if they are made not as rallying cries, but rather as serious invitations to deny the difference and delegitimate the vocabulary that makes us captives of this world of prejudice and injustice.

The centrality of the public/private distinction in feminist thought is underscored by the number of challenges to existing conditions that have been grounded in these terms. The discussion of these challenges will therefore illustrate both alternative ways of arguing about the effects of differences between private and public and the overall effect of using the terminology.

A. There is no difference

In this Part, I will not discuss the contention that identification of the difference referred to by the distinction is impossible due to the meaninglessness of the terms used. Nor will I discuss those versions of pragmatism or contextualism that suggest words have no meaning outside of their contexts.[24] Rather, I will deal only with criticisms which deny the existence or importance of a difference between private and public.

1. *Indeterminacy*. The first form of this argument criticizes the dichotomy for being so indeterminate that nothing follows from identifying anything as either 'public' or 'private'. As a result, the invocation of these terms becomes a rationalization for decisions rather than an independently valid justification. Legal scholars have used such an argument in the realm of labour law,[25] and Clare Dalton has challenged the distinction in a similar way from a feminist perspective.[26]

Here we must distinguish two arguments. The first is that because there is no rational way to identify what is private and what is public, such identifications *must* be arbitrary and conclusory. The second is that, while it is possible to identify and to agree upon what is private and what is public, it is not always clear what follows (or should follow) from the identification.[27] According to both arguments, the identification of something as 'private' or 'public' may be conclusory, a mere invocation to justify a conclusion actually reached on other grounds.

Despite their similarity, these challenges are different. Only the former supports the general indeterminacy challenge described previously. As for the latter argument, the fact that the same situation (or value) may require conflicting decisions is a well-known tenet in moral reasoning. This conflict in itself does not render the concept useless to clear thinking. For example, a possible rationale for limiting hate speech is that such speech silences others. This argument justifies limiting the free speech of some in order to expand others' freedom to speak. Similarly, to protect democracy, it is arguably necessary to outlaw political parties that advocate the abolition of democracy. It could be argued, however, that such action is antithetical to the ideal of democracy itself and is therefore self-defeating. Whatever the validity of these arguments, it is clear that they involve issues in which the same value can lead to different conclusions. Yet, I am not aware of any claims that either 'democracy' or 'free speech' are either necessarily indeterminate or conclusory.

Thus, it may well be that the identification of something as 'private' supports both a claim of noninterference (for example, it is best to let families try to work out their differences without external interference), and interference (since abuse within families is not highly visible, families should be closely scrutinized to prevent blatant abuse, especially to those family members who are vulnerable).[28] Though we must assess such conflicting arguments to reach a conclusion, the fact that the same feature (privateness) may point in both directions does not undermine its utility. In fact, it may be beneficial to see that the choice we have to make involves a serious conflict, even in terms of the same value.

On the other hand, if it *is* true that there is no rational way to distinguish between private and public, the distinction may indeed be misleading, and capable only of conclusory uses. The critical literature cannot, however, support this claim. Looking back to the list of meanings offered above,[29] we see that although some of them are all-or-nothing distinctions (for example, a public official compared to a private individual) most are matters of degree. Labels of 'privateness' and 'publicness' may be clear at the extremes, but become more difficult when we get to the grey areas where most actual cases are. In many situations, an entity can be described as private or public, or relatively private or public, in a number of different dimensions. Both the lack of a bright line between public and private and the existence of multidimensional analysis are cited as sources of the alleged fatal indeterminacy. But neither feature is unique to the public/private distinction, and in this, as in other contexts, the complexity of ascriptions does not entail either conclusoriness or uselessness.[30]

The dangers of conclusory uses are real and I shall return to them later. Practices which force us to identify entities with either one label or another encourage conclusory uses, especially if the application is premised on a rule mandating a particular result based on this identification. Such practices tend to distort the reality that these institutions are complex mixtures of private and public elements. The existence of these dangers should not obscure the fact that in many contexts we do use these terms confidently, usefully, and in non-conclusory ways.[31]

For example, voluntarily watching pornographic movies in the privacy of one's home is different from being exposed to pornographic posters on the public highway. The first activity can be described intelligibly as more private along several dimensions: It occurs in a private (inaccessible) place and is private (free) because it is voluntary. Moreover, both aspects of privateness can support a presumptive entitlement to be private (not-interfered-with). Yet this valid and useful ascription of privateness should not prejudge the question of whether the two activities should be treated differently in terms of legal regulation. The activities may be similar in respects that transcend the public/private difference. Such similarities may include common effects on public culture or on private conduct. Thus, it is arguable that such conduct is *not* private (self-regarding). As a result, the presumptive entitlement to noninterference may be defeated by the wish to prevent such harms. This discussion reveals how the ascription of privateness, with attention to different senses and moves on the normative-descriptive spectrum, therefore aids the discussion without prejudicing it. Thus, the general indeterminacy argument for denying all public/private differences must fail.

2. *Nothing is really private.* Here, the attack is directed at three senses of private noted above: private as self-regarding; private institutions based on norms of contract and property (the more voluntary parts of which are called 'private law'); and private as free. According to this argument, false beliefs are created when these three senses of privacy—which are, in fact, empty categories—are invoked. While the attack is not directed at all conceivable senses of public or private listed above, those targeted are the central and important ones. If the attack is successful, the utility of the distinction may be outweighed by its confusing and distorting effects.

Nothing is self-regarding. This challenge has become familiar from criticisms of J. S. Mill's *On Liberty*. A cornerstone of Mill's argument for liberty was the distinction he drew between self- and other-regarding activities. According to Mill, the former were outside the jurisdiction of society.[32] Mill's arguments for liberty were attacked by critics who contended that, because individuals do not exist as monads, independent of all others, no significant activity can be solely self-regarding.[33]

Some feminists sound like Mill's critics. In response to the claim that what happens within families is self-regarding, affecting only members of the family unit, feminists answer that the 'private' arrangements within families affect both nonmembers and society at large in important ways. Citizens of the state are socialized within the family, and evidence shows that child-rearing arrangements affect children in profound and complex ways. Consequently, the characteristics brought by children into their adult lives will eventually affect the general norms and expectations of their society. Furthermore, child-rearing arrangements affect not only the chances of particular family members to participate fully in the public world of work and politics, but also the general pattern of participation of women in society (including those women not raising children).[34]

Similarly, some feminists argue that activities that are commonly viewed as paradigmatically self-regarding, such as an individual's decision to watch pornography alone in the privacy of her home, are in fact other-regarding in important ways.[35] According to this argument, such decisions presuppose the availability and permissibility of the activity, as well as society's toleration of the possible consequences of the choice to view pornography. A society in which such outlets not only exist, but are tolerated, is a society that permits the creation of images portraying women enjoying abuse and pain. It is also a society in which it is more likely that people will respond to pornography and abuse others.

No controversial activity can be purely self-regarding. The very fact that an activity creates a controversy indicates that it has an effect on others. Moreover, it may be true that no significant activity is completely self-regarding, because any conduct may have some effects, however remote, speculative, or diffuse, on others. Additionally, while consent, freely given, may entitle participants in an activity to noninterference in some contexts, it does not make the activity self-regarding. The real question, however, is whether we can intelligibly distinguish among activities according to the quality, magnitude, probability, and irreversibility of the effects that they may have on others. Herein lies the strength of Mill's intuition. Any individual's decision to violate a social norm in the privacy of her home may contribute to the demise of that norm (and thus may not be fully self-regarding). This conduct, however, differs from a public denial or violation of that same norm. Such public denial, in turn, is very different from conduct which harms individuals directly.

This objection to the public/private distinction serves as a reminder that the extent to which activities are self- or other-regarding may be a matter of degree. Consequently, the objection is of the same status as the argument from indeterminacy.[36] Although most entities are neither clearly public nor clearly private, important normative conclusions may still follow from the *degree* of self- or other-regarding. For instance, it may be legitimate to dub activities which are primarily self-regarding as 'private' and to establish a presumption of noninterference on this basis.[37]

No social institution is private. Critical Legal Studies scholars took this argument about contract and property from the Realists and their mentors,[38] and it was subsequently applied to the family.[39] This argument seeks to undermine the presumption of noninterference with private institutions by showing that these institutions are in fact public in important respects. In doing so, the criticism demonstrates how the presumption of noninterference arises: We label property, for example, as private to signify that it depends on voluntary transactions between relatively equal private adults. When coupled with a general respect for the voluntary activities of individuals, this description creates a presumption of noninterference.

According to the criticism, contract, property, and marriage are public because they are defined and regulated by the law and social norms, both public creations. The law determines the initial endowments of property. The law confers the 'private' powers of deciding whether to make a contract, to sell a piece of property, to get married, or to enter into a co-habitation agreement. The State also grants and, when necessary, enforces powers such as the prohibition on nonowners to enter, use, or sell. The implication is that the presumption of noninterference is misguided: What the public created and maintains, the public can take away. The ultimate decision about what should be private is, and should be, public.

While this important insight should be conceded and even stressed, it neither follows that there is no important sense in which 'private property' is private nor that there are no good reasons for the presumptive entitlements of private arrangements to noninterference. There is (and probably should be) a difference between property that is controlled, maintained, and managed by individuals and property that is held by collectives or the state. It is true that the decision about the property regime in a given society is a public one. Though the decision will be public irrespective of the content of the regime which is adopted, the difference between property arrangements is significant, and some such arrangements can intelligibly be dubbed 'private'.[40] So private property is indeed 'private' in an important sense.

Moreover, the conceded fact that what is private is determined by public norms and laws does not invalidate the presumption of noninterference with private arrangements. Although the public realm may be the final arbiter of what remains immune from interference, public norms and laws should grant private arrangements this immunity where these are transactions between full and informed individuals. This follows from the belief that it is desirable to leave individuals an area in which they can act free from governmental interference.

Nothing is free. This argument, too, has general and feminist versions. According to the general version, nothing we decide is really 'free' in the sense that it is determined only by our own wishes and preferences. We are constrained by various limits: opportunities, socialization, expectations, resources and perceptions. Many of these constraints are person-made and not inevitable.[41] Similarly, nothing is voluntary and equal. The worker who *must* earn a living and can sell only his labour is not free to choose unemployment, even if the only available work is humiliating and exploitative. Consent becomes anything but the product of bargaining between free and equal adults.[42]

The feminist version of the argument ranges over a number of areas. When women 'choose' to marry, when women 'want' sex, when women 'choose' to stay home and spend time with their children rather than pursue their careers in 'workaholic' ways, women are not choosing freely, but rather are selecting from choices mandated by social constraints and norms. The fact that many women feel happy and fulfilled in these 'choices' is not evidence that these 'choices' are free. Rather, the feeling of fulfilment is the insult added to the injury of the initial programming. Society has induced these feelings in women so that women will not rebel against their exploitation and oppression. Basically dependent upon men as breadwinners and sources of power and status, women are free to 'exit' and are therefore unable to negotiate the conditions of their relationships from positions of freedom and equality.[43]

It is an important insight that many decisions not subject to state regulation or physical coercion are not authentic exercises of individual autonomy and choice; much of what determines our conduct stems from external constraints with diverse and pervasive sources. It must further be conceded that these constraints may have important political implications, often obscured by descriptions of these activities as 'free' or as 'equal'.

None the less, the truth of these insights should not be taken to require either of the following conclusions: first, that all attempts to quantify freedom, or to distinguish between areas of freedom and areas of its absence, are necessarily false and misleading; and second, that freedom from *legal* regulation is not an important and useful distinction.

It may be an interesting empirical claim that women are systematically subordinate to men in their available options and expectations. This situation may well call for redress. Yet, though it may be interesting to claim that women are not free,[44] this is a far cry from saying that nothing is ever free. In fact, the complaint that women are not free presupposes that men may be free and that women should strive for this level of freedom. Implicit in the complaint, therefore, is an ideal which assumes that some form of political and social liberty is possible and desirable. For these reasons, the feminist complaint does not allege that nothing is free. Rather, the error is either that something is deemed free when it is not (women's consent to sex and marriage is seen as free when it is induced by constraints and brainwashing), or that some men oppress women, denying women's freedom in order to perpetuate their own.

If nothing is free anyway, the difference between legal regulation and other ways of guiding behaviour disappears. A qualification in this statement is therefore needed to remind us of the distinctness of using the *law*, or the power of the State, to regulate aspects of human conduct. It is hardly a trivial move to advocate or justify using the law to prohibit conduct which does not cause physical or economic harm to others. One important contemporary political debate revolves around such questions, as applied to conduct such as homosexuality, taking soft drugs, voluntary sadomasochistic practices, and the voluntary or solitary watching of pornography. Often the argument against legal regulation in these fields has been made in the name of freedom. Even if the argument *could* be based on other grounds, however, it is a mistake to assume that legal regulation is indistinguishable from social pressures or economic needs.[45]

3. *The personal is political.*   This claim in slogan form, so typical of the women's movement and of feminism, appears as a radical denial of the difference between two central senses of private and public.[46] In some contexts, it is related to the claim that nothing is self-regarding or free in the sense of autonomous, unconstricted, or unaffected by cultures and social norms. Many of one's most 'personal' decisions, such as whether to marry, how to mourn, and what kind of career to choose, are obviously affected both by political constraints and by the availability of legitimate options. For example, in a time of social or political crisis, the decision not to engage in political activity may be much less permissible than the same decision during a time of prosperous and 'normal' politics. The fact that both personal and social factors affect individuals' decision-making is in no way unique to feminist perspectives or insights. More importantly, this fact does not seek to undermine the importance of identifying such decisions as personal. Usually, such identification relates to a combination of factors, such as the importance of the decision to the individual's life or identity, the relative absence of identifiable and direct harm to others or the public at large, the power the individual has to make the decision, and the absence of a social expectation of accountability for the choice.

But there is at least one context, central to the feminist challenge, in which the slogan does seek to deny these differences and to negate the implications which usually follow from calling something 'personal'. One of the functions of dubbing something 'personal' is to define that activity, decision, or complaint outside of the social, political, or public arena, and to connect it with the particular circumstances and responsibilities of the individual or individuals concerned. This definition, in turn, identifies the proper way to address the complaint or the problem: The individual suffering from personal difficulties may need aid or therapy. Although the general availability of such help may be a social concern, the particular problem is of no public interest or concern.

Feminists, especially radical ones, attack the classification of things into personal and political, arguing that many personal problems are deeply political.[47] For these feminists, the slogan does not act as a mere reminder of interdependence between the public and private realms. Rather, it is used to challenge the *existence* of alleged differences: The 'personal' should not be allowed to stop conversations, critique, or accountability; the 'persona' should not be seen as an improper theme for concern and possible public interference. It is against the background of *this* interpretation of 'personal' that the slogan identifying the personal with the political should be understood. When women are harassed in the workplace, it is not just the predicament of the individual women who are unfortunate enough to work for exceptional male employers. When women are battered at home, it is not because each particular victim has triggered an unfortunate 'individual' tragedy. When women feel constrained and bored in their expensive suburban homes, with nothing to do but wait for their husbands and children so that they may cater to their needs, it is not because these women fail, as individuals, to adjust to their natural feminine roles. Social structures are involved, social structures which are not simply 'natural'. They are person made, and they benefit males.[48]

Furthermore, the argument goes, dubbing certain activities or choices as 'personal' is in itself part of the mechanism used to perpetuate the anomalous and unjust situation, by obscuring the injustice of the structure, and instead highlighting individual adjustments within the status quo. For this reason, feminist consciousness-raising groups, meeting to discuss the lives of their individual members, are not properly understood as an indulgence in the personal. Such groups are a way to give the experiences of women more visibility and to make women understand that their 'individual' problems are actually the reflections of undesirable social structures.[49]

One part of this argument must be valid: To recognize effectively that the structures are partly responsible for these 'personal' problems, society must first identify the symptoms as part of a social problem. We should then seek to make the underlying problem visible (instead of encouraging the secrecy and shame which are too often the accepted approaches to personal inadequacies) and to mobilize individuals to regard the situation as political, enlisting the forces of political and social reform for change.

More questionable is the attempt to conclude from 'the personal is political' that *nothing* should be immune from public scrutiny, discussion, and accountability. This is a substantive question of political morality, which should be discussed on its merits. It cannot be decided simply by identifying the effective preconditions of putting something on the public agenda and by evaluating it against its social and political background.[50]

I shall return to the issue of whether, since many so-called 'personal' issues are actually caused by social and political facts, the fact that the designation of 'private' hides this fact supports a conclusion that public/private *language* should be delegitimized. Nothing in this claim are identical or that the use of the terminology is never useful. This claim does not affect the basic intuition that our particular struggles with our activities, loves, and work are what make our lives our own. Of course we are affected and constrained by available options and social norms, and our own struggles may well help to reinforce political and social processes. But most of us feel that there are aspects of our lives which are 'private' and 'personal', and thus should not be accessible to others without our consent; they should not be matters dealt with by the public, be it media or politicians. This intuition presupposes some distinction between private and public, between personal and political. It is not affected by the validity of the insight that 'privatization' may be, at times, a cause of invisibility and paralysis.

B. *Too much difference*

Even feminists who advocate versions of the 'no difference' claims agree that, in our social reality, pervasive differences exist between private and public, and that these differences, real and perceived, greatly affect the situation of women. The paradigmatic private sphere contains the realm of domestic and family life, whereas the paradigmatic public sphere encompasses the realm of politics—decision-making concerning the welfare of society as a unit. The economic realm, which includes production and marketing, lives in-between. While for the Greeks and for most liberal political theorists, the economic is an element of the private, for

Marxists, CLS scholars, and radical and socialist feminists, it is an important part of the public.

The claim that differences exist between the public and private is
reflected in the history of Western society. Before the industrial revolution, a distinction existed between politics and war, on the one hand, and
the complex of family and household work on the other. Though women
and slaves were excluded from the former, they dominated the latter
realm, which expanded well beyond family matters. During this period,
most of the products necessary for survival, both for consumption and
for barter or commerce, were produced within the household, and
women and children had primary responsibilities for these tasks. As a
consequence of this mingling of work and family life, more decisions
were made in the household, and the balance of power and responsibility
within the family was more egalitarian. In public/private terms, we can
describe this either as a more extended private, or as a period of mingling
of private and public.

After the industrial revolution, the social difference between the
domestic and the market appeared and intensified. Though the distinction between the domestic realm and that of politics remained, a further
distinction emerged: that between the world of work, removed from the
household, and the world of the family, in which children were raised
and the physical needs of members were met.

These post-industrialization distinctions are still in effect today, and,
against the background of this relatively noncontroversial description,[51]
feminists raise several claims. In different ways, each of these claims
invokes the public/private distinction.

1. Relegation to private, exclusion from public.   The first feminist claim is
that the privatization of women has resulted in their marginalization. In
modern, post-industrial societies, women have remained relegated to the
private, while this realm has become increasingly impoverished and limited. The private now excludes not only politics, but also bread-winning
work.[52]

Exclusion of women from the public occurred in many ways. First,
many legal systems excluded women politically by denying them the
vote and even withholding legal status independent of their fathers or
husbands. In addition to these exclusions, women were granted only limited economic and property-holding rights, and, in many countries,
women were banned from many professions, including medicine and
law. Even today, without many of the formal legal hindrances to equal

participation in the political or professional worlds, women are represented unequally. Finally, in most families, women still take primary responsibility for raising children and for providing unpaid services in the home while men are expected to earn a living outside the home.

Feminists argue that this relegation of women to the 'private' is unjust because it burdens women in many ways.[53] It denies them positive liberty, visibility, rewarding lives, and independence, without acknowledging the distribution as unjust and deserving of discussion and redress. The 'private' becomes simultaneously invisible and purely 'self-regarding', and therefore of no public interest.

2. The myth of difference.   According to feminists, the problem is more than the creation of the public and private realms and the relegation of women to the latter. Another problem lies in the way the realms have been *differentiated*. Feminists argue that the differences are either nonexistent or exaggerated, resulting in the continued oppression of women.

One frequently criticized characterization views the market, like the hunt or war, as cruel and harsh, governed by self-interest and power. The family, on the other hand, is the realm of affection, love, harmony, and cooperation. Under this perspective, men, because they are stronger, volunteer to face the harsh 'outside' world, and women, grateful to have been spared, provide the warmth and support that enables the men to return to the harsh world of money-making.

Another characterization relates to the degree of freedom from regulation within the family, as compared to the 'outside'. Because the family realm is one of love and harmony of interests, there is no need for legal interference. According to this perspective, 'natural' familial instincts and common interests will ensure the welfare of everyone. Noninterference can also be explained and justified because intra-family arrangements have been reached by free and equal adults. Therefore, respect for the autonomy and integrity of familial relationships requires suspension of interference.

Feminists challenge all of these characterizations of the realms. Though the world of work and politics may be competitive and harsh, they are often rewarding and challenging, providing meaning and importance in one's life. Furthermore, though much behaviour in the worlds of work and politics may be motivated by self-interest, one can also find nobility, charity, and friendship in these worlds. Participation in the public realm should not be seen as a sacrifice, and the exclusion from it, even if voluntary, should not be seen as an advantage.

Similarly, according to feminists, the family is far from being a place of simple affection and harmony. Despite the love and commitment which are central to family associations, the interests of family members often conflict. These conflicts are often resolved by power, rather than by a benevolent consideration of everyone's interests. Furthermore, though the work in the home may not be as competitive as that in the market, it is often routine and tedious, not to mention lonely and isolating. Because it is usually not paid for, the work generates no financial benefit to foster independence and control. To top it all, work within the home has little visibility.[54] Descriptively, for feminists, the 'private' is much less attractive, and the 'public' much less threatening, than the common story allows. With this in mind, a bargained-for division of labour that excludes women from the public becomes much less acceptable.

As we have seen, feminists also charge that families are not in fact 'free' in any important sense of this term. First, we consider 'free' in the sense of unregulated by legal or social norms. While it is true that there is a reluctance in the law to interfere with the ongoing management of family life and to supervise or enforce 'intimate' arrangements, there is much regulation of the institution of marriage and discouragement of alternative family groupings. Competence to marry and default arrangements are often regulated by law, while norms of appropriateness are enforced through social pressures and counseling.

Second, we consider 'free' in the sense of emerging from bargains and agreements between equal and free adults. Children, who are clearly not equal and free adults, suffer the consequences of familial arrangements that cannot be described as 'voluntary' in so far as they are concerned. But, claim feminists, women too are neither equal nor free. Because of their dependence on men, which is partly economic and partly psychological, women are afraid to exercise the 'exit' option, or to behave in ways that will increase the chances that their husbands will 'exit'. Family 'bargaining' therefore proceeds under the shadow of this dependence. Furthermore, the family is not an inviolate area for women. In fact, we know that the problems of domestic violence and abuse are all too real in modern society.

Finally, feminists challenge the conclusion that the family *should* be free from interference by the state. They argue that this conclusion rests on false premises about the nature of family life. Once these false assumptions are exposed, it becomes clear that families should be scrutinized, and that interference may be justified when necessary to protect the vulnerable: women and children. According to this argument, the 'privacy' of the family is often invoked to mask the exploitation and battering of family members. Such exploitation and violence should be matters of public concern, and the fact that they occur within the family should not be used to provide them with immunity.

3. The myth of autonomy. In addition to differentiating between public and private, a common interpretation makes them separate and autonomous: What happens in private concerns only the family or its individual members and does not affect society at large. The belief that private acts are relatively inconsequential helps to justify noninterference as well as to perpetuate low visibility and an absence of public concern. The events of private life are, in the terms of the familiar slogan previously discussed, merely personal. Feminists emphatically challenge the purported independence of the two realms, arguing with great force that private arrangements profoundly affect the public realm and its social structures.

In Part III.A.2 above, I rejected the broader feminist argument that nothing could, in principle, be self-regarding. But there is great merit in the narrower claim concerning the public importance of the consequences of arrangements that are superficially self-regarding and considered private. One significant function of this feminist claim is to give these consequences visibility and, thus, to make them a matter of public knowledge, attention, and concern.

For example, familial relationships, in large part, shape the individuals who will become citizens and workers. The basic ingredients of public life are traceable to the ways in which families raise children, including the inculcation of gender-based expectations and perceptions. In addition, the relative disadvantages of women in the world of politics and work stem from their disproportionate burdens in the private realm, especially with respect to child-rearing. The interdependence of public and private indicates that changes in public limitations on women will have little effect unless they are accompanied by changes in private relationships and by correlative changes in the interaction between public and private realms.

Interdependence provides another argument against the presumptive entitlement of noninterference in the family realm. Because private family arrangements may well be among the most consequential factors in individuals' development and may largely determine their options in the public world, public attempts to optimize these arrangements may be desirable. The need for public influence becomes evident when we consider the inequality of bargaining powers and the prevalence of many prejudices and stereotypes. As usual, these reasons may be balanced against other constraints, including the wish to protect, to some extent, the privacy of families, and the limited effectiveness of public regulation in this area. But these are very different from 'jurisdictional' objections to interference with private lives.

4. *Assessing the private.*   The difference between private and public is not only a matter of relegating parts of life to different realms and claiming that these realms are autonomous. The two realms, typically, are also valued and assessed differently. Three approaches to this valuation process compete in the general literature. The first devalues the private as unimportant and unchallenging, lacking the nobility and courage demanded by involvement in the public. The second makes the private not only the 'haven in a heartless world', but also the ultimate source of meaning and satisfaction in life. A third approach views both as candidates for satisfaction and reward, with individuals needing access to both realms, although possibly in different mixes.[55]

Most feminists believe that the world as we know it systematically leans to the first approach, devaluing the private as a woman's realm based in nature as distinguished from culture. Anthropologists point out that this tendency is cross-cultural; exclusively male tasks, whatever they may be in a given society, are considered more important than tasks performed by females.[56] Feminists tend to accept this first approach as an accurate description of current attitudes, but they are ambivalent as to the correct normative approach. They feel a life exhausted by the private is impoverished and that many of the tasks connected with care-giving and housekeeping are indeed less valuable and less creative, less the stuff of great drama, than other human activities. They would agree that the painting of the *Mona Lisa* is rightly seen as a great human achievement and would consider the endeavour a greater contribution to our culture than that provided by the support and sacrifice of many mothers.[57] At the same time, however, many feminists feel that something is wrong with this devaluation of activities associated with private life. They see a society in which there is no glory, pay, or prestige in the daily task of raising children, but in which waging a bloody war is a great human achievement. They believe that ours is a less humanistic society, a worse society, than one in which the essential human tasks receive more prominence, recognition, and respect.[58]

Many feminists regard the second description, which claims to value the private above all else, as disingenuous. They see talk of love's importance and centrality in the lives of men as either a way of masking lust or a part of the 'opium' necessary to keep women marginal, servile sex objects. It is a way of making an otherwise undesirable fate more appealing. After all, they say, men's lives are rarely exhausted by their loves,[59] whereas the lives of women who love 'important' men are frequently exhausted in a secondary role.[60] Consequently, many feminists deny that anyone really considers love and family to be the ultimate sources of satisfaction.

Finally, most feminists find no fault with the third account as an ideal. Their complaint is that, in social life as we know it, the two sexes do not share access to the same range of choices. While some feminists concentrate on the injustice done to women in this respect,[61] others stress that present arrangements harm both women and men.[62] While men usually operate in both realms, their unique role in the public realm causes them to be distanced and alienated from the values of the home. Some radical feminists, however, see the focus on choice between private life and pubic commitments as legitimating the decision to lead one's life without political involvement.[63]

5.The myth of inevitability. Finally, the division of life into two realms and the currently prevalent family structures are often portrayed as inevitable or natural. Often this portrayal is coupled with a claim that existing arrangements are desirable, either because women have a special disposition or ability to raise children (they are more attached, compassionate, and caring), or because men are better at the tasks of work and politics (they are more oriented to justice, intellectual creativity, abstract thought, and sophisticated technology, and have the physical ability to deal with heavy equipment), or both.

The inevitability and desirability of some division of life functions along gender lines is a central controversy for feminism. First, there is an internal debate over the question of whether there are differences in tendencies and capacities between men and women. Some feminists, notably Carol Gilligan and her followers, argue that there is indeed a tendency among women to prefer an 'ethics of care'. Others deny that such a difference exists, or argue that the difference results from socialization rather than from innate and inevitable differences between the sexes. Most feminists are sceptical of claims of inevitability, since they believe that such claims are attempts to silence women, and, thereby, to perpetuate existing arrangements, discouraging critical examination.[64]

Another heated debate within feminism concerns the desirability of arrangements that assign different responsibilities and functions to men and women. Most classical and radical feminists advocate equal access for women to the public realms of work and politics. Some feminists, however, are willing to concede that women have special responsibilities to their families, and that these responsibilities may imply some inequality between the sexes.[65] This controversy provides a natural transition to the next subject: the desirability of a difference between public and private.

C. *There should be no difference*

We saw that a challenge to the public/private distinction may be motivated by the belief that its invocation promotes undesirable social arrangements, or hinders their reform. This kind of challenge presupposes a specific normative position: It is desirable that there be no difference between private and public, or, at least, that the differences be reduced.

Some of the claims challenging existing arrangements and perceptions of private and public as they relate to women are uncontroversial. The claim, for example, that domestic arrangements matter and should be integrated into political philosophy and considerations of justice is generally accepted. In public/private terms, this may be formulated as a combination of descriptive and normative claims—the private (domestic) has been invisible, not fit for public concern. This invisibility contributed to the devaluation of the private and to the failure of theories of justice to address its structure. It also led to the silencing and imposed privatization of women and their activities. The normative implication is clear: These arrangements deserve more attention and should become matters of public scrutiny and concern. Theories of political and social justice should address them. And the 'privateness' of domestic arrangements should not deter scrutiny, or imply inviolability.[66]

There is much less agreement on the desirability or feasibility of more specific changes in the balance between private and public. Usually, when the dichotomy between private and public is challenged, the argument is that all is (or should be) public. But once we look at particular questions, it is rare to find feminists who argue consistently either that everything should be regulated by the state, or that the family and all other forms of intimate relationships should disappear in favour of public communities that provide for the needs of members, make political decisions, and police the different ways in which members interact. When pushed, feminists explicitly deny that this is their ideal.[67] They advocate only local changes in the existing mix of private and public and in the existing institutionalization of both realms, with more equal access to the two realms for both genders. They also want the freedom to explore these questions boldly and creatively.[68]

While there are particular contexts in which a feminist agenda can be identified as advocating a change in the public/private mix, it is hard to specify even one context or dimension of the distinction in which the claim is that the whole category of the private is useless, or that private structuring should be discontinued. The normative debates concern relationships between private and public, but their conclusions do not assert that the differences should be obliterated or even greatly reduced.[69]

D. The role of language

Having reviewed the many ways in which feminists have attacked the present uses of the public/private distinction, we must now return to the external critique. Internal challengers have argued that political arrangements should be critically discussed and that changes should be made in private and public structures, including the traditional reluctance to interfere in the private realm of the family. The external challenge makes the further claim that the public/private distinction and its invocation, as such, are partially responsible for the undesirable state of affairs. Consequently, the *terminology* that distinguishes private and public and that invokes the value of privacy should be abandoned or delegitimated.

Feminists agree that, in Western society, there is a difference between private and public realms, and that this difference is reflected in language. Some feminists argue that the distinction is not gender-neutral; the distinction 'keeps the private beyond public redress and repoliticizes women's subjection within it'.[70] This argument is complex: The public is simultaneously a source of power and a fundamental structuring concept that affects beliefs and expectations. It is difficult to divide the argument into more distinct elements while maintaining the integrity of the argument. On the other hand, the assertions being made are difficult to understand without being broken down into component parts. The following is my attempt to separate our identifiable elements from the critique and evaluate them individually.

1. Bad results.   The first, and primary, complaint of the external critique is that the use of public/private language somehow leads to undesirable consequences. People who use public/private talk get the problems, not the terms, wrong. They tend to reach solutions that systematically disadvantage women. The best way to examine this claim is by studying a number of examples that allege such bad results.

Abortion. MacKinnon's critique of *Roe* v. *Wade*[71] shows both the difficulty of separating the complex argument into discrete elements as well as the importance of doing so.[72] The bad result MacKinnon discusses is *Harris* v. *McRae*,[73] in which the Supreme Court ruled that a state has no obligation to finance medically required abortions *and* that this conclusion does not affect the privacy rights of women. MacKinnon argues:

> [T]he *Harris* result sustains the ultimate meaning of privacy in Roe: women are guaranteed by the public no more than what we can get in private—that is, what we can extract through our intimate associations with men. Women with privileges get rights.[74]

This complaint should be analysed in light of the general claim, made by MacKinnon and others, that the liberal ideal of the inviolability of the private uses the doctrine of privacy to protect the status quo. Because liberals assume that what happens in the private is equal, free, autonomous, and intimate, they assume that these activities should be protected against violation by the public. Liberals, the claim goes, do not realize that private inequality can, and often should, be redressed by the state. Equality can only be achieved if there is public interference, not public abdication.[75]

In the abortion context, MacKinnon argues, this background inequality is systemic and profound; women cannot control their sexual availability and are often discouraged by social norms from protecting themselves against unwanted sex, and its possible consequence—pregnancy.[76] The primary fight should be over ways in which women can gain control over their own sexuality, not over ways to deal with unwanted pregnancy.[77] This fight requires state intervention, intervention that will speak to intimate and private transactions between the sexes.

MacKinnon's critique of the doctrinal choice of privacy in *Roe* is very different from the objections raised by other privacy scholars.[78] The latter highlight the distinction between freedom from intrusion and publicity on the one hand, and freedom in the sense of noninterference on the other. These privacy scholars would have been content had the abortion decision been analysed in terms of (negative) liberty. MacKinnon's critique, however, pertains equally to liberalism's ideal of liberty (as in the liberty of the homeless to sleep under bridges).

Under this view, the tension between *Roe* and *Harris* exists for all standard liberty rights. One illustration should suffice. Everyone has the freedom to travel, but only those who can pay the fare can effectively exercise the right. The state prevents unjustified interference designed to limit one's physical freedom of movement, but does not provide funding for travel. Although most people will argue that this supports the conclusion that freedom of movement is protected, it is also clear that this freedom can and does coexist with deep inequalities.[79]

MacKinnon argues that the abortion issue should be viewed in terms of equality rather than privacy or liberty.[80] The fact that women bear the burdens of reproduction, combined with the fact that they often cannot control their sexual availability, constitutes one critical cause of the inequality of women.[81] Since the right to an abortion is necessary to mitigate this inequality,[82] it becomes a matter of substantive equality, not a claim to liberty or privacy.

MacKinnon is wrong, however, in arguing that the privacy language was not important for the decision in *Roe*. She incorrectly claims that *Roe* only gave women what they could have obtained through private negotiations with men, and she is wrong in asserting that the *Harris* decision became more likely because of *Roe*'s privacy rationale. Finally, the privacy framework used in *Roe* can be justified in three significant ways.

First, the use of privacy terminology helped secure for women the positive outcome found in *Roe*. A 'liberty' rationale would have been a less attractive and less likely candidate, since the Court needed to distinguish the substantive due process rationale established in *Lochner* v. *New York*.[83] But the privacy rationale was, in fact, a limited liberty rationale that the court was willing to use. The Court was not ready to endorse the more radical and controversial analysis viewing abortion as a matter of equality or as following from the woman's right to control her own body.[84]

Second, *Roe* gave women a lot more than they could have obtained in private. Most obviously, *Roe* and its progeny released women from the costs of illegality—both the extremely high prices charged for abortions by doctors who risked their licences by performing the procedure, and the grave health risks faced by women undergoing abortions in substandard conditions. *Roe* and its progeny also made a woman's choice largely independent of the approval or consent of her father or husband. Women could not have achieved these advances in their intimate negotiations with men. These benefits were derived from the public decision to decriminalize abortion.

The third, and perhaps most significant, point in this context is that the *Harris* decision was not made more likely by the *Roe* privacy argument. The concept of liberty contains the very same tensions and could have justified the same result. Furthermore, a commitment to fight against inequality between the sexes may be very different from a commitment to fight against inequality based on class or wealth. The equality argument MacKinnon puts forward is expressed in terms of gender. Even if it had been accepted by the Court, the argument would have been unlikely to produce a commitment to economic equality.[85] The *Harris* holding may be one possible implication of basing a woman's right to an abortion on the desirable limits of legal interference. But we should recall that neither privacy nor liberty reasons, on their own, justify noninterference. To justify noninterference, we must show that the reasons for not interfering are not outweighed by reasons supporting interference. *Roe*, then, stands also for the proposition that this situation does not exist in the case of abortion.

The difference between the liberty and the equality rationales is less stark than MacKinnon claims. Although noninterference is sometimes sufficient to protect liberty, at other times positive interference is required. Just as the full protection of equality may require some change in the underlying inequality, the full protection of liberty may require securing the preconditions for its meaningful exercise.

At times MacKinnon suggests that this is precisely where privacy *language* becomes responsible for these bad results:

The liberal ideal of the private—and privacy as an ideal has been formulated in liberal terms—holds that, so long as the public does not interfere, autonomous individuals interact freely and equally. Conceptually, this private is hermetic. It *means* that which is inaccessible to, unaccountable to, unconstricted by anything beyond itself.[86]

But, as we saw above, inaccessible, unaccountable, and unconstricted are different, even if they are all sometimes dubbed 'private'. If the private is that which is unaccountable to others, then privacy in this sense cannot be an ideal. It functions merely as a definition, or a description. When we talk about the ideal, we talk about the strong normative sense of the private: that which should not be subject to interference. The focus then becomes careful analysis of not only the activities and situations that should be free from interference, but also the reasons for providing that immunity from external regulation.

We have now discussed two different mechanisms that allegedly explain the manner in which language is responsible for the bad result in *Harris*. One is formal: Since 'private' is *defined* as that which is (or should be) inaccessible or uninterfered with, the use of privacy is simply conclusory. What appears to be a doctrinal choice is really explicable in Realist terms. MacKinnon, presumably, thinks this is a fancy way of protecting the status quo. But *Roe* was widely perceived as an extremely significant political change affecting the status quo, which allowed states to prohibit abortions. Indeed, if a doctrine is really conclusory, it *cannot* explain or justify the results reached through it. This is precisely what we mean by saying that the move is conclusory. The arguments offered for *Griswold* and *Roe* may have been wrong and confused, but the decisions are not conclusory. To say otherwise ignores the reasons actually presented in support of a woman's right to make her own decisions regarding contraceptives and abortion without state intervention.

The second alleged mechanism is substantive: Privacy language helped to make available a *bad* doctrinal choice. According to MacKinnon, the privacy rationale does not provide adequate protection, and it protects for the wrong reasons. The privacy rationale was employed because it offered a way out of the *Lochner* dead end. The privacy argument identified reasons for which noninterference was justified: the personal nature of the choice; the intimate area of life involved; and the centrality of the decision to one's self-identity. All of these reasons help to justify the choice of privacy over liberty arguments.

These reasons also raise several related questions. First, when we consider whether or not to prohibit abortion by law (a paradigmatic form of interference by the public), are the factors mentioned above relevant? Is there indeed a presumption in favour of noninterference in intimate and extremely personal aspects of one's life? Can the abortion decision be described in these terms? My answers to these questions are affirmative. The presumption mentioned is not irrebuttable. It should not, for example, grant immunity to those who are violent at home. But it does apply to the decision to abort, a decision which is central to a women's self-identity and her sense of control over her own life.[87] Furthermore, while we have described the reasons for granting the presumption for noninterference in nonprivacy language, the meanings of 'private' listed above indicate that there may be linguistic support to identify this cluster as having to do with privacy.

Second, could a woman's right to decide whether to abort have been based on different grounds by the Court in 1973? If so, would the alternative doctrine have better served women in 1980 or today? These are difficult counterfactual questions, but my reading of the history of the abortion issue is that the *Roe* Court did not want any version of equality protected. Moreover, the legislative, political, and judicial developments since then have not had much to do with the Court's particular doctrinal choice. If *Roe* had been justified in ways that would have precluded the result in *Harris*, the substantive right protected by *Roe* may already have been overruled. The choice of privacy/liberty over a more radical feminist analysis may have given *Roe* both its relative limitations and its great symbolic staying power.[88]

Third, does the choice of privacy language obscure the fact that abortion is really only a small part of broader and deeper social attitudes toward women and sexuality? Is much more than a woman's right to decide whether to have an abortion at stake? Does full equality for women require 'the explosion of the private', with its concomitant hidden assumptions of equality and freedom, and the exposure of the reality of inequality? It may. But the privacy rationale as formulated in *Griswold* and *Roe* was not intended to be the best formulation of feminism. It was meant to identify one *justification* for the decision to constitutionally protect the right to legal abortions. One can agree that privacy is not enough without concluding that the choice of privacy arguments in the *Roe* context was a setback for women.

It seems, therefore, that with respect to abortion there is no necessary connection between the use of the pubic/private distinction or privacy terminology in *Roe*, and the unfortunate holding of *Harris*.

Domestic violence. Domestic violence is another frequently cited example of the bad consequences resulting from the public/private distinction. Here, the argument is that family relations are seen as paradigmatically private. In part, this is based upon the assumption that family relationships are voluntary and equal. Consequently, there is a presumption that these private relations should be free from external interference. Often people, incorrectly, jump from the accurate description of family relationships as private to the conclusion that no interference is justified, without examining the truth of the initial assumptions or contrary considerations which might defeat the presumption.

Such a leap constitutes an obvious mistake in practical reasoning. In part, this mistake results from equivocation, and thus may be attributed to language or terminology. As we saw in Part II, the key term 'private' may be used in at least three different senses. First, 'private' may indicate the highly personal and intimate reasons for the presumptive entitlement of families to be free from interference. Second, ascription of privateness may be an invocation of the presumptive entitlement, to be weighed against other features of the situation. Third, its usage may indicate a *conclusion* that, all things considered, the activity should not be interfered with.

Public treatment of domestic violence is plagued by dubious uses of the notion of privacy. The police are often extremely reluctant to interfere in domestic disputes, even when violence is alleged. Often, the reason offered for this reluctance is the private nature of the marital relationship.[89]

The potential for confusion generated by this variety of uses is not unique to the public/private distinction or to the feminist context. In fact, this kind of problem is pervasive in legal reasoning, especially when the conclusion must be justified in terms of interpretations of authoritative texts.[90] Moreover, the confusion appears in many different fields of the law. Although these mistakes should be avoided, a reform of the language and the terminology is not necessarily the cure.

Reforming the language by delegitimating the use of 'private' and 'privacy' will not clarify distinctions between descriptive and normative claims. The descriptive-normative ambiguity exists for all alternative candidates. Some terms, such as 'highly personal', may not have a purely descriptive sense, because what is central to one's self-identity is probably a matter of constitutive rules and expectations. But all substitute terms have uses which refer to people's wishes and perceptions, as well as senses which refer to the conclusions of normative arguments. Adopting words other than 'private' and 'public' to discuss what should be free from state regulation may help us to avoid some potential sources of mistakes, but the new terms may generate their own ambiguities and risks.[91]

Although this argument cannot, therefore, support the external challenge, it does draw our attention to a context in which impermissible inferences in practical reasoning are likely to be made. Recalling that the private is sometimes that which is intimate and highly related to self-identity and, at other times, that which should not be regulated by the state or enforced by police action, we can carefully guard against unthinkingly conflating the different senses. But it is unlikely that there are alternative ways of expressing these ideas that will, by themselves, overcome the potential for confusion.

Another reading of the bad results argument associated with the problem of domestic violence does not depend on the notion of equivocation. The language of privacy, allegedly, masks a form of ethical confusion. Use of the language of public and private suggests that there are valid reasons for protecting the private from state regulation. But under present social conditions, and in contrast to this implication, women have no interest in such protection.[92] For them, the intimate and the realm of family life is neither a realm of freedom, nor a haven in which the dignity of self-direction can be cultivated. To the contrary, in private, women are exploited and abused with impunity.[93] Women should, therefore, recognize that invocations of the value of privacy are a means of perpetuating their oppression by creating the false impression that the protection of privacy is good for women, by isolating them, and by depoliticizing their struggle.[94]

This assertion raises a substantive moral and political question. In private, women may be vulnerable in ways that are beyond the scrutiny and censure of the public. Does it follow, then, that women have no interest in the values of privacy and intimacy, or that there are no contexts in which women would want to keep the state out of their lives? Presumably, even for MacKinnon, the answer is no. Therefore, we must differentiate between good arguments, derived from the values associated with privacy, and bad arguments, in which reference to the same values is used to mask exploitation and abuse. This distinction is not a matter of language, but a matter of the features of the specific situations involved.

Some legal scholars may then response that what is protected is not *really* privacy or intimacy, but the value of what is done within them. Intimacy, importance to self-identity, and choice are not necessary, on the one hand, to justify protecting activities which are valuable in themselves. On the other hand, when the activities in question are destructive, their inaccessibility or possible intimacy should not count as reasons for protecting them. In other words, the substance of the activity, rather than its public or private context, determines its value.

This response is misleading in two ways. First, while privacy and intimacy should not provide blanket immunity from public interference, it does not follow that we *always* look at the substance of the activity rather than its context. The value of privacy and inaccessibility includes not only the protection of activities which are desirable, but also some activities which are undesirable. This is especially true for activities that many regard as victimless sins, such as homosexual conduct between consenting adults. We do *not* want to reduce the question to a debate about the morality of the conduct. Politically, it is quite clear that such debates could result in prohibitions, even though many people who believe that this conduct is immoral may oppose criminalization due to its close relation to self-identity and physical intimacy.

Such considerations provide powerful arguments against perspectives which examine only the substantive morality of conduct. Generally, we want to afford immunity for voluntary consensual associations where consent and freedom are not illusory. If we accept that such situations exist even in our gendered, unequal society, then intimacy and privacy do operate, presumptively, to limit interference without requiring that we publicly judge all behaviour on its moral merits.

We may also wish to protect the privacy or the intimacy of relationships among individuals. Some of these relationships are institutionalized, such as the family and small clubs; others provide the background against which individuals grow up and live (various affective communities). The protection of such associations and groups requires a measure of state noninterference if such associations are to provide the functions for which we value them.[95] Small associations are protected through the restraint of external force. Interference only occurs in the case of blatant violations of members' rights, while it seems to insure the voluntariness of the association, and the viability of exit as an option.[96]

Finally, many feminists concede that privacy is, and ought to be, important to men as well as women. The substantive challenge to the private made by some can be linked to a challenge familiar from communitarian critiques of liberalism: While viewing privacy as valuable highlights the importance of individualism and the freedom to be left alone, it obscures the dangers of loneliness and alienation—the second face of privacy.[97] This attack on privacy though, identifies the wrong culprit. The freedom to decide when and with whom to associate is more often than not exercised by the choice to be a member of a strong affective association or network. What is kept private and what is shared with others may change, but some sense of privateness and identity is a necessary presupposition of healthy relationships and communities. It is not through respect for privacy that people become alienated and lonely.

2. Dichotomization and reification. Another charge is that linguistic frameworks and distinctions pervade our thinking and limit our vision and our hopes. In this vein, Frances Olsen has made a powerful argument concerning the distinction between the privateness of families and the publicness of markets.[98]

Olsen is aware that 'the personal is (the) political' may be seen as an invitation to a totalitarianism in which all, indeed, is political.[99] While at times she alleges that the inherent conflict is unique to liberalism,[100] at others she concedes that the conflict between individuality and relatedness, and the differences between work and social interaction, are immanent features of the human conditions as we know them.[101] Olsen identifies the inherent conflict in terms of dichotomies that 'stunt human growth by avoiding and displacing conflict—conflict within the individual psyche and among people'.[102] Since the dichotomies serve to externalize the conflict through compartmentalization, we must transcend them if we are to resolve the actual conflict.

According to Olsen, the dichotomies polarize our world into the public and the private.[103] Our efforts at reform become attempts to give markets more of the strengths of families (for example, limiting the right to fire at will) and to give families some of the strengths of markets (protection against exploitation and abuse). These reforms will inevitably result in some gains and some losses. If, instead, we transcend the dichotomy, we will be able to reform the situation in more creative and integrative ways.

Can we transcend the dichotomy? As Olsen herself stresses, real markets and families are more complex than their 'ideal types'.[104] One can agree with Olsen that, if we see the world outside as heartless, we are forced to seek happiness in a private haven; conversely, those who are disappointed with their families and love lives invest their energies in their work.[105] But this seems to be a natural reaction to failure in achieving the ideal shared by all: a life with a good balance between intimacy and success, between personal and public commitments. This ideal is integrated and whole; it does not require a transcendence of dichotomies. It is simply the rich life based on a mixture of different experiences, all of which are valuable.

Dichotomies confuse only if we believe that we must choose in an either-or fashion. They point out that we cannot have everything, and that any balanced life requires an ability to give up things that are incompatible with others that we value more. For instance, complete freedom cannot coexist with meaningful commitments and relationships. Similarly, one cannot both pursue a demanding career and always be available to and supportive of others. I believe, however, that the problems Olsen describes are of the second type. If so, then transcendence is a dangerous illusion rather than a liberating release from constructive vocabularies and habits of thought.

3. Inevitability and naturalness. Perhaps Olsen's point is that words may create misguided feelings of naturalness and inevitability and that these, in turn, may affect our ability to move toward change. The private and the public, when distinguished, become reified and seem to be part of reality, a given to be reckoned with, not a person-made construction which can be challenged and transformed.

Feminist anthropologists have helped us to see both the strengths and the limitations of these claims. People, clearly, can structure the content of their public and private lives differently, and men and women can adopt different kinds of relationships. Particular arrangements, therefore, are neither natural, nor inevitable. On the other hand, some features are disturbingly persistent across cultures. The presence of these persistent features cannot be explained merely by the fact that women bear children, concededly a natural fact in the strongest sense.[106]

Again, we are not looking at the obvious, though complex, effects of perceptions of naturalness and inevitability *per se*. Rather, we are trying to identify the contribution of conceptual schemes and distinctions to these feelings. If all terms and concepts came with ontological commitments, we would have difficulty asserting that something does not exist, or should not exist. Clearly, our language is more flexible than that. Olsen's ideal reflects an integrated, not alienated, human existence, one that is not compartmentalized into distinct and autonomous realms. I fail to see how identifying the various elements which together form human well-being undermines the realization of this ideal.

As mentioned above, feminists often concede that their ideal is *not* a state of affairs in which nothing is private. Consequently, the public/private dichotomy does not discourage the perception of the feminist ideal. Moreover, since the ideal life requires some minimum of both private and public aspects, even the weaker argument—that language makes perceiving and articulating options and visions more difficult, rather than impossible—does not seem to apply to the public/private pair.[107]

4. *Paralysis and isolation.* Finally, the external critique of public/private terminology rests on the claim that it has been used as one of a number of tools obscuring and, thereby, perpetuating the oppression and subordination of women. This was achieved by privatizing women in a combination of ways that together made them invisible, isolated, powerless, devalued, ashamed, and more likely to perceive their predicament as individualized and personal.

This paralysing effect is achieved by invoking different connotations of the private. Women internalize an understanding of the private which presupposes its identification with female roles, as well as an acceptance of that role as natural and inevitable. What is dubbed 'private' should not be shared. Instead, it should be kept 'in the family'. If something is wrong there, it is the individual's fault; individual problems should be hidden, repressed, and managed.

As I have already mentioned, I believe feminists have succeeded in identifying and documenting real and dangerous patterns here. Clearly, we want to make language users aware that unjustified inferences are often made, and we want to minimize faulty inference. However, if there are differences between private and public that must be maintained and invoked, the delegitimation of the distinction and the corresponding vocabulary will make meaningful communication and discourse more difficult. Furthermore, as we have seen, the move to the external challenge creates additional dangers. For instance, we want to fight the sense of shame which makes women unable to express their private tragedies, but do we also want to eradicate the notion of shame?[108] Where we identify undesirable processes, we should seek to change them. Where language constitutes or facilitates undesirable processes, we should fight against these as well. But it is self-defeating to throw away important conceptual tools which are essential to clear thinking about these issues.

IV. Conclusions

The feminist challenge to the public/private distinction and the ways in which the distinction has reinforced social trends is fascinating and revealing. It provides a rich illustration of the senses of privateness and publicness, as well as insight into the ways in which the ambiguity of terms may lead to errors in practical reasoning. Furthermore, the feminist challenge highlights both the costs of coerced privatization, and the importance of public cultures in the personal lives of individuals. It provides a strong reminder that 'out of sight is out of mind', that low visibility and suppression distort public perceptions of what is important. Finally, the feminist challenge raises important questions concerning what the ultimate values and institutional structures of human life in society can and should be.

Feminists are aware of the importance of privacy, intimacy, and the sense of human dignity, all of which are connected to the values of the private. In fact, the intensity of their arguments flows from the belief that women deserve more of these goods than they present receive.

Against this background, the appeal of external challenges should be clear. Women feel that for too long we have been ignored, because we have been seen as private and unimportant. Furthermore, we feel that for too long our lives and our complaints have been ignored because they lacked visibility. We are now extremely reluctant to endorse a voluntary privateness, and to see it as a value. It seems right that the very language in which these suggestions are couched, the very naturalness of talking and thinking in these ways, are part of what we would want to rebel against.

However, fighting the verbal distinction between public and private, rather than fighting invalid arguments which invoke them, or the power structures which manipulate them in unjustifiable ways, is as futile as seeking individual therapy for problems of social structure. Some women are angry that their energies have been channelled toward futile individual therapy and away from political struggle. We should be just as angry at those who invite us to fight against words and ways-of-seeing, instead of fighting the real obstacles obscuring our visions of the good life. Even more disturbing, this new vision of the good life is often missing, while its absence is not noticed in the intensity of the preoccupation with an oppressive and rejecting present.

Some uses of words are not innocent. They are not mistakes. They are not tools necessary to remind us of important differences and values that are occasionally also abused and misused. They are so natural that they mask undesirable habits of thought and facilitate unsupported inferences. Their costs are clear, and they have no redeeming benefits. These usages, images, and metaphors should be identified and exposed.[109] The public/private distinction, and the vocabulary reflecting it, however, are not of this type. Their *ascription* may be bad, but not their existence and use. The cure should be to make ascriptions more carefully, in a way that will help us keep our thoughts straight. 'Exploding the private', or claiming that 'the personal is the political' may be effective slogans that highlight a danger or mobilize people, but they have dangers too. Perhaps, in some contexts, we can make a choice about vocabulary and stop using public/private talk. It may well be that, in some contexts (although I have yet to encounter one), there are good strategic reasons for preferring a different way of making claims and arguments. But even if this is the case, the all-out fight against the vocabulary of public and private is unjustified, because the terminology is uniquely suited, precisely because of its richness and ambiguities, to make and clarify many of feminism's most fundamental claims.

One difficulty in discussing feminist challenges is that the vantage point of the challenges is not always clear. Philosophical claims about reality and truth are not adequately distinguished from political-strategic claims about the best means to achieve desirable results in the present, imperfect world. Moreover, the distinction between the two enterprises is often criticized by those who argue that scholarship is to be enlisted in the cause of some political vision. They argue further that those claiming neutrality are supporting the status quo. The result is frustration: Whatever one says, no joinder is created. When we remember the urgent social problems that call for resolution, it is more than just frustrating to be stuck in the realm of theoretical polemics.

I expect that many feminists who endorse an external critique of the public/private distinction may dismiss this article as yet another misunderstanding of their claims. At times, I have felt that maybe there was an important argument that I somehow failed to see. So I write this as an invitation to do what must be done if we are not to talk forever past each other: to unpack the claims, distinguishing between those which are empirical, social, and causal, and those which relate to visions of ideal worlds. We must argue about the truth or adequacy of the first, and the details and feasibility of the second. Finally, we must make claims about the relationships between language, conceptions, social reality, and social change less elusive, more intelligible, and more accessible to reasoned judgement.

Notes

1. For a collection of various treatments of the public/private distinction, see *Symposium on the Public/Private Distinction*, 130 U. Pa. L. Rev. 1289 (1982). See also Patrick Devlin, *The Enforcement of Morals* (1965) (discussing the distinction between private and public moralities).
2. See, e.g., Margaret Jane Radin, 'The Pragmatist and The Feminist', 63 S. Cal. L. Rev. 1699, 1707–8 (1990) (stating that while both pragmatists and feminists are suspicious of the distinctions between thoughts and actions, and theory and practice, only the feminists criticize the public/private distinction).
3. As Carole Pateman has argued, 'The dichotomy between the private and the public is central to almost two centuries of feminist writing and political struggle; it is, ultimately, what the feminist movement is about.' Carole Pateman, 'Feminist Critiques of the Public/Private Dichotomy', in *Public and Private in Social Life* 281, 281 (S.I. Benn & G.F. Gaus eds., 1983). For the centrality of this challenge to feminism, see Will Kymlicka, *Contemporary Political Philosophy*, 247–62 (1990); Susan Moller Okin, *Justice, Gender, and the Family*, 110–33 (1989). This distinction has also been used as a means of classifying feminist theorists. See Alison M. Jaggar, *Feminist Politics and Human Nature* (1983).
4. Catharine A. MacKinnon, *Toward a Feminist Theory of the State*, 191 (1989). For a detailed discussion of some of MacKinnon's views, see notes 71–104 *infra* and accompanying text.
5. Although even one who believes that there is no difference between 'private' and 'public' might concede that the linguistic or conceptual distinction is necessary to expose the false beliefs of others.
6. These connections between external and internal challenges can be generalized. See Duncan Kennedy, 'Form and Substance in Private Law Adjudication', 89 Harv. L. Rev. 1685 (1976). Kennedy maintains that much of

traditional legal theory is built on a distinction between (the use of rules or standards) and substance (the content of the arrangement). He argues that the two are in fact intertwined, making the distinction, with its implication of autonomy between form and substance, completely misleading. For a further example of Kennedy's thesis, see Duncan Kennedy, 'The Structure of Blackstone's Commentaries', 28 Buff. L. Rev. 205 (1979). For a sophisticated (and somewhat modifying) discussion of Kennedy's arguments, see Mark Kelman, *A Guide to Critical Legal Studies*, 15–63 (1987).

7. The standard grounds for nondiscrimination in human rights documents present an interesting case. These documents usually declare that people should not be discriminated against on the basis of race or religion. Clearly, this policy does not mean to suggest that race and religion do not represent differences between individuals. On the contrary, these documents often affirm the value of pluralism and of cultural and ethnic differences. Instead, the claim arising from the nondiscrimination policy is that these acknowledged differences should not be considered relevant with regard to the treatment of individuals.

8. I realize that this presupposition is controversial. Nevertheless, I consider the differentiation of these types of questions to be an essential element of any attempt to make sense of our world. It is compatible with many approaches to the question of the relationships between reality (natural or social) and language. It is not, however, compatible with the approach that reality *is* a text, and that there is no way to distinguish between reality and the way we talk about it.

9. Descriptions such as these, coupled with critical evaluations, are common in communitarian literature. See, e.g., Hannah Arendt, *The Human Condition* (1958). For descriptions with a more balanced evaluation, see Albert O. Hirschman, *The Passions and the Interests: Political Arguments for Capitalism Before Its Triumph* (1977); Albert O. Hirshmann, *Shifting Involvements: Private Interest and Public Action* (1982) [hereinafter *Shifting Involvements*].

10. For a comprehensive discussion, see John D. Donahue, *The Privatization Decision: Public Ends, Private Means* (1989).

11. See Devlin, *supra* note 1.

12. See, e.g., Stanley I. Benn, 'Private and Public Morality: Clean Living and Dirty Hands', in *Public and Private in Social Life*, *supra* note 3, at 158–9.

13. See H. L. A. Hart, *The Concept of Law* (1961).

14. Id.

15. For a similar discussion on the various senses of the public/private dichotomy, see S. I. Benn & G.F. Gaus, 'The Liberal Conception of the Public and Private', in *Public and Private in Social Life*, *supra* note 3, at 31.

16. See Ruth Gavison, 'Privacy and the Limits of Law', 89 Yale L.J. 421, 428–33 (1980).

17. For examples of information-centered definitions, see Alan F. Estin, *Privacy and Freedom* 7 (1967); Charles Fried, 'Privacy', 77 Yale L.J. 475, 482–3 (1968).

18. Richard Parker defines privacy as control over those who can sense us. See Richard B. Parker, 'A Definition of Privacy', 27 Rutgers L. Rev. 275, 280 (1974); see also Gavison, *supra* note 16, at 432–3.

19. But, as I shall discuss later in this article, 'public' and 'political' share, to some extent, the same ambiguities. See text accompanying note 55 *infra*.

20. Confusions based on this ambiguity abound in the laws of defamation and privacy, in which public interest is a defence. See, e.g., Note, 'The Right of Privacy: Normative-Descriptive Confusion in the Defense of Newsworthiness', 30 U. Chi. L. Rev. 722 (1963).

21. An example from the feminist context will illustrate this point: My wish to become sexually aroused by watching pornography alone in my home may be private (intimate) and thus presumptively entitled to noninterference. But, as some feminist scholars argue, such conduct may be extremely harmful in ways that consent of the parties does not remove; this harm may therefore defeat the presumptive entitlement. See text accompanying notes 98–104 *infra*.

22. For ways in which accessibility and freedom may be interrelated, see Robert K. Merton, *Social Theory and Social Structure* (1949); S. I. Benn, 'Privacy, Freedom and Respect for Persons', in 13 Privacy 1 (J. Roland Pennock & John W. Chapman eds., 1971); Gavison, *supra* note 16, at 446–7.

23. This is one explanation of *Bowers* v. *Hardwick*, 478 U.S. 186 (1986) (rejecting privacy challenge to Georgia's law prohibiting sodomy).

24. Such extreme positions are self-defeating. By questioning the very possibility of using language to convey messages or meanings, these critics undermine their own attempts at communication. We should distinguish these extreme positions from others that *are* compatible with the presuppositions that I have adopted in this article: that meaning is related to usage; that pragmatics and semantics coexist; and that languages may (or must) derive their meaning from human experience. For a position stressing the relativity of language, see Richard Rorty, *Contingency, Irony, and Solidarity* (1989). For an in-depth critique of related positions, see Michael S. Moore, 'The Interpretive Turn in Modern Theory: A Turn for the Worse?', 41 Stan. L. Rev. 871, 892–905 (1989).

25. Karl Klare provides a detailed account of this claim as it pertains to labour law. He concludes that:

> [I]t is seriously mistaken that legal discourse or liberal political theory contains a core conception of the public/private distinction capable of being filled with determinate content or applied in a determinate manner to concrete cases. *There is no 'public/private distinction'*. What does exist is a series of ways of thinking about public and private that are constantly undergoing revision, reformulation, and refinement. . . . The public/private distinction poses as an analytical tool in labor law, but it functions more as a form of political rhetoric used to justify particular results. . . .
> . . . [T]he use of such rhetoric obscures rather than illuminates, and . . . the social

function of the public/private distinction is to repress aspirations for alternativepolitical arrangements by predisposing us to regard comprehensive alternatives to the established order as absurd.

Karl Klare, 'The Public-Private Distinction in Labor Law', 130 U. Pa. L. Rev. 1358, 1361 (1982).

26. Clare Dalton, 'An Essay in the Deconstruction of Contract Theory, 94 Yale L.J. 997, 1038 (1985).

27. See generally Duncan Kennedy, 'The Stages of the Decline of the Public/Private Distinction', 130 U. Pa. L. Rev. 1349 (1982) (stating that a successful distinction must permit identification of things between the poles and an examination of the distinct consequences that follow from such an identification).

28. It should be noted that different senses of 'privacy' are used here. The family's privacy (inaccessibility) and its privacy (limits on interference), together with its acknowledged importance as an institution, provides a justification for public attention. This attention may result either in publicity as knowledge (about the family as an institution and about particular families) or in actual public interference. This interference, in turn, may take the form of legal regulation or of less institutionalized forms of influence. Ideas about the family unit may justify a presumptive entitlement to privateness as noninterference. For example, elements of intimacy which bind the family could be harmed by wholesale legal interference. In addition, since family life cannot be realistically conducted under the constant shadow of the law, it is better to seek arrangements that will have internal strength, independent of constant observation and enforcement by others.

29. See notes 15–20 *supra* and accompanying text.

30. A famous illustration of the difficulties of ascription is the adjective 'bald': Whereas Yul Brenner was bald by all standards, there are many cases in which the adequacy of the ascription is questionable. None the less, the word remains an effective adjective. For a discussion of the limits of indeterminacy challenges in the context of the personhood of fetuses or the ascription of 'life', see Bernard Williams, 'Which Slopes Are Slippery', in *Moral Dilemmas in Modern Medicine* 126 (Michael Lockwood ed., 1985).

31. Dalton makes a powerful argument that 'private' and 'public' are used in a conclusory manner in contract law. Dalton documents how arguments from both 'privateness' and 'publicness' have been used to deny women's claims to property rights upon the termination of nonmarital intimate relationships. Such decisions to not enforce agreements between cohabitants can be based on a variety of grounds: an interpretation of the actual intent of the parties themselves (a private matter, the enforcement of which is a matter of public policy); a policy decision that the relationships involved are too intimate (cohabitation in this sense is more intimate than are business transactions); or a reluctance to allow and thereby encourage alternative forms of relationships outside of publicly supported and regulated marriage. Dalton's conclusion is

142 *The social and conceptual context*

that the 'availability of this range of intention-based and policy-based arguments makes possible virtually any decision'. Dalton, *supra* note 26, at 1100.

Dalton is correct that many arguments are possible and that some will invoke notions of privateness and publicness. She is also correct that 'privateness' may at times be a reason both for enforcement (we want to give force to free agreements between parties) and nonenforcement (we want to remove the possibility of enforcement from certain relationships and negotiations). This illustrates the many senses of 'privateness' as well as the fact that some values may be implemented, at times, in different ways; it does not support the view that the use of privateness (intimacy) or privateness (voluntary and consensual) is conclusory.

32. John Stuart Mill, *On Liberty* 13 (Emery E. Neff ed., 1926).
33. A related critique of liberalism is the claim made by communitarians that liberalism is based on a misguided picture of the individual as existing prior to inclusion in a particular society. See, e.g., Charles A. Taylor, *Sources of the Self* (1989).
34. See Okin, *supra* note 3, at 131–3 (relying on, among others, Nancy Chodorow, *The Reproduction of Mothering: Psychoanalysis and the Sociology of Gender* (1978)).
35. This argument is distinguishable from the assertion that voluntary viewing of pornography by women is not really voluntary, so that the right to watch pornography at home protects 'men's right to inflict pornography upon women in private'. MacKinnon, *supra* note 4, at 205. More applicable here is MacKinnon's description of pornography as 'an industry that mass produces sexual intrusion on, access to, possession and use of women by and for men for profit'. Id. at 195.
36. See text accompanying notes 25–31 *supra*.
37. This might be a major qualification of Mill's argument if he believed that self-regardingness was an all-or-nothing concept which established a conclusive reason for noninterference. In the context of challenging the public/private distinction, however, the broader position suffices. See text accompanying note 32 *supra*.
38. See Kelman, *supra* note 6, at 102–13 (citing the works of Realists including Robert Hale); see also Morris R. Cohen, 'The Basis of Contract', in *Law and the Social Order: Essays in Legal Philosophy* 69 (1933) [hereinafter *Law and the Social Order*]; Morris R. Cohen, 'Property and Sovereignty', in *Law and the Social Order*, *supra* at 41.
39. Much literature documents the fact that the family is regulated quite heavily. See, e.g., Christopher Lasch, *Haven in a Heartless World* (1977); Frances Olsen, 'The Myth of State Intervention in the Family, 18 U. Mich. J.L. Ref. 835 (1985).
40. See, e.g., Jeremy Waldron, *The Right to Private Property* (1988) classifying forms of property, including private property, and justifying the institution of private property).

41. See Robert C. Post, 'The Social Foundations of Privacy: Community and Self in the Common Law', 77 Cal. L. Rev. 957 (1989).

42. The first challenge—that nothing is really free—is much more sweeping than the second challenge—that nothing is voluntary. Under the first challenge, most aspects of our lives are not free. The second challenge is more local and presupposes that in some contexts people may act freely and voluntarily. For a denial of the voluntariness and justice of many work agreements under capitalism, see Allen Buchanan, 'Exploitation, Alienation, and Injustice', 9 Can. J. Phil. 121, 122–4 (1979) (discussing Marx's view that exploitation is prevalent in the labour process).

43. For the illusory nature of the freedom of women to choose marriage and sex, see MacKinnon, *supra* note 4, at 160–70. For the actual constraints on the ability of women to exit from and negotiate in marriage, see Okin, *supra* note 3, at 137–8.

44. Although some feminists make this broad claim, I doubt its truth. For a more detailed documentation, see note 54 *infra* and accompanying text. It seems that the feminists who make such a claim do so rhetorically, to draw attention to an important (partial) truth and do not intend to make a serious empirical claim. Even on the rhetorical level, there is a tension within feminist thought concerning this claim. For example, abortion is often defended as providing a woman with the power to make a choice to control her own life. But, if women's choices are *never* free, this argument fails. Debates about surrogacy also illustrate this tension. Some feminists regard surrogacy as the ultimate exploitation of women—it commodifies them by treating them as 'birth machines'. Other feminists recommend leaving the decision in the hands of individuals, emphasizing the independence of women to make choices about personal resources such as their bodies. See Carmel Shalev, *Birth Power: The Case for Surrogacy* (1989).

45. This is well illustrated by a debate within feminism. While 'liberal' feminists object to the regulation of pornography, among other things, because of a distrust of the state *qua* state, 'radical' feminists distrust the state *qua* male. See Jaggar, *supra* note 3, at 180, 283. Liberal feminists typically argue that women should decide for themselves whether or not to indulge in, for example, voluntary sadomasochistic practices, but will urge women that such practices are undesirable. Id. at 274. Radical feminists often welcome strong social and group pressure which mark such practices as inconsistent with 'true feminism'.

Therefore, while both liberals and radicals agree that privacy or freedom properly excludes *legal* interference, only the liberal feminists also want to exclude *social* pressures. For the liberals, freedom of choice or autonomy justifies this exclusion. On the other hand, some radical feminists see lesbian sadomasochism and pornography as private cases of the general wrongs of pornography, deserving of unambiguous social condemnation and possible legal prohibition. Id. at 274–5.

MacKinnon, whose analysis of pornography suggests the latter view, made a strategic decision to advocate legislation that did not prohibit 'private use'. Compare the general analysis with the explanation of the proposed ordinance in Catharine A. MacKinnon, 'Francis Biddle's Sister: Pornography, Civil Rights, and Speech' in *Feminism Unmodified: Discourses on Life and Law* 163, 171–77 (1987) [hereinafter *Feminism Unmodified*].

46. In fact, some feminists treat the statements 'the private/public distinction must be challenged' and 'the personal is the political' almost interchangeably. As Okin has stated, ' "The personal is political" is the central message of feminist critiques of the public/domestic dichotomy.' Okin, *supra* note 3, at 124; see also Catharine A. MacKinnon, 'Privacy v. Equality: Beyond *Roe* v. *Wade*', in *Feminism Unmodified*, *supra* note 45, at 93, 100 ('This is why feminism has had to explode the private. This is why feminism has seen the personal as the political. The private is the public for those for whom the personal is the political.').

It is interesting to note that one sentence of this passage reads differently in MacKinnon's 1989 book: 'The private is public for those for whom the personal is political.' MacKinnon, *supra* note 4, at 191. Both formulations abound in feminist literature. Whereas the first statement presupposes the distinctness of the realms and claims that everything that belongs to the personal is also political, the second formulation denies altogether the distinctness of the realms. For a discussion of the difference, see Frank Michelman, 'P̶r̶i̶v̶a̶t̶e̶ Personal but Not Split: Radin Versus Rorty', 63 S. Cal. L. Rev. 1783 (1990). For my purposes, either formulation will suffice.

47. See Carol Hanisch, 'The Personal Is Political', in *The Radical Therapist* 152 (Jerome Agel ed., 1971).

48. This is an important part of the reason why Betty Friedan's best-selling book *The Feminine Mystique* was so influential: It argued that the factors affecting women's lives were systemic rather than personal.

49. See Hanisch, *supra* note 47, at 152 (defending the practices of some consciousness-raising groups against the challenges of more radical and activist feminists).

50. A topical example is the heated debate among feminists as to whether the names of rape victims should, against their wishes, be made public. A recent instalment of the debate came in the wake of the disclosure of the name of the woman claiming that William Kennedy Smith raped her in 1991. See, e.g., Andrea Dworkin, 'The Third Rape', L. A. Times, Apr. 28, 1991, at M1 (objecting to disclosure); Susan Estrich, 'The Real Palm Beach Story', N.Y. Times, Apr. 18, 1991, at A25; 'Respect Rape Victims' Privacy', Wall St. J., Apr. 24, 1991, at A14 (recounting a rape victim's view of the debate).

We should not automatically choose greater disclosure, even if we accept that more disclosure will more effectively fight the misguided shame and stigma presently connected with being a rape victim and the falsehood that rape is an individual tragedy rather than part of a social pattern.

51. Zillah R. Eisenstein, *The Radical Future of Liberal Feminism* 14–30 (1981).
52. One of the interesting features of feminist scholarship is that it consciously fights its own class and colour biases. This description seems true primarily of middle class women, the subjects of the modern analysis given by Betty Friedan. Feminists recognize, however, that some women have always worked to earn a living.
53. See, e.g., Shulamith Firestone, *The Dialectic of Sex: The Case for Feminist Revolution* (1970); Okin, *supra* note 3, at 128–33 (citing instances of sexual divisions of labour within the home as well as in the outside world).
54. Feminists have done important work documenting women's lives. They often detail the lives of exceptional women who successfully break out of their traditional roles and achieve lives of distinction. But they have also documented private lives, attempting to show their unappreciated and undervalued richness. For an example detailing the lives of 'regular' women, see Fran Leeper Buss, *Dignity: Lower Income Women Tell of Their Lives and Struggles* (1985). For a sensitive discussion of the impact and importance of such documentation, see Mari J. Matsuda, 'Pragmatism Modified and the False Consciousness Problem', 63 S. Cal. L. Rev. 1763, 1766–8 (1990).
55. I use private and public loosely here, with 'private; and 'personal' focused on family and intimate relations as well as social and recreational activities, which are more central to feminist concerns. There are different assessments of private and public when the latter is depicted more narrowly to include only political and public involvements. For instance, compare the Greek idealization of the nobility of politics, reflected in contemporary literature that mourns the shift to 'privatization', see e.g., Arendt, *supra* note 9, with the more cautious approach of liberals such as Benjamin Constant. See, e.g., Hirshman, *Shifting Involvements, supra* note 9.
56. See, e.g., Michelle Zimbalist Rosaldo, 'Woman, Culture and Society: A Theoretical Overview', in *Woman, Culture and Society* 17, 19 (Michelle Zimbalist Rosaldo & Louise Lamphere eds., 1974) (arguing that even in societies where women have power, they lack authority, and the activities of men provide the sources of value).
57. Great individual sacrifice can also become the subject of drama and can be seen as the highest of human achievements. For example, the lives of saints are certainly considered paradigms of human sacrifice and achievement. One of the 'public relations' problems of the private and the caring activity that is done there is that there is so much of it. Although such continued sacrifices are essential to human life, it is hard to find exceptional cases to serve as role models.
58. While most political philosophers who stressed the importance of the public were men, some women joined the group. A notable example is Hannah Arendt, who endorsed both the perception of the public (i.e. politics) as ennobling and the willingness to exclude women and workers from this

sacred realm, relegating them to the world of family and work. See Arendt, *supra* note 9; see also Hannah Pitkin, 'Justice: On Relating Private and Public', 9 *Pol. Theory* 327 (1981). Within feminist scholarship, much of the debate, both descriptive and normative, relates to Gilligan's distinction between ethics of justice and ethics of care. See Carol Gilligan, *In a Different Voice: Psychological Theory and Women's Development* (1982). For a recent application of these themes to judicial work, see Judith Resnik, 'Housekeeping: The Nature and Allocation of Work in Federal Trial Courts', 24 Ga. L. Rev. 909, 953–63 (1990) (documenting how lower-echelon work is often dubbed 'housekeeping' and thus devalued through connection to domestic, female roles).

59. Emma Bovary's husband is one of those rare exceptions. For an eloquent description of the role of romantic love in the lives of women see Kate Millett, *Sexual Politics* 36–7 (1970). See also MacKinnon, *supra* note 4, at 67.

60. This ambivalence does not apply to that form of privatization against which Arendt fought, the perception that many people prefer private life—work, family, and play—to a life of political involvement. Men as well as women face this choice, and, in a world in which most political actors are men, it may apply more aptly to them. While some feminists advocate political activism, there is nothing in feminism as such that necessarily values political involvement more highly than enjoyment of the private (although feminists want women to have the choice). This is why I have argued that the feminist politicization of the private should not serve as a denial of all possible or desirable difference.

61. See, e.g., Catherine Hall, 'Private Persons versus Public Someones: Class, Gender and Politics in England, 1780–1850', in *British Feminist Thought* 51 (Terry Lovell ed., 1990) (documenting the ways in which women were excluded from politics).

62. For those who talk about harms to both males and females, see Chodorow, *supra* note 34. For a similar position, but from a male perspective, see John Stoltenberg, *refusing to Be a Man: Essays on Sex and Justice* (1990).

63. See, for example, the position of socialist feminist Barbara Haber, as described in Jaggar, *supra* note 3, at 345–6.

64. See Sherry B. Ortner, 'Is Female to Male as Nature Is to Culture?', in *Woman, Culture and Society*, *supra* note 56, at 67. For a recent discussion of these issues offering a more pragmatic approach to the construction of gender, including feminist criticism of the dichotomies claimed by Gilligan, see Joan C. Williams, 'Deconstructing Gender', 87 Mich. L. Rev. 797 (1989).

65. See Jean Bethke Elshtain, *Public Man, Private Woman* (1982); Judith Stacey, 'Are Feminists Afraid to Leave Home? The Challenge of Conservative Pro-Family Feminism', in *What is Feminism?* 208 (Juliet Mitchell & Ann Oakley eds., 1986).

66. This view is shared by liberal feminists such as Susan Moller Okin as well as

conservative feminists like Jean Elshtain. See Elshtain, *supra* note 65; Okin, *supra* note 3; see also Pateman, *supra* note 3.

67. See, e.g., Frances E. Olsen, 'The Family and the Market: A Study of Ideology and Legal Reform', 96 Harv. L. Rev. 1497, 1568 (1983) (declaring that she is not, in fact, advocating totalitarianism). For her vision of more complete males and females in an ideal society, see id. at 1577–8. See also Alan Freeman & Elizabeth Mensch, 'The Public-Private Distinction in American Law and Life', 36 Buff. L. Rev. 237 (1987).

68. Even one of the most radical feminist visions, that of Shulamith Firestone in 'The Dialectic of Sex: The Case for Feminist Revolution', see note 53 *supra*, keeps child-rearing in the framework of an egalitarian household, and accept the importance of intimate relations and love between individuals. Radical feminists today argue for communitarian feminist structures, but maintain that these should be governed by the woman culture, and not regulated by the state. In addition, they resist ideas that the state and the law should regulate sexual practices among women. See Jaggar, *supra* note 3, at 270–82. Other feminist visions advocate different relationships between the family and the worlds of the market and politics. Some, like Okin, seek primarily to make the classical nuclear heterosexual family more egalitarian, while others criticize her for not giving sufficient weight to alternative intimate relationships. See Will Kymlicka, 'Rethinking the Family', 20 Phil. & Pub. Aff. 77 (1991) (reviewing Okin, *supra* note 3). For both Okin and Kymlicka, intimate relationships are, and should remain, private in important respects.

69. Surrogacy provides a dramatic context in which the competing feminist positions are formulated in terms of the desirable mix between public and private. Feminist opponents of surrogacy view the practice as an undesirable intrusion by the market into the sacred realms of the intimate and the highly personal. See, e.g., Debra Satz, 'Markets in Women's Reproductive Labor', 21 Phil. & Pub. Aff. 107, 108 (1992). Feminist supporters of surrogacy, however, see the question as one of constitutional privacy: Women's control over their lives and bodies requires the autonomy to make economic (private) choices, free from state (public) interference. See, e.g., Shalev, *supra* note 44.

70. MacKinnon, *supra* note 46, at 102. For another illustration of the belief that the public/private distinction between private and public is instrumental in the oppression of women, see Linda J. Nicholson, *Gender and History: The Limits of Social Theory in the Age of the Family* (1986). See also Hester Eisenstein, *Contemporary Feminist Through* (1983) (the second chapter is titled 'The Public/Domestic Dichotomy and the Oppression of Women').

71. 410 U.S. 113 (1973) (holding that a woman's right to have an abortion falls within the due process privacy right).

72. The most systematic account appears in MacKinnon, *supra* note 46, at 93–102.

73. 448 U.S. 297 (1980).

74. MacKinnon, *supra* note 46, at 100.
75. Id. at 94–100.
76. Id. at 94–5.
77. Id. at 95–6.
78. See, e.g., Alan R. White, *Misleading Cases* 99–111 (1991); Gavison, *supra* note 16.
79. Recent abortion decisions are very careful not to mention privacy and talk instead of the woman's 'liberty interest'. Webster *v.* Reproductive Health Servs., 492 U.S. 490, 520 (1989). This change in terminology, in itself, has changed neither the *Roe–Harris* tension, illustrated once again in Rust *v.* Sullivan, 111 S. Ct. 1759 (1991), nor the unclear fate of the *Roe* decision.
80. See MacKinnon, *supra* note 4, at 246; see also Frances Olsen, 'Unravelling Compromise', 103 Harv. L. Rev. 105 (1989).
81. MacKinnon, *supra* note 46, at 94–6.
82. See id.
83. 198 U.S. 45 (1905). The detailed substantiation of this point goes far beyond the scope of this paper. It should, nonetheless, be noted that any difficulties with invoking liberty in *Griswold* v. *Connecticut*, 381 U.S. 479 (1965), and in *Roe* were not logical difficulties. A distinction could be made between issues of personal liberty (as in contraceptives and abortion) and those of economic freedom (the freedom of contract in *Lochner*). Those who seek to justify the *Griswold* progeny make precisely this distinction. Acknowledging that invoking simple liberty as a justification for *Grisworld* was not an attractive route is a concession to external critics. The choice of terms and metaphors does matter.
84. The question of the best way to formulate or present an issue is not unique to abortion. Compare the difficulties feminists and others are having in dealing with pregnancy and child-birth benefits for women. For an attack on gender-neutral discussions of abortion, see MacKinnon, *supra* note 4, at 184–94. For an analysis of the struggle to enact a law guaranteeing childbirth leave, including the question whether it should be conducted in terms of the welfare of women, or in terms of the welfare of all persons with family responsibilities, see Christine A. Littleton, 'Does it Still Make Sense to Talk About "Women"?', 1 UCLA Women's L.J. 15, 19–37 (1991).
85. However, had *Roe* been decided using an equality rationale, it would have been more difficult for the Court to argue in *Harris* that the *Roe* Court merely engaged in noninterference while refusing to deal with background conditions. Accepting the right to an abortion as a condition of gender equality would mean accepting the necessity of addressing unequal background conditions. Nevertheless, the history of equal protection shows that the different sets of background conditions that generate inequality are seen as distinct for purposes of state interference. Some of these differences may be justified.
86. MacKinnon, *supra* note 46, at 99.

87, My argument does not deny the relevance of the personhood or life of the fetus. I am *not* suggesting that abortion is private (self-regarding). The presumption in favour of liberty may be defeated if abortion is indeed murder. This may counterbalance the desire women have to control their bodies and their lives. But see Judith Jarvis Thomson, 'A Defense of Abortion', 1 Phil. & Pub. Aff. 47 (1971) (suggesting that even if abortion is the killing of an innocent person, a woman's right to control her body trumps the right of that innocent person to be kept alive).

88. MacKinnon might concede this. But then she would also need to acknowledge that the doctrinal choice was helpful in facilitating the recognition of a right to abortion.

89. See, e.g., MacKinnon, *supra* note 46, at 101 ('[T]he legal concept of privacy can and has shielded the place of battery, marital rape, and women's exploited labor.').

90. These difficulties lead to the scepticism of the Legal Realists. One form of this scepticism was the claim that key terms attain conclusory meanings. For example, because the Constitution provided that property shall not be taken without compensation, the *meaning* of property became that which should not be taken without compensation. For the general programme of the Realists, see Karl N. Llewelyn, 'A Realistic Jurisprudence—The Next Step', 30 Colum. L. Rev. 431 (1930).

91. This point is illustrated by Michelman's suggestion that 'personal' replace 'private'. See Michelman, *supra* note 46. Michelman correctly notes that what *should* be kept free from interference (the private) is a public question. Id. at 1794. He opposes the idea that the mere use of the term 'private' should preclude further debate on the matter of interference. Id. at 1792–4. The way to avoid this, he suggests, is by talking about 'personhood' rather than 'privacy'. Id. at 1790.

It is not clear why identifying things as 'personal' will be less susceptible to conclusory and mistaken arguments. Margaret Jane Radin's article, 'Property and Personhood', 34 Stan. L. Rev. 957 (1982), which Michelman cites, provides an apt illustration: Which aspects of property involve personhood? Rather than pointing the way out, Radin's work exhibits a tension between her emphasis on the values of personhood and the risks of commodification on the one hand, and her endorsement of the feminist invitation to abolish the distinction between private and public on the other. For a similar critique, see Jed Rubenfeld, 'The Right of Privacy', 102 Harv. L. Rev. 737 (1989).

92. See MacKinnon, *supra* note 46, at 101.

93. Id.

94. Id. at 101–02. This is related to the point made above regarding the identification of the personal and the political. It is no accident that MacKinnon connects the two. Id. at 100.

95. For the importance of privacy to groups, see Kenneth L. Karst, 'The Freedom

of Intimate Association', 89 Yale L.J. 624 (1980). It is ironic that feminists would challenge this, since they have been acutely aware of the importance of the consciousness-raising group with its intimacy and exclusion. At the same time they have successfully challenged, on grounds of illegal discrimination, the exclusionary provisions in some exclusively male social clubs. Thus, women know well the benefits and difficulties of independent social groups. For the centrality of consciousness-raising to feminism, see MacKinnon, *supra* note 4, at 83–105; Katharine Bartlett, 'Feminist Legal Methods', 103 Harv. L. Rev. 829 (1990).

96. I believe that the feminist movement should have a similar goal; we should strive to make intimate relationships truly voluntary, and then provide them relative autonomy and immunity. Note, though, that this struggle may be much more difficult than the struggle to regulate existing relationships. Clearly, much long-term work is needed, including the extension of notions of acceptable relationships beyond the heterosexual marriage. The process would not be complete without a more careful understanding of the limits of the presumption of immunity. But I believe that not only will this process result in a net gain to women's (and men's) freedom, but it will also avoid the dangerous course of eliminating the presumptive privacy of personal relations.

97. See, e.g., Freeman & Mensch, *supra* note 67.

98. Olsen, *supra* note 67. The argument is similar to that found in Klare, *supra* note 25.

99. Olsen, *supra* note 67, at 1568.

100. Id. at 1564.

101. Id. at 1568.

102. Id. at 1569.

103. Cf. notes 24–30 *supra* and accompanying text (feminist critique of common themes that stem from the public/private distinction).

104. Olsen, *supra* note 67, at 1565–6.

105. Id. at 1566.

106. Technology can make a difference, of course. Previously, it seemed not only natural but inevitable that women must nurse children. Now, this is no longer necessary. Still, in most cultures, mothers carry a large part of the responsibility of caring for young children. Some feminists, notably Shulamith Firestone, have indeed argued that women cannot be equal unless they are freed of childbearing. See Firestone, *supra* note 68.

107. Olsen switches, at the end of her paper, from talking about the distinction between private (or family) and public (or market) to that between man and woman—a distinction that is more heavily laden with stereotypical and limiting associations and nuances. See Olsen, *supra* note 67, at 1560–78.

108. See, e.g., Carl D. Schneider, *Shame, Exposure, and Privacy* (1977) (criticizing early feminists for their indiscriminate challenge of shame).

109. A good example of success, though still awkward, is the unwillingness to accept the use of 'he' in writing. The awkwardness, however, is not too high a price to pay in the fight against the naturalness of the identification of individuals of achievement as exclusively male. Similarly, the portrayal of certain professions in gendered ways—e.g., doctors as males, nurses as females; professors as males, secretaries as females—restricts our freedom to imagine different worlds and orders. The complex and frustrating nature of the problem can be illustrated by the fact that no solution seems capable of resolving the problem completely. First, feminists sensitized readers to the effects of using exclusively male language. Now, however, when female pronouns are used to describe persons of status and achievement, this usage is sometimes attacked as misleading when there are relatively few women in high status professions and occupations. We can agree that there are few women in positions of power or prestige. We may even agree that it is desirable to change this situation, or at least its appearance of inevitability, but it seems difficult to agree on the linguistic recommendations that should follow.

2.2 Regulating families or legitimating patriarchy? Family law in Britain*

CAROL SMART

The relationship of law to the family is a complex one and the function of law in the reproduction of patriarchal relations is, as yet, inadequately theorized. However both law and the family have been central to the tradition of feminist politics and remain a major concern and a focus for struggle in the present. It is therefore of considerable importance that law and the family, and the relationship between the two, should be critically examined and that the presumed role of law in the oppression of women should not rigidify into a feminist conventional wisdom that is received uncritically. But even to pose the issues in this way is problematic. As Cousins (1980) has argued, it is inaccurate to posit the law as a unitary category. On a simplistic level, law is divided into its various branches such that one branch of law (i.e. social security law) may attempt to impose a particular set of regulations on the family or the individual that are in contradiction with another branch of law (i.e. family law).[1] Moreover, law is not simply synonymous with either legislation or the body of the judiciary. For example, in family law, as with some aspects of criminal law and social security law, the operation or enforcement of law is increasingly administered or influenced by quasi- or non-legal personnel such as probation officers, social workers, and even school teachers. Decisions regarding the custody of children are one instance of this shift away from judicial decision-making towards a practice where social workers and probation officers effectively make the decisions about what is in the best interests of the child. So it would be increasingly inaccurate to analyse the law simply in terms of a combination of judicial rulings and legislation. Where non-legal criteria such as the 'best interests of the child' begin to predominate in the legal forum, necessarily other professions besides the legal profession begin to influence the development and implementation of law.

* An earlier version of this paper was presented at the European Conference on Critical Legal Studies, London, March 1981.

But if the relationship of law to the family is complex, the relationship of law to structures of patriarchal relations[2] is even more difficult to pose theoretically. Any analysis that posits law as a tool of patriarchal oppression is bound to fail because a close examination of law in general will reveal that although some laws are particularly patriarchal (i.e. laws on rape and prostitution) others (i.e. equal pay and abortion legislation) may be more progressive in intent or application. Even within one area of law, such as family law, it is possible to observe contradictions. Recent Law Commission recommendations on illegitimacy[3] for example would, if accepted, impose a father figure on a one-parent family, even against the wishes of the mother, in order to eliminate illegitimacy. Hence illegitimacy would not be abolished by raising the status of the one-parent family, but by providing a father's name on a child's birth certificate and supplying a father's nationality. The solution to illegitimacy is posed as a reconstruction of the single-parent unit and an extension of the rights (and obligations) of marriage to the unmarried. Similar attempt to treat illicit unions as if they were lawful unions have occurred in other ways in recent years. The cohabitation rule is the most notorious and the most objectionable to women because it forces them to be financially dependent upon the men they are living with even if they are not married to them. But, within family law, certain other regulations and rights that previously only applied to wives are being extended to unmarried women, and not all of these are to the disadvantage of women. For example the 1976 Domestic Violence Act extends the same protection to cohabitees as to wives; moreover, cohabitees (male and female) can now more easily (than 20 years ago) establish a claim to property that has been shared as a home. So although the law is undoubtedly extending the rights and obligations of the marriage contract to the unmarried this cannot simply be depicted as an extension of patriarchal controls. The purposes of bringing illicit unions within some form of State regulation are therefore not always synonymous with an extension of male domination, and the motivations for legislative reforms and developments may be, in some instances, to protect public spending rather than simply to control women, even though the consequences of legislation affect wives and husbands, mothers and fathers, women and men differentially.

To help to understand the complex relationship of contemporary family law to the family and to the issue of the reproduction of patriarchal relations it is valuable to adopt an historical perspective. Although matrimonial law in England and Wales has changed considerably over the last century, and most dramatically over the past 10 years, the genesis of

contemporary legislation resides in canon law and common law.[4]
Moreover the primary aim of matrimonial law, which is to regulate and
maintain the family (albeit that the legal ideal of the perfect family structure has been modified) has never changed. What has changed, however,
is the *extent* to which the law has directly involved itself in family life and
the *modes* of regulation of family members that have been employed.
Broadly speaking, it is possible to trace a transition in these two axes of
regulation. On one hand the law has become more willing to invade the
private sphere of family life (for example recent legislation on domestic
violence and the introduction of powers to vary the ownership of the
matrimonial home) whilst it has abandoned, to a considerable extent, its
negative and punitive response to extra- and non-marital relations. I shall
consider some of these developments in an historical context before discussing their particular relevance in the post-war period.

Historical developments in family law

The punitive obsession

Diana Leonard (1978), in her work on marriage, has shown that the secular state became increasingly involved in the regulation of personal,
familial relationships during the eighteenth century. Although the
Established Church exercised its jurisdiction over marriage and separations it was not until the secular state established a system of registering
marriages, births, and deaths in 1836 that an effective and enforceable
method of centrally regulating the entry into (and exit from) marriage
became available. It was only when the State could confirm who was
married to whom that legally specified dependants could begin to be
identified. As long as the State itself did not routinely provide financially
for the dependants created by the social organization of reproduction and
the sexual division of labour it was of no particular importance to specify
the individuals who had the legal responsibility for providing maintenance and support. But with the development of Poor Law provisions,
national assistance, and eventually social security, the need to identify the
person responsible for this maintenance (known now as the liable relative) became more pressing. The strict legal and financial obligations of
marriage therefore expanded with the growth of a welfare state, as have
the State's requirements to regulate and supervise marriage and divorce.
The maintenance of lawful children and lawful wives has been increasingly removed from the sphere of individual benevolence and placed in
the sphere of legal compulsion. Moreover this duty to maintain, and the

legal process of specifying the individuals who are to assume this responsibility, is being gradually extended beyond actual biological relatives and beyond wedlock.

From the first inception of civil regulation over marriage and the introduction of divorce, the relationship of law to the family via marriage and divorce has been essentially control oriented; applying negative and punitive sanctions. It is in fact only recently that matrimonial law has begun to abandon its punitive treatment of those who fail to marry in certain circumstances and those whose marriages fail. One example of this movement away from a punitive, negatively controlling orientation towards the family and its members has been the development of the law governing illegitimacy. The formal and bureaucratic regulation of marriage introduced in the nineteenth century necessarily strengthened the legal, as opposed to moral or religious, categories of legitimacy and illegitimacy. The easier it became to identify who was married to whom, the simpler it became for a legal administration to declare a person illegitimate. Such a declaration could have very serious consequences in the nineteenth century as an illegitimate child could not inherit intestate from his parents or other blood relations. But the consequences of illegitimacy were not only felt in the properties classes; indeed, they were felt more keenly, as might be expected, amongst the poor. The position of the poor unmarried mother worsened during the nineteenth century (R.O.W. 1979) because the Poor Law insisted on forcing the main burden and support of the illegitimate child on to the mother. Fathers could be made to contribute financially to the upkeep of their illegitimate children, but unwed mothers had to enter the workhouse, or leave their children there, if they could not support them by their own efforts.

During the nineteenth century and at the beginning of the twentieth century the legal category of illegitimacy operated as one of the major bulwarks of the family. The deprivations and hardships that were imposed on women and children as a consequence of the legal construction of illegitimacy were justified on the grounds that such sanctions discouraged extra-marital sexual relations and encouraged couples to enter into legally recognized unions. As I shall argue below, similar justifications were attached to the legal stigma and hardships associated with divorce at this time. Family law, in conjunction with the Poor Laws, was therefore quite clearly operating to maintain a particular patriarchal family structure through the implementation of punitive sanctions against those, particularly women, who attempted or were forced to adopt a different lifestyle.

This negative form of control operated by the law was modified slightly in the first half of the twentieth century with the introduction of the Legitimacy Act of 1926. This allowed an illegitimate child to inherit intestate from his or her mother and it also allowed for the legitimation of the child if the parents subsequently married. This was only possible however if neither of the parents was married to another partner at the time of the child's birth. In this way the law could show a certain amount of compassion towards the child, which was in keeping with the emergent family law principle of safeguarding the welfare of the child (Brophy & Smart, 1981). But at the same time it could still discourage and punish adulterous relationships that resulted in the birth of a child. In post-war Britain, however, the balance between these two principles of punishment and welfare altered and I shall return to this issue below.

If the legal status of illegitimacy provides one example of the negative and punitive orientation of legal control over the family in the last century, the legal process and consequences of divorce and marital breakdown provide another. As the primary objective of family law was the preservation of marriage and the family structure, with its unequal sexual hierarchy and sexual division of labour, and as it sought to achieve its objectives by punishing its failures and deviants, it was quite logical that divorce, like illegitimacy, should carry considerable stigma and economic penalties. During the nineteenth century and much of the twentieth century, a divorce (in the High Court) or a noncohabitation order (in the magistrates' courts) could only be granted if one spouse established that the other was guilty of a matrimonial offence. The sole ground for a secular divorce was originally adultery or, if a wife was petitioning, adultery combined with some other offence. These were gradually extended to include desertion and cruelty but the whole basis of divorce or separation rested on the concept of the matrimonial offence and the guilt of one party contrasted with the innocence of the other.

The fact that divorce and separation were based on establishing the existence of an offence necessarily meant that legal proceedings constituted a punishment for the guilty spouse. If a husband was guilty his punishment was an order to pay maintenance to his wife as well as a loss of conjugal rights (Reiss, 1934). The penalty for a guilty wife was much more severe however. She could lose all rights to maintenance as well as (prior to 1882) all the property and money she might have brought to the marriage or earned throughout its duration. She could lose not only the custody of her children but also all access to them (Brophy & Smart, 1981). The stigma and punishment of divorce was therefore not distributed evenly across the sexes and the burden, as with illegitimacy, fell hardest on women. Moreover, while husbands were entitled to compensation for loss of conjugal services if their wives were guilty of adultery, this right was not reciprocal.[5] This differential treatment of husbands and wives was most usually justified by reference to the dual standard of morality. For example in 1912 one member of the Royal Commission on Divorce maintained that,

I do not think that an act of adultery on the part of a man has anything like the same significance that an act of adultery on the part of a woman has; and most men, I think, or all men, know it perfectly well. An act of adultery on the part of a man may be more or less accidental . . . (it) is not inconsistent with his continued esteem and love for his wife (Royal Commission, 1912, Sir J. Bigham).

Such chauvinistic utterances are very common in legal discourse[6] and family law is a particularly fertile ground for such statements. Undoubtedly the double standard affected the way in which family law responded to extramarital sex and infringements of the monogamous ideal. However the double standard of morality is not in itself a sufficient explanation of why women were selected out for extra punitive treatment if they offended against sexual and marital norms. The double standard of morality is in fact a practice rather than an explanation and it does not provide an answer to the question of why women were identified as so central to the preservation of the family and why the consequences of women's conduct were seen as potentially far more damaging to social stability than those of men.

One possible reason why the conduct of women and the stability of the family and the nation became so closely linked is related to the changing perception of children during the nineteenth and early twentieth centuries. As both Davin (1978) and Donzelot (1980) have argued, the State began to identify children as a valuable national asset which should not be squandered. In consequence, mothers as child rearers rather than simply as child producers became increasingly central figures. Davin maintains that,

The family remained the basic institution of society, and woman's domestic role remained supreme, but gradually it was her function as mother that was being most stressed, rather than her function as wife. . . . Moreover the relationship between family and state was subtly changing. Since parents were bringing up the next generation of citizens the state had an interest in how they did it. Child-rearing was becoming a national duty not just a moral one (Davin, 1978, pp. 12–13).

In a similar vein, Donzelot argues that,

In point of fact, this transformation of the family was not effected without the active participation of women. In working-class and bourgeois strata alike . . . women were the main point of support for all the actions that were directed toward a reformulation of family life. For example, the woman was chosen by the medical and teaching professions to work in partnership with them in order to disseminate their principles, to win adherence to the new norms, within the home (Donzelot, 1980, p. xxii).

Women as mothers or potential mothers therefore carried a particular responsibility, the abrogation of which led to punitive sanctions. The changes in law relating to child custody are a very clear example of this process. Prior to the 1839 Custody of Infants Act mothers had no statutory or formal rights to the custody of their legitimate children. However this Act, followed by a number of Guardianship Acts, created a legal recognition of the significance of the mother/child relationship. Mothers could then apply for custody although at first it was only for young children. However, adultery on the part of the mother barred her from applying for, and later when she could apply, from winning, the custody of her children. Her adultery made her an unfit mother who should not be entrusted with the care of children. As Donzelot argues, the idealization of motherhood, although it increased the powers of women within the family to some extent, had the undesirable consequence of creating greater penalties for the so-called unfit mother because family law was still at this time locked into its negative mode of regulating family life.

The punitive mode of regulating family members and sustaining marriage therefore had differential consequences for men and women. The extra responsibilities placed on women-as-mothers and as the socializers and care takers of the next general subjected them to a new, emergent form of containment within the family. Legally their status simply as their husband's property was diminishing as women's legal rights to own property, to sue in actions for damages, to lave the matrimonial home against their husbands' wishes, to enter the professions, and to use the franchise increased. However, simultaneous with these developments and the undermining of traditional, legally supported, patriarchal relations was the enhancement of the role of the mother. Through this newly reconstituted role women remained as closely bound to the family as before, albeit that there was some slight shifting of the power structure within the household.

Legal intervention in the family

The negatively controlling function of family law in the nineteenth and early twentieth centuries tended to preclude direct legal intervention in the family. The law defined very clearly the boundaries of marriage and the family and policed those boundaries in an authoritarian fashion. However it did not enter into the private sphere of the family to any great extent. The family was the domain of the head of household and he was granted the authority by law and tradition to act much as he pleased within that domain. It was only gradually, towards the end of the nine-teenth century, that ordinary women were, for example, granted any kind of legal relief from wife-beating, while the introduction of mainte-nance for separated wives at this time was still resisted on the grounds that it interfered with the authority of the husband.

This rigidly non-interventionist stance began to be modified, however. On the one hand it was challenged by feminists such as Frances Power Cobbe, Caroline Norton, and later Millicent Fawcett (Bauer & Ritt, 1979) who recognized that legal intervention in the authority structure of the autonomous family was one way of reducing the autocratic power of the head of household. And on the other hand the State itself initiated a degree of intervention on behalf of children who were identified as neglected and unlikely to develop into healthy, useful citizens. Of course legislation and legal reforms, particularly in the area of Poor Law legisla-tion and protective employment legislation, had affected the family before the nineteenth-century family law reforms, but these effects were often unintentional or unpremeditated. Deliberate changes to family law had a different significance as they were always conducted in line with the pol-icy of preserving the family and marriage. The reforms that occurred took place within clearly defined ideological debates about the correct roles of the different members of the family and the function of marriage and reproduction of the State. It was therefore particularly significant when family law began, on principle, to tolerate a certain degree of intervention into the private sphere. The degree of permissible intervention in the nineteenth and early twentieth centuries was slight, however, and it was not until the latter half of this century that the consequences of this shift in policy became apparent. Only with the changing social, economic, and political climate in Britain after the Second World War did family law fully embrace these different strategies to stabilize the family and contain its members. And as the form and content of the legal regulation of the family were modified and even transformed so the relationship between law and the reproduction of a patriarchal family structure became increasingly obscured and difficult to identify. Patriarchal authority *is* diminished by legal reforms and women *are* granted greater freedoms inside and outside the family. Moreover the law itself is seen to champion women's rights and to protect wives and mothers against the worst excesses of masculine abuse. Under such conditions it is clearly inappropriate to identify a unitary relationship between law and the family in which the interests of law, the State, and the family coincide. Indeed such a model might always have been inadequate, but it became increasingly so with the nature of the changes that took place after the war. It is to these developments that I shall now turn.

Family law in post-war Britain

There is a further factor in the problem of marriage breakdown, which is more dangerous, because more insidious in its effects, than any of the others. In fact, we believe it lies at the root of the problem. There is a tendency to take the duties and responsibilities of marriage less seriously than formerly . . .
Unless this tendency is checked, there is a real danger that the conception of marriage as a life-long union of one man with one woman may be abandoned. This would be an irreparable loss to the community (Royal Commission on Marriage & Divorce, 1956, pp. 9, 11).

In Britain after the Second World War a widespread concern developed that the institution of the family was in the grip of a major crisis. The Royal Commission on Marriage and Divorce which sat between 1951 and 1955 expressed deep concern over the tide of events and predicted disaster for the nation if the divorce rate kept on rising. In addition the illegitimacy rates were causing concern and it appeared by all conventional measures of family and national stability that social and ideological changes caused by the war, education, the emancipation of women, and housing problems were undermining the family in a very profound way.

The initial response of the legislators and their legal advisers was to fall back on traditional methods of control in order to achieve a re-stabilization. The Royal Commission therefore recommended no changes to the divorce law which had in fact, hardly changed in principle since its inception in 1857. Changes, the Commissioners felt, would only worsen the situation and while they did not advocate greater controls, some anticipated that it might become necessary in the future to abolish divorce altogether and to return to a pre-1857 situation. The Commission's response to proposals to liberalize the laws on illegitimacy received similar treatment. It refused to accept the proposal that subsequent marriage should legitimate all illegitimate children, including adulterine bastards. In fact it maintained that,

It is unthinkable that the State should lend its sanction to such a step, for it could not fail to result in a blurring of moral values in the public mind. A powerful deterrent to illicit relationships would be removed, with disastrous results for the status of marriage as at present understood (Royal Commission, 1956, pp. 304–5).

When challenged by changing social conditions and demands for liberal reforms the legislators in the immediate post-war period looked for pre-war solutions. The Royal Commission sought to preserve the negative forms of regulation that family law had traditionally implemented, and recommended the continued use of deterrence to promote stable family life. It refused to abolish the concept of matrimonial offence and continued to treat divorce as a punishment of the guilty spouse. Yet only a decade later the Law Commission[7] was putting the opposite view and recommending the abolition of matrimonial offences as the basis of divorce. Moreover, it began to extol the benefits and virtues of facilitating remarriage and reducing illegitimacy through the vehicle of lawful marriage. In little more than 10 years the formal position of family legislation was completely changed and the policy of deterrence largely abandoned.

This apparent reversal in legal policy raises the issue of why such a dramatic change should occur over such a short space of time. On one level it would appear that the law in this area became subject to the same philosophy of liberalization and permissiveness as other branches of law. There were, for example, liberal reforms in other areas such as abortion (Abortion Act 1967), contraception (National Health (Family Planning) Act 1967), homosexuality (Sexual Offences Act 1967), pornography (Obscene Publications Acts 1959 and 1964), and theatrical displays (Theatres Act 1964). As Hall has argued, 'Descriptively, we may agree that the tendency of the legislation was to shift things in the general direction of a less rigid, looser, more "permissive" moral code' (Hall, 1980, p. 2).

But although these reforms were liberal and permissive, in that they permitted people to do things or to behave in certain ways that were morally, socially, and legally condemned a generation previously, the boundaries of conduct were still policed and regulated by law. Hall refers to this process as a 'shift in the modality of moral regulation'; in other words there was a qualitative change in the mode of legal regulation, but the law did not abandon its regulatory function. The concept of permissiveness implies a loosening of regulation and control, and suggests that law retreated from an involvement in the conduct of individuals and family members. However a closer examination of law in relation to the family does not support support this view. As matrimonial law became less deterrence-oriented it intervened more in the relationships between spouses, unmarried couples, parents and children, and it adopted positive modes of regulation that encouraged the formation of lawful family units by facilitating divorce, remarriage, and the legitimation of children and by extending a certain degree of legal recognition, as well as duties and obligations, to the unmarried. In the 1960s and 1970s there was a discernible shift in the two axes of regulation of family law. The Royal Commission of 1956 was, in retrospect, a final attempt to re-establish the old, traditional methods of regulation. However it failed and its strategies proved to be inappropriate to the changing conditions of the family in the post-war period. I shall briefly outline these changing conditions before discussing the post-war shift in the modality of regulation.

Post-war changes in family structure

Family life in Britain changed considerably after the Second World War but it is important to stress that the origins of these developments pre-date 1945 and in fact had been in process for a long time. Child-centredness, for example, which became almost an obsession after the war, did not suddenly materialize with the work of John Bowlby (1951) in the 1950s. The emphasis on child development and the stress on the mother–child bond have a tradition that stretches back beyond the beginning of the nineteenth century (Ariès, 1979; Donzelot, 1980). However it was with the post-war growth in education and health provision that this child-centred ideology really became a major force in family life and social policy. The welfare of children appeared to become a national obsession.

As the position of the child in the family changed significantly so did the position of the mother. But, as Wilson (1980) argues, she was subject to two opposing forces. On one hand her role of mother and home-maker was idealized and stressed while on the other her waged labour was required to assist the post-war reconstruction of the economy. In every decade since the war the proportion of married women in the labour force has increased. Both of these trends affected the family. The enhancement of motherhood gave women a special relationship to their children (whether they want it or not). This relationship had many disadvantages in that it curtailed women's economic independence and ability to earn a reasonable wage. But it also gave many women a legally recognized prior claim to their children should their marriages fail. This is not a point that should be overstated as there have been numerous examples of mothers failing to win the custody of their children because of moral judgements by the courts. But none the less there has been a very important shift away from the automatic rights for fathers which existed in the nineteenth century.

The increase in the numbers of working wives also had an important impact on the family. As with child care, this trend has brought significant problems such as the double-shift, where women have to do both waged and domestic work. But it has also brought certain advantages besides the obvious financial ones. It was, for example, when midde-class women began to earn an income and to contribute towards the financial costs of home-making that the law began at last to intervene in the virtual male monopoly of property ownership. Although family law valued the wife who stayed at home and performed her 'natural', unwaged, domestic function, until recently it was only the 'less-natural' wage-earning wife who could reap any financial reward from her labours in the form of a share in the husband's property on divorce. The law exalted domestic labour but refused to give it a pecuniary value. The recognition that wives contributed directly, in a financial way, towards the accumulation of family property, was therefore a first step towards a later recognition of the pecuniary value of indirect contributions like housework and childcare.

The pattern of married women working had one other important implication for the family and ultimately for family law. For middle-class women at least marriage ceased to be the moment when they gave up independent, waged work. As Westergaard & Resler (1975) have argued, working class women did not necessarily stop working at any stage of their lives so this trend did not necessarily affect them or their families. But for the middle classes, marriage ceased very gradually to be the point at which a woman underwent, in all practical terms, a major change in status. She did not, financially speaking, become automatically dependent upon her husband, even though important changes may have occurred such as the loss of her name or being treated as a dependent for tax or social security purposes. The moment at which wives unavoidably became economically dependent upon their husbands gradually shifted away from the moment of marriage to the moment of parenthood. As a number of feminists have pointed out, although wedlock entails a number of legal and other disadvantages for women, it might be argued that (the) responsibility for childcare, inscribed in the economic and ideological relations of capitalism, constitutes a more significant source of the oppression of women than the marriage relationship itself (Barrett & McIntosh, 1979, p. 102).

The significance of the shift away from marriage, as the crucial rite of passage into economic dependency for many women, to the onset of biological reproduction as the threshold of a new economic status, gradually undermined the law's insistence that marriage *per se* should differentiate men and women, mothers and fathers, parents and children, into distinct, discrete categories. Increasingly in practice, and in law, the distinction between marriage and nonmarriage became somewhat blurred because of the changing involvement of married women in waged-labour. However these processes took several generations before they were reflected at all in family law. In fact marriage is still treated as a desirable goal for women, and marriage remains extremely popular. As the Society of Conservative Lawyers maintains,

A stable family life lived within the bonds of matrimony is still the popular ideal. If there is a failure to live up to that ideal, if marriages break down or are unstable, then the whole of society is weakened. The State is therefore vitally concerned in the preservation of marriages, and when there are children, vitally concerned to preserve a *stable two-parent family united in marriage* (Society of Conservative lawyers, 1981, p. 11, emphasis added).

Notwithstanding that much of this statement is accurate in that marriage is probably still a popular ideal and that the State is concerned to preserve the stable, two-parent legally recognized unit, there has been a blurring of categories between the married and unmarried and the legitimate and the illegitimate and it is to these issues that I now turn.

The axes of regulation

The punitive obsession abandoned

In 1964 two Private Members' Bills were introduced into the House of Commons. The first of these was entitled The Strengthening of Marriage Bill, the second was The Family Preservation Bill. Their titles make them sound virtually identical but the first was an attempt to introduce divorce by consent after five years' separation while the second aimed to ban information relevant to divorce by making it an offence to 'give teaching or instruction calculated to encourage husband or wife to break mutual obligations'. The first wanted easier divorce, the second wanted to make it more difficult to acquire; both aspired to strengthen marriage and to preserve the family. These two Bills symbolized the struggle between the new, positive approach to regulating the family and the old negative and punitive approach.

By 1969 the objectives of the Strengthening of Marriage Bill had been incorporated into the Divorce Reform Act which transformed the basis of divorce in England and Wales away from a system based on matrimonial offences, guilt, and punishment towards one based on irretrievable break-down, mutual responsibility, and need. This Act, as I have argued above, was greeted as a liberal, permissive measure that would increase the sum of human happiness. But during its passage through Parliament the arguments that appeared to have the greatest sway concerned the plight of illegitimate children and the need to preserve the popularity and the voluntary nature of marriage and its commitments.[8] It was argued convincingly that the best solution to illegitimacy was to allow the parents of illegitimate children to marry. The solution was not seen in terms of the removal of the legal status of illegitimacy but in terms of reducing obstacles to a second or legitimating marriage. Marriage and remarriage therefore became elevated to the status of solutions, while at the same time it was argued that divorce was only a stage in the process of remarriage and the chance to contract an even better, happier, more permanent union. Divorce was depicted not so much as an end as a new beginning through which, it was argued, the family as an institution would benefit. This idea presented a novel dislocation between the family and the institution of marriage. Prior to this it had really been unthinkable to separate the two, a high divorce rate necessarily meant that the family became unstable. During the 1960s, however, it became possible to argue that a high divorce rate merely reorganized families because the majority of divorcees remarried.

The main purpose of the new divorce law therefore was to facilitate remarriage rather than to free individuals from the responsibilities of marriage itself. Its aim was to ease the redistribution of men, women, and children round units that were capable of legal recognition. During the 1960s family law did not recognize cohabitees and, although social security legislation operated as if a woman cohabiting with a man was maintained by him, she could not legally claim maintenance from him during or after cohabitation. If she had children she could only claim maintenance for them through an affiliation order and they could not inherit automatically from their fathers. If these problem unions could be more easily recognized by law through the process of facilitating remarriage, it followed that the economic dependence of mothers and children, created by the social organization of childcare and domestic labour, would become the responsibility of individual men rather than becoming the responsibility of the state. Hence the solution to the financial and social problems caused by single parent families could be eradicated. As Land & Parker have pointed out, 'Interestingly, in Britain, the solution to the problem of lone mothers is perceived more in terms of how best to remove barriers to their remarriage rather than to overcome obstacles to their increased participation in the labour market' (Land & Parker, 1978, p. 336).

Regardless of the benefits of remarriage to the individuals concerned, remarriage was positively desirable for the State because only under those conditions could the problems of economic dependence be contained within the family. As long as the State made remarriage difficult, or even absolved husbands of their duty to maintain wives who were guilty of a matrimonial offence, it was creating categories of women and children whose main source of support would almost inevitably be the State.

This is not to argue however that the shift in the mode of regulation was a simple reflection of a new economic rationalism. The reforms to family law that occurred at this time were not easily achieved and would not have succeeded if it had not been for the struggle of feminists and women MPs who appreciated that the old system of divorce and separation disadvantaged wives and mothers far more than men. Neither would these reforms have occurred if there had not been major shifts in the doctrines of the established church which allowed the regulation of divorce to become a secular matter. But although these shifts in legal policy did improve the position of women and children when marriage broke down they did very little to alter the fundamental power structure within the family. The reforms celebrated the existing division of labour between the sexes and reinforced the structures of dependency that existed by reducing slightly the social and economic consequences of that dependency. The expectation that women should fulfil the domestic role, whilst men remained the providers for the family, was at no point seriously challenged.

The growing legal intervention

The other axis of regulation along which family law developed and changed concerned the growth of intervention into the privacy of the family. Traditionally, family law has tended to treat the family as a private sanctuary that should be protected from public or legal interference.

Other branches of law have been less particular in their dealings with the family. Poor Laws, for example, did not concede the same privacy or consideration to families and employment legislation in the nineteenth century did much to undermine working-class families. But family law, particularly divorce law, developed in the context of middle-class and aristocratic families where the privacy of the individual family was not only accorded great respect but elevated to an absolute principle of law. Even now this principle remains, although in practice it has been breached.

The main assault on the principle of non-intervention into family life, which has also played an important role in the decline of the punitive approach, is related to the growing concern over the welfare of children. Safeguarding the interests of children is now a priority in divorce and separation proceedings and before a decree absolute can be granted a judge has to declare him or herself satisfied that the provisions made for the children of the family are adequate. This has led to a steady increase in the demand for welfare reports on families to assist the judiciary or the bench to make decisions about the future of children which are based on welfare, rather than legal, criteria. Such reports entail a probation officer visiting the family, interviewing its members separately and together, assessing the nature and standard of the accommodation in the home, interviewing schoolteachers and even neighbours (Murch, 1980). Under certain conditions the probation officer can also recommend that a supervision order be attached to the parent who is eventually given custody. The family with young children can therefore be subjected to a very close degree of scrutiny once it comes in contact with the legal processes of divorce or separation. Moreover, others who are working are frequently put under particularly close scrutiny by the courts who tend in consequence to perpetuate the view that mothers with the care of children should not work outside the home.

The growth of intervention into the privacy of the family is not restricted to the issue of children, however. Gradually the domestic and divorce courts have acquired greater power of enquiry into the financial standing of family members. In fact their powers are no similar to those of the criminal courts and the element of compulsion has increased. Attachment of earnings orders for example, which were once viewed as a major infringement of privacy as they deducted money from a man's income before it reached his pocket and because they entailed informing employers about a man's domestic affairs, can now be attached without a man's consent if he falls into arrears. Such strategies are of course not always effective.[9] However the existence of such powers is an indication that the hallowed principle of privacy has been overwhelmed by the need to reduce the financial burden of broken marriages on the State. Arguably it is this economic motivation that has also helped to blur the old rigid distinction between the married and unmarried and to modify the concept of *legal* relatives. One example of this blurring is the concept of the 'child of the family'. In a situation of high divorce rates men and women are increasingly finding themselves married to a spouse with children from a previous marriage. If he or she should then financially support those children because their other natural parent does not, he or she may find him or herself financially responsible for the children until they reach adulthood should the second marriage fail. In this way the State avoids the cost of maintaining those children and the financial burden remains a personal problem dealt with by a new form of extended family.

It is quite possible that a similar motivation may also encourage family law to dispense with the distinction between cohabitation and marriage altogether. At present social security law treats a cohabitee as a dependant although tax law and family law do not. If a cohabitation breaks down a woman cannot expect the man she was living with to support her, although her children can in certain circumstances. If she cannot support herself she has to turn to the State and the financial burden of supporting single parent families is one that the State appears to be increasingly unwilling to undertake. A solution for the State could be to pass the responsibility back to the former cohabitee. As Deech has pointed out,

It can be seen that to regard any relationship other than that of marriage as one of intimacy and dependency is comparable to the throwing of a stone into a lake. The circle of logical claimants is ever widening and their number cannot be ascertained in advance by the giver of benefits (Deech, 1980, p. 307).

It may be that the State would wish to extend the 'circle of logical claimants' however, as the costs of a high divorce rate and the increasing numbers of unsupported families increase. It may be that the present strategies of family law, far from moving towards a principle of individual support for everyone, are deliberately reconstructing an extended family to support its weaker members. Such an extended family might not be based on kinship however, so much as the acquisition of legal and financial obligations arising out of living in a particular household structure. The consequence of this type of strategy for women is that the possibility of achieving economic and financial independence within the family structure is reduced further and the vulnerability of wives and mothers is sustained. It would however be misleading to argue that such an outcome was the deliberate intention of family law policy. As I have tried to argue, developments such as these are more complex than a simple reassertion of patriarchal control.

Conclusions

In this paper I have attempted to argue that there are problems in assuming that there is a simple, instrumental relationship between law and the structures of patriarchy. I have concentrated on family law because it is this branch of law which exerts a significant influence on the structure of the family which in turn constitutes a primary site of the oppression of women.[10] But I have not been concerned here to reveal the extent of sexual discrimination or stereotyping which operates within family law, nor to discuss the issues of women's rights in law, as these issues have been discussed more fully elsewhere.[11] Rather I have been concerned to outline the complexities of the relationship between the law, the family, and the position of women, and to trace major legislative developments that have occurred over the last century which have obscured this relationship.

It is no longer possible to assert that family law is oppressive of women in a simple and direct fashion. That relationship is directed through the family and, inasmuch as the structure of the family has been modified, so the directly oppressive impact of law has been deflected. Donzelot (1980) has argued that,

The family was also transformed in its exterior status by the modification of family law. By the terms of the new law, the ancient or monolithic authority of the father gave place to a dual regime, which took the form of a simple alternative: either the system of *tutelage*, or that of the *contract* (Donzelot, 1980, p. xxi).

It is not necessary to accept the totality of Donzelot's argument, namely that patriarchal authority in the family has now disappeared, to appreciate that it has been modified. Certainly there still exist very many overt instances of the operation of that authority, such as with wife-beating. But the law no longer condones such behaviour, it even provides remedies, albeit that agents of the law do not always provide very effective protection. But we cannot say that the law has not shifted since the days when it proclaimed that a man had every right to beat his wife.

Family law now apparently provides for a great deal of individual liberty. It no longer confines people to unhappy marriages, it no longer punishes wives for their adultery as it used to, and it now attempts to protect divorced wives who are disadvantaged through marriage and motherhood. But in so doing it has reinforced the very structure of the family which is so oppressive of women because it has extended and perpetuated the legal status of dependency. It has failed to facilitate the development of a household structure in which dependency need not arise. Ironically these developments have however benefited wives and mothers; they have even been in line with feminist demands for reform to the divorce law in the nineteenth and twentieth centuries. But although family law has changed considerably since the nineteenth century, most especially in terms of the axes of regulation along which it operates, the economic and social vulnerability of wives (and increasingly cohabitees) has been preserved. Moreover the popularity of marriage has been preserved too because the grossest abuses of patriarchal authority are no longer condoned. What remains unchanged however, and this is of the utmost significance to women, is the way in which,

the domestic hierarchy continues to be justified . . . by the 'inherent' weakness and defencelessness of the subordinates (women need protection because they have to care for children etc., and they cannot earn as much as men anyway) and because they consent to it (marriage is what women 'want' and 'choose') (Leonard, 1978, p. 261).

In Diana Leonard's terms, family law has become more benevolent, it is no longer the simple vehicle of an oppressive patriarchal system, it even talks of an equality between the sexes and of reciprocal rights and duties. Family law rarely promotes what can be identified as traditional patriarchal values now. Judges may still voice the odd chauvinistic utterance on the position of women in an attempt to reassert traditional strategies of regulating the family, but these are not a true reflection of the content of modern family law. Instead law regulates women through the ideology of their primacy for the welfare of children, through the extension of the dependent/breadwinner dichotomy, and through the continuing, engineered but real, popularity of marriage.

Notes

1. An emphasis on the disciplinary subdivisions of law has of course itself been a focus of criticism from Marxist scholars. In many ways these divisions can be said to disguise the functioning of law as a whole (or unity) such that an examination of theft and criminal law is meaningless without a knowledge of

property law, and a knowledge of the whole is necessary to grasp the significance of the ownership of property to the social formation. This is a powerful argument but it does not justify ignoring the contradictions within law itself.

2. The use of the term 'patriarchal relations' raises immediate problems. I agree with Michèle Barrett that 'as a noun the term "patriarchy" presents insuperable difficulties to an analysis that attempts to relate women's oppression to the relations of production of capitalism' (1980, p. 19). However I do not agree that terminology such as patriarchal relations should be expunged from our vocabulary, neither would I agree that we can only refer to patriarchal ideology.

3. Law Commission, *Working Paper on Illegitimacy* (1979).

4. For example the $1/3$ 'rule' as a method of dividing property and income between spouses was used by the ecclesiastical courts (McGregor *et al.*, 1970).

5. 'The husband is entitled to compensation for the loss of his wife and for the injury to his feelings and the hurt to his family life. Factors to be taken into account in assessing the loss of the wife are her fortune, her assistance in the husband's business, her capacity as a housekeeper and her ability in the home, and her character and conduct generally' (Royal Commission on Marriage and Divorce, 1956, p. 120).

6. The courts have traditionally taken a far more serious view of a wife's adultery than a husband's. The usual reason put forward for this is the threat that her adultery might mean the introduction of illegitimate heirs into the family.

7. Law Commission, *Report on the Reform of the Grounds of Divorce*, 1966.

8. For example Leo Abse used this argument to considerable effect in the Divorce Reform Bill in 1969. Ronald Fletcher (1966) provided sociological and empirical arguments to support this view.

9. The Campaign for Justice on Divorce has reproduced figures from a written answer given by the Secretary of State for Social Services in 1979 which indicate that £72 million is spent to recover £20 million from ex-husbands. See *All Disquiet on the Divorce Front*, 1980.

10. See for example the work of Barrett (1980), Beechey (1979), or McDonough & Harrison (1978).

11. Examples of recent developments in a feminist analysis of law can be found in Allat (1981), Brophy & Smart (1981), and O'Donovan (1979).

References

ALLATT, P. (1981), 'Stereotyping: familism in the law'. In *Law, State & Society* (Fryer, B. *et al.*, eds.) (Croom Helm: London).

ARIES, P. (1979), *Centuries of Childhood* (Penguin: Harmondsworth).

BARRETT, M. (1980), *Women's Oppression Today* (Verso: London).

BARRETT, M. & McINTOSH, M. (1979), 'Christine Delphy: towards a materialist feminism?', *Feminist Review* 1.

172   The social and conceptual context

BAUER, C. & RITT, L. (eds.) (1979), *Free & Ennobled: Source Readings in the Development of Victorian Feminism* (Pergamon: London).

BEECHEY, V. (1979), 'On patriarchy', *Feminist Review 3*.

BOWLBY, J. (1979), *Maternal Care & Mental Health* (W.H.O.: Geneva).

BROPHY, J., & SMART, C. (1981), 'From disregard to disrepute: the position of women in family law', *Feminist Review 9*.

Campaign for Justice on Divorce (1980), *All Disquiet on the Divorce Front* C.J.D.).

COUSINS, M. (1980) 'Mens' rea: a note on sexual difference, criminology, and law'. In *Radical Issues in Criminology* (Carlen, P., & Collison, M., eds.) (Martin Robertson: Oxford).

DAVIN, A. (1978), 'Imperialism & motherhood', *History Workshop 5*.

DEECH, R. (1980), 'The case against legal recognition of cohabitation'. In *Marriage and Cohabitation in Contemporary Society* (Eekelaar, J., & Katz, S., eds.) (Butterworths: Toronto).

DONZELOT, J. (1980), *The Policing of Families* (Hutchinson: London).

FLETCHER, R. (1966), *Family & Marriage in Britain* (Penguin: Harmondsworth).

HALL, S. (1980), 'Reformism and the legislation of consent'. In *Permissiveness and Control* (ed.) (National Deviancy Conference, Macmillan: London).

LAND, H., & PARKER, R. (1978), 'Family policy in the U.K.' In *Family Policy* (Kamerman, S., & Kahn, A. J., eds.) (Columbia University Press: Guilford).

Law Commission (1966), 'Report on the Reform of the Grounds of Divorce', *Paper 6* (H.M.S.O.: London).

Law Commission (1979), 'Illegitimacy', *working Paper 74* (H.M.S.O.: London).

LEONARD, D. (1978), 'The regulation of marriage: repressive benevolence'. In *Power & the State* (Littlejohn, .G., et al., eds.) (Croom Helm: London).

MARSDEN, D. (1969), *Mothers Alone* (Allen Lane: London).

McDONOUGH, R. & HARRISON, R. (1978), 'Patriarchy & relations of production'. In *Feminism & Materialism* (Kuhn, A., & Wolpe, A. M., eds.) (R.K.P.: London).

McGREGOR, O. R. et al. (1970), *Separated Spouses* (Duckworth: London).

MURCH, M. (1980), *Justice & Welfare in Divorce* (Sweet & Maxwell: London).

O'DONOVAN, K. (1979), 'The male appendage: legal definitions of women'. In *Fit Work for Women* (Burman, S., ed.) (Croom Helm: London).

REISS, E. (1934), *The Rights & Duties of English Women* (Sherratt & Hughes: Manchester).

Rights of Women (1979), *Illegitimacy* (R.O.W.: London).

Royal Commission on Marriage & Divorce, 1951–1955. *Report 1956* (H.M.S.O.: London).

Society of Conservative Lawyers (1981), *The Future of Marriage* (Conservative Political Centre: London).

WESTERGAARD, J. & RESLER, H. (1975), *Class in a Capitalist Society* (Heinemann: London).

WILSON, E. (1980), *Only Half Way to Paradise* (Tavistock: London).

Part Two

Substantive aspects of family law

3. Partnership: entrances and exits

3.1. Marriage: An unnecessary legal concept?

E. M. CLIVE

In a book concerned with the underlying assumptions of modern marriage law it may be of interest to challenge the very prevalent assumption that marriage law is necessary. I shall do this from the point of view of a legislator in a western industrial state where there is a high marriage rate, a high divorce rate, and an unknown but growing number of cohabitations outside marriage. I shall draw my examples from the laws of the United Kingdom, because those are the laws I know best, but I believe that similar examples could be drawn from the laws of other countries. The question which I wish to confront is whether it is conceivable that a legal system might ignore marriage altogether, regarding it as a private or religious matter, no more regulated by law than friendship or entry into a religious order. I am not attacking or defending the social institution of marriage. I am concerned only with the legal concept of marriage, a technical matter which has no necessary relationship to the social institution.[1]

It seems fairly clear that marriage is not a necessary legal concept with regard to the personal effects of a couple's living together. There is no reason why the couple should not have complete freedom with regard to their name or names and the name or names of their children.[2] There is no reason why they should not be free to separate and set up other relationships as they please.[3] There is no need for any special rule on the nationality,[4] domicile,[5] or residence[6] of married persons. The rules formerly found in many legal systems to the effect that the wife owed obedience to the husband and that the husband could moderately chastise the wife are clearly unnecessary and intolerable.[7] The traditional obligations of married couples to live together and be sexually faithful to each other are manifestly unenforceable in modern conditions and could be discarded without any difficulty.[8]

It is also clear that marriage is not a necessary legal concept in relation to children. In many countries children are now in exactly the same legal position whatever their parents' marital status. There is a growing realization in other countries that it is unjust to discriminate against children because of their parents' non-compliance with the marriage laws. Illegitimacy is on the way out.[9]

In relation to the laws of contract and tort or delict, marriage can easily be disregarded. Liability for household supplies can be left to depend on ordinary legal principles applying equally to any cohabiting couple, whether married or not.[10] Claims for damages for wrongful death can be allowed on the basis of factual dependency, or compensation based on tort or delict can be abolished altogether and replaced by benefits under a national insurance scheme which concentrates on factual dependency.[11]

In many systems there are special rules affecting spouses engaged in litigation. There is clearly no need for any rule that spouses cannot sue each other in the courts in the normal way.[12] Nor is there any difficulty about various archaic privileges in the law of evidence—such as privileges attaching to evidence of marital communications or marital intercourse. These can be swept away with advantage.[13] There is more difficulty about the rule that one spouse cannot be compelled to testify against the other in criminal proceedings. Many people would find the abolition of this rule repugnant. There are two questions here. First, should the state, out of decency or a shrewd estimation of the value of the evidence foregone, renounce the evidence of certain people having a close relationship with the accused? That involves a value judgement and the answer could go either way. Secondly, if the answer is Yes, what relationships should be taken into account? It is not immediately obvious that marriage is the best or only criterion which can be used. There seems no real reason for the state to do without the evidence of an estranged spouse, or a spouse who has been party to a marriage of convenience designed purely to prevent his or her evidence being used.[14] On the other hand the considerations which suggest that a loving wife should not be compelled to testify against her husband apply equally to a loving cohabitee. Indeed if cohabitation outside marriage became as common as marriage the present rule would become indefensible.

Marriage may have certain effects in the criminal law. Again some of these may be archaic rules which could be discarded with advantage, such as the rule that a husband cannot be charged for raping his wife, or the rule that a husband and wife cannot be convicted of conspiracy where they are the only parties to the conspiracy.[15] Some people would feel less happy about discarding the rule, found in some legal systems, that intercourse with a step-daughter is incest. Yet some countries have no such rule[16] and, quite apart from the broader question whether incest should be a criminal offence at all, it is very hard to justify a rule which makes sexual relations between consenting, genetically unrelated *adults* a crime. There are other ways of protecting vulnerable children and young people. Clearly marriage is not a necessary concept in this area. In relation to bigamy the question to be asked is not whether marriage is a necessary prerequisite for this crime. It clearly is: the two stand or fall together. The real question is whether the abolition of marriage and bigamy together would leave a vacuum in which women would be dangerously exposed to exploitation by men falsely claiming to commit themselves to a long-term relationship. It is doubtful whether marriage and bigamy provide any real protection at present. The danger of exploitation in personal and sexual relationships is always present but there is very little that the law can do about it. My own guess is that the abolition of the legal concept of marriage and the crime of bigamy would make very little difference in this area.

In tax law and social security law the concept of marriage is already widely supplemented by reference to factual cohabitation.[17] There is no reason why non-contributory systems concerned with needs and means should not disregard legal relationships and concentrate on factual relationships. Nor is there any reason why contributory benefits for dependants should not be paid on the basis of actual dependency. There is something absurd about paying a widow's pension to a woman who has been separated from her husband for 40 years after, say, one night's cohabitation and not paying it to the woman with whom the deceased has cohabited for the last 40 years.

Indeed if the object is the relief of need it is not immediately obvious why the old widow or the old cohabitee should be preferred to the old spinster who has never cohabited with anyone, while if the object is the payment of benefits bought by contributions it is not immediately obvious why the contributor should not be allowed to nominate the beneficiary. On either view, marriage is irrelevant. It may be objected that while a man can have only one wife he may have several cohabitees and that the state could not afford to abandon the 'one man–one woman' system. Two answers may be ventured. First, a man may already have several wives successively in a contribution career. So nothing would change in that respect. The one man–one woman system has already been abandoned. Secondly, if one man has several concurrent cohabitees then the chances are that some other man has none. Unless large numbers of cohabitees are drafted in from overseas it is unlikely that the pool of dependent women would be increased by abolishing marriage. There is, in any event, something fundamentally repulsive about this whole idea of dependent women. The long-term goal in this area should be the abolition of private dependency, by encouraging independence and treating poverty as an individual rather than a family phenomenon. Even before that goal is reached, however, it does not seem necessary to preserve the legal concept of marriage for the purposes of tax and social security laws.

Nothing in the above is very new or very surprising. The three great trends—towards liberty, equality, and secularity—have been around for a very long time.[18] The removal of most legal effects from marriage is just their culmination. In relation to finance and property, however, the matter is not so simple. It can be argued that real liberty and real equality require that wives be given maintenance and property rights against their husbands and that there are very good reasons for not extending these rights to unmarried cohabitees. The classical form of this argument is that husbands earn money and accumulate property while their wives do unpaid work looking after the home and the children. Therefore justice requires that the wives be given maintenance rights and claims against the husbands' income and property, at least on the breakdown of the marriage. There is obviously something suspect about this argument. It is a bit like saying that the remedy for slavery is to give the slaves rights to maintenance and rights to share in the master's property if he dies or goes out of business. I shall return to this point later. For the moment I am concerned only to point out that, while few family lawyers with any claims to liberal or egalitarian views would argue that a wife's domicile should automatically follow her husband's or that a wife should owe a duty of obedience to her husband, there are plenty to argue that a wife should have generous maintenance rights, succession rights, and matrimonial property rights. We are obviously in a more difficult area here.

In a very theoretical sense, of course, marriage is obviously not a necessary legal concept in relation to finance and property. The state could base a private law right to maintenance on factual criteria such as the existence of dependent children or the length of dependent cohabitation or, more radically, it could provide a guaranteed maintenance allowance for all citizens who are not self-supporting, thus removing the need for any private law right of maintenance. It could decline to provide for any financial adjustment on divorce[19] or could provide a form of adjustment equally appropriate to cases of cohabitation without marriage. It could ignore marriage completely in relation to the ownership and management of property during life,[20] and could give succession rights, in so far as it resisted the temptation to confiscate for the common good, only to those who were factually, rather than legally, in a close relationship to the deceased. All these things would be legislatively possible, but it would be unsatisfactory to stop at this theoretical level. What has to be asked is whether the abolition of the legal concept of marriage would lead to such undesirable consequences in relation to finance and property as to be a practical impossibility.

The obligation of maintenance or support is often regarded as one of the fundamental effects of marriage. Its abolition would be viewed by many people with horror. Yet several factors have to be borne in ind in considering this question. First, most couples support each other willingly and gladly so long as their relationship continues. They would continue to do so if legal obligations based on marriage were removed. Second, maintenance claims are notoriously difficult to enforce once the relationship has broken down. Third, there is a close relationship between private maintenance and social security. It has been shown, for example, that in the United Kingdom most separated spouses are better off on supplementary benefit than on maintenance awarded by the courts.[22] Fourth, there is a close relationship between private maintenance and patterns of employment. If both sexes have genuinely equal employment opportunities and if there are generous child-minding allowances for the years devoted to bringing up dependent children, there is at the very least a much diminished need for a private law of maintenance. Fifth, there is an interesting relationship between private maintenance and tax policy. Let us assume that from the point of view of society it does not matter which set of dependants a wage earner supports so long as he or she takes a share in the cost of bringing up the next generation. If this is so, then the obvious way of dealing with those who do not share this burden is to tax them heavily.[21] If a man walks out on his wife and young children and does not acquire a new family it may make more sense to extract his share of the social cost of dependency by taxation than by trying to recover maintenance specifically for his abandoned family. There would certainly be much less moral indignation about men 'getting off with it' by walking out on their dependants if they were walking into the rapacious arms of the tax collector. In passing it may be noted that if a man does acquire a new set of dependants it makes more sense to let him support them than to try to force him to support the old family and neglect the new.[23] In the light of these observations let us consider what would actually happen if the private law obligation of maintenance between spouses were abolished. The position would vary from country to country. In the United Kingdom it would be as follows. First of all, millions of happily married couples would continue to support each other as at present. Second, the many thousands of separated spouses who rely exclusively or mainly on supplementary benefit would continue to do so.[24] Third, the many thousands of separated spouses who support themselves by working would continue to do so.[25] Fourth, those in receipt of maintenance for children would continue to receive it. That would leave a comparatively small proportion of spouses (in practice almost entirely wives) worse off because they would no longer have a claim for maintenance. In the case of those without dependent children who had not lost anything by the marriage there would be no good reason for conferring a right to claim maintenance. In the case of those with dependent children or those who were otherwise in a worse position[27] as a result of the marriage there would be a good reason for conferring a right to some sort of maintenance or financial provision *but the reason would be equally applicable to cohabitees in a similar position*. In short, the abolition of maintenance obligations between spouses would not be an unthinkable or undesirable proposition (even if we accept the dependent position of many women in present circumstances), if maintenance or financial provision were awarded on the basis of dependent children and loss suffered as a result of cohabitation. And this would, to my mind, be a sensible basis. It would be unjustifiable to extend to cohabitees rights to maintenance and financial provision based on the idea of voluntary assumption of liability.[28] Often this would be lacking. It would be perfectly justifiable to give them rights (unless they expressly contracted out) based on child-related dependency and other losses resulting from the relationship.

Exactly the same considerations apply to financial provision on divorce except that here the notion of a continuing obligation of support based on a voluntary assumption of the burden is even less appropriate if it is accepted that the object of divorce is to terminate the legal relationship resulting from the marriage. In the words of the Scottish Law Commission 'financial provision on divorce should not be based on the principle that there is a continuing alimentary relationship between the parties. Rather, its purpose should be to adjust equitably the economic advantages and disadvantages arising from the marriage, in so far as this adjustment is not made by other branches of the law.'[29] Although the Commission did not consider the question of financial provision for cohabitees on the break-up of the relationship their equitable adjustment approach is eminently suitable to that situation.

I have no wish to add to the extensive literature on the merits and demerits of different systems of matrimonial property. I would merely like to submit that a system which ignores marriage is perfectly practicable and can be reasonably acceptable. My evidence for this submission is the Scottish experience. Since 1920 the general rule in Scots law has been that marriage has no effect on the ownership and management of property. With a few very minor and unimportant exceptions married couples are treated in exactly the same way as cohabiting couples who are not married. Couples are free to opt out b ante-nuptial or post-nuptial marriage contract but such contracts, although common before separate property was introduced, are now virtually unknown in practice. Many couples do, however, have their houses and their investments, if any, in joint names.[31] This system has proved to be practicable. In recent years, however, its harshness has been criticized. The main criticism has been that the spouse who happens to be owner or tenant of the matrimonial home can turn the other spouse out on to the street like an uninvited guest and cannot himself be ordered to leave the home no matter how violent he may be. The Scottish Law Commission has suggested a system of occupancy rights and exclusion orders to remedy these defects in the law.[32] The Commission appeared to concede that there was a case for extending protection against violence to unmarried cohabitees and invited views on how this could best be done.[33] They concluded, however, that 'the law should not concede to an "unmarried spouse" with whom the owner or tenant of a dwelling is cohabiting the same occupancy rights as are proposed for spouses'. They argued first that the case had not been made out for a general principle of extending matrimonial property rules to couples cohabiting without marriage. They pointed out that 'one of the reasons why some unmarried cohabiting couples do not enter into marriage is that they wish to retain the freedom and other advantages associated with single status. They may not want, for example, to be subject to the powers of the courts to adjust property rights on divorce. If this assumption is correct, then arguably it is unduly paternalistic and inappropriate for the state to claim that it knows better and to foist the trammels of marital property law on them. There is a lot of force in this argument in so far as it relates to the extension of a full community property system to unmarried couples, and some force in it in relation to the complicated and far-reaching system of occupancy rights proposed by the Commission. There is, however, no force in the argument if all that is proposed is a limited protection against being thrown out on to the street. That is all that is required to remedy the worst feature of the present system and such an elementary protection could, and in my view, should be extended to unmarried cohabitees. It is a simple question of choosing between protection of property interests and a minimal protection of personal security, and it is hard to see that marriage has anything to do with it. The Commission's second argument was that 'to give unmarried cohabitation the same property consequences as marriage itself would sooner or later mean the end of marriage as an institution'. On this I would make two comments. First, if by 'institution' the Commission meant 'social institution' then I simply do not believe their assertion. It seems to me to be absurd to suggest that nowadays people marry exclusively or primarily for property reasons. Secondly, if the Commission was referring to the end of marriage as a legal institution, then my comment would be, so what? There is nothing in the statute setting up the Commission which requires them to preserve the legal institution of marriage even if this means inflicting hardship and injustice on certain individuals. We may have here a very good example of an underlying assumption about marriage law—the assumption that it must be preserved at all costs.

There has been some interest in Scotland in the idea of joint ownership of the matrimonial home by operation of law, on the lines recommended by the English Law Commission.[35] The usual arguments in favour of such a scheme are (1) that it recognizes the wife's work in the home and (2) that it expresses the idea of fair sharing which underlies marriage.[36] The first argument is patently unsound if it amounts to the claim that all wives do work in the home which can be fairly recompensed by, and only by, giving them a half-share in it. Some wives do less work in the home than they would if they were employed and live at a higher standard of living than they would if they were employed. Generally speaking the wealthier the husband the less housework the traditionally oriented housewife does, so that the effect of this proposal is that the housewives who work most get least and those who work least get most—a curious form of justice. The fundamental objection to this argument based on the value of the housewife's work is that it assumes the continuance of sex roles which are becoming obsolete. The second argument—that co-ownership expresses the idea of fair sharing which underlies marriage—is more attractive. Certainly a social survey carried out in England revealed massive support for the proposition that the home and its contents should legally be jointly owned by the husband

and wife irrespective of who paid for it. Ninety-one per cent of husbands and 94% of wives agreed with the proposition. This, of course, invites the reply that if spouses are so keen on sharing they can always share voluntarily. There seems little need for very complicated legislation which would apply only to those spouses who own their homes,[38] who do not voluntarily take the title in joint names,[39] and who do not jointly opt out of the new scheme. I do not wish to elaborate on this question which is a difficult and controversial one. I wish only to observe that the 'housewife's contribution' argument is based unsoundly on a view of marriage which is not now universally held and that the 'imposed fair sharing' argument would have more force if voluntary fair sharing not so readily available and so clearly approved of by an overwhelming majority of couples. At the very least it can be said that the arguments for statutory co-ownership of the matrimonial home are not overwhelming. As there is not a strong demand for more extensive forms of community property, my conclusion is that a separate property system, which ignores marriage, is not only workable but also reasonably acceptable and defensible provided that certain minor adjustments are made. I have already mentioned protection against precipitate eviction and domestic violence. This should apply to unmarried cohabiting couples as well as to married couples. Adjustments are also needed in relation to the ownership of household furniture and effects. At the moment in Scots law the ordinary principles of property law are applied. The process of deciding, on the basis of such principles, which spouse owns which piece of furniture is artificial in the extreme. There should be a presumption of joint ownership of the household effects of cohabiting spouses. Again, however, the difficulties are due to the factual situation—the shared life, the pooled resources—and not to the legal tie of marriage. They exist also in the case of unmarried cohabiting couples. The presumption should apply in such cases also. In short, marriage is not a necessary legal concept in relation to the ownership and management of property.

The law of succession has reflected different traditions, values, and policies at different times and places.[40] The prevailing view in the United Kingdom seems to be that the law of succession in general should strike a balance between the wishes of the deceased and a reasonable provision for family members and dependants,[41] and that the law of intestate succession should be based on the supposed wishes of the ordinary testator. It should make for him the sort of will he would have made for himself if he had got round to it.[42] In so far as the law is based on the actual wishes of testators it is clear that marriage is an unnecessary concept. In relation to the supposed wishes of testators it seems to be the case that most testators do in fact make their surviving wife or husband their main or only beneficiary, but this fact must be interpreted with caution. It is likely that it is not the legal tie of marriage which is important in the minds of these testators, so much as the emotional tie. It would be very surprising if the average testator would prefer his separated wife to his actual cohabitee. Without further investigation we cannot be sure that a will in favour of 'my wife' is not really a will in favour of 'the woman with whom I have shared my life for the last 40 years'. The position of the surviving spouse under the laws of intestate succession in the United Kingdom has improved dramatically in the present century, to such an extent that he or she very often takes the whole estate, but it may be that the improvement has been based on insufficiently precise information and that it should have been directed towards cohabiting spouses or cohabiting 'unmarried spouses'.

A question in the social survey recently commissioned by the Scottish Law Commission on Family Property in Scotland will explore attitudes to succession by cohabitees. It will be interesting to see the results. In so far as the policy of the law is to ensure a reasonable provision for family members and dependants, it is again arguable that marriage is not a necessary legal concept. The English Law Commission has come close to recognizing this. In their Report on Family Provision on Death they recommended that 'the class of applicants entitled to apply for family provision should be extended to include any person who was being wholly or partly maintained by the deceased immediately before his death'.[43] This would include the cohabitee. The Commission thought that such a solution would often reflect the wishes of the deceased.[44] However, the Commission also recommended that the non-judicially separated spouse should be in a preferred position. He or she would not need to prove dependency and would have a claim not just for reasonable maintenance (as in the case of other applicants) but for 'such financial provision as it would be reasonable in all the circumstances of the case for a husband or wife to receive, whether or not that provision is required for his or her maintenance'.[45] The Commission gave no reasons for requiring cohabitees, but not spouses, to prove dependency. They gave three reasons for giving the surviving spouse a claim not limited to reasonable maintenance. The first was that a social survey indicated that 'the general public were prepared to see it [i.e. family provision on death] assume a wider role in the case of a surviving spouse'.[46] However, the survey in question was limited to married and formerly married people and did not ask

them about their attitudes to family provision for cohabitees or other factual dependants. Nor did it distinguish between cohabiting and separated
spouses. It therefore provided no basis at all for a conclusion that the general public wished the new extended role of family provision to be confined to surviving spouses. The second reason for giving surviving
spouses a claim to more than reasonable maintenance was that they
could get more than this on divorce and that the position of the surviving
spouse should be no less favourable than that of the divorcing spouse.
This would be a satisfying reason only if one were satisfied (*a*) that the
analogy with divorce is helpful[47] (*b*) that the law on the objectives of
financial provision on divorce was satisfactory,[48] and (*c*) that adequate
consideration had been given to the question of extending the adjustment mechanisms of divorce to terminated cohabitations. The
Commission's third reason was that nothing had emerged in the course
of their consultations to suggest that 'in the case of persons other than
the surviving spouse the function of family provision legislation should
be extended beyond making reasonable provision for their maintenance'.[49] As the general public were not asked about cohabitees' claims
it is not surprising that they expressed no view on them. The Commission's arguments for placing the surviving spouse (even, it should be
noted, the factually separated spouse) in a privileged legal position in
relation to family provision are not convincing. It would clearly be possible to devise a system on the English model which would protect the reasonable claims and expectations of surviving cohabitees whether married
or not.

I have been talking so far about the legal effects of marriage and I hope
I have shown that there need be none. The codes, the statutes, and the
textbooks all devote just as much, if not more, space to the rules on
entering into marriage and on getting out of it by divorce or annulment.
If marriage disappeared as a legal concept all these would disappear.
There would be no rules on under-age marriages, on marriages between
near relatives, or on marriages with mental defectives. However, where
there is a real danger of harm the criminal law can provide sanctions[50]
and where there is no real danger of harm there is no need for any restriction. It is not the law of marriage which protects young and weak-
minded girls from sexual exploitation.[51] Divorce would also disappear if
there were no marriage. Is there anyone, apart from those with a financial interest in it, who would regret its passing? I have already dealt with
the question of financial adjustments on divorce. Some may think that
divorce is an opportunity to protect the interests of children. By all means

let us protect the interests of children but let us not imagine that all children of separating couples need our officious intervention, or that all children of cohabiting couples do not; or that divorce, which may come months or years after the period of maximum stress, is the best occasion for intervention in those rare cases where intervention is necessary.[52]

If marriage is not a necessary legal concept, is it none the less a convenient legal concept? This, I think, depends entirely on the extent to which the category 'marriages' overlaps the category 'cohabiting couples'.

If almost all married couples are cohabiting and if almost all cohabiting couples are married (Fig. 1) then it is convenient enough to frame rules on the various matters I have discussed in terms of marriage. If, say, 50% of married couples are not cohabiting and 50% of cohabiting couples are not married (Fig. 2) it would be inconvenient and unjust to frame rules on these matters in terms of marriage. If almost all married couples were not cohabiting and almost all cohabiting couples were not married (Fig. 3)—an unlikely position—then it would be absurd to use marriage as a test in relation to laws on, for example, evidence, damages for death, pensions, property, presumptions of paternity, or taxation.

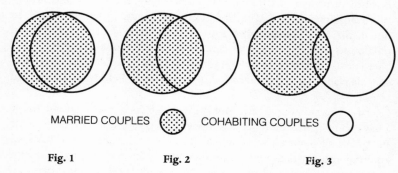

MARRIED COUPLES ⬚   COHABITING COUPLES ◯

Fig. 1   **Fig. 2**   **Fig. 3**

It may be that in the future marriage will become both an unnecessary and an inconvenient legal concept in various European countries. If so we shall have to give some thought to Article 12 of the European Convention on Human Rights which states that 'men and women of marriageable age have the right to marry and to found a family, according to the national laws governing the exercise of this right'. What are the underlying assumptions of that provision? Would it be breached if a country abolished marriage as a legal concept but gave its inhabitants complete freedom to participate in such religious or social marriage ceremonies as they thought fit?

Notes

1. There are legal marriages in which there is not even any cohabitation or sexual intercourse. Such limited purpose or sham marriages are treated in different ways in different legal systems but I am not aware of any legal system which regards them all as void. I am not aware, for example, of any legal system which would regard as void a marriage entered into solely to legitimize a child, even if there was no cohabitation or sexual intercourse after the marriage.

2. In the United Kingdom a person is free, as a general rule, to use whatever name he or she wishes. Names are a matter of usage, not law. The English courts, however, have got into a bit of a mess over the names of children after divorce. See e.g. *D.* v. *B.* [1979] All E.R. 92.

3. In the United Kingdom they are free to do so *in fact* at the moment whether married or not.

4. In the United Kingdom the present law is that marriage has no automatic effect on citizenship although a woman who has been married to a citizen of the United Kingdom and Colonies can acquire such citizenship by registration under s. 6 (2) of the British Nationality Law (Cmnd 6795, 1977) canvassed the possibility that wives should be required to take out naturalization in the ordinary way. This would solve the problem of sham marriages for nationality purposes and if the naturalization rules are flexible and generous would not cause hardship.

5. In the United Kingdom the rule that the wife took her husband's domicile was abolished by the Domicile and Matrimonial Proceedings Act 1973.

6. There has never been any rule in the United Kingdom that a wife's residence or habitual residence followed that of her husband, one of the attractions of these concepts being their freedom from legal technicalities.

7. As late as 1951 a leading Scottish textbook claimed that such rules still formed part of Scots law. See Walton, Frederick P., *Husband and Wife* (W. Greer and Son, Edinburgh, 3rd edn. 1951), 101. This is no longer so. See Clive and Wilson, *Husband and Wife* (W. Greer and Son, Edinburgh, 1974, 178–9). It has been held in England that a husband has no right to prevent his wife from having an abortion. See *Paton* v. *Trustees of B.P.A.S.* [1978] 2 All E.R. 987.

8. In England the remedy of restitution of conjugal rights, which had become meaningless, was abolished by the Matrimonial Proceedings and Property Act 1970, s. 10. In Scotland an action for adherence—to order the other spouse to cohabit—is still competent but will not be enforced. In both countries the right of a husband to claim damages from anyone committing adultery with his wife has been abolished. See law Reform (Miscellaneous Provisions) Act 1970 s. 4; Divorce (Scotland) Act 1976, s. 10.

9. The English Law Commission has published a Working Paper tentatively favoring the complete abolition of the legal concept of illegitimacy. Published Working Paper No. 74, *Illegitimacy*, 1979.

10. In England the so-called wife's agency of necessity was abolished by the Matrimonial Proceedings and Property Act 1970 s. 41 (1). As a result the special chapter on the 'Agency of Married Women etc.' has been deleted from the latest edition of Bowstead on *Agency* (Sweet and Maxwell, London, 14th edn., 1976) as 'the position of a wife in the law of agency no longer requires separate treatment' (p. 94). In Scotland liability for a spouse's debts depends on ordinary principles of the law of contract and unjustified enrichment—See Clive and Wilson, op. cit. 253, 263.

11. Neither of these results has yet been reached in the United Kingdom. The Royal Commission on Civil Liability and Compensation for Personal Injury considered the cohabitee's claim sympathetically but decided to make no recommendation for or against it. Cmnd 7054—I (1978) para. 405.

12. The Law Reform (Husband and Wife) Act 1962 (applying to England and Scotland) removed the last restriction on litigation between spouses by allowing spouses to sue each other in tort of delict. The court has a power to dismiss the proceedings if no substantial benefit would accrue to either party by their continuation. This power seems to be rarely, if ever, used and is unnecessary. There are other disincentives to frivolous litigation.

13. The Civil Evidence Act 1968 s. 16 abolished, for civil proceedings in England, the privileges attaching to marital communications and to evidence of marital intercourse. The Criminal Law Revision Committee recommended that in England a spouse should be a competent witness for the prosecution but should be compellable only in certain cases (e.g. family violence). See the Committee's Eleventh Report (Cmnd 4991, 1972) para. 153.

14. Cf. *Hoskin* v. *Commissioner of Police* [1978] 2 All E.R. 136 (accused married his victim two days before trial).

15. Cf. *Midland Bank Trust Co. Ltd.* v. *Green* [1979] 2 All E.R. 193 (where the rule was held not to apply to civil liability for the tort of conspiracy). There is no trace of this rule in Scots law and it has been vigorously rejected in the United States. See *U.S.* v. *Dege* 364 U.S. 51 (1960).

16. See generally on this question the papers by Peigné, Manchester, Cooper, and Senaeve presented at the Second World Conference of the International Society on Family Law and reproduced in *Family Violence*, edited by Eekelaar, John M., and Katz, Sanford N. (Butterworths, Toronto, 1978).

17. In the United Kingdom the best known example is the rule that, for purposes of supplementary benefit, 'where a husband and wife are members of the same household their requirements and resources shall be aggregated and shall be treated as the husband's, and similarly, unless there are exceptional circumstances, as regards two people cohabiting as man and wife'. Supplementary Benefits Act 1976, Sch. 1 para. 3. There are many other examples. See Clive and Wilson, op. cit., pp. 390–404.

18. See Rheinstein, 'Trends in Marriage and Divorce Law of Western Countries', 18 *Law and Contemporary Problems* (1953) 3.

19. This was the Scottish position, in relation to wage or salary earners without capital, from the 16th century until 1964.

20. This has been the Scots law since 1920, with some very minor and unimportant exceptions. See Clive and Wilson, op. cit., 289.

21. The question, from another point of view, is who should pay for the upbringing of the next generation—only those who have children or everybody? The existence of free education, health, and other social services means that the idea that only those who have children should bear this burden has long been discarded.

22. Report of the Finer Committee on One Parent Families, pp. 98–99 (Cmnd 5629, 1974).

23. This has been recognized in the United Kingdom for some time and is reflected in the policies of the Supplementary Benefits Commission and their predecessors the National Assistance Board. See the Finer Committee Report (cit. *supra*) pp. 132–7.

24. See the Finer Committee Report (cit. *supra*) p. 244. Fifty per cent of fatherless families other than widows' families had supplementary benefits as their main source of income.

25. Thirty-five per cent of the above families had earnings as their main source of income. Ibid.

26. Only $12^1/_2\%$ of the above families had maintenance as their main source of income. Ibid.

27. I am assuming here the absence of those radical changes in employment, tax, and social security laws which might ensure that people were not normally in a worse position as a result of marriage.

28. Cf. the Scottish Law Commission's Memorandum on *Aliment and Financial Provision* (Memo No. 22, 1976) para. 2.11 where they express the view that the basis of an alimentary obligation should not be the mere existence of a blood tie but 'for instance, that the person in question has himself assumed the liability (by marriage, for example, or by bringing a child into the world, or by adopting a child) or may be equitably bound to aliment someone (such as an aged parent) who has supported him at an earlier stage in life'.

29. Op. cit. para. 3.7. In retrospect the major weakness of the Commission's approach is the importance placed on the distinction between aliment between spouses and financial provision on divorce. The distinction is legally relevant: in the one case a legal relationship exists; in the other it is terminated. But it is doubtful if it is factually important. There would be much to be said for applying the Commission's 'equitable adjustment on breakdown' approach to all cases.

30. See Clive and Wilson, op. cit., 289.

31. Exact figures are not available although a survey on Family Property in Scotland is currently being carried out for the Scottish Law Commission by the Office of Population Censuses and Surveys. A recent survey in England found that 52% of spouses in owner-occupied accommodation had the house

in joint names. Todd and Jones, *Matrimonial Property* H.M.S.O., Office of Population Censuses and Surveys, London, 1972).

32. Scottish Law Commission, *Occupancy Rights in the Matrimonial Home and Domestic Violence* (Memorandum No. 41, 1978).

33. The Family Violence (Scotland) Bill 1979, introduced by George Reid M.P., would have applied equally to married couples and couples cohabiting without marriage. This Bill fell on the dissolution of Parliament.

34. Memo, No. 41, cit. *supra*, Vol. 2, p. 140.

35. See the Law Commission's *Third Report on Family Property: the Matrimonial Home (Co-ownership and Occupation Rights) and Household Goods* (Law Com. No. 86, 1978). The Scottish Law Commission has the question of matrimonial property and succession law on its agenda and has commissioned a social survey on the topic. This will include couples cohabiting outside marriage and attitudes towards the effect which cohabitation should have on property.

36. See the Law Commission's *First Report on Family Property: A New Approach* (Law Com. No. 52, 1973) paras. 12–18, 21–30.

37. Ibid. para. 22.

38. In Scotland only 32.8% of dwellings are owner-occupied, 53.7% are public sector tenancies.

39. Increasing numbers of couples do so. See Todd and Jones, op. cit., 79. Where the spouses bought their home before 1940 only 20% had it in joint names. Where they bought it in the 1970s 74% had it in joint names.

40. See Fleming J. G., 'Changing Functions of Succession Laws', 26 *American Journal of Comparative Law* (1978), 233.

41. This balancing exercise is performed in different ways in England and Scotland. In England the general principle is freedom of testation but spouses, children, and other dependants (including cohabitees) can apply to the court for a financial provision out of the deceased's estate. Inheritance (Provision for Family and Dependants) Act 1975. In Scotland the surviving spouse and children can claim fixed legal rights out of the moveable estate of the deceased. The cohabitee has no claim. See Meston, Mildred C., *The Succession (Scotland) Act 1964* (W. Green & Son, Edinburgh, 2nd edn., 1969).

42. In England the rules of intestate succession were modelled on the provisions of the typical will in the central repository of wills. Fleming, loc. cit. *supra*. The Mackintosh Committee on the Law of Succession in Scotland based its recommendations expressly on the principle stated in the text and received evidence from solicitors about the contents of typical wills. (Cmd 8144, 1963, para. 6).

43. Law Com. No. 61 (1974) 92.

44. Even if it ran counter to his will, his will may have been stale or may have operated in a way he did not anticipate. If he had been living with a woman and had children by her it would, the Commission thought, be unlikely that he would wish the children to inherit to the exclusion of their mother. Ibid. para. 90.

45. Ibid. p. 82, now in the Inheritance (Provision for Family and Dependants) Act 1975, s.1.
46. Ibid. para. 13.
47. The two positions differ fundamentally in that on divorce the interests of the other spouse have to be taken into account whereas on death they do not. If the analogy were helpful it would still seem strange to analogize from divorce to death rather than the other way about.
48. It is not, in England, as it is still torn between providing continuing support and adjusting the consequences of a dead relationship on the basis of accrued rights. See Cretney, S. M., *Principles of Family Law* (Sweet and Maxwell, London, 3rd edn., 1979), 334–5.
49. Law Com. No. 61 para. 24.
50. In the United Kingdom, for example, it is a criminal offence to have sexual intercourse with a girl under 16, with certain near relatives, or with a mentally defective female (as defined).
51. Indeed in Scotland the position is quite the reverse. It is a defence for a man accused of unlawful intercourse with a young girl or mentally defective woman to prove that she is his wife. See *Henry Watson* (1885) 5 Couper 696.
52. In the absence of a custody dispute between the parents (which could, of course, be brought to court as an independent process) the courts in the United Kingdom very rarely disturb the arrangements made by the parties themselves for the children. See Eekelaar and Clive, *Custody after Divorce* (Centre for Socio-Legal Studies, Oxford, 1977).

3.2. Australia: A proposal for reform

KATHLEEN FUNDER

In Australia, as in many Western countries (OECD 1990), the economic hardship of marriage breakdown falls heavily on women with dependent children. Recognition of this economic burden and of its unequal division, can be seen in recent inquiries and reviews, including the Maintenance Inquiry (1986), and the Social Security Review (1986a). Actual and proposed reforms appear to have three main objectives: the alleviation of poverty, a reduction in public costs associated with the support of lone-parent families, and a more equal distribution of the hardship of divorce.

The dimensions of hardship

The Australian Family Law Act 1975 introduced non-fault divorce and marked a watershed in marriage dissolution, with the rates in the 1980s plateauing at a very much higher level than would have been predicted a decade before. By 1987 the crude divorce rate in Australia was 2.1 divorces per 1,000 population, a figure which has been fairly stable in recent years. The Australian Institute of Family Studies (AIFS) estimates indicate that 30–3 per cent of marriages contracted in the 1970s will end in divorce, with a small decline predicted in the future, based on a tendency towards later marriage and a lower marriage rate. The divorce rate in 1987 was 11 per 1,000 married women, with the highest rate of 18.7 per cent applying at ages 25–9. In that year 39,700 divorces were granted, involving 44,000 dependent children.

In 1985 Australia had about four million families, 2.18 million (54.6 per cent) of which were families with dependent children. Of these families with dependent children 315,000 (14.4 per cent) had only one parent, and 261,000 (83.0 per cent) of the lone-parent families were receiving some social security payments (Social Security Review 1986b). Most lone-parent families (278,000 or 88.2 per cent) are female-headed, and these women and their children are more likely than male-headed families to be in receipt of pensions or benefits.

Lone-parent families are more likely to be poor. In 1981–2, 56.2 per cent (177,000) of female lone parents were in the lowest decile of unit incomes, compared with 17.2 per cent (6,200) of their male counterparts and 3.5 per cent of married couples. Thus being female increases by almost thirtyfold the chances of being a very poor lone parent. Most (63.2 per cent) female lone parents received their main income from social security/welfare sources (Social Security Review 1986b). In the decade 1978–88 the number of beneficiaries had more than trebled, with a commensurate growth in costs.

The Family Law Act—provisions for financial settlements

Three means of achieving just and equitable financial outcomes are available under the Family Law Act. First, property can be reallocated between the parties. Secondly, adjustment may be made through the award of spousal maintenance, subject to the twin conditions of the needs of one spouse and the capacity to pay off the other. Thirdly, child maintenance orders may transfer money from the non-resident parent to the resident parent on the basis of continuing shared responsibility for the financial support of children of the marriage. A major difference between the property and maintenance orders is that maintenance orders may be adjusted according to changing needs and capacities to pay, while property settlements are immutable.

Under the Australian Family Law Act 1975 marriage does not change the property rights of the individual. Without an assumption of community of property, no base line for its division applies. In Mallett's case, the High Court rejected a 50 : 50 baseline for property division, leaving judges with wide discretionary powers in allocating property in order to arrive at a just and equitable outcome. Two broad sets of considerations are applied in reaching such a settlement: the contributions each party has made to the economy of the marriage and their respective needs after the dissolution. Contributions to the economic partnership of the marriage may be both financial and non-financial, direct and indirect. Thus home-making and child-rearing, as well as contributions from the money economy, are included in assessing how much each has invested (Family Law Act, s. 79 (4)). A list of possible sources of need may also be weighed by the court in arriving at a fair and equitable settlement (FLA s. 75 (2)). Basically, needs are assessed in terms of post-separation circumstances, whereas contributions concern the efforts of the parties during the marriage. Such a neat division serves a useful purpose in dividing the law into manageable segments for reference; it is rarely so easy to divide life circumstances into pre- and post-separation phases, or into contributions without consequences or needs unrelated to marriage.

Under section 81 of the Family Law Act the court shall, as far as practicable, make such orders as will finally determine the financial relationships between the parties to the marriage and avoid further proceedings between them. This section is an endorsement of the clean-break framework. Whether by design or by accident, spousal maintenance orders, as they are currently used, fit more or less well within the clean-break principle. Orders are relatively rare and ongoing orders are commonly complied with only until property settlements are finalized (Harrison 1986).

Child maintenance orders are made on the basis of the needs of the children and the responsibility of both parents to provide care and support for them. Orders are not final in intent, since they are meant to be responsive to children's changing needs and parents' changing circumstances. In practice, however, the AIFS survey data show that such orders, when made, were commonly not varied and thus remained at their original level, or were simply not complied with (Harrison and McDonald 1988). The new Child Support Scheme, introduced in 1988, is designed to increase both compliance with orders and the amount of child maintenance paid.

Problem areas of the law under review

Criticisms of the operation of the law received by a Joint Select Committee of the Federal Parliament (1980) were that wide discretion resulted in uncertainty, inconsistency, and excessive legal costs. In 1983 the Attorney-General referred the issue of Matrimonial Property to the Australian Law Reform Commission. An AIFS survey, designed to provide a representative picture of the economic consequences of marriage breakdown and the role of the law, showed that for families with dependent children economic hardship fell disproportionately on women (Weston 1986).

Women living alone or as lone parents experienced a drastic fall in living standards three to five years after separation. Their average household income was just over 50 per cent of the pre-separation income; men who had not repartnered had about 80 per cent of their pre-separation household income. However, as in this study most women who had not repartnered were caring for two children, over half still ended up living in poverty in spite of any maintenance paid. Only 13 per cent of single men were similarly poor, and many were better off on an income–needs ratio than before separation. Contrary to the myth, women were 'asset rich and income poor', since 92 per cent of the group received a property allocation below the limit which entitles a woman to full social security benefit.

Rules for the systematic allocation of property between spouses, many of whom bargain in the shadows of the law were difficult to find, and many respondents reported divisions of property outside the 60 : 40 range. Outcomes which are so variable may indicate the flexibility of the law to deal with individual circumstances, though such an interpretation was not supported in a survey of disputed cases before judges and registrars (Schwartzkoff and Rizzo 1985). Although Family Court judges and registrars reported weighing up contributions of spouses to the marriage, they cited property-settlement outcomes at about 50 : 50. The AIFS study, however, showed that the needs of the custodial parent for housing appeared to be an important factor, weighing shares in the property in favour of the custodian. When businesses or farms were part of the property, however, shares were more variable, with valuation of these assets posing a problem (McDonald 1986). Contributions made to the business and ownership were important in deciding how much each party received.

In addition to documenting the inequitable distribution of property, the AIFS study showed that some property, such as superannuation benefits, were omitted or inconsistently treated in property settlements, although they were often of significant value (McDonald 1986). The implications are that the law must consider both the definition of property and the rules for its division.

Systematic inequalities in outcome, resulting in serious hardship for many, were redressed neither by property settlement nor by spousal maintenance payments, which were very rarely reported by the surveyed men and women. Moreover, child maintenance was not regularly ordered or paid, and when paid was at an almost uniformly low level. Thus property settlements, spousal maintenance, and child maintenance appear ineffective in achieving a fair distribution of the financial burdens of divorce.

Gender gap and opportunity costs of children

The disparity in standard of living between men and women is largely due to their different earning capacities, which does not appear to be offset by maintenance paid, or property transferred, and to the woman's disproportionate burden of financial and care responsibility for the children of the marriage. There are two components to the disparity in income. The first concerns the gender gap in earnings which exists in Australia; the second is related to the differing effects of marriage, child-bearing, and child-rearing upon the income-earning capacity of men and women (Funder 1986).

It is unrealistic to expect individuals, and the legal system, to attempt to redress structural inequalities (i.e. gender differences) in employment and earnings. Thus, discussion of the impact of the present law on the economic circumstances of men, women, and children after divorce must distinguish between the general social and economic influences on income, which account for continuing differences between average earnings for men and women, and those factors which are particular to marriage and the law relating to its dissolution.

In Australia, in spite of legislation phasing in equal pay since the mid-1960s, by 1984 adult women's full-time, ordinary hours' earnings were still only 80 per cent those of men (Australian Bureau of Statistics (ABS) 1987). Causes of this discrepancy include sex differences in education (particularly in science and technology), sex segregation in the job market, and associated differences in opportunity for on-job training and career advancement. Moreover, although the importance of sex discrimination is debated, there is strong evidence that gender, net of credentials, years of experience, and hours worked account for some of the income differential (Jones 1983).

Differences in men's and women's earnings are also influenced by family-related interruptions to work, which are reflected in the broken-work histories of married women with children (less than 1 per cent of the women in the AIFS study had uninterrupted work histories compared with 96 per cent of men), and their common return to work part time. In the clerical, sales, and service occupations, women make up 65 per cent of the workers, but almost half are part time. Time out of work depreciates human capital measured by earning capacity (Mincer 1980), and tailoring work to children's needs seems to involve downward occupational mobility, further depressing earnings (Funder 1986; Joshi 1984).

Marriage-related effects on women's earnings were described in the AIFS study of divorced women (Funder 1986). Lone mothers who had spent more than two-thirds of their married life out of the workforce were $50 per week (25 per cent of the average net income for this group) worse off than those who had been out of the workforce less than one-third of the marriage. This difference persisted when other factors such as education, occupational level, and time since separation were statistically controlled and all income transfers between the partners included. Women withdrew from the workforce almost exclusively to bear and rear children, and it is to this that their lower earnings are attributable. Although it seemed plausible that property transfers made under the Family Law Act, section 8, might have offset some or all of this imbalance, no evidence for such counter-balancing transfers was found.

Past and continuing care of children was a powerful influence on earnings, yet couples chose to reduce the wife's participation in the paid workforce to give her more time to care for the home and children—an arrangement confirmed in an AIFS national study of maternity leave (Glezer 1988). Women rarely indicated that lack of job opportunity or child-care provisions was the most important hindrance to their employment. The high value put on the quality of parenting for young children clearly runs counter to economic independence of women. Within marriage, however, partners make their priorities, including the child-rearing conditions for their children, and share the benefits and costs of their decisions.

The balance between paid work and work in the home is a powerful determinant of the inequities observed in the settlement of the economic aspects of the marriage partnership. Time, tasks and resources, and the location of residence are commonly organized as part of a strategy to maximize the security and earnings of the husband, usually the higher earner. The wife will normally be an integral part of the productive unit, giving precedence to employment obligations, assuming major responsibility for the children and home-making. The cost and benefits of these arrangements are shared during the marriage.

It is evident, however, that the benefits of investing in the husband's career—his security of employment, his increasing earning capacity based on continuous employment, experience, and efforts in the work place— are not to the wife's advantage after separation. Conversely, the costs borne by the marriage partnership of the depreciation of the wife's earning capacity through interrupted participation, downward occupational mobility, and part-time participation (which tends to be in sectors without career paths) are not passed on to the husband after separation.

Opportunity costs and family law

The fact that financial settlements under the Family Law Act, 1975, in Australia systematically, leave women with dependent children bearing the greater burden was acknowledged by the Australian Law Reform Commission (1986). A major cause of this inequality was seen in the discrepancy in income–needs ratios between men and women which derived in part from the division of labour—past and present—in the care of children.

Two avenues for redress are possible under the Family Law Act: first through spousal and child maintenance provisions, and second through property division. At first sight, the maintenance approach appears logical and direct. Under section 77 (2) (k) one of the matters to be taken into account in awarding spousal maintenance is 'the duration of the marriage and the extent to which it has affected the earning capacity of the party whose maintenance is under consideration'. Women who have reduced earnings associated with having assumed primary responsibility for the care of children during the marriage could claim a transfer from the spouse, thus equalizing or at least sharing the deficit as they had done during the marriage. Moreover, the earning decrement which is associated with the ongoing care of children after the separation might be seen as part of the costs of maintaining children, albeit indirect costs, and be taken into account in calculating periodic child maintenance.

Objections to using the maintenance provisions to share the opportunity and direct costs of children relate to the violation of the clean-break principle which is widely espoused. Moreover, at a pragmatic level, the court's record for enforcing any sort of maintenance order has been so poor that this course has been largely eschewed; lawyers frequently recommend 'a bird in the hand' approach. In the new Child Support Scheme the assumption has been made that the indirect costs of children are a component of the resident parent's support of the child. In general, however, the notion of open-ended or very long-term spousal support is commonly rejected by both men and women (Harrison 1986). Alimony cuts across the psychological meaning of divorce as the severance of interdependent spousal relationship at all possible levels.

In practice, clean break has come to mean settlement day, whether in court, a lawyer's office, or elsewhere; any continuing transfers are seen as a violation of the principle. In some cases, however, because of the complexity of business, or the lack of liquid assets, payments are made over time in order to reach a fair financial settlement. Thus there are precedents for the clean break being achieved over a limited period of time. The principle of severance of interdependencies is thus observed, but not at the expense of an equitable settlement. The door is open for finite spousal maintenance—not recurrent—as a means of obtaining fair outcomes in some cases where to insist on a settlement-day approach would risk injustice to one of the parties.

The unequal burden may also be redistributed through the property settlement. Precedent exists for this, in that custodial parents tend to receive more of the basic assets than non-resident parents (McDonald 1986). This often secures the children's home and may well represent a lump-sum child maintenance component (although legally it is not seen as such). Securing housing for children and their resident parents is important psychologically, socially, and economically, and has been shown to accelerate re-entry into the paid workforce (Wulff 1988). Where hardship is unequally shared and there is sufficient property, a component might be transferred to the party who bears the greater burden of past and future child-care responsibilities. Where insufficient property exists, periodic payments could be made over a specified time.

If family law is to play any part in redressing the inequalities which currently exist, that component of inequality which derives from structural features of the Australian workforce must be distinguished from that part which derives from the marriage. It is only the latter which may fairly be considered the responsibility of the parties to the marriage, and hence come under the domain of family law.

Differences in earnings between men and women reflect a variety of causative factors, but are none the less consistently described. Some differences exist even when education, occupation, and continuity in the workforce are held constant. Fig. 1 shows a schematic representation of the lifetime earnings of men and women who have had continuous work experience. The 'gender gap' in earnings is represented by the difference between the two lines. This gap, although a serious inequality, cannot be attributed to the marriage. Children are, however, part of the business of a marriage. Their care and financial support are the responsibility of the two partners who must allocate time and effort to children's needs. The way in which they do this, although constrained by gender differences in wage rates, is a private matter. It is part of the conduct of the marriage and is assumed to be a joint decision, maximizing the benefits of the partnership. The usual pattern is for the mother to withdraw from the paid workforce to bear and rear children, returning part time as their needs diminish.

When women withdraw from the workforce to care for children, the opportunity costs they incur from child-rearing may be expressed in terms of lifetime earnings *vis-à-vis* women of similar background who have had continuous work experience. It would not be appropriate to

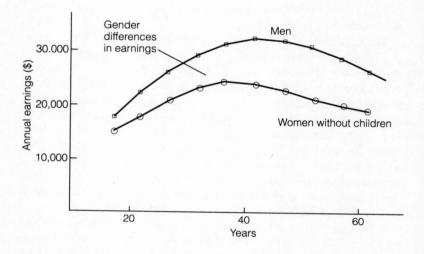

Fig. 1 Average earnings of men and of women without children

count these costs in comparison with the earnings of men, since there are structural differences which explain at least some of the differences in earnings between men and women, shown in Fig. 1. Opportunity costs of women who withdraw from the workforce to care for children may be calculated by comparing the earnings of women who have children with those of like women who have uninterrupted work histories. Fig. 2 shows how these opportunity costs are defined. Fig. 2 shows a hypothetical comparison between the lifetime earning streams of women with similar educational and occupational backgrounds. The gap between the two reflects the wage losses attributed to the efforts and time devoted to children and resulting in loss of earnings. This loss is referred to as the opportunity costs of children.

Some of these costs are shared in the marriage partnership, and losses of income are counted against the quality of life for all family members and the parents' investment in the children. The benefits of children and quality of life are shared, as are the loss of all or part of one spouse's income. This is not the subject for reallocation. These costs, however, continue in the future in two ways which are relevant to the financial settlement of the marriage partnership. First, the depreciation of earnings originating in the care of children of the marriage continues to be felt in the post-separation period. Secondly, this is commonly exacerbated by

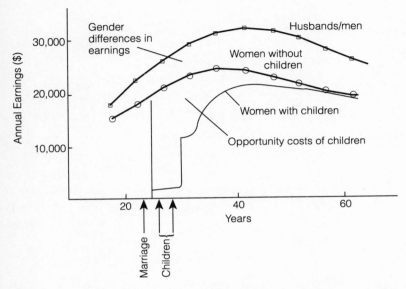

Fig. 2 Average earnings of men, women without children, and women with children

the demands that dependent children continue to make on the custodial parent, who is most often the same parent who has taken prime responsibility for them during the marriage. Although it is recognized here that these two components are separate, and that the continuing indirect costs of children after separation might be treated as a factor in calculating child maintenance, they are considered together at this point.

Fig. 3 shows how opportunity costs, calculated against the lifetime earnings expected for like women, may be estimated. Also shown is the allocation of these opportunity costs into two categories: those which were shared during the marriage and those which were borne solely by the woman, who took the primary role in rearing the children. As the lost earnings during the marriage were shared by the partnership, they are not the concern of settlement. Only the deferred costs borne solely by the wife are considered as a debt against the marriage partnership.

An alternative approach

Any alternative approach to settlement of the marriage partnership should conform with a number of principles:

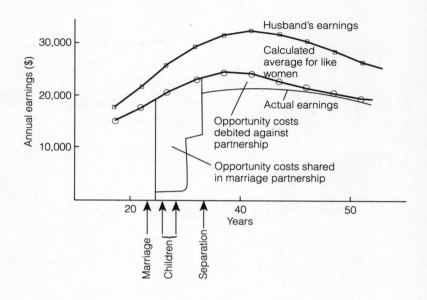

Fig. 3 Estimated opportunity costs

1 it should produce just and equitable outcomes;
2 it should be consistent with the principle of marriage as a partnership of equals which does not exploit one partner at the expense of the other;
3 it should be predictable and accountable, making public the principles and means of calculating the shares;
4 it should include a means of putting a money value on one of the most significant determinants of present inequalities—the depreciated earning capacity of women who have assumed the primary responsibility for rearing children and who have withdrawn or modified their workforce participation to fulfil this role;
5 it should cover most cases in a fair and equitable way but allow the right of appeal against the application of the system to unusual cases where outcomes would be unjust.

At the heart of this proposal is the concept that labour invested in raising children and making a home detracts from present or future efforts in the paid workforce. The withdrawal from the workforce has immediate costs to the marriage partnership in terms of lost earnings which are shared during the marriage, as are the attendant advantages of having happy children, a secure income, and a certain quality of life. As with the whole working economy of the marriage and the various contributions of the parties, this loss is not the subject of the settlement.

When a marriage ends, the costs of the depreciated earnings which were previously absorbed by the partnership are carried by the partner whose paid work has been interrupted and whose individual earnings are reduced. The partner who has stayed in the workforce, usually the husband, has typically increased his earning capacity through experience, extra training, earning increments which come with years of service, reputation as a worker, goodwill in business, etc., all of which can only be earned with years of uninterrupted service to a profession. This means that, instead of the assets (increased earning capacity) and the losses (depreciation in earnings) being shared, since they were in part or whole acquired during the marriage, the husband is left with the assets and the wife with the loss.

Fairness demands that the debt of continued depreciated earnings be claimed against the total assets of the partnership and by virtue of contributions to it. The debt should not be claimed against the husband, in as much as both parties decided to apportion their roles on the tacit understanding that the benefits and costs be shared. It is thus a debt to be claimed against the marriage partnership at the time of settlement. The principle suggested here differs from the current thinking in several important ways.

It assumes that ex-wives, among whom are many poor and welfare recipients, have earned the right to some deferred payments against the losses they incurred in making their contributions to the marriage. They are thus reclassified as debtors asserting their claim against the marriage partnership, rather than as being in need of support (either from the ex-spouse through maintenance or from the government through public benefits). This approach is a powerful endorsement of the notion of marriage as a partnership between equals.

It does not require a tallying of contributions during the marriage, but assumes that the partnership was a shared enterprise. When the partnership is dissolved, however, debts which were carried in unison cannot be allocated to one party. Similarly, the whole orientation of the approach is retroactive, and not directed to guessing at future needs and circumstances; the debt once assessed and paid cannot be claimed again. The approach is thus consistent with the desire of people for the swiftest severing of financial ties.

Calculating the debt against the marriage partnership

There are several econometric models for calculating the opportunity costs of children. Opportunity costs may be broadly defined as 'the earnings that a woman might have had, but had to forgo, because of the need to care for her children' (Reed and McIntosh 1971). Costs are estimated by comparing the lifetime earnings of groups of women who have had no children, and no child-induced interruptions to their workforce participation, with those of women who have borne children.

The bases for these estimates are large nationally representative samples of women and the collection of statistics on their workforce participation, earnings, and fertility. Calhoun and Espenshade (1986) in Australia have calculated the costs of having children. All conclude that the presence, age, and number of children have estimable effects on women's earnings. The availability of national scales for these costs means that estimates can be made of the costs for a woman of particular socio-economic, fertility, and labour force characteristics. Joshi (1984) demonstrates that interruptions to women's work are primarily associated with children and that the cost of these interruptions, measured by gross cash earnings forgone as a result of family formation, is about double the loss of actual woman-years in the labour force.

Although there are differences in methods and estimates, these approaches provide statistical estimates of the opportunity costs of children which lessen women's earning capacity in comparison with childless women of similar educational, occupational, and regional characteristics; both suffer from a number of limitations. Any extrapolations made from a group to an individual will contain errors. Observations of particular cohorts of people will not take account of changes in, for example, women's workforce participation rates. This is a weakness shared, however, by all insurance tables and compensation estimates. For example, recent estimates of the life expectancy for young Australian men aged 18 in 1985 were revised upwards to 73.6 years from 72 years, the estimated life span in 1970–2 (ABS 1987).

Beggs's and Chapman's (1988) estimates provide a base for calculating opportunity costs of children and generating tables of costs under a range of demographic, socio-economic, family formation, and family dissolution circumstances. Such tables could then be made available to the public and used by the court as standards against which to assess the outstanding opportunity-costs estimates to be borne by the carer of the children. As with all insurance and compensation tables, each set of circumstances would be assessed within a band of values. The band would be set to cover about 95 per cent of cases, outside of which there could be a system of appeal. Negotiations would be possible on the basis of individual variations, but the parameters would be set.

Allocation of opportunity costs to the partnership

To be both effective and equitable the following principles in compensating for lost earning capacity from the net property of the marriage might be considered:

1 that the compensation is for prospective loss of income post-separation, to compensate for the cumulative loss following the lowered point of entry back into the workforce. It is *not* for the retrospective losses during the marriage; where losses during the marriage and the prospective cumulative loss post-separation are similar, however, is that they are a charge on the joint economy of the marriage;
2 that the compensation is calculated and finite, since ideally the compensation should be levied as a once-and-for-all debit against the net joint property of the marriage at the time of separation.

An outline of the procedures for the payment of compensation for opportunity costs might be as follows:

1 Determine the net property of the partnership after all other liabilities have been accounted for.
2 Deduct from that net amount another debt—that of the opportunity costs, payable in this case to one partner.
3 Divide the remaining property equally between the partners.

An example of this process, constructed for an average case in the AIFS study, might be as follows. Average net property value before calculating opportunity costs was $50,000. Time out of the workforce for a woman married ten years with two children aged 7 and 9 at the time of separation was about five years. Future opportunity costs of a clerical worker from the time of separation through the normal working life (we have no scales, but would estimate this on the basis that these costs would be diminishing over the working life between 34 and 60). Let us set this at $20,000. On the assumption that these costs be based on the difference

between her full-time earnings and those of a matched woman without
children, the calculation would be as follows:

Total net assets	$50,000	
Less opportunity costs	$20,000	
Remaining net assets	$30,000	
50 : 50 shares of remainder	husband	wife
	$15,000	$15,000
Final settlement of matrimonial property	$15,000	$35,000

In the AIFS study the average net annual income differential between
men and women after tax and maintenance payments was $7,800 in
favour of the man at the time of interview, three to five years after separation. This difference comprises both an amount attributable to the general income differences between men and women, and an amount
attributable to support in the workforce by the marriage partnership, as
well as the opportunity costs of children on the career. In this hypothetical case, the man would recoup in under sixteen months (through the
earnings differential) the net amount paid out of 'his' share of marital
property to compensate the wife for her lowered earnings. In this example, as in most cases, there are clearly resources to pay the compensation
entirely out of assets or to charge some of the debt against the husband's
earnings in the years immediately following separation.

Further questions

Although the Australian Family Law Act of 1975 includes specific recognition of the opportunity costs of children, and national scales of costs
have been developed, there are several further questions to be addressed.
Possible conflicts between compensation claims and child maintenance
responsibilities must be explored. There is very poor evidence for earning
advantages of married men over single men (Calhoun and Espenshade
1986); similarly Joshi (19894) reports that marriage *per se* has little effect
on women's lifetime earnings. Thus, in spite of the US cases exploring
the value of wives' efforts in augmenting husband's human capital, the
evidence is not strong for specifically marriage-related costs and benefits
for either sex.

Reforms confront a complex array of economic, social, and legal structures which embody social norms of the past and present. Social values
are not, however, unified and harmonious. They are a pastiche of carry-

overs from previous generations and recent additions. Not surprisingly, reforms relating to marriage and divorce highlight, as they confront, the many inconsistencies which are the very fabric of Australian social mores. Contentious issues include the division of labour in managing the marriage economy, equality of opportunity in paid employment, and the role of the state in supporting lone-parent families which result from divorce. As Ellwood (1987) has argued, reforms will only come about if they can resolve value conflicts.

This proposal endorses marriage as a partnership of equals. Its focus is on settling debts, not on establishing dependency needs. Much of this rhetoric is commonplace in Australia; it remains to be seen if its practical expression will be accepted by the decision-makers within the community and by the community as a whole.

References

Australian Bureau of Statistics (ABS) (1987), *Lifetables: The Labour Force in Australia* (Canberra).

Australian Joint Select Committee on the Family Law Act (1980), *Family Law in Australia*, Report (Canberra), vol. i.

Australian Cabinet Sub-Committee on Maintenance (1986), *Child Support: A Discussion Paper on Child Maintenance* (North Ryde, NSW).

Australian Law Reform Commission (1987), *Matrimonial Property*, Report No. 39 (The Hambly Report) (Canberra).

BEGGS, J., and CHAPMAN, B. (1988), 'The Forgone Earnings from Child-Rearing in Australia', paper commissioned by the Australian Institute of Family Studies, Australian National University Centre for Economic Policy Research, Discussion Paper No. 190 (Melbourne).

CALHOUN, C. A., and ESPENSHADE, T. J. (1986), 'The Opportunity Costs of Rearing American Children', Projects report, The Urban Institute (Washington, DC).

ELLWOOD, D. T. (1990), 'Valuing the United States Income Support System for Lone Mothers', in OECD, *Lone Parents: The Economic Challenge* (Paris).

FUNDER, K. (1986), 'Work and the marriage partnership', in P. McDonald (ed.), *Settling Up: Property and Income Distribution on Divorce in Australia* (Sydney).

—— 'The Value of Work in Marriage: Options for Compensation after Marriage Breakdown', in D. Ironmonger (ed.), *Households Work* (Sydney).

GLEZER, H. (1988), *Maternity Leave in Australia* (Melbourne).

HARRISON, M. (1986), 'Maintenance, custody and access', in P. McDonald (ed.), *Settling Up: Property and Income Distribution on Divorce in Australia* (Sydney).

—— and McDONALD, P. (1988), 'Parents and Children after Marriage Breakdown: The Price of Child Maintenance', paper presented to *Bicentenary Family Law Conference*, Melbourne, 16–20 March, Business Law Education Centre.

JONES, F. L. (1983), 'Income inequality', in D. H. Broom (ed.), *Unfinished Business: Social Justice for Women in Australia* (Sydney), ch. 5.

JOSHI, H. (1984), *Women's Participation in Paid Work: Further Analysis of the Women and Employment Survey* (Department of Employment Research, Monograph No. 45; London).

MCDONALD, P. (1986), 'Property Distribution: The Shares of Each Partner and Their Determinants', in P. McDonald (ed.), *Settling Up: Property and Income Distribution on Divorce in Australia* (Sydney).

MINGER, J. (1980), 'Human Capital and Earnings', in A. B. Atkinson (ed.), *Wealth, Income and Inequality* (2nd edn., Oxford).

ORGANIZATION FOR ECONOMIC CO-OPERATION AND DEVELOPMENT (OECD) (1990), *Lone Parents: The Economic Challenge* (Paris).

REED, R. H., and MCINTOSH, S. (1971), 'Costs of Children', in E. R. Morse and R. H. Reed (eds.), *Economic Aspects of Population Change* (Washington, DC).

SCHWARTZKOFF, J., and RIZZO, C. (1985), *A survey of Family Court Cases in Australia* (Matrimonial Property Law Research paper No. 1: Sydney).

Social Security Review (1986a), *Income Support for Families with Children*, Background Paper No. 1 (Canberra).

Social Security Review (1986b), *Australian Families' Current Situation and Trends: 1969–1985*, Background Paper No. 10: (Canberra).

WESTON, R. (1986), 'Changes in Household Income Circumstances', in P. McDonald (ed.), *Settling Up: Property and Income Distribution on Divorce in Australia* (Sydney).

WULFF, M. (1988), 'Demographic Change and Housing Policy: An Analysis of a Government Home Ownership Scheme on Female Sole Parents', paper presented at the 4th National Conference of the Australian Population Association, 31 Aug.–2 Sept. (Brisbane).

4. Parenthood and the position of children

4.1. Child support reassessed: limits of private responsibility and the public interest

HARRY D. KRAUSE*

I. The setting

Looking back at twenty-some years of work with the legal parent-and-child relationship and, more specifically, the child support obligation,[1] I am increasingly concerned about current trends. Tension is mounting between (1) society's continuing need for a functioning family infrastructure, (2) the 'me-generation's' emphasis on the individual's *rights* ('liberty and happiness'), (3) traditional financial responsibility for dependents (spouse and children), and (4) the care-giving capacity of the one-parent family. These tensions have become greater than the loosened framework of the modern family (or less formal, more casual relationships now competing with marriage) can reasonably handle.

At least since President Johnson, politicians have concerned themselves with the 'breakdown' of the American family and have emphasized the importance of family policy.[2] Even sharper ideological disagreement now divides the political right and left.[3] They have one thing in common: neither side's proposals are likely to reconstitute the 'American family', whatever that was.[4] Standing alone, current proposals

* This article was originally presented at a symposium, *Divorce Reform in Retrospect*, sponsored by the Earl Warren Legal Institute, University of California at Berkeley, and the Institute for Research on Women and Gender, Stanford University, November 4–5, 1988. This paper also will be published by the Yale University Press as part of a collection edited by Professor Stephen D. Sugarman. My thanks go to participants in that conference, especially to Professor Stephen D. Sugarman and Frank Zimring, for constructive criticism and thoughtful suggestions, and to Marion Benfield as well as Eva and Peter Krause for their comments on earlier drafts. Copyright © Harry D. Krause 1989. All rights reserved.

to grant pregnancy leave[5] or to subsidize day care[6] are inadequate to that task—as inadequate as are calls to return to a moral past[7] that has been superseded by new facts.[8]

In the 1970s, divorce reform and child support reform seemed revolutionary. Looking back, those 'reforms' amended traditional approaches and brought adjustments, but left in place many traditional concepts—perhaps too many. True, no-fault divorce ended the state's role in the divorce decision, but divorce by consent had been available all along.[9] Moreover, the state soon reasserted its interest by reregulating the financial consequences of divorce, which strengthened the legal meaning of marriage where it matters: after divorce. The (consequent?) increase in premarital, nonmarital, and postdivorce cohabitation,[10] has led to the demand—somewhat successful in several states—that cohabitation give rise to legally enforceable economic rights and obligations parallel to marriage.[11] And the enormous increase in births to unmarried mothers—which strained the welfare system to the breaking point—has led to the multibillion dollar, government-assisted child support enforcement industry.

Child support is my immediate topic. I shall put aside exciting, related questions regarding the continued legitimacy of interspousal support liability in the ongoing marriage and after divorce. I shall put aside concerns as to what reasonably should be the treatment of property accumulation in the modern marriage.[12] My focus will be on the rationale of the parental child support obligation (1) in the ongoing family, (2) after divorce, and (3) when the absent parent has never participated in a family or a similar social setting.

The very success of the federal child support enforcement legislation[13] (four billion dollars are now collected annually),[14] raises provocative new questions. What level of support obligation is consistent with modern perceptions of family ties? Is the father's demotion from cherished patriarch to absent parent entirely irrelevant to his obligations? Should a 'second class' (noncustodial) parent pay 'first class' support? Is the 'mere existence of a biological link' enough?[15] How much support is enough? Will rigid enforcement of high levels of child support, along with the risk of easy divorce and consequent *de facto* termination of the father–child relationship, deter responsible men from fathering children? Do we need a better balance between individual and social responsibility—in the children's *and* in society's best interests?

II.   The past: little interest in child support

In 1934, the American Law Institute's (ALI's) *Restatement of Conflict of Laws* characterized support obligations and their enforcement as 'of no special interest to other states'. The Restatement continued '[s]ince the duty is not imposed primarily for the benefit of an individual, it is not enforceable elsewhere . . . .'[16]

Twenty-five years ago, child support was not a public issue. Absent parents were not pursued. Even for a legally established child support obligation, the absent father could all but choose not to pay. The obligation was rarely enforced effectively—especially not across state lines. Paternity—where in doubt—was rarely ascertained.[17] Dominant social work doctrine proclaimed that the father should *not* be brought face-to-face with his (theoretical) support obligation, because enforcement might inconvenience the mother. In any event, since the AFDC system was paying for the child, support enforcement seemed quite unnecessary.[18] Feeble attempts to bring deserting fathers to accept responsibility were discounted with the argument that the funds thus collected would not benefit the children, because collections would only be offset against AFDC entitlements.[19] Some went further and suggested that child support enforcement actually harmed the fragile black family structure by driving away fathers—fathers who liked the social tie but not the financial responsibility.[20] When Congress enacted the federal child support enforcement legislation in the mid-1970s, opposition came from many respected quarters—including even the League of Women Voters—and remained strong for a time.[21]

To be sure, not all the blame rested on social workers. When a welfare-related support action *was* brought, judges often saw fit to impose only token obligations, such as $10 per month. In short, despite widespread enactment of the *Uniform Reciprocal Enforcement of Support Acts* of 1950, 1958, and 1968, and explicit references to child support collection in early AFDC legislation,[22] *in practice* American law remained deeply insensitive to the enforcement of child support obligations.

Indeed, only thirty-five years ago, American law provided a shaky basis for imposing a child support obligation on the father. An illustrative New Jersey case involved a medical necessity and arose within an *ongoing* family. Here are a few words from that case:

Suffice it to say that it appears that the question to be resolved here has not yet been passed on in the court of last resort, but that there are divergent views at law and in equity as to the fundamental nature of a parent's obligation to maintain an infant child awaiting decision.[23]

In the 1750s, Blackstone had said:

The duty of parents to provide for the *maintenance* of their children, is a principle of natural law. . . . By begetting them, therefore, they have entered into a voluntary obligation, to endeavour, as far as in them lies, that the life which they have bestowed shall be supported and preserved. And thus the children will have a perfect *right* of receiving maintenance from their parents.

. . . [A]nd the manner, in which this obligation shall be performed, is thus pointed out. The father, and mother, grandfather, and grandmother of poor impotent persons shall maintain them at their own charges, if of sufficient ability, . . . and if a parent runs away, and leaves his children, the churchwardens and overseers of the parish shall seize his rents, goods, and chattels, and dispose of them toward their relief.[24]

III.   The present: enforcement!

Looking now at Blackstone's last sentence, we see the federal child support enforcement legislation and corresponding state law reforms. The intermediate past has been overcome.

A.   *The federal enforcement initiative of 1974*

The Office of Child Support Enforcement (OCSE) of the United Stated Department of Health and Human Services provides the following statistics for 1987: (10 812,661 support orders were entered; (2) 268,766 paternities were established; (3) nearly 1.4 million parent-locate requests were filed, and eighty per cent were filled within two weeks; (4) nearly four billion support dollars were collected, bringing to twenty-three billion dollars the total collected since the inception of the program twelve years before; and (5) on average, one dollar was spent to collect $3.68.[25]

When Congress enacted the sweeping legislation to strengthen enforcement of child support obligations across the nation, the primary goal was to reduce the federal cost of the AFDC program. Since then, the scope and purpose of the enforcement program have been broadened. It was recognized early that the objective of reducing the cost of AFDC programs could be secured more successfully if potential recipients were kept off welfare by extending the support enforcement programme to them. But the programme now reaches well beyond this group: support enforcement is available to anyone for a reasonable fee.[26] In terms of 'middle class' family support, this has made a significant difference—more than one-half of the total collections are going to children who are not on welfare.[27]

State authority and state laws remain primary vehicles, but state enforcement agencies—now commonly known as 'IV-D agencies', reflecting their location in title 42 of the United States Code—must meet standards imposed by federal law. OCSE is the stimulator, overseer, and financier of state collection systems. The 'stick' waved at the states is loss of some of their federal AFDC funding. The 'carrot' is federal funding for a considerable portion of the states' support enforcement programs, but only if they meet federal standards.

B. The federal enforcement process

To summarize:[28] federal law requires state AFDC agencies to collect data, use the social security numbers of all AFDC applicants as identification, notify state child support enforcement agencies when benefits are granted to eligible children, and open their records to support enforcement officials. Applicants must assign their rights to uncollected child support to the state and must agree to cooperate in locating absent parents, in establishing paternity, in obtaining support judgments if none are outstanding, and in securing payments. In case of an applicant's unjustified failure to cooperate, AFDC benefits are withheld from the applicant, though not from children.

The states maintain parent locator services equipped to search state and local records for information regarding the whereabouts of absent parents. OCSE maintains a sophisticated, computerized federal parent locator service based in Washington, D.C., with access to social security, internal revenue, and nearly all other federal information resources, except census records. When the absent (or alleged) parent is located, the state establishes paternity (if necessary and possible), obtains a support judgement, and enforces the obligation through either in-state or inter-state proceedings. All states must cooperate fully with their sister states. Access to federal courts is provided, if necessary, and so if collection by the Internal Revenue Service. After collection, the state disburses child support payments, keeping detailed records and reporting to OCSE. To encourage local participation in child support enforcement, the state turns a portion of the proceeds over to the collecting unit of the local government.

C. The 1984 child support amendments: mandatory withholding and discretionary guidelines

In 1984, significant federal amendments asked the states to sharpen their laws and strengthen enforcement powers.[29] State laws now must require employers to withhold child support from the paychecks of parents delinquent for one month.[30] State laws must provide for the imposition of liens against the property of defaulting support obligors, and credit companies may be informed of unpaid child support in excess of $1,000.[31] Unpaid support obligations must be deducted from federal and state income tax refunds. Expedited hearings—judicial or administrative—are required in support cases. Following, extending, and anticipating various United States Supreme Court decisions,[32] statutes of limitation for the establishment of paternity must allow at least eighteen years after a child's birth for suit. To give families receiving welfare some direct benefit from the father's support payments, the first fifty dollars per month are now paid directly to the family and not deducted from the family's welfare cheque.

The 1984 amendments announced that Washington will play a more active role in defining standards for acceptable state law on these questions. The amendment achieves one important objective—long and effectively championed by David Chambers:[33] more effective methods of support enforcement will become the rule, specifically wage deduction to avoid default, rather than (often counterproductive) jail and loss of job after default.

At least as importantly, the 1984 amendments require states to establish discretionary guidelines for child support awards. Toward that end, the amendments provide:

(a) Each State, as a condition for having its State plan approved under this part, must establish guidelines for child support award amounts within the State. The guidelines may be established by law or by judicial or administrative action.

(b) The guidelines established pursuant to subsection (a) shall be made available to all judges and other officials who have the power to determine child support awards within such State, but need not be binding upon such judges or other officials.

(c) The Secretary shall furnish technical assistance to the States for establishing the guidelines, and each State shall furnish the Secretary with copies of its guidelines.

(b) [sic] The amendment made by subsection (a) shall become effective on October 1, 1987.[34]

In response to the House Ways and Means Committee's request, a national panel was set up to advise the states upon support guidelines.[35] That Panel comprised a divorced women's advocate, a divorced men's advocate, a state support enforcement director, a child support judge, a state legislator, a court systems child support administrator, an economics professor, and a law professor (myself). After long debate and much compromise, we endorsed the following basic principles:

(1) Both parents share legal responsibility for supporting their children. The economic responsibility should be divided in proportion to their available income.

(2) The subsistence needs of each parent should be taken into account in setting child support, but in virtually no event should the child support obligation be set at zero.

(3) Child support must cover a child's basic needs as a first priority, but, to the extent either parent enjoys a higher than subsistence level standard of living, the child is entitled to share the benefit of that improved standard.

(4) Each child of a given parent has an equal right to share in that parent's income, subject to factors such as age of the child, income of each parent, income of current spouses, and the presence of other dependents.

(5) Each child is entitled to determination of support without respect to the marital status of the parents at the time of the child's birth. Consequently, any guideline should be equally applicable to determining child support related to paternity determinations, separations, and divorces.

(6) Application of a guideline should be sexually non-discriminatory. Specifically, it should be applied without regard to the gender of the custodial parent.

(7) A guideline should not create extraneous negative effects on the major life decisions of either parent. In particular, the guideline should avoid creating economic disincentives remarriage or labour force participation.

(8) A guideline should encourage the involvement of both parents in the child's upbringing. It should take into account the financial support provided directly by parents in shared physical custody or extended visitation arrangements, recognizing that even a fifty per cent sharing of physical custody does not necessarily obviate the child support obligation.[36]

The establishment by the states of reasonable guidelines for setting child support obligations will assure less arbitrary and diverse conceptions of the needs of the child and the father's ability to pay than have been applied in the past. The states' responses to the federal mandate are being evaluated.[37] For now I refer and defer to the analyses of others, and add only one point: more consistent and coherent results would be achieved if federal (not state-by-state) standards would set a national standard, with adjustments for regional variations in the cost of living. With the movement to OCSE-sponsored national support enforcement, continued federal deference to state-by-state discretion seems misplaced.

The 1984 amendments injected federal initiative and authority more deeply into matters that previously had been viewed as reserved to the states. Nevertheless, when Congress signalled this policy by passing a sense-of-congress resolution, it still insisted that 'state and local governments must focus on the vital issues of child support, child custody, visitation rights, and other related domestic issues'.[38] Specifically:

(a) The Congress finds that—

   (1) the divorce rate in the United States has reached alarming proportions and the number of children being raised in single parent families has grown accordingly;

   (2) there is a critical lack of child support enforcement, which Congress has undertaken to address through the child support enforcement program;

   (3) Congress is strengthening that program to recognize the needs of all children;

   (4) related domestic issues, such as visitation rights and child custody, are often intricately intertwined with the child support problem and have received inadequate consideration; and

   (5) these related issues remain within the jurisdiction of State and local governments, but have a critical impact on the health and welfare of the children of the Nation.

(b) It is the sense of Congress that—

   (1) State and local governments must focus on the vital issues of child support, child custody, visitation rights, and other related domestic issues that are properly within the jurisdictions of such governments;

   (2) all individuals involved in the domestic relations process should recognize the seriousness of these matters to the health and welfare of our Nation's children and assign them the highest priority; and

   (3) a mutual recognition of the needs of all parties involved in divorce actions will greatly enhance the health and welfare of America's children and families.[39]

D.   The 1988 child support amendments

The 1988 child support amendments[40] provide that, beginning in 1994, for all new or modified support orders, child support payments are to be withheld from absent parents' wages automatically and without regard to whether they are in arrears. Support guidelines must be used to determine child support obligations, and child support orders are to be reviewed every three years. Federal standards for the establishment of paternity must be met, and the federal government will pay ninety per cent of the cost of laboratory tests to establish paternity. Moreover, such tests may be required by the contesting party.[41] The legislation also mandates automatic tracking and monitoring systems, provides additional sources for the parent location service, and authorizes the establishment of a commission on interstate child support.

E.   How much room is left for improved enforcement?

Room for improvement remains. There are unexplained, wide variations in collection performance from one state to another, arising from incomplete federal, state, and local implementation.[42] Better collection figures can and will come out of administrative improvements, stimulated by federal pressure. In August 1988, Wayne Stanton, the Director of OCSE, admonished:

> While collections have increased, child support agencies must become even more proficient at using every tool available to collect support from parents who are now simply walking away from their children. Much more State attention must be paid to collection efforts, such as using liens on personal and real property, as well as reporting delinquents to credit bureaus to cloud their credit.[43]

Despite OCSE's proud macrorecord described earlier, dismal microstatistics involving child support collections have been reported in numerous studies, prominently Professor Weitzman's[44] and Professors Bruch's and Wikler's.[45] These studies focus not on how much more is now being collected, but show that in the samples the authors studied, a lot of child support remains uncollected. OCSE reports that '[t]he aggregate amount of child support payments due for 1985 alone was $10.9 billion but payments actually received amounted to only $7.2 billion'.[46]

F.   Why is that support not collected?

To concentrate on the really hard cases, we might put aside the cases in which the custodial parent supports the child adequately and, for reasons of her own, does not wish to impose on the absent parent. Ignoring such cases leaves only two alternative explanations of inadequate support. One is that the state makes an inadequate effort to enforce existing law, law that increasingly is up to the task. But as implementation of existing law is—as it surely will be—perfected, only one explanation why absent fathers do not pay will remain: they do not have the money to render adequate child support. Even now, I suspect that a large number of defaulting fathers do not have (and never had) the missing money. Many a defaulting father's obligation, even if originally assessed fairly, does not correspond to his current economic circumstances, and current law or practice does not afford him an adequate opportunity to effect an appropriate modification.[47]

Looking carefully at statistics and reality, it is reasonable to conclude that many fathers are not alone able to provide the support their children need to get a decent start in life, even if many try.[48] And to the extent we are now driven to see child support enforcement as the sole solution to child poverty, we are as wrong as those in the 1960s who saw the AFDC program as the sole appropriate source of support for female-headed families. To refresh my memory, I occasionally go to our local courts—in a relatively affluent midwestern community, nothing like the big city courts I also have studied—and spend a few hours seeing the parade of unemployed, and often unemployable, teenagers being confronted with unmeetable financial obligations, arising, ironically, out of constitutionally protected conduct.[49] For those who have not seen these proceedings, David Chambers has described them graphically.[50]

I fear that our current emphasis on enforcing the father's obligation is clouding our judgement as to how much money we can realistically expect the father to provide. Looking more carefully at detailed collection statistics at the bottom of the social pyramid, the fact is that at the AFDC level we currently spend nearly as much on collection as we collect—and in many states more.[51] Child support collection actually has been turned into an income transfer programme from poor fathers to lawyers and welfare bureaucrats—something I had hoped we would avoid.[52]

On the fix-it-fast level, I have suggested that we institute facilitated, semiautomatic modification of prospective support payments to reflect the typical low-income father's often quickly changing ability to pay.[53] That would reduce or eliminate the accumulation of the hopeless arrears many fathers owe the government—by that I mean arrears that, short of winning the lottery, the father has no hope of ever being able to pay. We should consider reinstituting forgiveness of such arrears, at least in the context of bankruptcy.[54] Nor am I completely at ease with the work product of our National Panel on Child Support Guidelines.[55] These issues continue to concern me, but not here and not now.[56]

Summing up what I see, the 'next issues' in child support include (1) the reality that many defaulting fathers simply do not have what it takes to support their children—as enforcement becomes comprehensive, fewer defaults will be due to irresponsibility, (2) my growing (if heretical) notion that it may not be fair to ask all absent fathers to foot the entire bill, and (3) the need to understand that children have a direct claim on society at large, along with their parallel claim on their parents. Let me now risk offering some caveats about overemphasizing the paternal support responsibility.

IV. The future

A. *Toward a better balance between private and public responsibility: the impecunious father and his welfare child*

In August 1988, the Census Bureau reported that, in 1987, the poverty rate (income below $11,612 for a family of four) for all children stood at 210.6%. Forty-nine per cent of black children under the age of six were poor—one in two![57] I happily stipulate that the poverty measurement is subject to numerous doubts, ranging from its unrealistic derivation (three times a basic food basket) to its perverse disregard of the value of in-kind programs, such as food stamps, subsidized housing, medical care, and school lunches. Still, the poverty figure does provide a rough measure of well-being or its opposite. AFDC, in most states, does not come close to meeting this minimum. In 1987, Alabama provided $147 per month for a family of four, the Mississippi provided $144.[58]

Our success in child support enforcement has not significantly improved the poorest children's lot! And it cannot, until we share between the poorest fathers and the taxpayer the cost of supporting all children at a responsible minimum level. My, I think not extravagant, recommendation which the 1984 amendments were proposed was that the welfare father's child support payments should not be deducted from his children's public welfare cheque until the father's payments have moved his children up to the poverty level.[59] Instead, we got the current fifty-dollar-per-month disregard[60]—a 'foot in the door', but hardly enough in terms of the children's realistic needs.[61]

The concrete reality of child poverty speaks for itself, but who is listening? Along with the rest of our economy and shifting ideology, children have been 'privatized'. Why? The perception has taken hold that the absent father is solely responsible for support of his children, and that if he does not pay enough, he is irresponsible, but worse, no one else is responsible. The realities predicted for the future, however, increasingly point away from the father.

In the so-called single-parent family, one parent (typically the mother) with one or more children constitutes a household unit. Either she is divorced, or she has never had a legal (and often not much of a personal) tie with the other parent. Increasingly, this is the social setting in which a significant proportion of our next generation is raised.[62] But easy-come, easy-go marriage and casual cohabitation and procreation are on a collision course with the economic and social needs of children. This may sound like a moral value judgement, but it is a pragmatic assessment. The last two decades of piecemeal adaptations of traditional law to a changing society are not meeting the challenge. If the traditional social structure—the traditional, ongoing two-parent family—no longer exists, can its ghost support traditional financial responsibility?

Senator Moynihan points out that by the year 2000:

[W]e project that about three-quarters of American families will be of the 'traditional' sort, whereas in 1960 nearly nine of ten families could be so described. In less than two generations the proportion of families headed by single persons will have doubled. . . .

In the final two decades of the century we project the number of families will increase from 59.5 million to 72.5 million, which is to say a net of 13 million families. But of these additional households, only 5.9 million are expected to be 'traditional' husband–wife families. Female-headed families will account for 5.8 million of the net increase, and male-headed families for 1.3 million. Put another way, in the period 1980–2000 the number of female-headed families will increase at more than five times the rate of husband–wife families.63

Can we afford to continue treating a phenomenon as widespread as one-parent child rearing as deviant? Can all problems attending one-parent child rearing be corrected simply by strict enforcement of child support obligations? Can we continue to limit social intervention to the prevention of outright starvation—at a level well below our official definition of a minimum standard? Are we dealing only with the failure of private responsibility?

As much and as long as I have worked to raise child support consciousness and have been criticized for that,[64] I now find it remarkable—even a

little frightening—that the absent welfare father's child support obligation has become so fast, so deeply, the only true faith. Arguably, this was
due in no small measure to an unlikely—if unwitting—political alliance
between women's groups and a basically conservative, anti-welfare legislative constituency, the latter drawing its support from many real and
more perceived excesses of the Great Society of the 1960s and 1970s.
Whatever the reason, and putting it very bluntly, in the late 1980s the
emphasis seems to be more on immorality—the culpability of the
father—than on the needs of the child. This has dissipated any sense of
urgency for legislative action to secure the financial welfare of children.
By voting for tougher child support enforcement, legislators, state and
federal, can congratulate themselves that something has been done for
children—and at no public cost. In sum, our current intense preoccupation with the absent father's fault and irresponsibility has displaced
awareness of the reality of the limited resources of many absent fathers.
It has made much more difficult a responsible dialogue over public
responsibility. Our justified insistence on the enforcement of the father's
unmet legal obligation has unjustifiably eclipsed our need to understand
that, ultimately, the adequate support of children is a public necessity.

B. *The rationale of the parental child support obligation*

On a more fundamental level than sheer inability to pay, I now want to
have another look at the current validity of the traditional parental child
support obligation. As Mary Ann Glendon,[65] Martha Minow,[66] Herbert
Jacob,[67] and many others have pointed out, the dominant dilemma is that
family loyalties today are less close than they used to be. Consequently,
family responsibilities are understood as less binding than they were even
a generation ago. But in contradiction to these facts of modern life,
recent child support doctrine reflects a sharpening of traditional values
and concepts governing family responsibility.

I do not have a clear answer to the question of what is the most intelligent legal response to still evolving new perceptions of the family and
new sexual-procreative lifestyles. But I am fairly sure that now, after
divorce reform, the answer must involve a radical redefinition of society's
economic and social involvement with the parent-and-child relationship.

1. Tradition: social and economic reciprocity   When Blackstone formulated
the support obligation for the common law world,[68] he was looking at a
world that was centred on the ongoing family. Divorce did not exist—
even if the law did not entirely comport with London reality.

Choosing to rest most of his case on natural law and what we now call sociobiology,[69] Blackstone did not say that the support obligation he saw was founded on the reciprocal relationship of parent and child in the ongoing family, but I think it was. This reciprocity had an economic and a social component.

Economically, the support-obligated parent was entitled to the child's earnings until the child reached majority.[70] Support received by the young child morally and legally obligated the adult child to support the aged parent. Before was had social security, child support was an 'investment' the parent made, to be recovered if needed. The law took this reciprocity quite literally: a child who unjustifiably had not been supported when young as absolved from the obligation later to support the parent.[72]

Socially, parent and child reciprocity involved an ongoing family life. Supporting parents had the emotional satisfaction of seeing their offspring grow up. They shaped their child's life. And their financial responsibilities were fairly minimal. Blackstone said:

No person is bound to provide a maintenance for his issue, unless where the children are impotent and unable to work, either through infancy, disease, or accident, and then is only obliged to find them with necessaries, the penalty on refusal being no more than 20s. a month. For the policy of our laws, which are ever watchful to promote industry, did not mean to compel a father to maintain his idle and lazy children in ease and indolence: but thought it unjust to oblige the parent, against his will, to provide them with superfluities, and other indulgences of fortune; imagining they might trust to the impulse of nature, if the children were deserving of such favours.[73]

In short, the father did not owe much beyond food and clothing, and even that not for long. Today's 'budget busters' were not yet in the picture. Long before medical bills could have seriously accumulated, the child would have died under then prevailing standards of medical care. Education, if there was any, consisted of one-room schools. The main expense of schooling was the loss to the family of the child's earnings or potential contribution around the farm or in the family business. Today, ineligible for loans or tax breaks, middle-class parents often expend $20,000 per year for seven years—four years of undergraduate college followed by three years of law school—and that after having invested upwards of another $100,000 in the same child before it turned eighteen.[74]

2. Modern reality: illegitimacy, divorce, and de facto loss of parental rights
Today, fathers increasingly have assumed an active parental role in the

ongoing family. In stark contrast, the typical custody adjudication on divorce terminates the father's parental status,[75] at least in any meaningful sense.[76] This *de facto* termination of parental status comes at the very time we impose on the absent parent a child support obligation that typically is potentially far larger than what he might have shouldered, or was legally obligated to provide, in the ongoing family. *Married* parents do not legally owe their children a lifestyle that is consistent with their income and station in life. They may choose to rear their children in any reasonable way they see fit. When the parents separate, the practicalities change. The decision-making power now is exercised by the custodial parent who, more often than not, is not the paying parent. In that situation, the custodial parent's reasonable choice of lifestyle largely controls. Without custodial control, the noncustodial parent may thus find himself (and in the future, herself) paying amounts well in excess of those the law would require him to provide if he had custody of his children. Further down the scale, unwed fathers typically never had, and even today rarely obtain, a social relationship with the children they are asked to support. Yet an Illinois court recently ordered an unmarried father to provide a college education for his nonmarital child,[77] whereas the married father in the ongoing marriage has no such obligation.[78]

The point is that the absent parent may fairly claim that he is not getting his 'money's worth' for the support he is obligated to pay, not on the economic and not on the social level. Today's enlarged child support obligation does not resemble what Blackstone was talking about.

Of course, times do change and traditional concepts take on new meanings. If the original rationale no longer holds, this does not mean that a new rationale might not support what we want to do. Let us consider this next.

3. *The weakened rationale of the absent parent's support obligation* I see a contradiction between lifting all 'prior restraint'—social and criminal sanctions[79]—on consensual nonmarital sexual activity and then insisting on strict enforcement of a civil liability that often amounts to eighteen years of potentially extreme restriction on the occidental (or in any event, absent) parent's lifestyle. I see an equally important contradiction on divorce, when we terminate the noncustodial parent's parental interest *de facto* and impose on him a greater and less flexible support obligation than the burden he shouldered in the ongoing family.

In other words, it does not seem at all obvious that the same (or a greater) level of parental responsibility that makes sense in the ongoing family should be grafted (1) onto consanguinity based on what is understood as permissible recreational sex, or (2) onto the essentially terminated post-divorce relationship between the typical father and his child.

Please do not misunderstand, I was among the first to insist that financial responsibility be placed on absent fathers[80] and would be among the last to suggest that there be no responsibility. I am searching now for a level of responsibility that is commensurate with the social reality of the situation.

In a related context—where the unwed father seeks to assert his custodial right—the United States Supreme Court has seen fit to weave a pattern of preference for the social parent-and-child relationship. The biological father has been dealt 'odd man out'. The Court's crucial phrase is: '[T]he mere existence of a biological link does not merit equivalent constitutional protection.'[81]

Consanguinity has a basic place in our culture and law, but does not give all the answers.[82] In the Supreme Court's considered view, the absence of a social relationship is sufficient to deny the biological, but unwed, father a right to object to his child's adoption. Some adaptation is needed to bring this perception to bear on our—one might say mirror-image—context. Just possibly, however, the mere existence of a biological link without a social link, should similarly be deemed insufficient to justify imposing an unmitigated support obligation on the absent, especially the involuntarily absent father. Conversely, as David Chambers suggests,[83] perhaps it is time to impose support obligations on step-parents, on those who have the social relationship although they lack the biological.[84]

The correlation, in fact, between a father's willingness to pay support and the quality of his personal relationship with his child has been pointed out by Judith Wallerstein and Shauna Corbin.[85] In terms of law, I think that it may be time to reflect the involuntarily lacking or impaired social relationship in the duty to support.

The absent parent's support obligation should be pegged at a level at which the cost of family failure—whether through divorce or because a family was not established in the first place—is shared equally by father and mother. Of course, I say nothing different here than what has been said so insistently by many advocates of the ex-wife and mother—and said with the greatest popular publicity by Professor Weitzman.[86] So far we all agree. The problem is in the detail. What is a fair definition of equal cost, of equal sacrifice, to come out of family breakdown?

Even if many aspects of Professor Weitzman's influential study have been questioned,[87] the basic findings are obviously accurate. There *are* irresponsible fathers, and there *is* considerable economic suffering by divorced wives and their children. That is not news. Accordingly, it is not at all my intention to cast doubt on or to belittle the mother's side of the story.[88] My argument goes to maintaining a balance. Let us also look fairly at the responsible father's side of the case.

Professor Weitzman's oft-repeated[89] core charge that the father's standard of living after divorce goes up by forty-two per cent, whereas the ex-wife's and the children's standard goes down by seventy-three per cent,[90] is open to critical evaluation on a variety of levels. But I do not want to bog down in that dispute. I simply want to establish the obvious: the fractured family has three sides, child, mother, and father. With all my prior work having been on the side of child support enforcement, I never have wasted sympathy on the absent father. But now that national support enforcement has alleviated the traditional nonenforcement scandal, I have come to think that sympathetic consideration for the responsible father may not be wasted, but deserved.

What I suggest we seek is a fair equalization of the cost of the alternative family behaviour that has come to pass for normal, or at least acceptable, in our increasingly value-free social environment. I do not plan to develop here any specific adjustments to the child support formulas that have been enacted by the states in response to the federal mandate—and for which I may have some small measure of responsibility. Let us first consider whether there really is a third set of equities in the picture. If we accept the principle, specifics will readily suggest themselves for a 'social relationship factor' in the definition of appropriate child support.

The connection between visitation and child support has been noticed even by the support-enforcement-minded Congress:

The Congress finds that . . . related domestic issues, such as child visitation and child custody, are often intricately intertwined with the child support problem and have received inadequate consideration. . . . It is the sense of Congress that . . . State and local governments must focus on the vital issues of child support, child custody, visitation rights. . . .[91]

The states have not yet done so. So far, even when deprived of custody and visitation, the father finds little sympathy in the courts or legislatures when he argues that he should be allowed to retaliate by withholding child support.[92] And the counterargument is well taken: the child is not denying visitation, and the child should not suffer for the mother's disregard of a visitation order. Accordingly, courts have kept enforcement of child support and the issue of visitation separate,[93] with rare exceptions in unusual cases[94] and even more unusual statutes.[95]

And indeed, what about the child? I certainly do not want to short-change the child. But along with the need to pick up responsibility for the child of the father who is unable to pay, I think that there is a pragmatic 1980s rationale for reconsidering the level of personal sacrifice the absent father is asked to make for a child that is his in a biological sense only.

To be sure, the lack of a social link between father and child—or social reciprocity as I called it earlier—has somewhat different implications in the case of the unwed father who has not lived with the child's mother than it does in the case of a divorced father who has lost custody. The latter more often maintains some social link through visitation. But the difference is one of degree only.

V. Society's responsibility

A. *Debt, self-interest, and the social security system*

Former Secretary Bowen of the Department of Health and Human Services said:

Providing financial support for children is first and foremost a parental responsibility. A successful child support enforcement program enhances the lives of children who because of divorce, separation, or out-of-wedlock birth live with only one parent. Furthermore, collecting child support payments saves hundreds of millions for taxpayers who must provide for families on welfare.[96]

As I see it, Secretary Bowen's view of the matter is correct, but incompleted. Why should any part of the child support burden be put on society? The answer is that economic reciprocity, as once it existed in the old-fashioned family and helped to justify parental responsibility, today furnishes a pragmatic rationale for taxpayer subsidy. The modern system of social security provides old age support for all retired workers and their spouses, regardless of whether they 'invested' in children. Retirees who had no children are equally entitled to social security benefits—equally with those who shared their earnings with their children and had a hard time of it. To the argument that nonparents contributed to the system and that is the basis of their claim, my answer is that their contributions were paid out long ago to retire their own parents. The fact is that the pensions nonparents expect to receive will be paid to them by other people's children—other people's children who have been forced by taxation to substitute them for their own parents.

I am not quarrelling with the concept of social insurance. Nor am I advocating that childless retirees be cut off. We must also understand, however, that children are only in part the private folly of their parents. Taxation has removed old age provision from the family context. Taxation has nationalized that part of children's future earnings that might have gone to fund the retirement of their own parents. In exchange, the taxpayer should reciprocate by bearing an appropriate share of the cost of supporting those who will later bear the burden of old age support for all.

In short, I think that society owes a more active role in supporting the rearing of children. Social recognition of this as a debt, not as reluctant charity, seems to me as important a what we have already accomplished: raising the absent father's consciousness of his debt.

Drawing the elderly into this discussion has another dimension. In terms of family law, the elderly are becoming 'obsolete'.[97] Today's elderly no longer look first for help to their children, they look to the social security system, private pension plans, Medicare, Medicaid, home care, institutionalization, and other social provisions and services. In law even more than in fact, the extended family has given way to the nuclear family, even as—in fact but not yet in law—the nuclear family is giving way to the single-parent family.

Has society gone too far in the direction of accepting responsibility for the elderly[98] and fallen too short in what it does for children? The *New York Times* reports: 'In the first half of the 1980's, the nation's elderly saw their median income rise by about 16 percent while that of the rest of the population either rose slightly, stayed about the same or fell.'[99]

The economic share of children has been slipping. Senator Moynihan says: 'There are some 12 million poor children in the nation but for one reason or another, 5 million get nothing. A half century after the enactment of Social Security, we look up to find that insensate numbers of children are poor and that young children have seven times the poverty rate of the elderly.'[100]

A partnership in child support is the appropriate goal. Martha Minow and Deborah Rhode say that 'child support is a public concern, discharged primarily by parents but enforced and supplemented when necessary by the state, through judicial enforcement, social welfare programs, tax subsidies, and so forth'.[101] David Chambers and I have thought for some time that in a few decades, our society may conclude that the enforcement of individual parental child support obligations, at least at full support levels, may no longer be good social policy.[102]

In democratic western European welfare states, society insists on, but assists with, child support.[103] Typically, those systems accept the two most burdensome aspects of child support, health care and higher education, as primarily social, rather than private, responsibilities. Yet even the duties of providing sustenance and personal care are tempered by children's allowances, subsidized day-care arrangements, and subsidized housing.[104]

Abstract fairness in defining support obligations is not the only issue. A practical concern is that reproduction rates may drop to levels endangering our economy and the social security system. For women, the instability of modern marriage has raised to nearly unacceptable levels the economic risk of choosing the home and children over a career. For responsible men, rigorous child-support enforcement may turn out to be deterrent to 'assisting' in the 'production' of children. Given effective birth control, ready access to abortion, and the mutual risk of easy divorce, increasing numbers of couples even now choose to remain childless. Most already limit reproduction under the pressure resulting from both parties' pursuit of individual careers and the increasing expense of rearing a modern child. The time may be approaching when the opportunity cost of child rearing becomes prohibitive. Rational men and women may then choose not to have children, unless their economic security is assured by society at large. At that point, mothers and fathers who care or who have cared for children may have to be rewarded for their parenting services by meaningful tax reductions[105] and subsidies financed by an equalization-of-burdens levy on those who choose not to (or for any reason are unable to) accept the social responsibility of bearing, rearing, and supporting children.[106]

Our society's *de facto* delegation of the child-raising chore to the lower economic strata (especially unmarried, divorce, and unemployed women without adequate income)[107] requires a greater awareness on the part of couples with double incomes and no kids (so-called DINKS) that their own future is in jeopardy. They should be asked whether they want to live in the kind of society that will be formed by an ever-increasing proportion of social outcasts—the inevitable product of continued disregard for the social and educational needs of the already twenty-five percent of all (and fifty per cent of black) children who even now survive under the poverty line.[108] If that question elicits no constructive response, they should be told that their own retirement is directly in jeopardy. Only a healthy, educated, and willing working generation will generate the necessary income to provide retirement for their predecessors in the workplace. In short, *having* children is not just a private matter—and neither is *not* having children!

The problem of our neglected and impoverished children is not simply the result of the failure of private responsibility. The problem we face cannot be corrected solely by enforcement of private monetary responsibility. We should take from parents what they can pay, but not more than they fairly should pay. Society cannot continue to limit social intervention to bare survival at a level well below our official definition of a minimum standard. Adequate financial and social support will turn a child from a social liability into a social asset. All of us must assume a fair share of the burden of decently raising the next generation. We are not doing that.[109]

B. *The custodial parent's need for services*

Money is not everything. Improved standards of economic assistance, in terms of a partnership between public aid and the child's parents, are but one aspect of a new public approach giving priority to the best interests of the child. We also should take a critical look at the relationship between the child and the custodial parent, and at the manner in which the mother takes care of her fatherless child. We cannot expect the absent parent to carry faithfully a full load of child support and refuse to look at the expenditure side. This has two aspects.

First, in fairness to the child and in analogy to the paying parent whose lifestyle is, in the best interest of his child, subjected to intensive scrutiny and often severe curtailment, the custodial parent should be held accountable that the money paid for the child's support actually goes to the child's support.

Second, honest concern for child welfare reasonably requires a routine check into the fitness for child rearing of single-parent homes—or, indeed, any home—without the implication of punishment or moral condemnation. Unlike some current child neglect laws, new laws should allow for the genuine cultural diversity and divergent lifestyles that legitimately coexist in our society. We must develop new concepts of sharing caretaking responsibility between parent and assistance institutions. But a line against the inadequate parent must be drawn where the essential interests of the child are in jeopardy.

I learned long ago that the politics of this area are fierce and angry[110]— all the more so because help for the child would have a statistically disproportionate impact in the African-American community.[111] But we must not be distracted by statistical appearances. For the sake of the children, I still think we must intervene in settings that are clearly inadequate for rearing children[112]—in settings that violate the civil rights of children.[113] "Even if cocaine addicts had a right to their addiction, should they have the right to pass it on?[114] Should not children have a constitutional right not to be homeless,[115] not to live in welfare hotels,[116] not in Manhattan,[117] and not to be born drugged?[118] But here goes another article.[119]

C. What can we do in the high-deficit late 1980s?

Quite immediately, we should focus tax rates and reductions on dependent children, not on joint returns triggered by a marriage certificate.[120] Driven originally by state law definitions of community income,[121] family tax relief has come primarily through income splitting by way of the joint return. The value of exceptions for dependants, even with a recent increase, pales by comparison. Wholly in line with this emphasis on the joint return, the recent family tax reform debate has long focused on the so-called marriage penalty, the difference between income tax owed by married and unmarried couples in the same or similar circumstances— demonstrating the self-centred political power of childless couples.[122] That debate culminated in a two-earner bonus provided under the Economic Recovery Tax Act of 1981.[123] That has been superseded by new legislation, not least because the marriage penalty has been rendered less important by new nearly flat income tax rates.[124]

The real problem has been and remains: tax law has used marriage, not children, as the tax significant event. This approach has always been in conflict with the underlying justification of income taxation—ability to pay. Many modern forms of marriage have no bearing on ability to pay— or, more typically, marriage (or unwed cohabitation) reduces expenses through economies of scale and thus increases ability to pay.

For years, the marriage penalty debate has focused on the very reasonable question of why, for tax purposes, the married, two-earner, equal career partnership established for emotional and sexual satisfaction should not be equated with the unmarried, two-earner, equal career partnership established for the same purpose. Seen from that perspective, the marriage penalty complaint has obvious merit, even if the Internal Revenue Service and the courts have not agreed.[125] But this was the wrong question.

Properly, the question should be why our tax law does not make a distinction between (1) the two-earner, equal career partnership, married or unmarried, and (2) the wholly or partially role-divided family established for the purpose of raising children.

To both the wrong and the right questions, the appropriate answer is clear: married and unmarried DINKS should indeed be treated alike. We should discontinue the tax preference (or penalty) triggered by the technicality of legal marriage. Instead, tax recognition and relief should be focused on children, where they are (affecting ability to pay), and where they were (affecting the 'former' mother's ability to earn in step with her childless sister). That is, if our society (as I think it does) considers expenses for child rearing on a higher level of social utility than, say, love boat cruises.

Where tax reductions have no effect, we should provide subsidies. We must ensure appropriate and necessary flexibility at the workplace for those who choose to parent, in terms of constructive day care for the children of full-time workers and part-time work without loss of long-run opportunity for those who choose to care for their children themselves. We must change employment practices to assist reentry into the economy of those who have parented, for their sake and that of the economy. A network of laws designed for full-time workers and based on workplace seniority now discourages needed change.

As for the argument that the federal budget will not stand for such new burdens, the good news is that the deficit, and ultimately perhaps the underlying debt, will soon be absorbed by the rapidly growing Social Security surplus, scheduled to be collected under laws now in place.[126] Even now, the budget is balanced in terms of current tax receipts and expenditures. The current deficit is only interest on the national debt[127]—nearly two-thirds of which was borrowed in the last eight years.[128]

Besides, there is misspent welfare money even in the current budget. I reject the usual military target—defence is not welfare and furnishes no useful comparison. However, the taxpayer supplies more than twenty five billion 'welfare' dollars each year for 'farmers',[129] and not just to the romantic family farm of American history. The principal recipients of this 'welfare' are agribusiness corporations[130] and adult individuals who have made bad business decisions—typically by borrowing irrational amounts to speculate in farmland.

The point is that we really can afford a major effort in this area. Can we afford not to step in? Recently, Justice Brennan wrote:

In The Republic and in The Laws, Plato offered a vision of a unified society, where the needs of children are met not by parents but by the Government, and where no intermediate forms of association stand between the individual and the State. The vision is a brilliant one, but it is not our own.[131]

Indeed it is not. We seem to be moving not toward a 'unified society', but toward a fractured society in which the needs of children are 'met not by parents' *and not* 'by the government'.[132]

At the welfare level, appropriate concern for the child requires a much more effective public contribution in terms of services and dollars to assure basic necessities and give the child a fairer start in life. At the well-off level, the argument is irrelevant—actor Hurt is not hurt by paying $65,000 in annual child support for his six-year-old son, and the child has enough, even if the mother wants more.[133]

At the upper middle income level, the taxpayer would be wise to consider whether a proper public recognition of the social value of parenthood would not be the assumption of nonroutine health and higher education costs that now beggar responsible parents—and that contribute to many responsible would-be parents' decisions not to have children.

Above the welfare level and below the upper middle income level, my argument concerns the enormously wide strata of those whom we like to flatter with the designation 'middle class', but who all too often are but a notch removed from what we have come to call the 'working poor'. At that level, sympathetic concern with the financial plight of parents who are doing what they can and the argument for a better balanced role division between parents and public have their greatest strength.

VI.   Summary

Where we now are going is wrong. While very impressive progress in child support collection from absent parents has been made, the very progress seems to have led us to overestimate, and consequently overemphasize, financial support that can be obtained from absent parents. Perhaps, we also ask too much from those who have lost their social relationship with their child. Finally, it seems that we overestimate, and consequently overemphasize, the parental rights of the care-taking parent past the point where the latter's conduct conflicts with the best interests of the child. These three misunderstandings are displacing public consciousness of our shared responsibility for the unprecedented havoc that is threatening much of our next generation.

My thesis is simple: children have a right to a decent start in life. This right is the obligation of the father and equally of the mother, and in recognition of a primary and direct responsibility, equally the obligation of society.

(1) The absent parent owes support commensurate with (*a*) his or her ability to pay, (*b*) the marital and sexual realities and expectations our society encourages or tolerates, and (*c*) his or her past and present social relationship with the child.

(2) The custodial parent owes services and care in an environment conducive to the child's short- and long-term best interests, (*a*) commensurate with his or her means, and (*b*) subject to an objective minimum standard.

(3) Society has a direct duty to the child to make up any shortfall, (*a*) on the absent parent's side, by provision of money, and (*b*) on the custodial parent's side, by intervention when care is not provided at a level called for by a minimal definition of the child's best interests.

Notes

1. See H. Krause, *Child Support in America: The Legal Perspective* (1981) [hereinafter *Child Support*]; H. Krause, *Illegitimacy: Law and Social Policy* (1971) [hereinafter *Illegitimacy*]; Krause, 'Equal Protection for the Illegitimate', 65 Mich. L. Rev. 477 (1967) [hereinafter 'Equal Protection']; Krause, 'Bringing the Bastard into the Great Society—A Proposed Uniform Act on Legitimacy', 44 Tex. L. Rev. 829 (1966) [hereinafter 'Uniform Act'].

2. President Reagan issued an executive order to assess the impact of federal activity on the family. Exec. Order No. 12,606, 3 C.F.R. 241 (1987 comp.), reprinted in 5 U.S.C. § 601 note a 139–40 (Supp. V 1987) [hereinafter Exec. Order]. The order asked:

   (a) Does this action by government strengthen or erode the stability of the family and, particularly, the marital commitment?

   (b) Does this action strengthen or erode the authority and rights of parents in the education, nurture, and supervision of their children?

   (c) Does this action help the family perform its functions, or does it substitute governmental activity for the function?

   (d) Does this action by government increase or decrease family earnings? Do the proposed benefits of this action justify the impact on the family budget?

   (e) Can this activity be carried out by a lower level of government or by the family itself?

   (f) What message, intended or otherwise, does this program send to the public concerning the status of the family?

   (g) What message does it send to young people concerning the relationship between their behaviour, their personal responsibility, and the norms of our society?

   Id. at 242, 5 U.S.C. § 601 note at 139.

3. In the fall of 1988, presidential candidates competed hotly on family issues, such as day care. All-but-forgotten presidential aspirants called for an increase

in the American birthrate, e.g., *N.Y. Times*, 24 Oct. 1987, at 9, col. 1 (Reverend Pat Robertson), and pregnancy leave (Representative Pat Schroeder's proposal is still pending in Congress). Senator Pat Moynihan's 1988 welfare reform shows a family and child support enforcement focus. See, e.g. 'Welfare: Reform or Replacement? (Child Support Enforcement—II: Hearings Before the Subcomm. on Social Security and Family Policy of the Senate Comm. on Finance', 100th Cong., 1st Sess. (1987). The party platforms reflected different approaches to the problem of child care. *N.Y. Times*, 17 Aug. 1988, §A, at 20, col. 1. The Republicans:

In returning to our traditional commitment to children, the Republic Party proposes a radically different approach: establish a toddler tax credit for preschool children as proposed by Vice President Bush, available to all families of modest means, to help them support and care for their children in a manner best suited to their families' values and traditions . . . .

Id.

The Democrats:

We believe that Government should set the standard in recognizing that worker productivity is enhanced . . . by major increases in assistance making child care more available and affordable to low and middle income families, helping states build a strong child care infrastructure, setting minimum standards for health, safety and quality . . . .

N.Y. Times, 17 Aug. 1988, § A, at 20, col. 2; see also 'Governor Michael Dukakis on Family Policy', *Am. Fam.*, Oct. 1988, at 5; Moritz, 'Family Policy in the 1988 Campaign: More Than Patronage and Promise?', *Am. Fam.*, Oct. 1988, at 3; Rovner, 'Democrats Lining Up Behind "Family" Banner', 46 *Cong. Q. Weekly Rep.* 183 (1988); 'Vice President George Bush on Family Policy', *Am. Fam.*, Oct. 1988, at 4.

4. Consider '82 Key Statistics on Work and Family Issues', Nat'l Rep. on Work & Fam. (BNA) Spec. Rep. No. 9 (Sept. 1988).

5. See, e.g., S. Rep. No. 447, 100th Cong., 2d Sess. (1988). Compare the minority view of Senator Quayle. Id. at 64–9. See 'Parental Leave Bill Put on Fast Track in Congress by House and Senate Sponsors', 2 Nat'l Rep. on Work & Fam. (BNA) No. 5, at 1 (17 Feb. 1989); Rovner, 'Child-Care Debate Intensifies As ABC Bill Is Approved', 47 *Cong. Q. Weekly Rep.* 585 (1989).

6. See, e.g., Besharov & Tramontozzi, 'The Costs of Federal Child Care Assistance', *Am. Fam.*, Sept. 1988, at 10; 'Bush Calls for $330 Million Package of Child Care Initiatives and Tax Credits', 2 Nat'l Rep. on Work & Fam. (BNA) No. 5, at 1 (17 Feb. 1989). Proposals remain active: Rovner, 'Partisan Bidding War Erupts over Aid to Poor Children', 47 *Cong. Q. Weekly Rep.* 653 (1989); Rovner, 'Senate's Child-Care Measure Would Broaden U.S. Role', 47 *Cong. Q. Weekly Rep.* 1543 (1989).

7. See, e.g., Working Group on the Family, The Family: Preserving America's Future (Nov. 1986) (unpublished report transmitted with letter dated Dec. 2,

1986, from Gary L. Bauer, Under Secretary of the United States Department of Education, to President Reagan) (on permanent file with the *University of Illinois Law Review*); cf. Exec. Order, *supra* note 2.

8. See, e.g., Chambers, 'The "Legalization" of the Family: Toward a Policy of Supportive Neutrality', 18 J.L. Reform 805 (1985). But see Burt, 'Coercive Freedom: A Response to Professor Chambers', 18 J.L. Reform 829 (1985).
9. See generally M. Rheinstein, *Marriage Stability, Divorce, and the Law*, ch. 4 (1972).
10. See U.S. Dep't of Commerce, Bureau of the Census, Current Population Reports, Population Characteristics, Series P-20, No. 433, *Marital Status and Living Arrangements*, March 1988 (1989).
11. E.g., Krause, 'Legal Position: Unmarried Couples', 34 *Am. J. Comp. L.* 533 (Supp. 1986).
12. For example, is marital community property an idea that came 100 years too late? See Glendon, 'Is There a Future For Separate Property?', 8 *Fam. L.Q.* 315, 322–5 (1974).
13. The federal child support enforcement legislation is discussed *infra* Part III.A to III.D.
14. See *infra* Part III.A.
15. Lehr *v.* Robertson, 463 U.S. 248, 261–2 (1983).
16. *Restatement of Conflict of Laws* §458 comment a, at 548 (1934).
17. *Illegitimacy*, *supra* note 1, at 107–8.
18. See Stack & Semmel, 'The Concept of Family in the Poor Black Community', in *Staff of Subcomm. on Fiscal Policy of the Joint Economic Comm.*, *93d Cong., 1st Sess., Studies in Public Welfare, Paper No. 12, The Family, Poverty, and Welfare Programs: Household Patterns and Government Policies* pt. II, at 275 (Comm. Print 1973) (R. Lerman ed.) [hereinafter *Studies in Public Welfare*]; cf. H. Krause, *Family Law: Cases, Comments, and Questions* 935–6 (2nd ed. 1983) (quoting G. Cooper & P. Dodyk, *Income Maintenance* 285 (1973)):

Though consanguinity has been traditionally recognized as an acceptable basis for the allocation of support costs, that criterion is markedly discordant with the ability-to-pay notions which determine so much of the modern allocation of public costs. Particularly where an extended net of liable relatives is recognized under state law, the wisdom of departing from the normal general-revenue tax base may be questioned. Indeed, even where one is dealing with the relation of father to son, one finds the reports replete with cases in which the biological nexus is paralleled by no ties of familiarity, affection or support—cases which raise grave doubt as to the ultimate significance of simple blood relationship for the problems at hand.

Moreover, whatever the conclusions one may reach on such matters, one must contend with the fact that reluctance to precipitate enforcement of support obligations causes many applicants to refrain from seeking public assistance. The aversion to trenching upon the already stretched resources of another household has caused many, particularly among the elderly, to prefer private penury to public assistance. Whatever the gain derived from reliance upon support obligations, its cost is some degree of frustration of the central purpose of public assistance.

19. Sugarman, Roe v. Norton: 'Coerced Maternal Cooperation', in R. Mnookin, *In the Interest of Children: Advocacy, Law Reform, and Public Policy* 365, 415–17 (1985).
20. See Stack & Semmel, *supra* note 18.
21. *Child Support, supra* note 1, at 285–306.
22. Congress added 42 U.S.C. § 602(a)(11) (requiring notice to state child support collection agency of AFDC benefits) in 1950.
23. Greenspan v. Slate, 12 N.J. 426, 437, 97 A.2d 390, 395 (1953).
24. 1 W. Blackstone, *Commentaries on the Laws of England*, *447–8 (footnotes omitted).
25. 'Twelfth Annual Report Released to Congress', *Child Support Rep.*, Aug. 1988, at 3 [hereinafter 'Report'].
26. See *Child Support, supra* note 1, at 323–30, discussing the drawn-out controversy over the non-AFDC support collection feature of the enforcement legislation. It is well worth emphasizing the significance of the extension of the federal support enforcement legislation beyond the welfare context. The provisions concerning non-AFDC support enforcement alleviate the all-too-common lot of the abandoned mother who has sufficient productive capacity and pride to keep herself and her children above the welfare eligibility line, but whose earning capacity may have been impaired by a role-divided marriage and now is restricted by the custodial services she renders her children. While the typical father's earnings enable him to make a reasonable contribution to child support, he does not earn enough to do so without pain. Thus, unless seriously encouraged, many fathers are unwilling to make their proper contributions. These contributions, though significant in terms of their children's needs, too often are not enough to make it economical to involve lawyers in repeated enforcement forays under the cumbersome and correspondingly expensive traditional child support enforcement procedures.
27. 1 *U.S. Dep't of Health & Human Servs., Office of Child Support Enforcement, Twelfth Annual Report to Congress for the Period Ending September 30, 1987*, 7 (1988) [hereinafter *Report to Congress*]; 2 id. tables 3, 5.
28. The federal enforcement legislation is codified at 42 U.S.C. §§ 651–65 (1982). The text following this note briefly summarizes the federal enforcement process. For more detailed explanations, see *Child Support, supra* note 1, at 307–87; M. Henry & V. Schwartz, *A Guide for Judges in Child Support Enforcement* (M. Reynolds, 2nd ed., 1987); M. Henry & B. Schwartz, *Essentials for Attorneys in Child Support Enforcement* (M. Reynolds (ed.), 1986).
29. Child Support Enforcement Amendments of 1984, Pub. L. No. 98–378, 98 Stat. 1305 (codified as amended in scattered sections of 42 U.S.C.) [hereinafter 1984 Amendments]; see also *H.R. Rep.* No. 527, 98th Cong., 1st Sess. (1983). The text following this note summarizes important provisions of the 1984 amendments.

30. The 1988 amendments require immediate withholding by 1994. See *infra* Part III.D.
31. By August of 1988, eight states routinely reported child support debt to credit bureaus. 'States Report Child Support Debts to Credit Bureaus', *Child Support Rep.*, Aug. 1988, at 1.
32. Clark v. Jeter, 108 S. Ct. 1910 (1988); Paulussen v. Herion, 475 U.S. 557 (1986); Pickett v. Brown, 462 U.S. 1 (1983); Mills v. Habluetzel, 456 U.S. 91 (1982).
33. D. Chambers, *Making Fathers Pay: The Enforcement of Child Support* (1979).
34. 1984 Amendments, *supra* note 29, § 17, 98 Stat. at 1321–22 (codified as amended at 42 U.S.C.A. § 667 (West Supp. 1989)).
35. H.R. Rep. No. 527, 98th Cong., 1st Sess. 48 (1983):

> The Committee recommends that the report include a full and complete summary of the opinions and recommendations of an advisory panel to be comprised of at least one person who is representative of parents entitled to receive child support on behalf of their children, at least one person who is representative of absent parents obligated to pay child support, and at least two people with professional expertise in child support issues in the fields of law and economics, at least one person who is a member of the judiciary, at least one person who is a member of a State legislature, and at least one person with expertise in the administration of child support enforcement programs.

36. R. Williams, *Development of Guidelines for Child Support Orders: Final Report*, I-4 (1987).
37. See Brackney, 'Recent Development—Battling Inconsistency and Inadequacy: Child Support Guidelines in the States', 11 Harv. Women's L.J. 197 (1988); Dodson, 'A Guide to the Guidelines: New Child Support Rules Are Helping Custodial Parents Bridge the Financial Gap', *Fam. Advoc.*, Spring 1988, at 4; M. Minow & D. Rhode, On Divorce Reform: Reforming the Questions, Questioning the Reformers 21–27 (Draft Oct. 1988) (unpublished paper presented at a symposium, *Divorce Reform in Retrospect*, sponsored by the Earl Warren Legal Institute, University of California at Berkeley, and the Institute for Research on Women and Gender, Stanford University, 4–5 Nov. 1988, to be published by the Yale University Press as part of a collection edited by Stephen D. Sugarman) (on permanent file with the *University of Illinois Law Review*).
38. 1984 Amendments, *supra* note 29, § 23(b)(1), 98 Stat. at 1330.
39. Id. §23, 98 Stat. at 1329–30.
40. Family Support Act of 1988, Pub. L. No. 102–485, 100 Stat. 2343 (to be codified in scattered section of 42 U.S.C.). For a summary and text of the 1988 amendments, see 15 Fam. L. Rep. (BNA) 1047–8, 2001–8 (1988). The text following this footnote briefly summarizes important provisions of those amendments.
41. This paternity establishment provision comes 15 years after it was proposed to the Senate Finance Committee. See *Illegitimacy, supra* note 1, at 133–7;

H. Krause, *Family Law: Cases, Comments and Questions*, 985–6 (2nd ed., 1983). Then, the proposal was enacted by the Senate, but not by the House, and dropped in conference.

42. See 2 *Report to Congress, supra* note 27, tables 58–71.

43. 'Report', *supra* note 25, at 3 (quoting Director Stanton).

44. L. Weitzman, *The Divorce Revolution: The Unexpected Social and Economic Consequences for Women and Children in America* (1985); see 'Review Symposium on Weitzman's *Divorce Revolution*', 1986 *Am. B. Found. Res. J.* 757 [hereinafter 'Review Symposium'].

45. Bruch & Wikler, 'The Economic Consequences', *Juv. & Fam. Ct. J.*, Fall 1985, at 5.

46. 1 *Report to Congress, supra* note 27, at 5.

47. *Child Support, supra* note 1, at 431.

48. See U.S. Dep't of Commerce, Bureau of the Census, *Current Population Reports, Household Economic Studies*, Series P-70, No. 13, *Who's Helping Out? Support Networks Among American Families* (1988).

49. The study shows that half of the teen fathers lived with their child at least for some time after the baby's birth. However, only one-third of the fathers married the mother of the baby within twelve months of conception. The study also shows that teenage fathers who were married prior to conception were the least likely to have completed high school: 62 per cent of those fathers dropped out of school compared to about 37 per cent of those whose first birth was conceived outside of marriage whether they subsequently married or not.

'Teenage Fatherhood', *Am. Fam.*, Mar. 1988, at 19; see generally J. Smollar & T. Ooms, *Young Unwed Fathers: Research Review, Policy Dilemmas and Options* 52–3 (1987).

50. D. Chambers, *supra* note 33, at 3–9, 253. Senator Moynihan has a more 'optimistic' perception of the situation:

This is a matter to be pressed *to* the point of punitiveness. . . . Hunt, hound, harass: the absent father is rarely really absent, especially the teenage father, but merely unwilling or not required to acknowledge his children's presence. The Child Support Enforcement program has the great virtue of paying for itself as well as having the inestimable advantage of linking the issue of welfare dependency to the more general issue of women's entitlements. . . . And for the too-much-pitied unemployed teenage male there would be nothing wrong with a federal work program—compulsory when a court has previously ordered him to support his children—with the wages shared between father and mother. This latter is not likely to get started or to work very well if it does. The disorder of the times would likely enough defeat it. But it does make a statement about legitimacy: there must be an acknowledged providing male.

D. Moynihan, *Family and Nation*, 180–1 (1986).

51. 2 *Report to Congress, supra* note 27, table 49; see also L. Loyacono & S. Smith, *State Budget Implications: Child Support Enforcement*, apps. B & C (1988). Below

'par' AFDC cost effectiveness ratios for 1987 are reported for New Hampshire (.83), Delaware (.92), Maryland (.96), New York (.74), Nebraska (.85), Florida (.81), Kentucky (.93), Louisiana (.90), Tennessee (.97), Virginia (.59), Arizona (.53), New Mexico (.95), Oklahoma (.97), Texas (.84), Colorado (.94), Alaska (.75), Nevada (.62), the District of Columbia (.53), Guam (.73), Puerto Rico (.52), and the Virgin Islands (.28). Id. In assessing the true meaning of 'cost–benefit effectiveness,' many caveats are in order. See *Child Support, supra* note 1, at 422–31, 446–55.

52. Krause, 'Reflections on Child Support', 1983 *U. Ill. L. Rev.* 99, 106–11.

53. H. Krause, *supra* note 41, at 897–9; H. Krause, *Family Law: Cases, Comments, and Questions*, 897–9 (2nd ed., 1983) (quoting Krause, 'Automatic Adjustment Clauses in Support Agreements or Decrees', 1 *Fair Share*, 3–4 (1981).

54. 'Child Support Enforcement Program Reform Proposals: Hearings Before the Senate Comm. on Finance', 98th Cong., 2nd Sess. 454, 458, 460 (1984) [hereinafter 'Hearings'] (statement of Harry D. Krause, Professor of Law, University of Illinois). *Contra* Bruch, 'Developing Standards for Child Support Payments: A Critique of Current Practice', 16 *U.C. Davis L. Rev.*, 49, 62 (1982).

55. See *supra* text accompanying note 36.

56. We could debate at length the relative effectiveness of specific enforcement techniques, from wage withholding to extradition and imprisonment. See D. Chambers, *supra* note 33; *Child Support, supra* note 1, at 81–4. We could discuss the United States Supreme Court's recent struggle with contempt sanctions, civil or criminal, in Hicks *ex rel.* Feiock *v.* Feiock, 108 S. Ct. 1423 (1988). But I think that the 'better enforcement' debate is all but over. With mandated formula based setting of support obligations, with payroll deduction of support owed, and with computer-provided nationwide access to support-owing parents, the law now provides an effective arsenal for imposing the obligation as well as collecting child support. Continuing complaints that child support collections remain inadequate can no longer expect much response from better enforcement law, although there is always room for improvement.

57. *Champaign-Urbana News-Gazette*, 13 Aug. 1988, at col. 1. (42.7% of black children under the age of 18 were poor); see also *N.Y. Times*, 3 Sept. 1988, § 1, at 22, col. 1.

58. *N.Y. Times*, 12 Apr. 1987, § 4, at 5, col. 2, lists maximum fiscal 1987 monthly benefits for a family of four as of January 1987. Given in parentheticals are the figures as a percent of estimated median monthly income for a family of four. The highest paying states were Alaska: $833 (23%); California: $734 (26%); New York: $706 (26%); Connecticut: $688 (21%); Wisconsin: $649 (25%). The lowest paying states were: Mississippi: $144 (7.3%); Alabama: $147 (6.6%); Tennessee: $189 (8.5%); Texas: $221 (8.5%); Arkansas: $224 (11.6%).

59. 'Hearings', *supra* note 54, at 454, 464–6 (statement of Harry D. Krause,

240 *Substantive aspects of family law*

Professor of Law, University of Illinois); see also *Child Support, supra* note 1, at 456–65.

60. For more detail, see Disregard of Child Support Payments, 53 Fed. Reg. 21,642 (1988) (codified in scattered sections of 45 C.F.R. pts. 302 & 303).

61. Even this small step has proved to be expensive. The $50 disregard reduced the overall savings to the taxpayer from a high near $250 million in 1984 to less than $25 million in 1987, and more than tripled the federal programme deficit to about $300 million in the same period. 1 *Report to Congress, supra* note 27, at 12.

62. Cf. Bowen *v.* Gilliard, 483 U.S. 587 (1987) (AFDC provision which attributes child support benefits to the family unit is not unconstitutional).

63. D. Moynihan, *supra* note 50, at 147.

64. E.g., Gray, Book Review, 46 N.Y.U. *L. Rev.* 1228, 1233 (1971) (reviewing *Illegitimacy, supra* note 1):

> Professor Krause . . . errs in suggesting that poor illegitimate children can be benefited by a systematic effort to force their fathers to pay support. . . . First, such a program would not create more stable families. Rather, the effect would be to encourage fathers to desert their illegitimate children entirely. Second, many children would not benefit financially even if fathers did pay, since the support payments would be deducted from any welfare benefits.

65. Glendon, 'Modern Marriage Law and Its Underlying Assumptions: The New Marriage and the New Property', 13 *Fam. L.Q.* 441 (1980).

66. Minow, 'The Properties of Family and the Families of Property' (Book Review), 92 *Yale L.J.* 376, 379–81 (1982) (reviewing M. Glendon, *The New Family and the New Property* (1981)).

67. Jacob, 'The Changing Landscape of Family Policy and Law' (Book Review), 21 *Law & Soc'y Rev.* 744 (1988).

68. 1 W. Blackstone, *supra* note 24, at *447–8.

69. See J. Beckstrom, *Evolutionary Jurisprudence: Prospects and Limitations on the Use of Modern Darwinism Throughout the Legal Process*, 50–3 (1989); J. Beckstrom, *Sociobiology and the Law: The Biology of Altruism in the Courtroom of the Future* (1985).

70. 1 W. Blackstone, *supra* note 24, at *453.

71. An Act for the Relief of the Poor, 43 Eliz., ch. 2, § VII (1601); 1 W. Blackstone, *supra* note 24, at *453–4; cf. Swoap *v.* Superior Court, 10 Cal. 3d 490, 516 P.2d 840, 111 Cal. Rptr. 136 (1973) (statute requiring children to reimburse state for aid paid to parents is not unconstitutional); see also Garrett, 'Filial Responsibility Laws', 18 *J. Fam. L.* 793 (1979–80).

72. See, e.g., Cannon *v.* Juras, 15 Or. App. 265, 515 P.2d 428 (Ct. App. 1973) (facts did not establish abandonment which would absolve son from support of his mother).

73. 1 W. Blackstone, *supra* note 24, at *449 (footnotes omitted).

74. The *New York Times* reports:

A middle-income couple with two children will face total costs of about $130,000 per child in 1988 dollars by the time both children are 18 years old, said Thomas Espenshade, a senior fellow at the Urban Institute, a research organization in Washington, D.C. If the children go to college, the costs will significantly increase. 'Most prospective parents grossly underestimate the financial obligations of parenthood', Mr. Espenshade said.

N.Y. Times, 20 Feb. 1988, § 1, at 34, col. 1. ('Planners advise parents to begin saving for a child's college education as soon as possible. For a child born in 1988, four years at a public university might cost about $120,000 in tuition and other expenses', Id.). 'A study by the College Board indicates that from 1981 to 1987, the cost of attending a private university increased 81 percent, while median family income rose 40 percent.' *N.Y. Times*, 23 Mar. 1988, §B, at 8, col. 1.

75. The traditional presumption that favours giving custody to the mother is dying a very slow death. The great majority of custody dispositions still go to the mother. H. Krause, *supra* note 41, at 727–35.

76. Even in trend-setting California, the flirtation with joint custody seems to be ebbing. On 27 September 1988, Governor George Deukmejian signed a new law that declares that California has 'neither a preference nor a presumption for or against legal custody, joint physical custody, or sole custody, but allows the court and the family the widest discretion to choose a parenting plan which is in the best interests of the child or children'. Sherman, 'Doubts Grow on Joint Custody', *Nat'l L.J.*, 24 Oct. 1988, at 3, col. 1 (quoting California law).

77. Rawles *v.* Hartman, 172 Ill. App. 3d 931, 527 N.E.2d 680 (App. Ct. 1988), *leave to appeal denied*, 123 Ill. 2d 566, 535 N.E.2d 410 (1989).

78. See Kujawinski *v.* Kujawinski, 71 Ill. 2d 563, 578–80, 376 N.E.2d, 1382, 1389–90 (1978); see generally Moore, 'Parents' Support Obligations to Their Adult Children', 19 *Akron L. Rev.* 183 (1985).

79. E.g., Doe *v.* Duling, 603 F. Supp. 960 (E.D. Va. 1985) (Virginia fornication and cohabitation statutes declared unconstitutional).

80. See 'Equal Protection', *supra* note 1, at 504–6; 'Uniform Act', *supra* note 1, at 859.

81. Lehr *v.* Robertson, 463 U.S. 248, 261 (1983), and, very recently, consider Michael H. *v.* Gerald D., 109 S. Ct. 2333 (1989). In *Lehr*, the Court elaborated:

The intangible fibers that connect parent and child have infinite variety. They are woven throughout the fabric of our society, providing it with strength, beauty, and flexibility. It is self-evident that they are sufficiently vital to merit constitutional protection in appropriate cases. In deciding whether this is such a case, however, we must consider the broad framework that has traditionally been used to resolve the legal problems arising from the parent–child relationship.

. . . .

The difference between the developed parent–child relationship that was implicated in *Stanley* and *Caban*, and the potential relationship involved in *Quilloin* and this case, is both clear and significant. When an unwed father demonstrates a full commitment to the responsibilities of parenthood by 'com[ing] forward to participate in the rearing of his child', his interest in personal contact with his child acquires substantial protection under the Due Process Clause. At that point it may be said that he 'act[s] as a father toward his children'. *But the mere existence of a biological link does not merit equivalent constitutional protection.* The actions of judges neither create nor sever genetic bonds. '[T]he importance of the familial relationship, to the individuals involved and to the society, stems from the emotional attachments that derive from the intimacy of daily association, and from the fact of blood relationship.'

The significance of the biological connection is that it offers the natural father an opportunity that no other male possesses to develop a relationship with his offspring. If he grasps that opportunity and *accepts some measure of responsibility for the child's future,* he may enjoy the blessings of the parent–child relationship and make uniquely valuable contributions to the child's development. If he fails to do so, the Federal Constitution will not automatically compel a State to listen to his opinion of where the child's best interests lie.

Lehr, 463 U.S. at 256, 261–2 (citations omitted and emphasis added).
82. For the Court's most recent opinion on related issues, see Michael H. *v.* Gerald D., 109 S. Ct. 2333 (1989).
83. D. Chambers, Stepparents, Biologic Parents, and the Law's Perceptions of 'Family' After Divorce (Conference Draft Oct. 28, 1988) (unpublished paper presented at a symposium, *Divorce Reform in Retrospect,* sponsored by the Earl Warren Legal Institute, University of California at Berkeley, and the Institute for Research on Women and Gender, Stanford University, 4–5 Nov. 1988, to be published by the Yale University Press as part of a collection edited by Stephen D. Sugarman) (on permanent file with the *University of Illinois Law Review*).
84. See Ramsey & Masson, 'Stepparent Support of Stepchildren: A Comparative Analysis of Policies and Problems in the American and English Experience', 36 *Syracuse L. Rev.,* 659 (1985).
85. See Wallerstein & Corbin, 'Father–Child Relationships After Divorce: Child Support and Educational Opportunity', 20 *Fam. L.Q.,* 109, 115 (1986); see also Pearson & Theonnes, 'Supporting Children After Divorce: The Influence of Custody on Support Levels and Payments', 22 *Fam. L.Q.,* 319 (1988).
86. See L. Weitzman, *supra* note 44; Abraham, 'The Divorce Revolution Revisited: A Counter-Revolutionary Critique';, 3 *Am. J. Fam. L.,* 87 (1989).
87. See, e.g., 'Review Symposium', *supra* note 44.
88. See, e.g., Hunter, 'Child Support Law and Policy: The Systematic Imposition of Costs on Women', 6 *Harv. Women's L.J.,* 1 (1983).
89. See, e.g., Moss, 'No-Fault Divorce Hurts', *A.B.A.J.,* Dec. 1986, at 36.
90. L. Weitzman, *supra* note 44, at 337–43.
91. 1984 Amendments, *supra* note 29, § 23, 98 Stat. at 1329–30.
92. R. Horowitz & G. Dodson, 'Child Support, Custody and Visitation: A Report to State Child Support Commissions' (July 1985) (unpublished paper pre-

pared for the American Bar Association National Legal Resource Center for Child Advocacy and Protection, Child Support Project) (on permanent file with the *University of Illinois Law Review*).

93. See *Child Support, supra* note 1, at 58, 67.

94. See *In re* Marriage of Boudreaux, 201 Cal. App. 3d 447, 247 Cal. Rptr. 234 (Ct. App. 988) (where visitation rights are intentionally sabotaged, noncustodial parent may seek modification of original child support to enforce visitation); Washington *ex rel.* Burton *v.* Leysaer, 196 Cal. App. 3d 451, 241 Cal. Rptr. 812 (Ct. App. 1987) (custodial parent who concealed herself and her children from noncustodial parent could not recover child support arrearages for period of concealment); Biamby *v.* Biamby, 114 A.D.2d 830, 494 N.Y.S.2d 741 (App. Div. 1985) (trial court erroneously granted unpaid child support in light of interference with visitation rights); Hoyle *v.* Wilson, 746 S.W.2d 665 (Tenn.) (custodial spouse denied child support payments for period she disappeared with the children), *reh'g denied*, 14 Fam. L. Rep. 1259 (Tenn. 1988); Rohr *v.* Rohr, 709 P.2d 382 (Utah 1985) (wilful failure to pay child support justified lower court's refusal to modify custody and visitation rights).

95. *Mo. Ann. Stat.* § 452.340.6 (Vernon Supp. 1989):

6. A court may abate, in whole or in part, any future obligation of support or may transfer the custody of one or more children if it finds:
(1) That a custodial parent has, without good cause, failed to provide visitation of temporary custody to he noncustodial parent pursuant to the terms of a decree of dissolution, legal separation or modifications thereof; and
(2) That the noncustodial parent is current in payment of all support obligations pursuant to the terms of a decree of dissolution, legal separation or modifications thereof. The court may also award reasonable attorney fees to the prevailing party.

96. 'Report', *supra* note 25, at 3 (quoting Secretary Bowen).

97. Except for vestigial mention in relative responsibility laws, Schneider, 'Moral Discourse and the Transformation of American Family Law', 83 *Mich. L. Rev.* 1803, 1813 & n.31 (1985), scattered attempts to resuscitate such laws, Byrd,' 'Relative Responsibility Extended: Requirement of Adult Children to Pay for Their Indigent Parent's Medical Needs', 22 *Fam. L.Q.* 87 (1988); Garrett, *supra* note 71, a successful movement to allow grandparents visitation with their grandchildren, H. Krause, *supra* note 41, at 792–98, 1149–50, and one attempt to impose support liability on grandparents, *Wis. Stat. An.* § 49.90(1m)(a) 1 (West 1987) (effective 1 Jan. 1990), the law has all but excised the elderly from the family.

98. Life is not all roses for all elderly persons. Lawrence Swedley of the National Council of Senior Citizens provides the following data:

Fewer than half of all older people receive private or public pensions. For men, the median private pension is $3,190 a year; for women, it's $1,940. Social Security is the major source of income for the elderly, making up 38 percent on average. It is all that

> stands between nearly one-third of the elderly and poverty. The median annual benefit is $6,150. While 67 percent of retirees have income from assets, that constitutes just 26 percent of aggregate income. Median income for households headed by a person older than 65 is $14,334 (1987 Census). For single individuals, median income is $8,205. Lastly, even with the added protection Medicare will now provide against 'catastrophic' costs, in 1989 beneficiaries will spend about $1,525 out of their own pockets on health care. For an average retiree, that doesn't leave too much for basic needs—let alone bonbons.

Letter to the Editor, *N.Y. Times*, 2 Nov. 1988, at A26, vol. 4.

99. *N.Y. Times*, 23 Apr. 1987, at C1, col. 5.

100. *N.Y. Times*, 24 Jan. 1987, at 1, col. 1; see also D. Moynihan, *supra* note 50, at 94–6; Chakravarty & Weisman, 'Consuming Our Children?', Forbes, 14 Nov. 1988, at 222.

101. M. Minow & D. Rhode, *supra* note 37, at 19 (citing Minow, 'Rights for the Next Generation: A Feminist Approach to Children's Rights', 9 *Harv. Women's L.J.* 1 (1986)).

102. *Child Support*, *supra* note 1, at 299; see Chambers, 'Comment—The Coming Curtailment of Compulsory Child Support', 80 *Mich. L. Rev.* 1614 (1982).

103. See A. Kahn & S. Kamerman, *Income Transfers for Families with Children: An Eight-Country Study* (1983); Kamerman & Kahn, 'What Europe Does for Single-Parent Families', *Pub. Interest*, Fall 1988, at 70; S. Kamerman & A. Kahn, 'Family Policy: Has the U.S. Learned From Europe? (Apr. 28, 1986) (unpublished paper prepared for the Ford Foundation Seminar on Comparative Social Policy, Columbia University, Apr. 9, 1986) (on permanent file with the *University of Illinois Law Review*); see also 'Family Allowances', 12 *Ann. Rev. Population L.* 1985 § 420 (1988). Despite budget woes, the debate in Britain is over *raising* child benefits. See 'The Aid of the Family', *Economist*, 22 Oct. 1988, at 19.

104. Cf. M. Rheinstein, *supra* note 9, at 425 (footnote omitted).

> The impact of social welfare measures upon family stability is potentially enormous. Through well-considered use they could constitute an effective device of rational family policy and prove much more effective than manipulation of the laws on divorce. But much research is needed to render these tools more effective and to avoid adverse consequences.
>
> So far little is known either about the effects upon family stability of those legislative and other measures which have been taken in numerous foreign countries but for which the United States does not, or not yet, have exact counterparts. The most conspicuous of these devices is the system of family allowances, which in 1959 existed in no less than thirty-eight countries, among them Canada. Mostly such legislation has been motivated by a desire to reverse a declining trend in the birthrate or simply to encourage fertility. In the Federal Republic of Germany general considerations of social welfare have been emphasized.

105. Family policy and tax policy remain unreconciled, their interrelationship often unrecognized. For a summary review, see H. Krause, *supra* note 41, at

280–92. Detailed analysis of the problem is provided by Bittker, 'Federal Income Taxation and the Family', 27 *Stan. L. Rev.* 1389 (1975); McIntyre & Oldman, 'Taxation of the Family in a Comprehensive and Simplified Income Tax', 90 *Harv. L. Rev.* 1573 (1977); see also *Staff of House Select Comm. on Children, Youth, and Families, 99th Cong., 1st Sess., A Family Tax Report Card: Round II* (Comm. Print 1985).

106. This is not even a new idea. 1 Plato, *Laws* bk. IV, at 313 (R. Bury trans. 1926) (*circa* 347 B.C.) suggested:

> [H]e . . . that disobeys and does not marry when thirty-five years old shall pay a yearly fine of such and such an amount,—lest he imagine that single life brings him gain and ease,—and he shall have no share in the honours which are paid from time to time by the younger men in the State to their seniors.

Much later, 'Hartford taxed "lone-men" twenty shillings a week "for the selfish luxury of solitary living."' 2 G. Howard, *A History of Matrimonial Institutions* 153 (1904) (quoting from A. Earle, *Customs and Fashions in Old New England* 37 (1893)).

107. Harvard's Joint Center for Housing Studies reports that 'the median income of a single parent under 25 was $6,223 in 1988, down 15 percent in inflation-adjusted terms from 1974'. *Champaign-Urbana News-Gazette*, 22 June 1989, at B9, col. 4.

108. *N.Y. Times*, 15 Mar. 1989, at 16, col. 4 (quoting The Family Support Administration of the Department of Health and Human Services).

109. See Whitman, 'The Hollow Promise', *U.S. News & World Rep.*, Nov. 7, 1988, at 41.

110. See Gray, *supra* note 64, at 1233–4:

> Professor Krause's naive view of the role of law in the lives of poor families is reflected in his argument that poor children could be helped by a stricter enforcement of child neglect and dependency laws. He is apparently aware that neglect laws are generally vague and irrationally punitive statutes which are often applied by biased and poorly trained judges who, in any event, lack any resources with which to actually help poor children. Nevertheless, the author suggests that increased state intrusion into the lives of poor families is needed to protect their children. . . . The validity of this conclusion is, to say the least, doubtful. . . . Rather, public interferences in the lives of poor families tends to destroy the very family structure (although not a white, middle class one) which Professor Krause is at pains to encourage.

111. 15.3 million children live in one-parent households, and 1.9 million more live with neither parent. From 1980 to 1988, the proportion of white children in one-parent households rose from 15% to 19%; among blacks, from 46% to 54%; and among Hispanics, from 21% to 30%. *Wash. Post*, 16 Feb. 1989, at A7.

112. I am not alone. See 'Bringing Children Out of the Shadows' (Book Review), *Carnegie Q.*, Spring 1988, at 1, 7 (reviewing and quoting from L. Schorr, *Within Our Reach: Breaking the Cycle of Disadvantage* (1988)):

Summarizing her arguments, Schorr presents 'five pillars' on which, she believes, a 'new national commitment of consequence' with 'staying power' must stand:

First, the public must accept the evidence that favorable outcomes among high-risk children can be achieved by systematic intervention early in life. Interventions, to be effective, must offer a 'broad spectrum' of services and continuity of care to families and children in the context of the community in which they live. These programs must have skilled staff that can develop 'reciprocal' relationships of trust and respect.

Second, the public must understand that 'intensive and sometimes costly' preventive care for vulnerable families and children represents a sound allocation of resources. Such assistance, she maintains, is cheaper by far than the price society already pays for neglected health, unemployment, and crime. Americans, in other words, must 'recognize that investments to improve the futures of disadvantaged children represent a joining of compassion with long-term self-interest'.

113. Cf. Garrison, 'Why Terminate Parental Rights?', 35 *Stan. L. Rev.* 423, 436–7 (1983) (parental visitation rights for children in foster care); Sherman, 'Keeping Baby Safe From Mom', *Nat'l L.J.*, 3 Oct. 1988, at 1, col. 1 (making pregnant women legally responsible for their fetuses).

114. For medical studies of such phenomena, see Chasnoff, Griffith, MacGregor, Dirkes, & Burns, 'Temporal Patterns of Cocaine Use in Pregnancy', 261 *J. A.M.A.* 1741 (1989); Novick, Berns, Stricof, Stevens, Pass, & Wethers, 'HIV Seroprevalence in Newborns in New York State', 261 *J. A.M..* 1745 (1989).

115. 'A report by the National Academy of Sciences called the growing number of homeless children a "national disgrace".' *N.Y. Times*, 20 Sept. 1988, at A1, col. 1. 'The Report estimates that on any given night families with 100,000 children are homeless.' Id.

The report itself was written in the bland, moderate style typical of the academy, a private organization that advises the Government on policy issues in science and health. It analyzed the causes of homelessness and the health problems associated with it, and it recommended Federal action to improve health services, housing and income levels to reduce homelessness. But a more strongly worded supplementary statement, endorsed by 10 of the 13 experts on the panel that wrote the report complained that the report was 'too limited' in its language and approach.

Id.

116. 'Lost Generation in Welfare Hotels: Growing Up With Drugs and Despair', *N.Y. Times*, 22 Feb. 1988, at 1, col. 1. A New York City plan calls for the closing of welfare hotels sheltering homeless families. As a result, '[s]ince Aug. 1, [1988], city officials said, 720 families have been moved out of welfare homes; 2,586 families remain in 41 welfare hotels'. *N.Y. Times*, 3 Mar. 1989, at B3, col. 1.

117. Cf. Shapiro *v.* Thompson, 394 U.S. 618 (1969) (statute denying welfare benefits to residents of state for less than one year declared unconstitutional).

118. There is a delicate balance to be struck between the reproductive rights and lifestyle of the mother and the fundamental rights of the child. The choice is between education and coercion. At a November 1988 health law

conference in Boston, I heard Professor Martha Field eloquently rejecting coercion in favour of education. I would much prefer that route myself, but education has been tried. It is not working. See Field, 'Controlling the Women to Protect the Fetus', 17 *Law Med. & Health Care* 114 (1989). A summary of recent fetal abuse cases and controversy is presented by Jost, 'Mother Versus Child', *A.B.A. J.*, Apr. 1989, at 84; see also Sherman, *supra* note 113.

119. See Krause, 'Child Welfare, Parental Responsibility, and the State', in *Public Welfare*, *supra* note 18, pt. II, at 255, 266–73.

120. See *supra* note 105.

121. J. Cribbett & C. Johnson, *Principles of the Law of Property*, 96–7 (ed ed., 1989).

122. An early analysis and the history of the marriage penalty are in 'American Families: Trends and Pressures, 1973: Hearings Before the Subcomm. on Children and Youth of the Senate Comm. on Labor and Public Welfare', 93d Cong., 1st Sess. 204, 204–11 (1973) (statement of Dr. Harvey E. Brazer, Professor of Economics and Research Associate, Institute of Policy Studies, University of Michigan).

123. I.R.C. § 221(a)–(b) (1982) (repealed 1986).

124. See McIntyre, 'Rosen's Marriage Tax Computations: What Do They Mean?, 41 *Nat'l Tax J.*, 257 (1988); Rosen, 'The Marriage Tax Is Down But Not Out', 40 *Nat'l Tax J.*, 567 (1987).

125. See Druker *v.* Commissioner, 697 F.2d 46 (2d Cir. 1982) (marriage penalty is not unconstitutional); Barter *v.* United States, 550 F.2d 1239 (7th Cir. 1977) (same), *cert. denied*, 434 U.S. 1012 (1978).

126. Senator Moynihan summarizes the figures:

> The current [Social Security] reserve is approaching $100 billion. Between now and the year 2000 it will grow to $1.4 trillion. (As of 1987, the entire assets of private pension funds were about $1.49 billion.) This revenue stream must be deposited with the Treasury. If at the end of the day the Treasury has more money on hand than it needs, it simply retires privately held debt. . . . The national debt begins to shrink. Our present deficit 'path' takes us, in theory at least, to a zero deficit by 1993. If that happens, the revenue stream from Social Security will be sufficient to begin retiring debt by 1994. As public debt declines, private savings increase. By 2010 the Social Security reserve is projected to be nearly $4.5 trillion. ($4,600,000,000!). If we wanted to go all the way, we could probably have zero national debt by that time.

N.Y. Times, 23 May 1988, at A19, col. 2

127. 'Interest on U.S. Debt to Top Budgets' $150 Billion Deficit', *N.Y. Times*, 8 Oct. 1988, at 1, col. 4.

128. *Champaign-Urbana News-Gazette*, 18 Sept. 1988, at B-1, col. 1.

129. 'According to Agriculture Department finance officers, commodity price support operations rose to a record $25.8 billion in 1986.' *Champaign-Urbana News-Gazette*, 26 Nov. 1988, at 1, col. 3. Bovard, 'Farm Policy Follies', *Pub. Interest*, Spring 1989, at 75, calculates:

American consumers pay over $10 billion more for their food than they would in a free market. For the same aggregate cost, the government could give every full-time subsidized farmer two new Mercedes each year. With the $250 billion that government and consumers have spent on farm subsidies since 1980, Uncle Sam could have bought every farm, barn, and tractor in thirty four states.

130. 'In 1983, the nation's 24,000 superfarms with over $500,000 in annual sales received an average of $26,805 in direct government payments, while the smallest farms averaged $1,211.' 'Should We Save the Family Farm?', *Rep. from Inst. for Phil. & Pub. Pol'y*, Summer 1988, at 1, 5 (quoting from W. Galston, *a Tough Row to How: The 1985 Farm, Bill and Beyond* (1985)). In an ironic foreign policy twist, we provide the Soviet economy a price for our food exports that is below our own production cost. This does major harm to unsubsidized farmers in friendly countries, for instance, Australia.

131. Bowen *v.* Gilliard, 483 U.S. 587, 632 (1987) (Brennan, J., dissenting) (citation omitted).

132. Cf. C. Murray, *Losing Ground: American Social Policy, 1950–1980*, at 227–8 (1984), advocating:

> scrapping the entire federal welfare and income-support structure for working-aged persons, including AFDC, Medicaid, Food Stamps, Unemployment Insurance, Worker's Compensation, subsidized housing, disability insurance, and the rest. It would leave the working-aged persons with no recourse whatsoever except the job market, family members, friends, and public or private locally funded services. It is the Alexandrian solution: cut the knot, for there is no way to untie it.

Though pointing in the opposite political direction, Dr. Murray's medicine smacks of the infantile 1960s—if we trash what there is, the millennium will emerge. Senator Moynihan has explained what will emerge in 12 years. See *supra* text accompanying note 63.

133. *N.Y. Times*, 25 June 1989, at 7, col. 3; id., June 28, 1989, at B3, col. 1.

4.2. Divorcing children: roles for parents and the state

MARTIN RICHARDS

Introduction

The basic argument of this chapter is simple: that parental divorce often damages the life chances of children and the State could, and should, act more firmly to head off some of this damage. In Britain, as in most industrialized countries, the State does intervene at divorce, adopting the rhetoric of preserving or enhancing the best interests of the child. However, such good intentions usually fail because there is little understanding or agreement about what the best interests might be. Where there are clear policies they are usually more concerned at reducing government spending, whether on the judicial system or on direct or indirect support for post-divorce households with children. The chapter will begin by outlining the evidence about the effects of parental divorce for children, before turning to the issue of State intervention in the arrangements that may be made for children.

Consequences of parental divorce for children

Children of divorcing parents tend to show a period of disturbed behaviour—either acting-out disruptive behaviour or depressive and anxious patterns. This may last through the whole process of divorce beginning months or years before a separation and continuing some time after this. School work often shows some falling-off around the time of separation and, as effects for educational attainment may be cumulative, children are likely to leave school with fewer qualifications and have a reduced chance of going on to a university (e.g. Maclean and Wadsworth 1988; Hetherington and Arasteh 1988; Chase-Landsdale and Hetherington 1990; Elliott and Richards 1991; Wallerstein 1992; Kiernan 1992).

Some effects may persist into adulthood and studies in Britain and the United States have found lower occupational status and earnings, earlier marriage and divorce, and increased frequency of psychological and psychiatric problems (Amato and Keith 1991). In short, parental divorce may be associated with downward social mobility for the children.

Of course, effects of divorce are very variable, depending on many aspects of the particular circumstances and such things as the age of the children, the social position of the family, and the living arrangements after the separation. Not all children show significant persistent effects. However, these are sufficiently common and of such importance—we are talking of effects which in some cases influence the life-long chances for adults—that it seems reasonable that we should regard these as the prime concern which we need to consider when discussing interventions at divorce (Richards 1991).

Why should parental divorce have these long-term effects? Clearly, this is a very complex question and there are no simple answers. But we may point to a number of key interrelated factors which play a crucial role in a young person's journey from their childhood home into their independent life as a young adult. My approach is to consider the ways in which parental divorce may influence these. These factors are educational attainment and vocational training, leaving home and setting up an independent life elsewhere, forming a cohabitation or a marriage, and the beginning of reproduction. Parental divorce has been shown to influence all these factors. It is through varying combinations of these factors that divorce is likely to have its effect on social mobility (Richards 1991). But the significance of the divorce effect is variable, depending on both individual and social factors. The analysis of the follow-up study of the cohort of children born in 1958, for example, suggests that girls from middle-class homes show the strongest effects in early adulthood while boys from working-class backgrounds are least affected (Richards and Elliott 1992). Moreover, the links are certainly complex. Nevertheless we can point to a number of crucial effects of parental divorce. So, for instance, a child that does badly at school is more likely to leave at the minimum age with few or no qualifications and is less likely to proceed to further education or training and so has reduced job prospects. Children who have left education are more likely to leave home and live independently. Marriage and cohabitation are more probable for those living independently and, associated with these, are earlier reproduction, which in turn may further reduce employment possibilities, especially for women (Tasker and Richards 1992). The association between leaving home and marriage and cohabitation is probably the end-result of two different processes; leaving home because a decision has been taken to get married, and because those living independently may be more likely to form relationships that develop more rapidly into cohabitation or marriages. Where relationships are difficult or strained at home a young person may choose to leave earlier than otherwise. A poor relationship with a step-parent is a significant factor for some. Social class differences are very important here, not least because of the need for financial resources to find independent accommodation. We should also note that matters which are controlled by government action such as rules for job training allowances and welfare benefits may have a direct bearing on the financial consequences for parents and young people of the latter staying or leaving home (see Roll, 1990). Availability of jobs and housing are also of obvious significance.

Divorce is associated with a sharp drop in income for homes with children. In Britain, a majority of households containing divorced women and their children become dependent on State benefits for at least a period of time (e.g. Maclean 1991) and some remain caught in the poverty trap. Inadequate income reduces children's educational attainment and in many other ways has adverse effects on their life chances. While parental remarriage, and probably cohabitation, may improve incomes, the levels are seldom restored to those preceding the divorce. And even if these events have beneficial effects for household income, they may lead to further psychological and social disruptions for children. Follow-up studies (e.g. Kiernan 1992) tend to show small but consistently negative effects for children from remarriage homes as compared with those where a mother remained on her own after the divorce.

After divorce most children live with their mothers, and fathers become, at best, occasional visitors in their lives. Research in Britain and the USA suggests that within a short time of separation many children cease to have a relationship with their father (e.g. Seltzer 1991). The breaking of established relationships with fathers and other family members may have significant effects on a child's social development and their capacity to form and sustain relationships with others. When a father disappears from a child's life that child often feels a persistent sense of abandonment and loss which damages their self-esteem and sense of worth. Lack of self-esteem, in turn, has many psychological and social consequences. The loss of a parent and kin may also have economic and social effects for children which may continue into adult life. Fathers who are in contact with their children are more likely to be contributing towards their support and, though there seems to be no direct evidence to make the point, other transfers of money and practical support are likely to be reduced or cease where divorce ends effective contact (see Finch 1990).

Conflict between parents before and after divorce is associated with poorer outcome for children (Emery 1982, 1988). Where parents are living together, if the conflict is conducted in such a way that children are not directly involved, they seem to be protected from some of its consequences (see Rutter 1988). An important point here is that the effects of inter-parent conflict for children may be relatively benign if the children are able to see their parents settle their differences and restore good relationships. Conflict in the closing stages of a marriage or after separation may be more serious because it is less likely that this happens and because children, and the arrangements for their care, are more likely to be the subject of disputes. Conflict between parents will often erode parent–child relationships or end them.

Separating and divorced adults tend to have higher rates of psychological and physical illness (Elliott 1991). Parents who are ill, depressed, preoccupied, and generally under stress are less effective as parents and their children may lack sustained support and emotional engagement. Such parental difficulties may further exacerbate the psychological problems of the children of divorce.

These problems may also be increased by moves which may mean a change of school and loss of friends and familiar peers. Changes of school tend to be associated with poorer educational attainment. Divorce may not simply lead to a simple move but, for some, is the beginning of continued changes as a single parent moves in and out of further relationships (and households).

The analysis I have sketched out provides a set of clear issues which could become goals for policies related to divorce and children. Such policies should aim to encourage the maintenance of a child's existing relationships with parents and the wider family and kin, ensure an adequate income to post-divorce households with children, to reduce as far as possible conflict between divorcing parents or, at least, encourage its expression in areas that do not involve children, encourage the provision of emotional and practical support for divorcing parents who have the care of children and, finally, avoid as far as possible moves of house or school. On this latter point we should note that the availability of reasonably priced housing, whether to rent or buy, is of particular importance to divorcing couples and their children. I have necessarily stated the policy objectives in broad terms. It will not always be desirable to strive to maintain relationships with both parents. The evidence suggests that it is the breaking of already existing relationships which has ill effects for children. In rare cases, existing relationships may be detrimental to children if they continue. However, I suspect that such cases are much less common than many professionals working in the field choose to believe. It is also important to realize that the loss of a parent usually means the permanent loss of half of a child's kin relationships which may have profound emotional, social, and financial consequences.

Parental and kin relationships and maintaining children

Earlier in this chapter I argued that children are likely to do better in the long term if they maintain relationships with both their parents and the kin network on both sides of their family after a parental divorce. We know that in practice, in Britain, the United States, and elsewhere, the usual pattern is for children to live with their mother after divorce and for around half of fathers (at best) to remain in regular contact. As far as mothers are concerned, we should expect the post-divorce pattern we see, as it is simply the same situation as is found within marriage. The bulk of child care is provided by women in marriage, as it is afterwards. In only very few cases is the mother's position of the primary caretaker challenged at divorce. What had been the mother's role as principal caretaker in the joint household becomes that of residential parent in a single-parent household. While she may be faced with all sorts of increased difficulties in this new situation—juggling child care and employment, housing, and financial difficulties etc.—the basic role remains the same. The complications arise in trying to see how a father can fit into the post-divorce pattern when the mother's primary role within one household is translated into that of a single parent (or one with a new partner). Within a typical marriage the father is out at work each day while the mother is either at home as a full-time carer of children, or combines work and, importantly, the organization of substitute child care while she is working, with child care and domestic work. A father fits what caretaking he does, and his other time with the children, into the basic pattern set up and maintained by the mother. In most households fathers engage with their children when the mother is present too. This is unlike the typical pattern for a mother who will spend a lot of time on her own with her children. Or to put it in other terms, if a father is to maintain a relationship with his children his role *vis-à-vis* children is likely to change at separation much more radically than that of a mother. He has to become a sole caretaker for the times he is with his children, unless he simply passes on the care to a new partner or a relative.

A change for a mother is that there may be times when she is *not* with her children, if they are visiting their father. For some women this can pose a significant psychological threat to their role as a mother and it is frequently experienced as a loss. So at many separations a mother may not wish her children to go to see their father, and a father may be unable or unwilling to change his life to become a part-time sole carer. Control over visiting, and more generally over contact with a father, may be one of the few areas in which a mother may feel she has some power, so it is not surprising that so many disputes get focused on these issues. Where a divorce has been initiated by a mother and the father feels he is losing his marriage, wife, and his home, he may push for as much time with his children as possible as a way of retaining some element of his past life. Again, this may help to add emotional fuel to conflicts over children which stand in practical and symbolic ways as the bones for contention.

New partners may further complicate the picture. Father involvement tends to fall off if either he or his ex-spouse acquires a new partner. This is likely to be for somewhat different reasons on each side. The residential mother may have fantasies about creating a new family for which ties with the 'old' father may seem a threat best met by keeping the children around and denying them visits to the other parent. While for the non-residential parent, a relationship with a new partner may feel threatened by the occasional presence of children who are reminders of the old marriage and intimacy with another. Running through these situations is a very persistent prejudice that children should never have more than two parents and when a new one arrives, an old one has to go. I suggest that children have a much greater tolerance for non-standard family forms than adults (see Funder 1991). Indeed discomfort about such arrangements seem particularly strong among professionals who deal with children who often seem to regard such arrangements as 'confusing' for children (see Kelly, 1991). I suspect this is a matter of projection and the potential confusion lies more with the adults than the children. A parallel argument could be mounted here about the concept of adoption and the great adult fantasy that it is possible to create and end kinship relationships at the stroke of a court order.

It is usual to regard children as conservatives in their views of family life. Certainly they may resent change and can be very sensitive about the ways others may regard their living arrangements. However, children may have few presuppositions about the roles various adults in their lives should play. One can cite cases of children who see nothing but gain in the addition of further adult figures who can come to occupy quasi-parental roles in their lives. But we know too little about how children experience arrangements in non-traditional family structures and we should be very wary about assuming on their behalf the existence of strong views in favour of idealized family forms.

And there is also the issue of conflict between parents which may lead to a reduction in contact between parents and can erode parent–child relationship. I shall have more to say about this below.

Changing the world

Given the pervasiveness of a pattern which places little emphasis on the need for continuing relationships between children and non-residential parents, and the strength of the beliefs and institutions that support this, change is not going to be easy. The evidence suggests that very little has occurred over recent decades in the United States (Seltzer 1991; Folberg 1991) and the situation seems similar here. A first step which we have begun to take in the Children Act is to make the legal change so that at least we do not take parental responsibility from most fathers at divorce.

But can we do more? Certainly if there are better ways of settling disputes between parents and conflict were reduced and some of the emotional tensions that so often continue between past spouses were addressed more directly, we might expect more fathers to stay in the picture. I will discuss this further below. Apart from this it seems a matter of creating a culture of expectation so that we accept, as the slogan goes, 'Divorce is for adults, not children'. We need small changes on many fronts. Schools, for instance, should be encouraged or even required to send information to both parents if they do not share the same address. Divorcing parents should receive written information about the post-divorce needs of children and the range of workable residence and visiting patterns.

In many jurisdictions, including our own, there have been recent changes in the law designed to increase child support from fathers after divorce. As yet, it is too early to say whether these schemes are likely to improve the economic standing of households with children after divorce. First indications are that they have little financial impact (e.g. Pearson, Thoennes, and Anhalt 1992) which may well be because they are more concerned with controlling government expenditure than with the welfare of children and those who care for them. However, it is possible that these schemes may serve a symbolic function in indicating to non-resident parents that their responsibilities toward them—financial and otherwise—do not end simply because they cease to share the same address.

Other effects that might follow more effective attempts to collect maintenance from fathers concern second families. At present, a father can effectively wipe the slate clean and start again with a second family. Ensuring transfers to existing children and giving them preference over subsequent ones might depress fertility in second families. Would that be an undesirable result?

A difficulty we should not duck here is the difference between his and her divorce. He is likely either to have been left or to be leaving for someone else. If the former, he may feel a strong sense of injustice at losing his marriage, children, house while continuing to pay support—or at least that is a way that a vocal minority will put it. If he is moving into a new relationship, guilt can provide some motive to pay, but a new partner may increasingly resent supporting another woman's children. Of course, not everyone is driven by such motives. However, the coming of legal 'no-fault' divorce has perhaps allowed us to believe that couples separate with a similar detached view of divorce. They don't. Blame, accusation, and strong feelings of injustice are the norm at divorce and they get in the way of couples making reasonable arrangements about children and money. Neither legal fiction of the lack of fault or imposed orders do anything to relieve the situation, rather the reverse.

Indeed, neither the public ordering of the court, nor most private ordering provide an adequate arena for the expressing of the feelings that accompany marital separation. Studies of the legal process of divorce (e.g. Davis and Murch 1988) show that many of the participants feel that the legal procedures do not engage what they see as the 'real' issues. Affidavits take instances from a private reality and present them in a context where they lose most of their meanings. There is always a deep sense of betrayal when events from a private and once shared reality are forced into public in the provocative legal prose of an affidavit. People are not allowed their say in a manner that fits their own sense of justice. They are told to look forward at a time when their prime concern is history and its rewriting. The wounds go very deep but they often feel that the doctor is not even interested in seeing them.

Most mediation takes the same stance. Agendas are strictly controlled and anyone who tries to talk about how the present situation came about is wrapped over the knuckles and told—directly or indirectly—to attend to the business at hand and look to the future (Dingwall and Greatbatch 1990).

Marriage, as Berger and Kellner (1964) argued in a perceptive paper that has deservedly become a classic, involves the joint construction of a private shared and exclusive reality. Identities are anchored in the shared meaning of the relationship (Askham 1984). Maybe legally we do not become one any more, but we aspire to a social and psychological fusion (Reibstein and Richards 1992). It follows, therefore, that the process of uncoupling is very painful and provokes powerful irrational feelings (Vaughan 1987; Weiss 1975). Yet we try to get people to divide their lives, children, and property without even acknowledging the deep sense of anger, love betrayal, and hate that most are feeling.

At separation many people are literally out of their minds. They will do things and treat people in ways they never have before and never will again. Any family lawyer can provide numerous examples of what has to be regarded of typical behaviour: he broke into her house and tipped the contents of the dustbin into the double bed where she and her new partner sleep; she went through the family photograph album cutting him out of each photo; he slashed the tyres of her, once their, car; she burnt the postcard he sent to the children while he was away on a business trip. We expect them both to be clam and rational, yet we present them with a system that allows them to take their irrational behaviour into the public arena of the court where it may be validated by the professionals who become drawn into their warring world. Court contests seem to be designed to allow the trivia of everyday life to become elevated to a point where it becomes the basis of long-term decision-making. The result is adults and children who may feel damaged and bruised by their experience, a great deal poorer, and not necessarily with any sensible solutions to their problems. I suggest that until we begin to address the feelings of the participants at divorce we cannot expect people to make sensible decisions about the long-term interests of their children.

My noting of the restrictiveness of some styles of mediation may have seemed rather dismissive. A major problem is that under this term is gathered together a very wide range of activities. It is not simply that there are many variants in practice, but there is dispute about some basic approaches and techniques. A common model is of a kind of public school debating contest with each team represented by one of the spouses and the neutral chair seeing that everyone keeps to the point and to time. There tends to be a polarization between those who come from the pragmatic dispute resolution tradition, often with a background of labour disputes work, and those who draw on more therapeutic frameworks. There is little thought about how the two might be combined in the very special circumstances of a dispute between two parties who were once intimate and emotionally interdependent and whose union may have represented a bridge between two kinship networks. Some of the influence from family therapy has been less than helpful as it puts little stress on the ambivalence of loss and love that may dominate the feelings of each warring spouse. Not surprisingly, mediation has had a somewhat mixed press in evaluation studies (see Bruch 1988). But not all evaluation has been negative (Kelly 1991). There have been concerns expressed by some feminists that women are disadvantaged by the 'privatization' of the law (e.g. Bottomley 1985), but such fears, at least judged by practice in the USA, seem unfounded (Kelly and Duryee 1992).

My guess, and it can be no more on present evidence, is that mediation can be effective if: (a) it is comprehensive and we get rid of the silly British fiction that we can sort out issues to do with children without discussing where they will live or how they are to be financially supported; (b) it does allow clients to express something of their feelings and so engage the private reality that was their marriage (drawing here on appropriate psychodynamic traditions); (c) it provides some help and encouragement to couples to see that their quarrels can be conducted in ways that are more or less damaging for them and/or their children; (d) it is offered in context where other services such as counselling and direct support for children are also available; and finally (e) deals in realistic and practical solutions for individual cases rather than idealized and generalized arrangements (see Richards 1990).

I think mediation is the best hope we have, but it needs more money, more experimental schemes, and more hard thinking about its dynamics and how they may relate to the psychology of uncoupling. When it is done in the spirit I am proposing it does have some interesting effects (see for example Johnston and Campbell 1990). Children receive higher levels of financial support, agreements are more likely to be kept, and there is more contact between non-residential parents and their children (Kelly 1991). But we need to be careful to judge post-divorce arrangements by appropriate criteria. Increased contact between children and non-residential parents may mean that there is more scope for continuing conflict between parents. Some continuing conflict may be a reasonable price that has to be paid for the better contact (Masheter 1991) but good mediation can help to ensure that it does not stand in the way of necessary discussions about children (Kelly 1991).

One other very important point needs to be made about the ways in which couples end their marriages. Most go on to further marriages or cohabitations after divorce and recoupling often stimulates fertility. Sadly, however, second and subsequent relationships are more prone to divorce than first-time marriages. It seems reasonable to assume the unfinished business of the first marriage—emotional as well as financial—is an important determinant of the stability of the second. Addressing the psychological issues of divorce and providing couples with a forum in which to do this might have significant benefits for any subsequent relationship and children that might be born in these.

I am sure it is right for the Law Commission (1990) to recommend that divorce is available on demand with a suitable delay in which to sort out arrangements about children and money and without the need to provide the usually fictional historical account of the marriage in a legal format. Courts are not the place in which to argue about the private world of intimate relationships. The present system seems to have the worst combination of offering opportunities through affidavits to rehearse all sorts of marital quarrels which break faith with an erstwhile partner but then to ignore these issues and give the divorce on the nod (see Burgoyne, Ormrod, and Richards 1987).

It is much more difficult to see how the courts might be used to settle those cases of disputes about children that mediation cannot shift. Perhaps we should try to follow the same kind of system as the proposed formula for determining levels of child support and we should define the areas of acceptable dispute in litigation over children. Perhaps the easier cases are the few where there is a straight dispute about residence (custody), about where the children should live. The vast majority of such disputes concern parents who are as fit and able to care for children as any other; i.e. they are what Winnicott might have called 'good enough' parents—who have both played some part in the care of the children before the separation. Relying on evidence of who did most during the marriage is not always very relevant as the divorce changes most things. Also the needs of children change through development and with the roles that the two partners may take. Perhaps all that is required is for each parent to establish that they have practical plans for how they would look after children under whatever scheme they are proposing for their future care. In these disputes parents often try to suggest, directly or indirectly, that their partner is unfit to have the care of children. I suggest that such evidence should be inadmissible. If there are such concerns, these should be dealt with by the appropriate child-protection procedures and only when any such issues have been resolved should a custody hearing take place. The principle of the primacy of the welfare of the children should still obtain in such situations but I suggest it should be given a single simple definition, that the children should reside with whichever parent is able to convince the court that they are the parent most likely to foster and maintain the children's links with the other parent and the wider family. Such a criterion has a long history (Solomon, 1 Kings 3. 16–28) and should ensure that attention is focused on the welfare of the children rather than the supposed moral worth of each parent.

One of the benefits of any clear guide like the Solomon principle is that it reduces the scope for argument. While few are likely to object to the concept of the best interests of the child, it is a concept which allows for the maximum range of disagreement. As the most cursory glance at what (married) parents do with their children (or indeed the changing whims of probation and social-work practice on judicial decision-making) makes clear, there is the widest divergence of views on what constitutes the best interests of children. That diversity of view means that bargaining in the shadow of the law provides maximum scope for disagreement. Leaving decisions to a court remains an uncertain gamble, but this allowing at least a ray of hope for the most unlikely cases and so encourages litigation.

The seeking of clearer guidelines or principles for resolution of custody disputes seems to be becoming an increasing preoccupation in the more progressive jurisdictions. The most favoured principle at present seems to be that of the primary caretaker. Essentially this means confirming the status quo—making the parent who provided the bulk of the caretaking within marriage, the residential parent after divorce. In most cases such a principle is simply a return to the maternal presumption which dominated in the days before the best-interests concept became established. Not surprisingly, those feminists who see child custody as an issue of gender politics have argued strongly for the primary caretaker principle (Smart and Sevenhuijsen 1989). In some jurisdictions in the USA, where the principle has been adopted, there have been problems and not all of the supposed benefits have been found (Crippen 1990).

The most detailed proposal for an approach of this kind has come from New Zealand (Hassall and Maxwell 1992). Here we might expect the results to be rather different from the USA because these would operate in the context of a family court system which places strong emphasis on the needs of children. The plan is a detailed one which is a development from the present mediation-based system. It places a family care conference—involving the parents, children, perhaps members of the wider family, an advocate for the children, and a mediator, but not lawyers—at the centre of the system. The proposal not only gives a list of tasks that can be used to define who is the primary caretaker but lays down norms for a 'standard' interim arrangement for children to be with their parents. Clearly, there is plenty of scope for argument about what principles decisions should be based on but two points about the New Zealand proposal are particularly attractive—the emphasis on providing a context for decision-making before the legal system is engaged, and the attempt to reduce uncertainty and set standards for appropriate arrangements. Of course, some cases will proceed to court and not all parents will behave in ways that remotely approach the standards set. But the proposals do seem to stand a good chance of reducing court cases (and so legal costs) and may help to protect the interests of children.

Disputes around access, and matters such as the removal of children from the jurisdiction are perhaps the hardest to resolve, not least because they are so often an arena in which the conflicting emotions of the once intimate are played out. It seems unlikely that there are any simple principles to guide solutions here. What about the father who consistently fails to turn up on agreed access days or the mother who refuses to let a father see his children despite access orders? In the latter case do we put the mother in prison as the occasional exasperated judge has tried or transfer the children to the father? Nothing is gained by the former and in the latter situation perhaps the father is unable or unwilling to take them. Similarly, heavy-handed treatment is unlikely to encourage a father to take his responsibilities more seriously. I think the best we can suggest is mediation, compulsory if necessary, and a court hearing at the very last resort where appropriate. The problem is, of course, that in the end, we cannot impose arrangements on parents who are determined to thwart an order. Such cases are rare but if everything has been exhausted—mediation with due attention to the psychodynamic agenda, a determined attempt to discover the reasons for the refusal, an informal meeting with a judge, and a court hearing—there is nothing for it but occasional supervized access visits until such time as children are old enough to make their own choices.

Acknowledgements

Some of my research on the consequences of divorce has been supported by a grant from the Health Promotion Research Trust. Jill Brown and Sally Roberts, as always, have provided excellent administrative and secretarial services.

262   *Substantive aspects of family law*

References

AMATO, P. R. and KEITH, B. (1991), 'Parental divorce and adult well-being. A meta-analysis', *J. Marriage and the Family*, **53**, 43–58.

ASKHAM, J. (1984), *Identity and Stability in Marriage* (Cambridge: Cambridge University Press).

BERGER, P., and KELLNER, H. (1964), 'Marriage and the construction of reality', *Diogenes*, **46**, 1–25.

BOTTOMLEY, A. (1985), 'What is happening to family law? A feminist critique of conciliation'. In J. Brophy and C. Smart (eds.), *Women-in-Law. Explorations in Law, Family and Sexuality* (London: Routledge & Kegan Paul).

BRUCH, C. S. (1988), 'And how are the children? The effects of ideology and mediation on child custody law and children's well-being in the United States', *Int. J. Law & the Family*, **2**, 106–26.

BURGOYNE, J., ORMROD, R., and RICHARDS, M. P. M. (1987), *Divorce Matters* (Penguin Books, London).

CHASE-LANSDALE, L., and HETHERINGTON, E. M. (1990), 'The impact of divorce on life span development: short and long-term effects'. In D. L. Featherman and R. M. Lerner (eds.) *Life-span. Development and Behaviour* (Erlbaum, Hillsdale, N.J.).

CRIPPEN, G. (1990), 'Stumbling beyond the best interests of the child: reexamining child custody standard-setting in the wake of Minnesota's four year experiment with the primary caretaker preference', *Minnesota Law Review*, **75**, 427–503.

DAVIS, G., & MURCH, M. (1988), *Grounds for Divorce* (Clarendon Press).

DINGWALL, R., and GREENBATCH, D. (1990), *Divorce conciliation: A Report to the Wates Foundation* (Centre for Socio-Legal Studies, Oxford).

ELLIOTT, B. J., and RICHARDS, M. P. M. (1991), 'Children and divorce: educational performance and behaviour, before and after parental separation', *Int. J. Law & the Family*, **5**, 258–76.

ELLIOTT, B. J. (1991), 'Divorce and adult health: the mediating effects of gender' (Unpublished paper: Child Care and Development Group, University of Cambridge).

FINCH, J. (1990), *Family Obligation and Social Change* (Polity Press, Cambridge).

FOLBERG, J. (ed.), *Joint Custody and Shared Parenting* (2nd edition, New York, Guilford Press).

FUNDER, K. (1991), 'Children's construction of their post-divorce families: a family sculpture approach'. In K. Funder (ed.), *Images of Australian Families* (Longman, Cheshire).

HASSELL, I., and MAXWELL, G. (1992), *A Children's Rights Approach to Custody and Access* (Wellington, NJ, Office of the Commissioner for Children).

HETHERINGTON, E. M., and ARASTEH, J. D. (eds.) (1988), *Impact of divorce, single parenting, and stepparenting on children* (Hillsdale, N.J., Lawrence Erlbaum).

JOHNSTON and CAMPBELL (1991), *The Impasses of Divorce* (New York, The Free Press).

KIERNAN, K. E. (1992), 'The impact of family disruption in childhood and transitions made in young adult life', *Demography* (in press).

KELLY, J. B. (1991), 'Mediated and adversarial divorce resolution processes. A comparison of post-divorce outcomes', *Family Law*.

—— (1991), 'Examining resistance to joint custody'. In J. Folberg (ed.) *Joint Custody and Shared Parenting* (2nd edition, New York, Guilford Press).

KELLY, J. B. and DURYEE, M. A. (1992), 'Women's and Men's Views of Mediation in Voluntary and Mandatory Mediation Settings', *Family and Conciliation Courts Review*, **30**, 34–49.

Law Commission, 1990. *The Grounds for Divorce* (Law Commission. No. 192. HMSO London).

MACLEAN, M., and WADSWORTH, M. E. J. (1988), 'The interests of children after parental divorce: A long term perspective', *Int. J. of Law and the Family*, **2**, 155–66.

MACLEAN, M. (1991), *Surviving Divorce. Women's Resource after Separation* (London, Macmillan).

MASHETER, L. (1991), 'Post divorce relationships between ex-spouses: the role of attachment and interpersonal conflict', *J. Marriage and the Family*, **53**, 103–10.

PEARSON, J., THOENNES, N., and ANHALT, J. (1992), 'Child support in the United States: the experience in Colorado', *Int. J. Law and the Family*, **6**, 321–37.

REIBSTEIN, J., and RICHARDS, M. P. M. (1992), *Sexual Arrangements* (London, Heinemann).

RICHARDS, M. P. M. (1990), 'Divorce Cambridge Style: New Developments in Conciliation', *Family Law*, 436–8.

—— (1991), *Children and Parents after Divorce*, Paper presented at the Seventh World Conference of the International Society on Family Law. Opatija, Yugoslavia, 1991, and to be published in the proceedings of the meeting.

RICHARDS, M. P. M., and ELLIOTT, B. J. (1991), 'Sex and Marriage in the 1960s and 1970s'. In D. Clark (ed.), *Marriage, Domestic Life and Social Change. Writings for Jacqueline Burgoyne* (Routledge, London).

—— —— (1992), 'The economic status of families before and after divorce' (in preparation).

ROLL, J. (1990), 'Young People: Growing up in the Welfare State' (London, Family Policy Studies Centre Occasional Paper No. 10).

RUTTER, M. (1988), 'Functions and consequences of relationships: some psychopathological considerations'. In Hinde, R. A., and Stevenon-Hinde, J. (eds.), *Relationships within Families* (Clarendon Press, Oxford).

SELTZER, J. A. (1991), 'Relationship between fathers and children who live apart. The father's role after separation', *J. Marriage and the Family*, **53**, 79–102.

SMART, C. and SEVENHJUIJSEN, S. (eds.) (1989), *Child Custody and the Politics of Gender* (London, Routledge).

TASKER, F. and RICHARDS, M. P. M. (1992), 'The attitudes to marriage and the marital prospects of the children of divorce: a review' (Submitted for publication).

VAUGHAN, D. (1987), *Uncoupling. Turning Points in Intimate Relationships* (London, Methuen).

WALLERSTEIN, J. S. (1992), 'The long-term effects of divorce on children: a review', *J. Amer. Acad. Child and Adolescent Psychiatry* (in press).

WEISS, R. (1975), *Marital Separation* (Basic Books, New York).

5. Domestic violence, child protection, and the law

5.1. Hype or hope? The importation of pro-arrest policies and batterers' programmes from North America to Britain as key measures for preventing violence against women in the home

REBECCA MORLEY AND
AUDREY MULLENDER

Introduction

The issue of men's violence against women in the home—'domestic violence' or 'battering'—was put on the public agenda in Britain and North America in the early 1970s by the refuge/shelter movement (Schechter 1982, Dobash and Dobash 1992). Based in feminism, the movement's core commitment to women's safety was (and is) part of a wider concern with personal and social transformation.

Since the mid 1970s, the issue has increasingly been recognized by governments internationally as a problem requiring urgent and systematic attention. The British Government has lent its voice to this concern—for example, through the European Community in the form of the First Conference of European Ministers on Physical and Sexual Violence Against Women which met in March 1991. Yet, to date, Britain has lacked a national strategy and funding base for a comprehensive approach to tackling the problem, and Women's Aid (the national federation of feminist-run refuges) has remained largely unsupported.

Within this context, this paper examines two notable British developments in public responses to preventing violence against women in the home: pro-arrest policies (Section A below) and batterers' programmes (Section B). These initiatives have both been imported into Britain from North America, often without recognizing that their widespread and established use in that continent is not uncontentious. The paper will explore the process of their adoption into Britain, together with the debates surrounding their effectiveness and their broader implications for women subject to this form of violence.

A. Pro-arrest policies

The development of pro-arrest policies in North America

The term 'pro-arrest policies' refers to policies which encourage or, less frequently, require police to arrest for domestic violence under certain circumstances. These policies originated in the USA, where they grew largely out of feminist critiques of and campaigns around the legal system's treatment of woman battering, beginning in the mid 1970s (Martin 1976, Schechter 1982).

Research (for example, Field and Field 1973, Eisenberg and Micklow 1977) corroborated feminist criticisms that police called to incidents of battering did not arrest the violent man even when the woman was in grave danger, had suffered visibly serious injury, and had explicitly requested arrest. Guided by non-intervention policies and training, police either responded slowly and reluctantly or not at all. Frequently women were told nothing could be done since the matter was a private, family one. Police often attempted to 'cool down' the situation by walking the batterer around the block, or to mediate or reconcile the 'couple', in so doing siding implicitly and often explicitly with the violent man. Perhaps the most dramatic evidence of the failure of police to protect women came from a Police Foundation study of domestic homicides and aggravated assaults in Detroit and Kansas City for the years 1970 and 1971 (Police Foundation 1977 in Dutton 1988: 128). Police records indicated that, in 90 per cent of homicides and 85 per cent of aggravated assaults, police had been called to the address of the incident during the previous two years. In 50 per cent of incidents of both homicide and aggravated assault, police had visited the address on five or more occasions.

Feminist campaigning centred around instituting legal reforms emphasizing that battering is a criminal rather than a private (civil) matter. Tactics included suing police departments for failure to comply with already existing assault laws (Gee 1983, Holden 1989). For many activists, increasing police powers to, and use of, arrest was an essential part of these campaigns. By July 1983 (Lerman and Livingston 1983: 3–4), eleven US states had made domestic violence a separate criminal offence to facilitate enforcement of the criminal law against batterers, some identifying dispositions in addition to fines and prison sentences: for example, protection orders and mandatory counselling for batterers. Thirty-three states had expanded police powers of arrest, most notably allowing arrest without warrant for misdemeanour (simple) assaults where probable cause exists or arrest without warrant for breach of protection orders where probable cause exists. In six states, arrest was made mandatory in these cases. Concurrently, a number of cities passed pro-arrest legislation, police departments began adopting pro-arrest policies, and a few jurisdictions adopted 'no-drop' policies which prevent victims and prosecutors from dropping charges, except under exceptional circumstances (Buzawa and Buzawa 1990).

However, the pro-arrest lobby received an enormous boost from the findings of the much publicized 'Minneapolis Experiment' (Sherman and Berk 1984). Sherman and Berk compared the effectiveness of three responses—arrest, advice/mediation, and separation—on misdemeanour domestic assaults. Arrest and initial incarceration was found to be the most effective police intervention in reducing repeat offending during a six-month follow-up period, independently of any other action by the criminal justice system. On the basis of their findings, the researchers recommended a *presumptive* arrest policy, whereby 'an arrest should be made unless there are good, clear reasons why an arrest would be counterproductive' (1984: 270). The Attorney General's Task Force on Domestic Violence, which reported in September 1984, referred to the Experiment in justifying its recommendation that arrest should be the *presumed* police response to 'family violence' (Hart *et al.* 1984: 24). Moreover, it has been argued (Sherman and Cohn 1989, Meeker and Binder 1990) that the Experiment was instrumental in the subsequent adoption of pro-arrest policies by many police departments across the USA recommending and, in some cases requiring, arrest for misdemeanour domestic assaults. A review of recent literature indicates that the study results have become widely assimilated into the thinking of academics, legislators, professional service providers, and feminist activists.

Meanwhile in Canada, activists were lobbying for change in a similarly unresponsive criminal justice system (MacLeod 1987). In 1983 the federal government responded by issuing a directive which, among other things, instructed police to lay charges in all domestic violence cases where sufficient proof exists, and the Crown to prosecute these cases in all but the most exceptional circumstances, even if the victim refuses to co-operate. Similar policies were adopted in many provincial and municipal jurisdictions. The city of London, Ontario, in fact pioneered the pro-charge policy in Canada by issuing its own directive in 1981 (Goyette 1990). In another well-publicized piece of research in London, Peter Jaffe and colleagues (Jaffe *et al.* 1986) reported that the policy had resulted in a dramatic increase of 2500 per cent in police-laid charges (measured over a five-year period from 1979 to 1983), and that charging resulted in a reduction in repeat violence. Further, contrary to common fears, victims appeared *not* to be more reluctant to call the police and the evidence suggested a significant decrease in charges being withdrawn or dismissed.

Thus, by the mid 1980s, an apparently happy agreement had been reached between activists, professionals and research evidence concerning the most appropriate police responses to domestic violence.

The importation of pro-arrest policies into Britain

British feminists, too, began campaigning in the early 1970s for changes in the policing of domestic violence to women (Hanmer 1989). The establishment of a Parliamentary Select Committee to examine all aspects of the issue of 'violence in marriage', which reported in 1975, was a victory for activists. With respect to policing, the Committee concluded that 'assaults in the home are just as serious as assaults in other places' and that police should be ready to arrest the assailant on the spot where there is evidence of any injury (Parliamentary Select Committee on Violence in Marriage 1975: para 44). The Committee's recommendations fell on deaf ears, however, and following some changes in the civil law, the issue of domestic violence largely disappeared from the public agenda until the second half of the 1980s. When it re-emerged, it did so in the context of an increasing tendency to view the police, and criminal justice system generally, as being in the forefront of solutions to the problem. And within policing, the new emphasis was firmly on domestic violence as a *criminal* act, and on *arrest* as the primary response to assailants.

Although feminists had continued to campaign vigorously for more sensitive policing following the Select Committee's report, it has been suggested (Radford and Stanko nd: 11) that the rapid change of tune by the British police towards domestic violence was not a direct response to feminist pressure, but part of a broader strategy to re-establish police credibility in inner city areas where uprisings and police abuses had, by the early 1980s, led to open hostility with local communities. By setting themselves up as protectors of vulnerable women, the police attempted to recapture public confidence, and ultimately to re-assert surveillance and control in these areas (see Southall Black Sisters 1989: 303–5). According to Radford and Stanko (nd: 11, 21) the British police sought advice on solving their policing problems generally, and domestic violence specifically, from their North American colleagues. It is almost certainly the case that the Minneapolis Experiment and London, Ontario study results contributed to the new pro-arrest leanings. Their influence can be seen in four key documents on policing: the Metropolitan Police Working Party report on domestic violence (1986), the Metropolitan Police force order on domestic violence (1987), the Metropolitan Police's *Domestic Violence Best Practice Guidelines* (1990), and the Home Office circular on domestic violence (1990).

The first three documents concern the London-wide Metropolitan Police Force. The earliest is a highly critical, and in some ways, radical report on the Force's policing of domestic violence (Metropolitan Police Working Party 1986), which was leaked but never released. The report gave detailed consideration to the London, Ontario, study and recommended a pilot scheme to test the viability of the London policy in the British context (54–5, 86–9), though the scheme never materialized. Shortly thereafter, the Metropolitan Police issued a policy statement (force order) on domestic violence which declared that 'a fundamental principle to be borne in mind is that an assault which occurs within the home is as much a criminal act as one which may occur in the street', and advised officers to use their powers of arrest (Metropolitan Police Community Involvement Policy Unit 1990: Appendix 1). It also suggested that, by virtue of a recent Act making spouses compellable witnesses, prosecution should be considered even when the victim is reluctant. The force order received a great deal of media publicity, much of which cited the London, Ontario, study (Sheptycki 1990: 3). In 1990, the Force's Community Involvement Policy Unit issued the *Domestic Violence Best Practice Guidelines* which devote a full page to describing the Minneapolis Experiment as demonstrating that 'arrest is the most effective way of dealing with Domestic Violence' (Metropolitan Police Community Involvement Policy Unit 1990: 45).

The final document is a circular published by the Home Office (the central government department responsible for policing and other legal matters) in July 1990. The Circular set out the most comprehensive policy guidelines to date on policing domestic violence. (The Scottish Office announced similar guidelines on the same day—Scottish Information

Office 1990). It stated that police should be aware of their 'extensive' powers to deal with domestic violence, and declared:

Experience in other countries suggests that the arrest of an alleged assailant may act as a powerful deterrent against his re-offending—at least for some time—and it is an important means of showing the victim that she is entitled to, and will receive, society's protection and support. The arrest and detention of an alleged assailant should therefore always be considered, even though the final judgement may be that this is inappropriate in the particular case (Home Office 1990: 6)

Home Office circulars make *recommendations* to Chief Officers (heads of the forty-three police forces in England and Wales) on policy, but they do not have the power to direct (see Bourlet 1990: ch. 5, and Thornhill 1989 for discussions of police structure and accountability in Britain). Nevertheless, an increasing number of forces, and divisions within them, are now adopting policies encouraging arrest. At the same time, many divisions are establishing specialized back-up domestic violence units, setting up computerized domestic violence registers, and getting involved in inter-agency work, sometimes performing the coordinating function. All these developments were recommended in the Circular.

Thus the rhetoric, if not the practice, of policing domestic violence to women in Britain has moved rapidly towards the pro-arrest orthodoxy, with the aid of a hefty push from North American research. Indeed, some would like to see Britain going further than simply *encouraging* arrest and prosecution, to adopting North American style presumptive/mandatory arrest and no-drop policies (for example, Horley 1988).

Evaluation of pro-arrest policies: North American experiences

The most common argument used to justify pro-arrest policies is that arrest is the best form of deterrent of repeat violence. But does arrest *really* deter? Paradoxically, given the aura surrounding the Minneapolis Experiment, the jury is still out on this issue. Although numerous US academics and activists have cited the Experiment as evidence that 'arrest is best' (for example, Langan and Innes 1986: 2, Buel 1988: 215, Hart *et al.* 1990: 6), it has been heavily criticized on methodological grounds (for example, Binder and Meeker 1988, Buzawa and Buzawa 1990). Some of these limitations are acknowledged by the authors themselves (Sherman and Berk 1984, Sherman and Cohn 1989). The National Institute of Justice has commissioned six replication studies in various parts of the USA, three of which are now complete. The Omaha, Nebraska (Dunford *et al.* 1989) and Charlotte, North Carolina (Hirschel *et al.* 1991) experi-

ments both failed to replicate the Minneapolis findings, showing no difference by disposition in frequency of re-offending. The Milwaukee,
Wisconsin experiment found some evidence of an initial deterrent effect
of arrest which had dissipated by six months (Sherman *et al.* 1991). All
three studies concluded that their results do not support mandatory or
presumptive arrest policies based on deterrence of repeat offending.

However there may well be other reasons for preferring arrest (see
Stanko 1989, Buzawa and Buzawa 1990: ch. 8). First, it is obviously the
case that arrest provides the victim with immediate protection by removing the assailant, and if he is held in custody long enough, may give the
victim time to make plans for her safety. Moreover, arrest gives the
police a tangible product for work which is conventionally viewed as a
waste of time, and thus may encourage them to take 'domestics' more
seriously. Finally, the authors of the Charlotte study (Hirschel *et al.* 1991:
159–60) echo many feminist activists in suggesting that arrest sends
important messages to assailants, victims and the community at large
that domestic violence is a serious *crime* which society will not tolerate.

On the other hand, some commentators have voiced concern that
arrest may not always be in a woman's interest (for example, Ferraro
1989*a*, 1989*b*, MacLeod 1989, Buzawa and Buzawa 1990: 92–3). For example, her economic survival may be threatened if her partner loses his job
by virtue of even a very short incarceration. If she is from an ethnic
minority community, formal involvement with the police may pose
the threat of deportation or racist abuse. Most crucially, without co-
ordination with other parts of the criminal justice system to control the
man and without adequate support and protection for the woman in the
community, arrest may in fact endanger the victim's safety due to
reprisals from an angry partner (for example, Davis 1988: 365, Steinman
1990). Indeed, fear of reprisal appears to be a major reason why many
women wish to withdraw charges against their assailants (for example
Bowker 1984: 92). And this fear may not be misplaced: in 1987 and 1988
more than 90 per cent of women killed by their partners in Minnesota
were actively trying to separate from them or seeking help from an outside agency (Pence 1989: 34–5).

In any case, discussions with researchers and activists both in the USA
and Canada indicate a growing awareness that an emphasis on
arrest/charge alone is not enough. Many jurisdictions are moving
towards a criminal justice response which is both internally co-ordinated
(between police, prosecution, and sentencing) *and* integrated within a
broader community response to provide women with a comprehensive

support system. Indeed, Jaffe *et al.* (1986, 1991) suggest that their very positive findings in London, Ontario, may have been grounded in the integrated community response to domestic violence in that city which includes not only co-ordination between police and prosecution, but also a battered women's advocacy clinic providing legal advice and counselling, a programme supporting victims throughout the court process, a treatment programme for batterers, and good provision of shelters and longer-term housing. Generally, those jurisdictions which report having achieved positive results with arrest are those which are part of a co-ordinated community response (for example, Pence and Shepard 1988: 292, Domestic Abuse Project 1991: 1, 3).

Perhaps the most controversial issue concerning tough criminal justice responses, particularly mandatory ones, is whether or not they *empower* the victim. The case supporting their empowerment potential (and a reason for preferring arrest over and above its immediate deterrent effect) is argued in two ways. The first centres around the symbolic function of the law and the rights of women. By sending a clear message to the abuser and society that woman battering is a crime unacceptable to the community which will therefore be fully prosecuted, a woman's right to equal protection is established and her sense of human dignity enhanced (for example, Buel 1988: 223–4, Currie 1990: 85). The second is based on the claim that if the decision to arrest and charge is left to the woman, it is actually *controlled* by the batterer since he has the power to threaten her into inaction. Policies which remove decisions from the woman thus remove control from the batterer, rather than from the woman (for example, Pence 1989).

However, others question whether handing over control to the criminal justice system can be defined as empowering (for example, Davis 1988, MacLeod 1989, MacLeod and Picard 1989). It may simply entail a transfer of control from the private realm: an individual male batterer; to the public: a largely male coercive institution. Both may be experienced as abusive. For example, compelling a woman to testify against her partner, and punishing her for contempt if she refuses, may be a 'choice' between testifying and being beaten or not testifying and being jailed or fined. More broadly, within the Canadian context, MacLeod (1989: 8) notes that women are sometimes forced to accept criminal justice intervention in order to qualify for other kinds of services. Women may perceive public control as even more dangerous than private, since it may entail surveillance, not only by the criminal justice system, but by other state agencies as well; for example, those dealing with immigration and child welfare which have the power to deport and remove children, respectively. This is a civil liberties issue of particular significance for poor, working class and ethnic minority women, since state surveillance is more likely to be forced upon them than upon their middle-class and/or white sisters. Rather than ensuring equality before the law, as some argue (for example, Buel 1988: 224), tough criminal justice policies may in fact divide justice even more strongly along race and class lines.

Regardless, many women either do not want the police to arrest/charge in the first place, or wish to withdraw charges at a later point (see for example, MacLeod and Picard 1989). Indeed, Ford (1991) argues that some women actively use the threat of prosecution as a power resource in negotiating safety and/or other desired outcomes with their violent partners. However, in order to utilize this power resource effectively, women need to be able to drop charges if their partners comply with their demands. Similarly, McGillivray (1987) maintains that women employ a variety of strategies to gain protection by the State without ending their relationship, including calling the police and then obstructing the prosecution process even in jurisdictions with tough police and prosecution policies: 'such behaviour may appear batterer-controlled or self-destructive but an observer cannot accurately assess either the degree of control the batterer has achieved or the destructive consequences of a decision to terminate the relationship' (McGillivray 1987: 23). No-drop policies, according to McGilligray, represent the 'consensus between reformers and the state that social interests are to take precedence over immediate interests of the victim' (31).

Of course, the surest way for women to maintain control of the criminal justice process is simply not to call the police in the first place. Data on arrest for domestic violence in Detroit (in Buzawa and Buzawa 1990: 103) suggested that the number of calls for assistance decreased following the implementation of an aggressive arrest policy, a finding attributed partly to victims' fear of losing control of the outcome of police intervention. On the other hand, in London, Ontario, the number of calls did not drop following the introduction of the pro-charge policy (Jaffe *et al.* 1986: 43, 46), and victims who had contacted the police apparently continued to call them after the target incident even though they knew that charges would probably be laid (Jaffe *et al.* 1991: 27–8). To date, however, there is very little empirical evidence on this issue. But growing concern is being expressed by policy makers, practitioners and activists in Canada that mandatory policies, in particular, deter women from calling the police, and there are calls to weaken charging policies so that women who want to drop their case may do so without being charged with contempt of court (personal communication from the Office of the Solicitor General, Ottawa, June 1991).

Perhaps most significantly, the debates concerning the virtues of tough policing policies are usually premised on the assumption that these policies translate into practice. However, there is overwhelming evidence that this congruence is not easily achieved (Stanko 1989, Ferraro 1989b, Buzawa and Buzawa 1990: ch. 3). The 'domestic' situations to which police respond are rarely clear-cut, and discretion is central to policing, even where policies are presumptive or mandatory. It appears that, in domestic violence cases, the decision to arrest (or more often not) is rarely made mainly with reference to legal factors or the wishes of the victim, although it may be justified on both these grounds. Instead, police operate on the basis of an array of inter-connected personally, occupationally, and organizationally relevant factors, all of which militate against arrest. Vastly oversimplifying a complex literature, these factors include the low status of 'domestics', which are not viewed as 'real' police work, so count little in promotional and other occupational reward terms; the realistic assessment of the difficulties in prosecuting these cases, which make arrests a lot of work for very little reward; the macho culture of policing; attitudes of individual officers to women who are beaten, which tend towards perceiving them as being to blame in some way for their situation. Stanko (1989) notes, too, that rank and file police tend to be resistant to policy changes imposed from above, in order to maintain a sense of control over the job.

As with the efficacy of arrest/charge in reducing repeat violence policies which have been most successfully translated into practice are those which form part of a co-ordinated intervention programme, both internally within the criminal justice system and externally within the community. Again, the London, Ontario, case is exemplary: its pro-charge policy produced an increase in police-laid charges of 2500 per cent over a five year pre-post policy period (Jaffe *et al.* 1986). By 1990, nearly 90 per cent of all 'wife assault occurrences' (recorded incidents meeting the legal criteria for charging) resulted in police laid charges, with only 3.6 per cent of those not charged being a response to victims' wishes not to lay charges (Jaffe *et al.* 1991: 22–3 and Table 3). Further, data from small samples of victims showed that the proportion of charges dismissed or withdrawn decreased from 38 per cent to 11 per cent in a ten year pre-post policy period (Jaffe *et al.* 1991: 29 and Table 28). Similarly dramatic effects of policy on practice have been reported in other jurisdictions with a co-ordinated response (for example, Gamache *et al.* 1988, Pence 1989: 21–5. See also Hirschel and Hutchison 1991: 54). Moreover, these jurisdictions report high levels of victim satisfaction with the criminal justice process.

There are a number of interesting examples in the USA of projects which co-ordinate the intervention of the criminal justice system with other legal agencies, welfare services, and advocacy programmes; notably the Domestic Abuse Intervention Project in Duluth Minnesota: DAIP (Pence and Shepard 1988, Pence 1989). DAIP, an independent monitoring agency, is grounded in a feminist understanding of violence against women and is accountable to victim advocates and groups of formerly battered women. Although it supports mandatory arrest and no-drop policies (now operating in Duluth) as essential to the primary objective of protecting victims by bringing an end to the violence, it takes very seriously the importance of empowering women, who are consulted throughout the prosecution process. Further, DAIP routinely monitors policies and practices, stressing the need to safeguard against race, class, and lifestyle bias in policy implementation. Significantly, the mandatory arrest policy in Duluth not only resulted in a substantial increase in arrests, but also in a decrease in the *proportion* of minority men arrested to levels more in keeping with their percentage in the population (Pence 1989: 22). The situation in Duluth suggests, then, that the potentially negative consequences of tough criminal justice responses can be successfully tackled, transforming them into positive interventive tools. However, as DAIP acknowledges, the project takes a great deal of effort and vigilance, and is able to operate successfully in large part because Duluth is a fairly small city which has a co-operative police department, a strong shelter movement, and a relatively progressive government.

However, even the most successfully implemented criminal justice policies cannot be relied upon as *the* key preventive response to domestic violence. Evidence for the positive effects of policy on practice tends to come from calculations of the increase in arrests/charges as a proportion of total *recorded* police incidents. However the proportion of the increase depends entirely on the size of the denominator. For example, Jaffe *et al.* (1986) show that the introduction of the pro-charge policy in London, Ontario, led to an increase in charging from 23 per cent to 72 per cent of recorded domestic *crimes*. However, recalculated to include the total number of 'family trouble' calls with 'elements of spousal violence contained in the written narrative of the incident provided by the investigating officer' (41), the percentage is reduced from 72 per cent to less than 13 per cent. If the calculation also takes into account the unknown number of calls for which no police records are made plus the unknown, but extremely large, number of assaults never reported to the police in the first place (estimates of the proportion of incidents reported to the police include less than 2 per cent, Dobash and Dobash 1980: 164, and 14.5 per cent, Dutton 1988: 136), the significance of the London, Ontario, results pales somewhat. This is not to diminish real achievements, but to suggest that even where practice appears to make a difference, it would be very unrealistic to expect that the police and criminal justice system can be relied on as the major solution to the problem of controlling men's violence to women in the home.

Hype or hope?

Many of the issues raised above are clearly relevant to the British context. Moves towards pro-arrest policies have not as yet been accompanied by changes in other parts of the criminal justice system (for example, Edwards 1989, Horley 1990b). Arrested men are usually released on bail, the Crown Prosecution Service is reluctant to prosecute, and in rare cases where convictions are achieved, sentencing is minimal and unimaginative: short or suspended sentences and, more often, fines. Moreover Women's Aid, perhaps even more than comparable feminist organizations in Canada and the USA, has been starved of funds. The most immediate result is that the demand for refuge space far exceeds supply, a situation which has been exacerbated in recent years by the deterioration of public housing stock. Underfunding also means that Women's Aid is unable to develop victim advocacy work to any substantial degree. Police officers from the specialist domestic violence units (DVUs) have to some extent jumped in to fill this breach. However it is questionable, given their location within a crime control institution, whether they can or should take on an *independent* and *confidential* advocacy role; and no overall coordination of units or agreed standards of operation exist.

Finally, there is minimal support for women from other welfare agencies, and even less co-ordination between them, although interagency domestic violence forums are being established by local councils or the voluntary sector in a few areas (see National Association of Local Government Womens Committees nd: 17–18, Wolverhampton Domestic Violence Initiative nd). Again some DVUs have jumped in, initiating and co-ordinating inter-agency groups. While these initiatives have been welcomed by some service providers and activists, with some refuge groups inviting DVU officers onto their management committees, others have expressed suspicion regarding the motivations behind the sudden police interest in inter-agency work, particularly with respect to civil liberties and the black community (for example, Southall Black Sisters 1989, Mama 1989: 303–5).

So what can be concluded about pro-arrest policies? It is clear that, historically, police on both sides of the Atlantic have failed women who contact them in times of great danger, and that many women in violent relationships will at some time desperately need good police intervention. No one concerned for the welfare of women wants to see the police returning to the old status quo. However, there is cause for concern about the way the police, as well as many others involved with the issue in Britain, have jumped onto the pro-arrest bandwagon often without due recognition of the possible dangers involved and with an accompanying assumption that the criminal justice system can and should be *the* major social response to domestic violence. Indeed, there are inherent limits to police reform because of the way the criminal justice system is structured in patriarchal capitalist societies, and because the system can only deal punitively with a minute proportion of violent men. Evidence from a study of women using shelters in Canada (in Currie 1990: 87) suggests that only a very small proportion of women see the police as the best means of stopping men's violence; many more believe provision of shelters and public education to be more desirable.

Campaigns for responsive policing must continue. The police must be required to do their job, but in a way which is sensitive to the realistic desires and needs of women who seek their help. What is absolutely clear is that all women who contact the police want protection and safety from violence. Beyond this basic need and right, there is unlikely to be a consensus. As Women's Aid insist 'the crucial point for us is that police officers must treat assaults in the home as a serious crime, and *listen* to the woman's point of view' (Hague *et al* 1989: 35, original emphasis).

B. Batterers' programmes

In some respects, batterers' programmes constitute a parallel case to pro-arrest policies. Working models have been introduced into Britain directly from North America, they are not uncontentious (Schechter 1982: 166–7, 258–67) and, in particular, they can be dangerous if not provided in a context which pays equal attention to ensuring women's safety. This second section of the paper looks first at the major North American intervention models in work with batterers, then at what is happening in Britain and how it has grown directly out of the American work, and finally at whether the empirical evaluations of the latter's longer-established programmes would seem to justify their replication elsewhere.

Intervention with batterers in America

In the USA, programmes of work with batterers had their roots in the mid-1970s (Nosko and Wallace 1988: 33) and, by the early 1980s, only nineteen States had no programmes running (Stout 1989: 25; see also Gondolf 1985: 48). The spread of this work has encompassed three broad settings: clinical responses by medical practitioners and therapists, formal schemes instituted within the criminal justice system either to divert men from prosecution on condition that they attend a programme or making such attendance a condition of sentence, and self-help or re-educational groups established by men's organizations.

Contrary to the apparent consensus reached over arrest as the most appropriate police response to battering, there has never been agreement between mainstream clinicians and feminist activists regarding appropriate goals and models of intervention with batterers. Indeed, a number of distinct interventive models exist which can be differentiated according to the explanatory models on which they are based. Adams (1988), in categorizing the various American models on intervention with batterers, distinguishes five models in terms of their underpinning assumptions (see also Gondolf 1985). The first four are non-feminist, and are distinguished from the pro-feminist model by their tendency, to varying degrees, to downplay the violence, to ignore the batterer's responsibility for his behaviour, and to implicate the woman's behaviour.

Broadly, using Adams' (1988) terminology, the *insight model* see violence as resulting from psychological inadequacies rooted in earlier developmental problems (examples include unresolved conflicts with violent parents, Schlesinger *et al.* 1982; and unmet dependency needs, Beninati 1989), together with past or current stress. Therapy focuses on these intrapsychic issues, rather than on the violent behaviour and the man's responsibility for it, allowing batterers to point to formative experiences outside their control and continue their violence. The *ventilation model* locates the cause of violence in supposedly unhealthy suppression of anger which leads eventually to violent explosions. Therapy, often in groups of couples, focuses on awareness of suppressed feelings, open communication, and expression of aggression, and may thus encourage the batterer to vent his anger towards his partner, rather than to take responsibility for controlling it.

Interaction models (for example, Geller 1982), based in family systems theory, see violence as the responsibility of both partners due to lack of communication skills or other relational 'dysfunctions'. It is these dysfunctional patterns of interaction and their underlying causes which are the focus of treatment in 'marital' or 'couple' therapy. Adams criticizes these models for suggesting that women should change their behaviour too, and for their lack of awareness that open and honest communication is not only impossible but perilous when one is living in constant fear of violence. Bograd (1984) offers a detailed feminist critique of family systems approaches, on grounds which include the negative effect of the batterer's unwilling attendance, and the exploitation of the greater malleability of the woman, thus reinforcing sex role stereotypes.

Unlike the above three models, *behavioural models* actually focus on the batterer's violence which is understood as learned behaviour reflecting a lack of social skills, and therefore capable of being unlearned and replaced by more socially competent behaviour. Therapy involves developing social skills through, for example, assertiveness and relaxation training and learning techniques of anger management (see for example, Saunders 1984 on groups for men, and Neidig *et al.* 1985 on groups for couples). Gondolf and Russell (1986) argue the case against anger control programmes on grounds that men tend to learn the techniques as a set of gimmicks without undergoing real change, and that society, too, is let off the hook by such a superficial approach. Wood and Middleman (1990: 3) argue that the model is flawed in that batterers actually have very good impulse control since they manage not to hit their bosses but go home and hit their partners. They recommend re-educational group-work employing confrontation and an alternative set of cultural norms to the ones which condone violence (e.g. not to hit someone smaller than yourself).

Here they share the stance of the *profeminist model* favoured by Adams himself. He sees men's violence and denial—both of the impact of their behaviour and of their responsibility for it—as endemic in patriarchal society and needing to be actively confronted in intervention. Within profeminist models, however, there are further subdivisions, with Project EMERGE, running in Boston since 1972 (Adams and McCormick 1982), using a self-help peer counselling model and other projects favouring an educational style, for example the Domestic Abuse Intervention Project in Duluth (Pence and Paymar 1986). There have also been numerous hybrid approaches to work with batterers such as those developed by Nosko and Wallace (1988) and Pressman (1989)—these authors all happening to be

Canadian. Moreover, Tolman and Edleson (1989) demonstrate that behavioural *techniques* have, in fact, become common to the majority of programmes, whatever their underlying theoretical orientation.

Practitioners favouring any of these theoretical models can offer case studies illustrating success. However, none outlines a rigorous evaluation of his or her own model at work. (This point will be developed further below.) Most importantly, as Adams argues, therapists who fail clearly to attribute sole responsibility to the male partner, may 'collude with batterers by not making their violence the primary issue or by implicitly legitimizing men's excuses for the violence' (Adams 1988: 177). This may actively lead to the abuse continuing. Pence (1987: 22), on similar lines, dismisses group work with batterers which focuses on psychology rather than placing the violence in its full social and cultural perspective since, if the phenomenon of male violence is inadequately analysed, dangerously inadequate solutions will be applied to try and prevent it and, again, the violence will continue. Conversely programmes, in whatever setting, which are based on a profeminist understanding which locates the violence in its social and cultural context, tend to place women's safety in higher profile through formalized links with women's organizations and effective integration with services for women.

The situation in Britain

In the UK, work with batterers is still new and exploratory. Of the three broad settings for such work in the USA, two—self-help and criminal justice—are represented in Britain, although programmes in both are still in their infancy. There appears to be no equivalent in Britain of North American clinical programmes aimed at abusing men. This influence may be yet to come however through, for example, a growing and rather uncritical interest in family systems therapy in social work and therapeutic settings.

Self-help men's groups appear to be spreading quite rapidly in Britain. As is the case in the USA (Schechter 1982: 261–2), criticism from women's organizations with a longer-standing involvement in this field arises where men fail to root their work in a thorough-going analysis of the causes of violence or to tie it in with any structured form of accountability to women. These criticisms have certainly been directed against one of the best known of such projects, the MOVE group in Bolton, which was established by an ex-batterer in 1988 (Waring and Wilson 1990). It is based on the behavioural, anger management techniques which have become the mainstay of American intervention (Tolman and Edleson

1989) and its influence appears to be spreading largely through media interest and personal appearances. The Men's Centre, a project based in London, blurs psychotherapeutic and self-help influences, whilst the Everyman Centre intends to offer a men-only helpline, as well as both individual and group work. The only overtly pro-feminist men's self-help group known to the present authors is PAX in Kidderminster, which is in the West Midlands.

To date, only two batterers' programmes linked to the criminal justice system have been established in Britain. Both are court-mandated programmes, using counselling as a sentencing option rather than as a pre-trial diversion. Both are located in Scotland, and the first of them started work only in 1990. A third is being planned in London. Unlike the vast majority of self-help men's groups, all three are explicitly pro-feminist, having been heavily influenced by the feminist based model developed in Duluth, Minnesota (Pence and Paymar 1986), though the British context of severe cuts in public funding has not allowed the response to batterers to be interwoven with other services, notably for women, as has been possible in Duluth.

The two established initiatives are the CHANGE programme in Stirling and the Lothian project, based in Edinburgh. Each has two workers, one male and one female, and uses mainly a group approach. The CHANGE project began to be planned in 1985 against a background of the much criticized failure of the criminal justice system to prosecute cases of domestic violence (blamed by police and the courts on women as 'unreliable witnesses' without perceiving their vulnerability to retaliation if they did pursue the matter) and where, if prosecution did occur, it resulted in very light sentencing such as short terms of imprisonment or fines which the women themselves might well end up paying out of their housekeeping (see Section A). Consequently, the project strongly emphasizes violence against women in the home as criminally prosecutable behaviour, and is itself located as a resource within the criminal justice system. Men are referred to the CHANGE programme as a requirement of a probation order, following screening for suitability, and not diverted to it as an alternative to prosecution as the Procurator Fiscal (the Scottish prosecutor) had initially wanted. (See Hamberger and Hastings 1990: 4, for a listing of the range of forms of court mandating available in the USA. One is a direct parallel of that used in Scotland.) Men are not accepted into groups outside of that structure. The project is, however, run independently by a committee encompassing legal and social work practitioners, Women's Aid and academics.

The CHANGE project has employed workers since early 1990 and took its first referrals in May 1990. It serves two Courts and had about thirty-four men referred as at 14/2/1991. The group meets weekly for two hours and each man attends for sixteen weeks. The work is conceptualized as re-education, involving the man being confronted with his own behaviour, taking responsibility for it, and 'working to eliminate violence and intimidation from his relationships with women' (CHANGE information leaflet, undated). The underpinning analysis is a feminist one ('violence in the home is a problem rooted in long established cultural norms which serve to maintain men's control over women') and group members are strongly encouraged to adopt this view.

The workers claim accountability first and foremost to the 'victim'. They seek the woman's views concerning her partner's participation in the programme though they are not bound by it, they feed back to the woman during the programme, and they seriously address the issue of the woman's safety. In addition, the workers claim accountability to he Courts who refer to social workers holding the probation orders, and to Women's Aid. (Presumably, having Women's Aid on the Management Committee is meant to ensure that CHANGE does not compete with Women's Aid for funding for work with women.) However, the workers offer no guarantees of success to any of these three parties. Interestingly, when the workers explored the unreliable witness issue and found that women would not give evidence against their partners because they feared retaliation, they realized that ensuring women's co-operation with prosecution required raising their confidence that other agencies would meet their needs. The project is not, as yet, accompanied by other inter-linking services for women. However, there is a commitment to developing training and educational materials, perhaps as part of building the 'community commitment' which the mentor project in Duluth stresses is absolutely essential (Pence and Paymar 1986: vii).

The second court-mandated programme, the Lothian 'Domestic Violence Probation Project', has grown up in the shadow of the CHANGE project because it started life slightly later. It opened in Autumn 1990 and took its first referrals in late November of that year. Like CHANGE, Lothian is a re-education programme with a feminist philosophy. It takes the safety of female partners seriously by making contact with them and issuing a leaflet which emphasizes that they should continue with plans to make themselves safe. Moreover, in an attempt to combat denial from the man, information from the woman is used to establish the baseline of the man's behaviour before he joins the group, and she is seen again at the three-month follow-up stage. As with CHANGE, however, there is no parallel structure of groups or advocacy/support services for women. The chief difference from CHANGE lies in the Lothian project's location in the statutory sector. It is a part of Lothian Regional Council and hence is a local government-managed project, though situated actually in the Court building. The impetus for its establishment came from the Women's Committee of the Council.

As with CHANGE, attendance at a group is made a condition of a probation order which means that men can be breached (returned to court) if they fail to attend. The precise level of attendance which may be deemed acceptable was still under discussion between the project and the prosecutors at the time of writing. However, the police keep group members' names on a special 'intelligence file' and immediately inform the project if there is a call-out involving any of them.

In Lothian, imaginative and committed work has been put into adjusting the Duluth materials to a working-class Scottish context. Videos have been produced featuring local people and the typical Duluth diagrams have been recast using local dialect expressions in place of the American slang with which local men might find it hard to identify. The words so be used have emerged from actual group sessions with the men so that, although the clientele had still not reached double figures at the time of writing, the project has begun to take on a distinctive identity of its own. This may be seen as one of the more positive examples of transnational influence being adapted to fit the importing culture and environment.

Empirical evaluations of programmes in North America: lessons for Britain?

Unlike most self-help men's groups in Britain, both of the Scottish court-mandated programmes have benefited from the expertise offered by direct Women's Aid involvement, although this has been far from unquestioning. A major research programme is being organized around the CHANGE programme by its originators. On a national scale, critics of work with batterers (Harwin 1990, Horley 1990a: 17) have argued that its efficacy is as yet unproven and that it deflects resources away from support for women. Certainly, while refuges continue to stagger from one funding crisis to the next, and other women's work remains underdeveloped and largely unfunded, new programmes for male abusers in various parts of Britain appear to be attracting money, media interest, and official approval. Some of the reasons may include the need to seek community alternatives to prison in a country where numbers of inmates are so high and unrest so common; the complete lack, until recently, of any constructive work with these men, who take up inordinate amounts of the time of criminal justice and social welfare professionals; and the possible bias of male budget holders towards doing something for men rather than shoring up the women's movement.

Consequently, it may be highly instructive to look to the North American experience, where offering treatment to batterers (or imposing it on them) is unexceptional, and to ask whether the findings of scholarly studies or evaluative processes lend backing to what appears likely to be the imminent explosion of such work in Britain. Across the Atlantic, there has been a proliferation of papers arguing the efficacy or otherwise of work with batterers, over and above those which simply describe the models currently in use, their philosophies and techniques. It should be remembered, though, that the majority of programmes have no follow-up evaluation (Shupe, Stacey and Hazlewood 1987). It is, of course, crucial to know whether violent men can change as a result of intervention because, even if their partners leave, there are frequent reconciliations and batterers are also often violent in a series of relationships (Gondolf 1987:96).

Evaluating the success of programmes is, however, fraught with difficulties which could be argued to invalidate most of the early attempts at measurement of success. Eisikovits and Edleson (1989: 392–400) review a literature of more than fifty publications on groups for men who batter and conclude that, although sophistication is increasing, there are still severe methodological shortcomings (407–8). The problems which they and others cite include the following:

- the weak link between interventive models and the theoretical literature on the causes of violence (Eisikovits and Edleson 1989);
- the mix of techniques, making it hard to isolate those which work, if any (Eisikovits and Edleson 1989: 394);
- the source of the study: too often this is the same person who ran the programme, giving no guarantee of objectivity (Chen *et al.* 1989: 310; Eisikovits and Edleson 1989: 407);
- the source of the data: since it is well established that female partners report more incidents of abuse than their abusers (Edleson and Brygger 1986; Poynter 1989: 138), it is essential to go beyond client self-report (Eisikovits and Edleson 1989: 396) and ask the woman what has happened since her partner attended the programme;
- defining violence: there is evidence that whereas physical abuse may

decline or stop, threats of abuse continue or even escalate so that the woman still lives in fear (Edleson and Grusznski 1989: 20–1; Eisikovits and Edleson 1989: 396, 397, reviewing a range of studies, and discussion on 399; Edleson 1990: 134, 141). One would hesitate to call this 'success' (Brygger and Edleson 1987: 334) and, indeed, the gravest fear about batterers' programmes is that they may replace physical violence with emotional or other forms of abuse. Yet several studies have used a measure of conflict which only incorporates physical violence (Poynter 1989: 134);

- the lack of control groups in many studies (Chen *et al.* 1989: 310; Tolman and Edleson 1989: 187);
- their frequent vagueness over key information such as the source of follow-up reports (Edleson 1990: 133, 135);
- the risk that a positive effect may have resulted from some other factor, such as the threat of a return to court, the partner having left, or other sources of support, rather than the programme of intervention itself (Eisikovits and Edleson 1989: 408);
- low response rates, low recruitment, and high drop-out from programmes (Chen *et al.* 1989: 310–11) which mean that those whose response is measured may not be typical, together with the fact that those sentenced to attend may not resemble those who do so voluntarily. Certainly, those who come through the criminal justice system tend to be from the lower educational and occupational strata of society (Johnson and Kanzler 1990: 21) and some ethnic groups are over-represented;
- the difficulty of measuring the rate of abuse where the partners are no longer together (Edleson and Grusznski 1989: 20) since, on the one hand, this may give less opportunity for violence but, on the other, men can indulge in severe harassment at such times. Also, studies may not divide off the separated from the other couples, nor account for the fact that couples may separate and reunite more than once;
- the fact that contact with a programme itself sensitizes both partners to the issue of abuse and may make them more likely to report it at follow-up (Edleson and Grusznski 1989: 20);
- the fact that evaluation studies have mainly been underfunded and hence small and not necessarily systematic (Edleson 1990: 144);
- the need for far longer periods of follow-up before it is known whether positive effects really are maintained over time (Poynter 1989: 141), particularly since the whole pull within society is towards male domination of women. Periods of three or six months are far too short. That

the picture can change fairly radically between a six-month and an eighteen-month follow-up is evident from a study which had first proclaimed self-help groups less effective than educational but later found that the latter's results improved to a surprising degree over time (Domestic Abuse Project 1989: 1–3, 1991: 1–3).

Taken together, then, although many studies do report successes—in the region of 59 to 75 per cent according to a review by Edleson (1990: 136)—the evidence is as yet far from firm. As Goldolf points out (1987: 106), both the partners of batterers and the wider society are perhaps being falsely reassured that something effective is being done: 'we must be very cautious about our claims for batterers programs, especially since the safety of so many women and children are at stake'. As with pro-arrest policies, this must be yet more the case when one considers how few men are ever likely to reach these programmes, even should they become as widespread in Britain as in North America. The case for large-scale introduction of such work in Britain does not appear to have been made, and certainly not as the first priority for any increase in public funding.

Conclusion

It has not been the intention of this paper to suggest that either pro-arrest policies or work with batterers should be rejected by British policy-makers or practitioners: that would be for a belated pendulum to swing too far in the opposite direction. Rather, it is intended to urge a careful reading of the results of research and a cautious approach to the introduction of new schemes.

Despite the doubts discussed above about the effectiveness of these responses, women do frequently have urgent need of police intervention and do wish to see violent men obliged to confront the consequences of their behaviour and to change it. Nevertheless, individualistic responses to male perpetrators who happen to come to public attention can never guarantee women's safety. The overwhelming need in Britain is still for Government to provide secure funding for a framework of services to support abused women and to control abusing men. As this paper has shown, research indicates that neither arrest policies nor batterers' programmes can make women safe except as part of an integrated community response grounded in accountability to women.

References

ADAMS, D. (1988), 'Treatment models of men who batter: a profeminist analysis', in Yllo, K. and Bograd, M. (eds.), *Feminist Perspectives on Wife Abuse* (Newbury Park, California: Sage).

ADAMS, D., and McCORMICK, A. J. (1982), 'Men unlearning violence: a group approach based on the collective model', in Roy, M. (ed.), *The Abusive Partner: An Analysis of Domestic Battering* (New York: van Nostrand Reinhold).

BENINATI, J. (1989), 'Pilot project for male batterers', *Social Work with Groups*, 12 (2): 63–74.

BINDER, A. and MEEKER, J. (1988), 'Experiments as reforms', *Journal of Criminal Justice*, 16: 347–58.

BOGRAD, M. (1984), 'Family systems approaches to wife battering: a feminist critique', *American Journal of Orthopsychiatry*, 54 (4): 558–68.

BOURLET, A. (1990), *Police Intervention in Marital Violence* (Milton Keynes: Open University Press).

BOWKER, L. H. (1984), 'Battered wives and the police: a national study of usage and effectiveness', *Police Studies*, 7(2): 84–93.

BRYGGER, M. P., and EDLESON, J. L. (1987), 'The Domestic Abuse Project: a multi-systems intervention in woman battering', *Journal of Interpersonal Violence*, 2 (3): 324–36.

BUEL, S. M. (1988), 'Mandatory arrest for domestic violence', *Harvard Women's Law Journal*, 11: 213–26.

BUZAWA, E. S., and BUZAWA, C. G. (1990), *Domestic Violence: The Criminal Justice Response* (Newbury Park, California: Sage).

CHEN, H., BERSANI, C., MYERS, S. C., and DENTON, R. (1989), 'Evaluating the effectiveness of a court sponsored abuser treatment program', *Journal of Family Violence*, 4 (4): 309–22.

CURRIE, D. H. (1990), 'Battered women and the state: from the failure of theory to a theory of failure', *The Journal of Human Justice*, 1 (2): 77–96.

DAVIS, N. (1988), 'Battered women: implications for social control', *Contemporary Crisis*, 12: 345–72.

DOBASH, R. E., and DOBASH, R. (1980), *Violence against Wives: a Case against the Patriarchy* (Open Books: London).

DOBASH, R. E. and DOBASH, R. P. (1992), *Women, Violence and Social Change* (London: Routledge).

Domestic Abuse Project (1989), *Research Update*, number 2, June (Minneapolis, Minnesota: Domestic Abuse Project Inc.).

Domestic Abuse Project (1991), *Research Update*, number 3, Winter (Minneapolis, Minnesota: Domestic Abuse Project Inc.).

DUNFORD, F. W., HUIZINGA, D., and ELLIOTT, D. S. (1989),*The Omaha Domestic Violence Police Experiment*, Final Report, National Institute of Justice and the City of Omaha, June.

DUTTON, D. G. (1988), *The Domestic Assault of Women: Psychological and Criminal Justice Perspectives* (Boston: Allyn and Bacon, Inc.).

EDLESON, J. L. (1990), 'Judging the success of interventions with men who batter', in Besharov, D. J. (ed.), *Family Violence: Research and Public Policy Issues* (Washington, DC: AEI Press).

EDLESON, J. L., and BRYGGER, M. P. (1986), 'Gender differences in reporting of battering incidents', *Family Relations*, 35 (July): 377–82.

EDLESON, J. L., and GRUSZNSKI, R. J. (1989), 'Treating men who batter: four years of outcome data from the Domestic Abuse Project', *Journal of Social Service Research*, 12 (1/2): 3–22.

EDWARDS, S. S. M. (1989), *Policing 'Domestic' Violence: Women, the Law and the State* (London:Sage).

EISENBERG, S. E., and MICKLOW, P. L. (1977), 'The assaulted wife: "catch 22" revisited', *Women's Rights Law Reporter*, Spring/Summer.

EISIKOVITS, Z. C., and EDLESON, J. L. (1989), "Intervening with men who batter: a critical review of the literature', *Social Service Review*, 63 (3): 384–414.

FERRARO, K. J. (1989*a*), 'The legal response to woman battering in the United States', in Hanmer, J., Radford, J. and Stanko, E. A. (eds.), *Women, Policing, and Male Violence: International Perspectives* (London: Routledge).

FERRARO, K. J. (1989*b*), 'Policing woman battering', *Social Problems*, 36 (1): 61–74.

FIELD, M. H., and FIELD, H. F. (1973), 'Marital violence and the criminal process: neither justice nor peace', *Social Service Review*, 47 (2): 221–40.

FORD, D. A. (1991), 'Prosecution as a victim power resource: a note on empowering women in violent conjugal relationships', *Law and Society Review*, 25 (2): 313–34.

GAMACHE, D. J., EDLESON, J. L., and SCHOCK, M. D. (1988), 'Coordinated police, judicial and social service response to woman battering: a multiple-baseline evaluation across three communities', in Hotaling, G. T., Finkelhor, D., Kirkpatrick, J. T., and Straus, M. A. (eds.), *Coping with Family Violence: Research and Policy Perspectives* (Newbury Park, California: Sage).

GEE, P. W. (1983), 'Ensuring police protection for battered women: The *Scott v. Hart* Suit', *Signs*, 8 (3): 554–67.

GELLER, J. (1982), 'Conjoint therapy: staff training and treatment of the abuser and abused', in Roy, M. (ed.), *The Abusive Partner: An Analysis of Domestic Battering* (New York: van Nostrand Reinhold).

GONDOLF, E. W. (1985), 'Fighting for control: a clinical assessment of men who batter', *Social Casework*, January: 48–54.

GONDOLF, E. W. (1987), 'Evaluating programs for men who batter: problems and prospects', *Journal of Family Violence*, 2 (1): 95–108.

GONDOLF, E. W., and RUSSELL, D. (1986), 'The case against anger control treatment programs for batterers', *Response*, 9 (3): 2–5.

GOYETTE, C. (1990), 'The patchwork policy', *Vis-à-vis*, 8 (1): 4–6.

HAGUE, G., HARWIN, N., McMINN, K., RUBENS, J., and TAYLOR, M. (1989), 'Women's

Aid: policing male violence in the home', in Dunhill, C. (ed.), *The Boys in Blue: Women's Challenge to the Police* (London: Virago).

HAMBERGER, L. K., and HASTINGS, J. E. (1990), 'Different routes to mandated spouse abuser counselling II: a cross validation study': paper presented at the meeting of the American Society of Criminology, Baltimore, Maryland, 10 November 1990.

HANMER, J. (1989), Women and policing in Britain, in Hanmer, J., Radford, J., and Stanko, E. A. (eds.), *Women, Policing, and Male Violence: International Perspectives* (London: Routledge).

HART, B., STUEHLING, J., REESE, M., and STUBBING,E. (1990), *Confronting Domestic Violence: Effective Police Response* (Reading, Pennsylvania: Pennsylvania Coalition Against Domestic Violence).

HART, W. L., ASHCROFT, J., BURGESS, A., FLANAGAN, N., MEESE, U., MILTON, C., NARRAMORE, C., ORTEGA, R., and SEWARD, F. (1984), *Attorney General's Task Force on Family Violence* (Washington, DC: US Department of Justice).

HARWIN, N. (1990), 'Inter-agency cooperation: working with Women's Aid', *Nottinghamshire County Council 1990 Domestic Violence Conference Report* (Nottingham: Nottinghamshire County Council).

HIRSCHEL, J. D., and HUTCHISON, I. (1991), 'Police-preferred arrest policies', in Steinman, M. (ed.), *Woman Battering: Policy Responses* (Cincinnati, Ohio: Anderson).

HIRSCHEL, J. D., HUTCHISON, I. W., DEAN, C. W., KELLEY, J. J., and PESACKIS, C. E. (1991), *Charlotte Spouse Assault Replication Project: Final Report*, January, no publishing details.

HOLDEN, H. R. (1989), 'Does the legal system batter women? Vindicating battered women's constitutional rights to adequate police protection', *Arizona State Law Journal*, 21: 705–28.

Home Office (1990), *Domestic Violence*, Home Office Circular 60/1990 (London: Home Office).

HORLEY, S. (1988), 'Homing in on violence', *Police Review*, 29 January.

—— (1990a), 'A shame and a disgrace', *Social Work Today*, 21 June: 16–17.

—— (1990b), 'No haven for battered women', *Police Review*, 17 August: 1634–5.

JAFFE, P., REITZEL, D., HASTINGS, E., and AUSTIN, G. (1991), *Wife Assault as a Crime: The Perspectives of Victims and Police Officers on a Charging Policy in London, Ontario from 1980–1990*, Final Report, April (London, Ontario: London Family Court Clinic Inc.).

JAFFE, P., WOLFE, D. A., TELFORD, A., and AUSTIN, G. (1986), 'The impact of police charges in incidents of wife abuse', *Journal of Family Violence*, 1 (1): 37–49.

JOHNSON, J. M., and KANZLER, D. J. (1990), 'Treating domestic violence: evaluating the effectiveness of a domestic violence diversion program': paper presented at the Tenth Annual Symposium on Social Work with Groups, Miami, Florida, October 1990.

LANGAN, P. A., and INNES, C. A. (1986), *Preventing Domestic Violence Against Women*

290   *Substantive aspects of family law*

(Bureau of Justice Statistics special report, Washington DC: US Department of Justice).

LERMAN, L. G., and LIVINGSTON, F. (1983), 'State legislation on domestic violence', *Responses to Violence in the Family and Sexual Assault*, 6 (5): 1–28.

MacLEOD, L. (1987), *Battered but not Beaten . . . : Preventing Wife Battering in Canada* (Ottawa, Ontario: Canadian Advisory Council on the Status of Women).

—— (1989), *Preventing Wife Battering: Towards a New Understanding* (Ottawa, Ontario: Canadian Advisory Council on the Status of Women).

MacLEOD, L., and PICARD, C. (1989), 'Toward a more effective criminal justice response to wife assault: exploring the limits and potential of effective interaction', working paper (Research and Development Directorate, Policy, Programs and Research Sector. Department of Justice Canada, June).

MAMA, A. (1989), *The Hidden Struggle: Statutory and Voluntary Sector Responses to Violence Against Black Women in the Home* (London: London Race and Housing Research Unit).

MARTIN, D. (1976), *Battered Wives* (San Francisco, California: Glide Publications).

McGILLIVRAY, A. (1987), 'Battered women: definition, models and prosecutorial policy', *Canadian Journal of Family Law*, 6: 15–45.

MEEKER, J. W., and BINDER, A. (1990), 'Experiments as reforms: the impact of the "Minneapolis experiment" on police policy', *Journal of Police Science and Administration*, 17 (2): 147–53.

Metropolitan Police Community Involvement Policy Unit (1990), *Domestic Violence Best Practice Guidelines* (London: Metropolitan Police).

Metropolitan Police Working Party (1986), *Report of the Working Party on Domestic Violence* (London: Metropolitan Police).

National Association of Local Government Women's Committees (nd), *Responding with Authority: Local Authority Initiatives to Counter Violence Against Women* (Manchester: NALGWC).

NEIDIG, P. H., FRIEDMAN, D. H., and COLLINS, B. S. (1985), 'Domestic conflict containment: a spouse abuse treatment program', *Social Casework*, April: 195–203.

NOSKO, A., and WALLACE, B. (1988), 'Group work with abusive men: a multidimensional model', *Social Work with Groups*, 11 (3): 33–52.

Parliamentary Select Committee on Violence in Marriage (1975), *Report from the Select Committee on Violence in Marriage together with the Proceedings of the Committee. Session 1974–5*, vol. 2: Report, Minutes of the Evidence and Appendices (London: HMSO).

PENCE, E. (1987), *In Our Best Interest: A Process for Personal and Social Change* (Duluth, Minnesota: Minnesota Program Development Inc.).

—— (1989), *The Justice System's Response to Domestic Assault Cases: a Guide for Policy Development* (Duluth, Minnesota: Minnesota Program Development Inc.).

PENCE, E., and PAYMAR, M. (1986), *Power and Control: Tactics of Men Who Batter. An Educational Curriculum* (Revised 1990) (Duluth, Minnesota: Minnesota Program Development, Inc.).

PENCE, R., and SHEPARD, M. (1988), 'Integrating feminist theory and practice: the challenge of the battered women's movement', in Yllo, K. and Bograd, M. (eds.), *Feminist Perspectives on Wife Abuse* (Newbury Park, California: Sage).

POYNTER, T. L. (1989), 'An evaluation of a group programme for male perpetrators of domestic violence', *Australian Journal of Sex, Marriage and Family*, 10 (3): 133–42.

PRESSMAN, B. (1989), 'Wife-abused couples: the need for comprehensive theoretical perspectives and integrated treatment models', *Journal of Feminist Family Therapy*, 1 (1): 23–43.

RADFORD, J., and STANKO, E. A. (nd), 'Violence against women and children: the contradictions of crime control under patriarchy' (Unpublished paper).

SAUNDERS, D. G. (1984), 'Helping husbands who batter', *Social Casework*, June: 347–53.

SCHECHTER, S. (1982), *Women and Male Violence: The Visions and Struggles of the Battered Women's Movement* (Boston, Massachusetts: South End Press).

SCHLESINGER, L. B., BENSON, M., and ZORNITZER, M. (1982), 'Classification of violent behaviour for purposes of treatment planning: a three-pronged approach', in Roy, M. (ed.), *The Abusive Partner: An Analysis of Domestic Battering* (New York: van Nostrand Reinhold).

Scottish Information Office (1990), *Guidance to Police on Domestic Violence*, Scottish office news release (Edinburgh: Scottish Information Office).

SHEPTYCKI, J. (1990), 'A report on innovations in the policing of violence against wives in London England': paper presented at the American Society of Criminology Annual Meetings. Baltimore, Maryland, November.

SHERMAN, L. W., and BERK, R. A. (1984), 'The specific deterrent effects of arrest for domestic assault', *American Sociological Review*, 49: 261–72.

SHERMAN, L. W., SCHMIDT, J. D., ROGAN, D. P., GARTIN, P. R., COHN, E. G., COLLINS, D. J., and BACICH, A. R. (1991), 'From initial deterrence to long-term escalation: short-custody arrest for poverty ghetto domestic violence', *Criminology*, 29 (4): 821–49.

SHUPE, A., STACEY, W. A., and HAZLEWOOD, L. (1987), *Violent Men/Violent Couples: The Dynamics of Domestic Violence* (Lexington, MA: Lexington Books).

Southall Black Sisters (1989), 'Two struggles: challenging male violence and the police', in Dunhill, C. (ed.), *The Boys in Blue: Women's Challenge to the Police* (London: Virago).

STANKO, E. A. (1989), 'Missing the mark? Policing battering', in Hanmer, J., Radford, J., and Stanko, E. A. (eds.), *Women, Policing, and Male Violence: International Perspectives* (London: Routledge).

STEINMAN, M. (1990), 'Lowering recidivism among men who batter women', *Journal of Police Science and Administration*, 17 (2): 124–32.

STOUT, K. D. (1989), '"Intimate femicide": effect of legislation and social services', *Affilia*, 4 (2) Summer: 21–30.

THORNHILL, T. (1989), 'Police accountability', in Dunhill, C. (ed.), *The Boys in Blue: Women's Challenge to the Police* (London: Virago).

TOLMAN, R. M., and EDLESON, J. L. (1989), 'Cognitive-behavioral intervention with men who batter', in Thyer, B. A. (ed.), *Behavioral Family Therapy* (Springfield, Illinois: Charles E. Thomas).

WARING, T., and WILSON, J. (1990), *Be Safe! A Self Help Manual for Domestic Violence* (Bolton, Lancashire: MOVE).

Wolverhampton Domestic Violence Initiative (nd), *Annual Report 1990/91* (no publishing details).

WOOD, G. G., and MIDDLEMAN, R. (1990), 're-casting the die: a small group approach to giving batterers a chance to change': paper presented at the Tenth Annual Symposium on Social Work with Groups, Miami, Florida, October 1990.

5.2. Law, policy and practice: an uneasy synthesis

LORRAINE FOX HARDING

I have outlined four different value perspectives on child care law and policy which, while sharing certain ideas in common, take different views of child welfare, the family, the origins of child care problems, the role of the state, the concept of rights, and society and social problems. While each perspective has a degree of internal coherence, and while each may be identified as influential in actual policy and practice at different times and in different places, the 'real world' of such policy and practice, it is argued, always represents an uneasy and incoherent synthesis of views. That is, the perspectives are not found in practice in anything like their pure forms, notwithstanding the broad prominence of particular perspectives at times. Many factors influence the movements in *actual* policies. Among these, nevertheless, are swings in professional and pressure group thinking which may correspond to the perspectives which have been outlined.

Such broad swings in thinking may be more apparent with hindsight than when considering contemporary and very recent change. For example, it is now fairly easy to identify the 1960s in England and Wales as the 'prevention' decade when policy and social work practice favoured supporting the natural family and minimizing time in care, and the 1970s as the time of 'child protection' spurred on by concern about child abuse. There may be a tendency to oversimplify the past, however. It is perhaps because the 1980s—at the time of writing—were not yet over, that it seemed harder to generalize about this decade. At the same time, it is submitted that the 1980s in England and Wales were genuinely a time of polarization, of contrasts, and of greater tensions and conflicts in child care policy.

Here I will attempt to accomplish two tasks. Firstly, the chief factors which seem to be influential in determining the shifting nature of child-care policy will be outlined. Secondly, a brief attempt will be made to analyse English child-care policy in the 1980s in the light of the four value perspectives. The brevity and superficiality of this account of the 1980s is acknowledged; this complex decade merits a far fuller treatment as an exercise in its own right. This brief account may however illustrate the extent to which the world of *actual* policy always represents an 'uneasy synthesis' of views.

Factors influencing law, policy, and practice

The following four broad areas are suggested as significant:

Scandals and enquiries and the response
Interest groups and their thinking
Reviews of legislation and policy
Wider policies and changes

(a) Scandals and enquiries and the response

It is impossible to overlook the impact of individual cases which achieve 'scandal' status, on the development of child-care policy, and difficult to overestimate their importance in English policy in the 1970s and 1980s. Even as far back as 1870, the case of Margaret Waters, a private foster mother or 'baby farmer' executed for the death of one of the neglected infants in her care, caused a wave of public consternation and prompted the infant life protection movement to press for legislative change to regulate private boarding out.[1] It was a scandal case, that of the foster child Dennis O'Neill, followed by a government enquiry,[2] which was one factor in the post-war realization that the child-care service was in urgent need of reform. Most famous of all scandal cases, perhaps, is that of Maria Colwell of 1973,[3] which was followed by a public enquiry and much media coverage hostile to social workers. In the fifteen years 1972–87 there were no fewer than 34 enquiries,[4] some public, some held in private, into deaths of children known to Social Services Departments. Most of these produced recommendations relating to the law, policy, and practice. Among these cases the most well-known are probably a cluster in the mid-1980s—Jasmine Beckford, Tyra Henry, and Kimberley Carlile; the latest scandal case at the time of writing was Doreen Mason (1987).[5]

Three points may be made about the significance of scandal cases, the enquiries into them, the reports, and the media and public response. The first is the degree to which blame for the child's death is popularly apportioned to the child-care agencies of the state rather than the actual killer of the child. The second concerns the determinants of public response to such child deaths and to the responsibility for them. The third point concerns the perception of such child deaths as preventable through the manipulation of the state's response.

Firstly, cases in the 1970s and 1980s have been marked by criticisms of the social workers deemed responsible for the care of the child at the time of her death, and also seen as largely responsible for not preventing the death. These workers have been publicly pilloried in the popular press with headlines such as 'They Killed the Child I Adored'[6] and 'Kimberley: Social Workers Failed her and the System Doomed her to die'.[7] The Social Services Director in the Beckford case—herself exonerated by the inquiry report—had to remind herself that she did not kill Jasmine, Morris Beckford did. Criticisms were based on the view—blindingly obvious with hindsight, but often only with hindsight—that the child victim should not have been left with, or returned to, the birth parent. That is, social workers were castigated for not being firm and authoritative enough in relation to birth parents and children at risk. (A reversal of this type of criticism was found in the suspected sex abuse cases in the county of Cleveland in 1987—not involving child deaths, but also the subject of an inquiry and report[8]—where social workers were portrayed by the press as over-zealous, as brutally removing children from their parents when there were no good grounds for doing so. These cases were an important influence on the emergency protection provisions in the Children Act 1989.) The issue raised here revolves round the location of blame in those state agents responsible for child protection—almost to the exclusion of the actual killer of the child. It is rather as though doctors were blamed for every death of a patient known to them.

A second and related point of significance is *why* the public response to children killed by their caretakers should have been as intense as it was, and should have taken the form it did. An often mentioned comment is that child cruelty and child murder are hardly historically new phenomena, yet it is in the years since the 1960s, when the phenomenon of 'baby-battering' was identified, that the public and the media have been highly sensitized to the occurrence of child abuse, and much publicity has been given to discoveries of individual severe abuse cases where social workers were involved. It is not clear whether in fact the incidence of serious abuse has increased or merely that there is more awareness of it. In any event, the degree and nature of social concern, sometimes even seen as a 'moral panic',[9] requires explanation. Parton[10] is one writer who has set this trend in context—that of a more generalized anxiety about the family and the social order. Another aspect of the context is a general attack on the public sector in the 1980s.[11] Child-abuse enquiries have apparently provided a useful weapon with which to attack one of the least popular groups of public servant. Of interest here also is the much lower profile given to children killed by foster and adoptive parents, than those killed by birth and step-parents.[12] The significance of this distinction must be left to speculation at this point however.

Thirdly, there is the assumption that severe child abuse and deaths from abuse *can* be prevented—by more vigilant social work, by changing the emphasis in social work, by changing the law, by improving training, and so on. Recommendations from inquiry reports assume that steps can be taken to reduce the danger of similar cases occurring again. There are problems with this assumption. Firstly, expectations of social workers are contradictory (as comparison of the child death cases and the Cleveland cases makes clear). Secondly, the crucial issue of resources in child-care work is often not adequately tackled.[13] Thirdly, it may reasonably be argued that because of the complexity and unpredictability of human behaviour, no child care agency or child-care law can ever completely eliminate severe abuse. Nevertheless, policy and practice have been subject to numerous changes because of scandal cases and their effects.

(b) Interest groups and their thinking

A second factor in policy is the influence of relevant interest groups such as professional and pressure groups. These groups are themselves influenced by research, practice experience, and ongoing discussion, and by the particular interests they represent, as well as by the scandal cases mentioned and the policy reviews and wider changes to be discussed below. From time to time new pressure groups appear, such as Justice for Children and the Family Rights Group in the late 1970s, and Parents Against Injustice (PAIN),[14] the Children's Legal Centre, and the Family Courts Campaign[15] in the 1980s. The thinking of certain groups may be broadly aligned with particular perspectives outlined in this book—for example, the British Agencies for Adoption and Fostering has been broadly identified with the protectionist, 'permanency' position, and the National Council for One Parent Families with the pro-parent view. The social work profession as expressed in the British Association of Social Workers has been, certainly at one time, associated with a position sympathetic to natural parents and preventive work;[16] although the effect of child-abuse enquiries on the social work profession should not be underestimated. These have resulted in great anxiety surrounding child-abuse work, and some defensive practice. Finally, professional and pressure group thinking is subject to changing trends or, to put it more derogatorily, 'fashions'. As has been suggested, in the 1960s the 'fashion', broadly speaking, was in favour of natural families and preventive work, and in the 1970s, protection and permanency. It may be that each swing of thinking sets in train its own backlash, giving rise to a 'pendulum' effect.

Interest groups and their thinking may have both a direct and indirect influence on policy and practice—a direct influence on individual decisions and practice at the micro level; and an indirect influence in so far as they feed into the policy-making process at higher levels.

(c) Reviews of legislation and policy

Apart from reports of individual case inquiries set up by government, other government documents which review child care policy in general are clearly influential. One category of review is the report of a government committee set up for a specific purpose. In the recent history of English child-care policy three reports stand out—the Curtis Committee report, on children in public care (1946),[17] the Ingleby Committee report, focusing on delinquency and child neglect and their prevention (1960),[18] and the Houghton Committee report, initially on adoption, but coming to include fostering, and children in care (1972).[19] The three reports laid the foundations of the 1948, 1963, and 1975 Acts respectively. Their significance lay, broadly, in the construction of a new and better quality service for children in the care of the state (Curtis), the introduction of preventive powers to act on family breakdown, child neglect, and delinquency (Ingleby), and the granting of greater powers of child protection (Houghton).

Another type of report is that of a standing body such as the All-Party Parliamentary Select Committee on Social Services (known for a time as the Short Committee), whose report on children in care in 1984[20] was influential in the setting up of the review of legislation which eventually led to the Children Act 1989. This review of legislation also demonstrates the influence of reviews and reports in the policy-making process. Consultation papers were issued in 1985 by an Inter-Departmental Working Party of civil servants set up immediately after the Short Report to look at options for the codification and amendment of the law. These papers formed the basis for further consultation, for costing, and for a White Paper on child-care law and family services published in 1987.[21]

At a later stage of policy-making, White Papers prepare the way for legislation but are also part of the process of consultation. In the 1960s two White Papers on juvenile delinquency[22]—the first of which met with considerable opposition—fed into the process which eventually produced the Children and Young Persons Act 1969. The 1987 White Paper just mentioned formed, after more consultation, the basis for the Children Act 1989.

Another category of government document which may be mentioned here consists of regulations, circulars, notes of guidance, and codes of practice. These may lack the legal standing of Acts of Parliament, but have considerable force in policy nevertheless. Examples would be a code of practice issued in 1984 on access to children in care, and a circular in the same year on the passing of parental rights resolutions.[23] Also worthy of mention are reports by non-governmental respected bodies such as the Law Commission. The latter has reported on aspects of private child-care law such as illegitimacy and custody after divorce.[24] Law Commission recommendations were incorporated into the Children Act 1989.

(d) Wider policies and changes

Two aspects of wider change which impinge on child-care policy can be referred to. Firstly, there are other aspects of government policy. One important aspect comprises government approaches to public expenditure in general and social expenditure in particular. Pressure on resources and the search for cheaper solutions have a long-standing history in the field of child-care policy, and both foster care and prevention have at times been identified as means of reducing costs.[25] Where governments seek to reduce state welfare spending in general, social work as a relatively expensive form of labour might be expected to be under scrutiny;[26] but the pressure of public interest in child protection makes it difficult for even an avowedly expenditure-cutting government directly and obviously to reduce work in the child-care field. *Indirect* curbs, however, may stem from reductions in local authority spending in general, adversely affecting child-care services unless local authorities choose to divert resources from other areas of work. Other relevant aspects of government policy include policies in the field of health care, social security, education, and housing. Many policies here may be said to have implications, short and long term, direct and indirect, for child welfare and child-care problems. A useful example of the intersection of policies in different areas is provided by homelessness. Affected by policies in both the income maintenance and housing fields, homelessness can have severe effects on the health and welfare of children—if families, for example, sleep rough, take refuge in grossly inadequate or overcrowded conditions, or are housed in squalid and dangerous 'bed and breakfast' hotels.

Some children come into the care of the state solely because of homelessness.[27]

More generally, government policy on welfare sets the context and general climate of thinking surrounding child-care policy. This is usefully illustrated by contrasting the situation in the late 1940s and in the 1980s in England and Wales. In the late 1940s newly popular collectivist ideas on welfare spread their influence to child care, where a much wider concept of state responsibility for children developed than had been accepted in the past. By the 1980s, although major Welfare State institutions were still in place, there was apparently an end to the post-War 'consensus' on a major state role, and prevalent 'new right' ideologies favoured free market economics, the reduction of the state's role in welfare, and the encouragement of independence from the state, of private and voluntary sector alternatives to state provision, and of family care. This was a totally different climate, and logically would not have supported a major state role in child care. However, the effect, as will be shown, was ambiguous, and actual policy did not take the *laissez-faire* form which might have bene expected from the ideology.

The other aspect of wider change which is significant for child care concerns wider economic and social change, including levels of prosperity, poverty, unemployment, and demographic change. To take two examples from the 1970s and 1980s: increased unemployment and changing family patterns both have profound implications for child care within families and thus for demands on the state child-care system. Unemployment has been shown to impose strains, both psychological and financial, on families, and there appears to be an association—though probably not a straightforward causal relation—between unemployment and referrals to child-care agencies.[28] The poverty associated with unemployment itself causes child-care problems, if the proponents of the third value perspective are correct. Secondly, changes in families connected with the increased incidence of marital breakdown and its consequences are significant—particularly more lone parent (usually mother-headed) families, and more 'reconstituted' or step-families often comprising a birth mother and 'step-father'. Lone parent families in general experience social, financial, and work-related problems, and their children are disproportionately likely to enter care;[29] reconstituted families often have severe problems of internal relationships[30] while the prominence of 'step-father' figures in notorious child-death cases has been notable.[31] Another family trend has been an increasing proportion of children born to lone mothers, and in cohabiting partnerships which may have less stability even than marriage.[32] Other factors in late post-war society which may be mentioned include smaller families, changes in sexual mores, changing gender roles, and the influence of feminism, increasing demands on the 'middle' generations by the elderly, the demands from vulnerable and dependent groups discharged from hospitals into society at large, ethnic and cultural diversity, inner city decline, the increase of indebtedness as a pattern of life, and the very pace of social and economic change itself. Many change factors could be listed, and no doubt the reader has her own list of those to be considered the most significant. The relationship of all these variables to child-care problems and the need for state intervention is complex, not clearcut; but the general point is that child-care problems and the response to them do not arise in a social vacuum.

English child care policy in the 1980s—the uneasy synthesis

To illustrate the extent to which actual policy is a pragmatic response reflecting a number of different, often conflicting positions, a brief account will be given of the 1980s in the light of *laissez-faire*, paternalism, the support of the family, and children's rights. The questions of conflict and balance will be briefly highlighted.

(a) Laissez-faire

As already suggested, less has been seen of *laissez-faire* in English child-care policy in the 1980s than might be expected from the government's declared ideology (or from the ideology of family 'traditionalists' like the Conservative Family Campaign). Rigid time limits after which a child must be returned to his family or adopted were not imposed, or at least not at a national level; the legal grounds for compulsory intervention were not clearly defined more narrowly as *laissez-faire* would require; the state did not withdraw from all but the most extreme cases; children were not all cut off from their family of origin after a change of home. Certainly, 'permanency' continued to be generally favoured (although with greater grounds for doubt emerging towards the end of the decade);[33] but permanency, as said before, can also be associated with the second, protectionist perspective or, if return to the birth family is preferred, with the third, pro-parent view. Interestingly, while effecting swingeing reductions in local authorities' powers in almost every other field, central government in England in the 1980s did *not* attempt to remove from local authorities the primary responsibility for child care and protection work.

One way, however, in which *laissez-faire* did manifest itself was in certain provisions of the Children Act 1989 (Section 1), which set out the principle of 'non-intervention' in both public and private law. The principle stated that a court should not make an order regarding a child unless it considered it better for the child than making no order at all. This would mean, for example, that in matrimonial cases parents' arrangements would not automatically be judged by the court, and in care proceedings a Care Order would not automatically be made just because the statutory criteria were made out.

(b) Child protection and state paternalism

While the 1970s in England and Wales have been shown to be the decade in which paternalism in its modern form made the greatest strides, in the 1980s the paternalist and protectionist approach was still influential, especially after the cluster of publicized child-abuse cases and the enquiries into them in the middle of the decade—Beckford, Henry, and Carlile.

The major legislative event of the decade was the Children Act 1989, which as, indicated, was the fruit of a lengthy period of preparation including the appearance of consultation documents and a White Paper. It was intended partly to clarify and codify a vast amount of fragmented legislation which had grown up in a confusing and incremental way. This Act contained *both* protectionist and pro-parent elements: it is the protectionist sections which will be considered here.

One change which may be seen as a step towards greater protection was a widening in the grounds for care proceedings: these now included *likely* significant harm to the child as well as such harm already inflicted (under Section 31). Where a Care Order was made, it would mean that mostly children would indeed be *in* care; the local authority would receive them into care (Sections 22 and 33). If a Supervision Order were made, it would give the social worker greater authority (Section 35). Another change was that the child's welfare should be the *paramount* consideration in court proceedings relating to a child's upbringing (Section 1); under the preceding legislation welfare was only the *first* consideration—not quite as strongly put.[34] An extension of local authority powers to care for and assist older 'children'—even up to the age of 21—under Sections 20 and 24, might be seen as a further expression of paternalism, and Section 20 in some respects was wider than previous provisions for 'voluntary' care, and did not include a reference to returning children to their parents (this responsibility being placed only in a Schedule to the Act). Another change, which may suggest a fundamental shift in ideology and emphasis, was that parents were no longer defined as having 'rights' but 'responsibilities' (Sections 2 and 3). The Act thus underlined parent-hood as a duty to care, although it also conferred the authority and power to do so (Section 3). This is in line with the general paternalist per-spective. Another aspect of the Act of interest here is the provision that the Emergency Protection Order—the new shorter order which under Sections 44–8 replaced the old 28-day Place of Safety Order protecting children in an emergency—included a provision for ordering a child's medical examination (Section 44). The EPO was backed up by a Child Assessment Order for non-emergency situations, lasting seven days, and allowing social workers to seek an order for medical assessment (Section 43). Residence Orders (Sections 8–14) also perhaps reflected a protection-ist emphasis, in that, for example, foster parents might ensure some secu-rity by this means.

As far as social work *practice* in the 1980s was concerned, planning for a permanent home for the child continued to be favoured in general, and it was the early 1980s which saw a considerable shift in this direction in many Departments' practices.[35] The social reaction to child abuse contin-ued to exercise a considerable influence, as has been indicated. Awareness of child sexual abuse expanded, partly influenced by greater openness among women abused as children, partly by developments among paediatricians,[36] and there was more action on this form of abuse by Social Services Departments; however in Cleveland the circumstance of a large number of children being removed compulsorily from their parents in a short time on suspicion of sexual abuse led to something of a public 'backlash' against social workers for being *too* ready to protect, on insufficient evidence. Another practice trend was that foster care became increasingly popular as a form of substitute care, with the percentage of children in care fostered being as high in the mid-1980s as it had been in the early 1960s.[37] Some authorities closed children's homes. This was at least partly linked with a desire to reduce costs. At the same time, how-ever, the total number of adoptions decreased.[38] The percentage of the child population in care also dropped.[39]

Meanwhile, notwithstanding 'traditionalist' defences of conventional family forms, and probably greater scepticism about the 'alternatives' to the nuclear family with which some had experimented in the 1970s, fam-ily diversity tended to increase: fewer children spent their entire child-hood in the conventional model of a stable nuclear family with breadwinner father and mother at home full time. As indicated earlier, marriages increasingly ended in divorce;[40] more children were born outside marriage, and of these, more it seemed were born in the context of co-habiting relationships.[41] Some women chose to have children alone.[42] The stigma of illegitimacy was all but eliminated.[43] Hence—in part—the lack of babies available for adoption; as a result some infertile couples sought out surrogate mothers to bear children for them instead.[44] Thus, too, perhaps, a greater move to the adoption of children who came into care. Instability in family life might be used to justify a more strongly paternalist role for the state; but another implication of family diversity and change is the calling into question of how far a child can *ever* find permanence. Foster and adoptive families are not necessarily immune to these processes of change.

(c) The defence of the birth family

In the 1980s the pro-birth family position also made its influence felt, although in a slightly different form from the 1960s, with more emphasis on parents' rights, and more action by aggrieved parents and pressure groups to defend these rights. In the early 1980s there was criticism of the administrative procedure used to take over parental rights by committee resolution, with the National Council for One Parent Families claiming that this was a contravention of 'natural justice'.[45] Two private member's bills sponsored by One Parent Families in 1982–3, which would have replaced the resolution procedure by a requirement to apply to the juvenile court for a Care Order, fell; but a circular in 1984[46] extended parents' rights in this procedure slightly by recommending that they be allowed to make representations to committee members. Meanwhile, a Section of the 1983 Health and Social Services and Social Security Adjudications Act (HASSASSA) extended the rights of parents of children in care a little by granting a right of appeal against termination of access to a child in compulsory care. A code of practice on access was also produced by central government.[47] However, the limited nature of the right of appeal, and the tendency for it to be pre-empted in practice by delays before hearings,[48] meant that it only marginally strengthened the power position of parents in relation to the local authority. The HASSASSA also facilitated parental objections in the parental rights resolution procedure by abolishing the provision for parental consent.

The 1980s saw other developments on the parents' rights front, including the formation of self-help groups such as PAIN, and appeals in child-care cases to the local government Ombudsman and to the European Court of Human Rights.[49] The mobilization of parents in the Cleveland sex abuse cases should also not be overlooked. Many fought the local authority's decisions on both the legal and a broader public front—there were wardship cases; some contacted the MP Stuart Bell who, as shown earlier, became very embroiled in the battle on the parents' side; and parents spoke to the media and involved other advocates such as a local clergyman. Some proceeded to sue for the damage they considered had been inflicted on their family life.[50]

The apparently 'pro-family' elements in the 1989 Children Act will now be considered. Firstly, it seemed that local authority 'preventive' powers, and powers of assistance outside the substitute care system, were being extended. Section 17 conferred a duty to safeguard and promote the welfare of children 'in need', and to promote their upbringing by their families, by providing services of various kinds, including, exceptionally, cash. Schedule 2 of the Act set out the details. This provision was broader than the old Section 1 of the 1980 Child Care Act (previously of the 1963 Act), in that the duty was not restricted to the diminishing of the need for children to enter care or go before a court. It therefore became easier to assist families, provided that these provisions were supported by adequate resources. However, the local authority had to consider the means of both parent and child, with an eye to repayment, which might be seen as a drawback from a pro-birth parent perspective. There were also some reservations about the possibly stigmatizing connotations of the term 'in need'.[51] Another important development on the 'preventive' side was that health, housing, and education authorities were placed under a duty to comply with requests for help from Social Services, if compatible with their own duties and functions (Section 27), and there was more provision for day care under Section 18.

Secondly, both parental rights resolutions and the need for a parent to give 28 days' notice of removal of a child in voluntary care disappeared with this Act. Care for the child—or 'accommodation' as it was now termed—was construed more in terms of partnership with the parents. However, the widened grounds for care proceedings, taking in the risk of harm, could be used to protect a child already in accommodation if the local authority thought a parental removal was inappropriate. Apart from this, the local authority was not usually to provide accommodation if the parent objected, and, in providing accommodation or care, the local authority had to consult the parents (Section 22).

Parental rights of access were further enhanced by the Act, and the shorter Emergency Protection Order might also be seen as a strengthening of parents' rights. Emergency protection (Sections 44–48) was now based on more explicit criteria, and the order lasted for a maximum of eight days rather than 28 (though with the possibility of extension for a further seven), with a right of appeal after three days in some cases (Section 45). The order carried a presumption of reasonable parental 'contact' (Section 44), this concept replacing 'access', and additional orders could be made regarding contact although it could also be refused. The time limit on police emergency protection was also reduced, from eight to three days (Section 46). The provisions helped to satisfy concern about the draconian nature of the former Place of Safety Orders.[52] There were also restrictions on interim Care Orders (Section 38). Where children were under Care Orders, the local authority was to be responsible for promoting reasonable contact with the parents, and the court could also order contact (Section 34). Contact could not be terminated without reference to the court. Under Section 26 a complaints procedure was to be set up by which parents, among others, could complain about the local authority in child care cases.

Local authority use of wardship proceedings was restricted (Section 100), and finally, the rights of unmarried birth fathers were enhanced, in that, for example, the father could obtain parental responsibility either through a court application or formal agreement with the mother (Section 4).

On balance, it appeared that the Children Act, while containing both state paternalist and pro-birth family provisions, leaned more heavily to the latter perspective. At the time of writing, however, it was too early to judge what effect the Act would have in practice. As mentioned, the adequate resourcing of the ostensibly wider powers is a crucial issue. The extra resources required to implement the powers could be considerable.[53]

A few additional points may be made about the pro-birth parent influence in the 1980s. Research evidence cast some doubt on policies of permanence;[54] and 'shared care' with parents was favoured to a greater degree in social work practice.[55] As noted, both adoptions and numbers in care dropped in the 1980s; it was also the case that fewer were in care under Care Orders than in the 1970s.[56]

(d) Children's rights and child liberation

The manifestations of a children's rights perspective in English child care policy in the 1980s, including the relevant changes in the 1989 Act, have already been referred to in discussing the rights perspective in practice in Chapter 5, and the reader is referred back to this section. It will be recalled that signs of responsiveness to this perspective were found in the 1980s in the formation of pressure groups representing children in care, complaints procedures, moves to end corporal punishment, greater scope for children's evidence in court, and the setting up of telephone lines for distressed children; and in the Children Act specifically, in the provisions to pay heed to the child's wishes, extend separate representation for children in court proceedings, enable the child to take certain actions herself, and set up local authority complaints procedures. There were some signs of the liberationist perspective in practice, then, although it cannot be regarded as a dominant viewpoint.

Conclusion: conflict and balance

The 1980s, as the author has attempted to show, were a period in which both the paternalist and birth-parent perspectives were in evidence, while *laissez-faire* and child liberation had a more minor influence. The 1980s appear, at the present moment of hindsight, to be somewhat polarized with no single perspective dominant. Concerns about *both* the child-care agents of the state doing too much, too coercively, *and* about them doing too little, too ineffectually, resulted in a wish for legislation and policy to attempt to proceed in two directions at once—both towards better protection of the child and better protection of the parent.

This bi-directional policy may be expressed in terms of *conflict*, or of *balance*. From one viewpoint, the two broad objectives are in conflict and cannot be realized simultaneously; more power for social workers in relation to children does mean that parents lose some of their rights, in this view. Therefore descriptions of the Children Act 1989 which refer to its providing both better protection for children and greater rights for parents[57] are simply a denial of conflict, an attempt to avoid the awkward dilemmas that the child-care field inevitably throws up.

From another viewpoint, however, what legislation and policy is all about here is *balance*. While there are some conflicting objectives, it is argued, a better balance can be achieved. Thus it is reasonable, and not inconsistent, for the Children Act to attempt to proceed in two directions at once, adding to the power of parents here, strengthening the courts and local authorities there. What will be achieved, it may be argued, is not simply a redistribution of muddle but a genuinely more effective balance correcting tendencies both to over- and under-react, while helping parents and children as a unit where it is appropriate to do so.

Notes and references

NB: Cross-references to chapters and footnotes shown below refer to the original text from which this chapter was taken.

1. See J. S. Heywood, 1978, *Children in Care*, 95–6. Chapter 3, footnote 49.
2. See Chapter 1, footnote 4.
3. See Chapter 1, footnote 2.
4. According to the Kimberley Carlile report 1987, *A Child in Mind* (Chapter 1, footnote 2) 34 child-abuse inquiries had been carried out in the previous 15 years. See also: DHSS 1982, *Child Abuse*, Chapter 1, footnote 2.
5. See Chapter 1, footnote 2. Doreen Mason was 16 months old when she was killed by her stepfather in 1987. An inquiry reported to Southwark Social Services Department in July 1989.
6. The headline in *The Sun* referred to Jasmine Beckford. It was placed next to the photograph of the social worker. See: B. Franklin (1989), 'Wimps and bullies; press reporting of child abuse' in P. Carter, T. Jeffs, ,and M. Smith (eds.), *The Social Work and Social Welfare Yearbook* 1 (Milton Keynes, Open University 6). Similar headlines included 'Social worker lemmings let Jasmine die', *The Daily Telegraph*, 3 December 1985; and 'Guilty ones who let Jasmine die', *The Sun*, 5 December 1985.
7. *Daily Mail*, reported by M. Fogarty (1987), *Social Work Today*, 21 December 1987. Franklin also quotes a headline from *the Star*, 'Man who let Kimberley Die'. See B. Franklin (1989), 'Wimps and bullies', footnote 6.
8. See Chapter 1, footnote 6.
9. For the term 'moral panic' see: S. Cohen (1973), *Folk Devils and Moral Panics: The Creation of Mods and Rockers* (St Albans, Paladin).
10. N. Parton (1981), 'Child Abuse, Social Anxiety and Welfare', and (1985), *The Politics of Child Abuse*. Chapter 2, footnote 53.
11. See references on the 'crisis' of the welfare state, chapter 3, footnote 78.
12. Chapter 3, footnote 37.
13. For example, the Kimberley Carlile report 1987 (Chapter 1, footnote 2) put the resource issue outside its remit.
14. PAIN was formed in the early 1980s.
15. The Family Courts Campaign was formed in 1985. See Chapter 2, footnote 7.
16. For example, during the passage of the 1975 Children Act BASW campaigned from a 'preventive' or pro-parent stance. See L. M. Fox (1982), 'Two Value Positions', Foreword, footnote 1.
17. Curtis Committee 1946, *Report of the Care of Children Committee*, Chapter 4, footnote 86.
18. Ingleby Committee 1960, *Report of the Committee on Children and Young Persons*, Chapter 4, footnote 96.
19. Home Office/Scottish Education Department 1972, *Report of the Departmental Committee*, Chapter 3, footnote 64.

20. House of Commons 1984, *Children in Care*, Chapter 4, footnote 20.

21. White Paper 1987, *The Law on Child Care*, Chapter 4, footnote 23.

22. Home Office 1965, *The Child, the Family and the Young Offender*, Chapter 4, footnote 102; Home Office 1968, *Children in Trouble*, Chapter 4, footnote 102.

23. DHSS 1983, *Code of Practice: Access to Children in Care* (London, HMSO); DHSS 1983 LAC Circular on Access: (83) 19; DHSS 1984 LAC (84) 15.

24. See Chapter 2, footnote 12.

25. See J. Packman (1981), *The Child's Generation*, Chapter 3, footnote 60; J. S. Heywood (1978), *Children in Care*, Chapter 3, footnote 49.

26. As for example when the then Secretary of State for Health and Social Services, Patrick Jenkin, set up the Barclay Committee to look into the role and tasks of social workers in September 1980.

27. For example, the National Children's Home claimed 600 children in care because of family homelessness, in March 1989; NCH 1989, *Children in Danger—Factfile 1989* (London, NCH), as reported in 'NCH report highlights dangers to children', *Social Work Today*, 30 March 1989 4.

28. For the effect of unemployment on families and child care, see for example: R. Rapoport (1981), *Unemployment and the Family* (London, Family Welfare Association); D. Piachaud (1986), 'a Family Problem', *New Society*, 13 June 1986; P. R. Jackson and S. Walsh (1987), 'Unemployment and the family' in D. Fryer and P. Ullah (eds.), *Unemployed People. Social and Psychological Perspectives* (Milton Keynes, Open University Press); J. Popay (1982), *Employment Trends and the Family* (London, Study Commission on the Family).

29. See Chapter 4, footnote 34.

30. For reconstituted families, see for example: J. Burgoyne and D. Clark (1982), 'Reconstituted Families' in R. Rapoport, M. Fogarty, and R. N. Rapoport (eds.), *Families in Britain* (London: Routledge, Kegan Paul), 286–302.

31. For example, Maria Colwell, Jasmine Beckford, Kimberley Carlile.

32. See Chapter 2, footnote 51. There is some doubt about the long-term stability of these co-habitations. See: A. Spackman (1988), 'Why the family is crumbling', Chapter 2, footnote 51.

33. See: J. Thoburn, A. Murdoch, and A. O'Brien (1986), *Permanence in Child Care* (Oxford, Blackwell). This study of a project run by the Children's Society found that, with some children, the new, 'permanent' family might need just as much help as the biological one if placement breakdown was to be avoided. Successful placement required considerable staff input, and finding families and settling children took up to two years. The scheme was a more costly method than had been thought. So 'permanency' is not necessarily a cheap option.
   Meanwhile, an emphasis on 'shared care' was increasingly found in the mid-1980s.

34. Under the Children Act 1975, Sections 3 and 59, and the Child Care Act 1980

Section 18, for children in care and adoption cases welfare was the *first* consideration. (Under the Guardianship of Minors Act 1971 Section 1, welfare was the *first and paramount* consideration.)

35. See for example: M. Adcock, R. White, and O. Rowlands (1983), *The Administrative Parent*, Chapter 3, footnote 20; P. Beresford *et al.* (1987), *In Care in North Battersea*, Chapter 4, footnote 27.

36. The pioneering work of Wynne and Hobbs in Leeds had influenced Higgs and Wyatt, the paediatricians at the centre of the Cleveland controversy 1987. See: C. J. Hobbs and J. Wynne (1986), 'Buggery in childhood—a common syndrome in child abuse', *The Lancet*, 4 October 1986.

37. While in 1980 only 37 per cent of children in care were fostered, by 1982 this had risen to 41.6 per cent, by 1984 to 48 per cent, by 1985 to just over 50 per cent, and by 1986 to 52 per cent. Sources: DHSS, *Children in Care of Local Authorities Year ending 31st March, England*, various years (London, HMSO; DHSS, *Health and Personal Social Services Statistics for England 1987*, London, HMSO); See Chapter 3, footnote 60.

38. The peak year for adoptions was 1968, when there were almost 25,000 adoption orders in England and Wales. By 1974 the number had dropped to 22,500, by 1976 to 17,600, by 1978 to just over 12,000, by 1980 to 10,600, and by 1983 (after a slight revival in 1982) to just over 9,000. The figure was just over 8,600 in 1984—in other words about a third of its 1968 figure. (It appears that it dropped further after this.) Sources: Home Office / Scottish Education Department 1972, *Report of the Departmental Committee*, Chapter 3, footnote 64; OPCS, *Adoptions in England and Wales*, various years (London, HMSO); OPCS Monitors, quoted in *BAAF Annual Review 1985/6* (London, BAAF).

39. In 1976, for example, 0.75 per cent of the under 18 population were in care; the percentage was 0.77 per cent in 1980, but it had dropped back to 0.75 per cent in 1982, to 0.7 per cent in 1983, to 0.65 per cent in 1984, to 0.62 per cent in 1985, and to 0.6 per cent in 1986. Most children in care in the 1980s were aged over ten. Sources: DHSS, *Children in Care of Local Authorities year ending 31st March, England*, various years (London, HMSO); DHSS, *Health and Personal Social Services Statistics for England 1987* (London, HMSO).

40. In 1979 there were over 11 divorces per 1,000 married persons; by 1984 there were 13. The latest figure given by the OPCS in 1988 was 13.4. See: OPCS, 1988, *Population Trends*, 52.

41. See Chapter 2, footnotes 50 and 51.

42. See for example: J. Renvoize (1985), *Going Solo: Single Mothers by Choice* (London, Routledge Kegan Paul).

43. See Chapter 2, footnotes 12, 50 and 51. Also see: R. Collins (1989), 'Illegitimacy, Inequality and the Law in England and Wales' in P. Close (ed.), *Family Divisions and Inequalities in Modern Society* (Basingstoke, Macmillan).

44. For surrogate motherhood, see for example: L. M. Harding (1987), 'The Debate on Surrogate Motherhood' Chapter 2, footnote 20; DHSS, 1984,

Report of the Committee of Inquiry into Human Fertilisation and Embryology, Cmnd 9314 (Chairman: Dame Mary Warnock) (London, HMSO); A. A. Rassaby (1982), 'Surrogate Motherhood: the position and problems of substitutes' in M. Walters and P. Singer (eds.), *Test Tube Babies* (Melbourne, Oxford, Oxford University Press), 97–109; J. Montgomery (1986), 'Surrogacy and the Best Interests of the Child', *Family Law* 16 (37).

45. NCOPF, 1982, *Against Natural Justice*, Chapter 3, footnote 38.
46. DHSS 1984 LAC (84) 15. This chapter, footnote 23.
47. DHSS 1983 LAC (83) 19. This chapter, footnote 23.
48. M. Southwell, Leeds University; research as yet unpublished.
49. See Chapter 4, footnote 56.
50. Parton and Martin (1989) state: 'At the time of writing it is unclear whether the parents are pursuing claims for professional negligence, assault and battery, or defamation.' N. Parton and N. Martin (1989), 'Public Inquiries, Legalism and Child Care in England and Wales', *International Journal of Law and the Family*, 3 21–39, footnote 11 38.
51. See M. Jervis (1989), 'The Stigma of "Children in Need"', *social Work Today*, 16 February 1989.
52. See for example: C. Ball (1989), '"Carlile factor" overlooked in proposed legislation', *Community Care*, 23 March 1989.
53. See for example: G. Stewart (1989), 'Who will foot the bill?', *Community Care*, 8 June 1989; J. Richards (1989), 'The Bill: Resource Implications', *Family Rights Group Bulletin*, Spring 1989.
54. See this chapter, footnote 33.
55. While the Short Report 1984 and the review of child care law 1985 favoured 'shared care', the White Paper of 1987 rejected the concept, feeling that the terms 'shared care' and 'respite care' were not advisable. (For these sources see Chapter 4, footnotes 20 and 23.)
56. While in 1975 45 per cent of children in care had been under (1969 Act) Care Orders, by 1980 this percentage had risen to 47.5 per cent, and by 1981 to nearly 48 per cent. There was then a decline, however, and by 1985 the percentage was down to 43 per cent, and by 1986 to 41.6 per cent. Sources: DHSS, *Children in Care of Local Authorities at 31st March 1986, England* (London, HMSO); DHSS, *Health and Personal Social Services Statistics for England 1987* (London, HMSO).
57. For example, the Prime Minister in introducing the Children Bill in the debate on the Queen's speech in November 1988 said: 'Children are entitled to protection from harm and abuse, and innocent families from unnecessary intervention by the state', as though the juxtaposition of these two aims was in no way problematic. See: J. Oliver (1988), 'Introducing the Children Bill', *Social Work Today*, 1 December 1988.

5.3. Responding to children's needs: an issue of law?

MICHAEL KING AND JUDITH TROWELL

We start with the effects of the law and the operation of the legal system upon those children and families who become the subject of legal proceedings.

The impression of the law that may have been gained by the cases that we have presented could well be that of a largely inflexible and insensitive institution which inflicts its rules and decisions upon families, social workers, and psychiatrists alike. At times, the outcome of legal cases may appear to have scant regard for the well-being of the children whose interests the law is trying to promote and at other times they may be based on a simplistic, rudimentary understanding of child psychology and, in particular, of the world as it appears to young children. Moreover, confrontations within the law appear to many non-lawyers who become involved in child-are cases as rather unpleasant and best avoided wherever possible. If they are unavoidable, then you have to play the game according to the arcane and artificial legal rules.

Yet, at the same time, there exists among most social workers and mental health workers a respect for the courts as necessary and important for the protection of people's rights and, alongside this respect, the hope, perhaps against all the odds, that some way out of the confusion over the child's future will emerge from the legal proceedings. The hope also abounds that things will get better, when judges and lawyers are more specialized and trained in child care, when the rules of evidence are changed, and, of course, when family courts arrive.

Yet much of these criticisms and hopes for change arise from expectations of the legal system which it can never realistically meet, given the inherent nature of law as a social institution. Only by ceasing to produce legal decisions can the legal system take on the role of therapist and promoter of children's interests. If we are to understand the limits of what law can do and what the legal system can become, we need to examine the functions that law performs in modern societies and then go on to see whether, or to what extent, these functions are compatible with the sensitive, child-responsive legal system that many who work in the childcare field want to exist.

Law's social functions

1 Maintaining social cohesion

Issues concerning child welfare and child protection presented by legal textbooks and by the reports of court cases tend to be simplified, sanitized accounts of reality as it is perceived from mental health clinics. Much of the complexity of interwoven emotional relationships is reduced and simplified by the legal process to dimensions that can be made to fit pre-existing legal categories. This process, far from reflecting inadequacies in the legal system that can be remedied by improvements in procedures and the quality of legal representation, is an essential part of the law's social role. Law, according to recent theoretical ideas about the nature of law as a social institution, needs to convey simple, straightforward moral messages to the external world. It does so in part by ignoring or simplifying just those complexities and ambivalences in human relationships that clinical workers thrive upon.

Just as in fairy stories the characters tend to be one-dimensional cardboard cut-outs, symbolizing different moral positions—the good fairy, the wicked fairy, the evil giant, the protective dwarfs etc.—so in legal stories real-life characters tend to be portrayed as caricatures. Moreover, as in fairy stories, legal stories contain a coded message or moral concealed in the narrative. The law's messages may be concerned with simple moral issues demonstrating, for example, how 'bad' parents lose their children or how 'innocent children' are protected against evil. However, the message is equally likely to celebrate the just nature of law itself. The law, for example, is fair because it protects the weak, rewards virtue and innocence, punishes the guilty, and seeks out where children's best interests lie.

This does not mean to say that all legal decisions are perfect. Law, like life, is imperfect—judges may from time to time criticize past legal decisions—but it is always presented as striving to improve its performance. Judges who fifty years ago may have minimized the effects of separating a young child from its mother are seen by today's judges as having been misguided. But today's judges are perceived as being 'correct' in maintaining that living with both parents is best for the healthy development of the child (except, of course, where one of the parents has sexually abused the child, in which case the parent is seen as 'evil' and generally denied contact with his children).

This, then, is not just a matter of judges keeping abreast of current knowledge about what is good and bad for children. Such knowledge is rather digested by the legal system and emerges as legal principles, over-laid with strong moral messages which serve to educate both litigants and people in general about what is and what is not acceptable behaviour in relations between parents and among parents, social workers, and chil-dren. These legal stories present a seemingly consensual view about chil-dren's needs and ways of meeting those needs through good practice and good parenting. The fact that in the external, non-legal world such a con-sensus does not exist has to be ignored in legal stories. For the law to enter into the controversies over psychological theory and the validity or otherwise of research studies would be both to generate uncertainty among parents, social workers, and other care takers and to undermine confidence in the law itself (as well as in psychological expertise) and its ability to resolve disputes in a just manner.

2. Promoting 'the public interest'

The degree to which the legal system has a responsibility for maintaining social order and promoting the public interest over and above its respon-sibility towards the parties to a legal dispute is a matter of much discus-sion among lawyers. In practice, the public interest as interpreted by the judges tends to prevail over the private interests of litigants, witnesses, etc. This, however, can conflict with the legal principle that children's welfare shall be paramount.

There are not many people who would be prepared to dispute that a young child of, say, six years, who had been the only witness to a mur-der, should wherever possible give evidence regardless of any possible trauma that could be caused by the child reliving his or her experience in court and being subjected to cross-examination. A balance has to be made between the harm likely to be caused to the child and the interests of law and order, of public safety. Where the crime is child sexual abuse and the suspected perpetrator is a stranger who is suspected by the police of having carried out several minor sexual assaults on different children, the same balancing exercise applies, only this time it may well be that the harm to the child in appearing as a witness outweighs the benefit to soci-ety from prosecuting the abuser. Let us change the facts slightly and make the perpetrator the child's father, and the abuse more serious. Does public interest now demand that the child give evidence, regardless of the likely harm that will be caused to the child?

Although we have deliberately avoided discussing criminal prosecutions, this does not entitle us to avoid difficult questions about how far the traditional (and, some would say, essential) roles of the law in our society should be curtailed by considerations about the effects on children's welfare. Our position is that where there is a serious risk of harm to the child through the use of the legal process, everything possible should be done to minimize that risk. This would involve not only such measures as video-links and the admissibility of previously recorded video evidence (Piggot Committee Report), but also a greater sensitivity to children's needs throughout the criminal justice system.

3. Conflict management

Where a couple are locked in battle over who should have the care of the children, are they not entitled to turn to the law, as the social institution charged with conflict resolution, and demand a determination of their dispute? Is not the law required to give that decision quite regardless either of the effects of the legal process upon the children or of the possibility that a cut-and-dried decision giving one parent custody may result in the loss for the children of all contact with the other parent?

In child abuse and neglect cases, is it not up to state agencies who wish to intervene in family life to prove in law that abuse has occurred and that action by the state is justified and necessary for the children's protection? If the law were to abdicate its responsibility, would this not leave the way open for tyranny by experts, with paediatricians, child psychiatrists, and social workers taking it upon themselves to remove children from parents whenever they pleased?

These are difficult policy issues. Clearly, there needs to be some control over the power of experts and the representatives of state agencies. This control may well take the form of legislation laying down strict limits for coercive intervention to protect children. This begs the question, however, over the distinction between persuasion and coercion. What Anglo-American systems have tended to do is to lay the emphasis upon the integrity of the family unit and to treat any threat to that integrity as potentially a matter of conflict for the courts to adjudicate upon. What several European countries, notably France, Belgium, and Holland, have done by contrast is to use the persuasive powers of officialdom so that the incidence of naked coercion is minimal and the number of cases requiring adjudication of a legal nature very small indeed.

The issue that concerns us here is not which of these approaches is fairer or more democratic, but which one is likely to cause the least harm to the children that the state is trying to protect. To insist as a matter of principle upon the legal adjudication through a full-blown courtroom contest of every matter where the state's representatives seek to protect children in ways which conflict with the parents makes little sense, if attempts to put the principle into practice actually hurt the vulnerable individuals that the law is trying to protect. What we would argue is that, in the understandable quest of lawyers, administrators, and politicians in Anglo-Saxon countries for a just and fair system, the harm caused to the relationships between parents and children and between families and their social worker or clinic is all too often ignored.

The other area of conflict which regularly finds expression in the courts involves parental disputes over children. Here again, on the strength of the case histories that we have presented, we would question the use of the law, particularly as it operates in Anglo-American systems, as necessarily the appropriate institution for managing conflicts of this kind. The problem with the systematic use of the legal process lies in its method of conflict management. By structuring as a legal contest the emotional tangle that often follows the break-up of close relationships, the law may succeed in channelling and so managing the conflict. In doing so, however, it allows the hostility and acrimony to find expression and feed upon the many opportunities that the legal process itself offers for humiliating, outwitting, and defeating the once-loved-and-now-despised former partner or the once-helpful-and-now-interfering social worker. In this paradox of conflict management, through the ritualized expression of conflict, it is the child once again who is likely to suffer, pulled in different directions by opposing parties.

Recent changes in the substantive law, such as the English Children Act, remove the obligation for parents to seek a court order for the children solely because they are divorcing. Nevertheless, whenever there is disagreement between them over the residence and visiting arrangements, the image of the child in a *Caucasian Chalk Circle*, on the point of being torn apart by rival carers intent on winning their claim to have the child living with them, has not been dispelled by the implementation in England and Wales of the Children Act 1989 or by the arrival in other countries of family courts.

Once again, from the child welfare perspective, persuasion is almost always better than coercion. The best conciliation services are able to offer education for parents on the deleterious effects on their children of unrestrained hostility and in doing so avoid the need to seek out a legal resolution of their conflict. However, other forms of conciliation may simply pressure parents into accepting compromises as an alternative to expensive and risky litigation. There may be agreement on paper, but no real commitment to work together for the sake of the children.

4. The protection of rights

There are important issues to be raised concerning the courts' role as protector of rights. In the first place we need to consider the concept of legal rights by dividing them into two, *substantive rights* and *procedural rights*. Substantive rights provide the rights-holder, whether a parent, child, or organization such as the family or social services, with the power, enforceable by law, to take action affecting others or to resist action taken by others against that individual or organization. Procedural rights, on the other hand, exist only to ensure fairness during the process of decision-making, whether in a court or elsewhere. Unlike substantive rights, they do not determine the outcome of the decision, but only the form of the decision-making process.

Substantive rights: The legal process works relatively well as a protector of substantive rights when it is asked to rule upon issues arising out of a contractual arrangement, such as landlord and tenant or seller and buyer. It may also work well when faced with such quasi-contractual situations as teacher–pupil or trustee–beneficiary. However, it works far less well for those relationships which are based upon a complex interweaving of emotional and economic factors such as one finds in family issues. While it may be able to regulate the economic relationship by deciding, for example, that the couple should share equally the proceeds of sale of the matrimonial home, it often has to leave emotional conflicts to be resolved outside the courtroom. In child protection cases, however, it is often not possible for law to renounce responsibility in the fraught area of emotions. To reduce the complexities to issues of rights and their infringement may be the only way that the legal process can give the impression of dealing effectively with such conflicts. The suspicion remains, however, that the rights rhetoric is covering up vast areas of human experience which law is ill equipped to tackle.

The recent Children Act for England and Wales deliberately avoids the use of the term 'rights' in relation to children, their families, and state agencies, preferring instead concepts such as parental 'duties' and 'responsibilities', children's needs and welfare. Despite this change in the terminology, the Act still gives social services departments the power to remove children from their parents where this is necessary for the child's protection. It gives parents the (procedural) legal right to challenge these decisions in court, and it asks the court to make a wide range of decisions where the rights of parents and families to self-determination have to be balanced against the rights of children to protection from harm. Furthermore, the courts, under the provisions of the Act, are still engaged in binary (right/wrong) decisions where parents attempt to protect their rights by denying that their child is in danger of significant harm and the social services department try to show that the child is indeed in danger of such harm and by doing so to secure through a court order the right of the child to protection. Although the terms may have changed, the essentials of the process remain largely unaltered whereby the complexities of intra-family relations continue to be simplified and reduced to issues that can be handled effectively by court procedures and decisions and by the intermittent nature of the court's involvement in the child's welfare. The change of vocabulary, then, does not in practice give rise to a change of substance in the kinds of decisions that courts are required to make.

This Act, like many other statutes existing in different countries, gives substantive rights to families to be free from interference by state agencies, as long as the children are not abused or in danger of harm. It also gives procedural rights to both parents and children. Few people would argue with the need to restrain agencies from the arbitrary use of state power or with the objective of protecting children. Yet the very fact that issues concerning children's welfare are, as we have shown, defined as a conflict between state and parents which only the courts can resolve, raises serious questions over whose interests are in fact being served by this use of the legal process. Similarly, nobody would deny that procedural rights for parents and children are important, but they do not mean that every disagreement between parents and social services departments should provide the opportunity for a full-blooded court trial with lawyers representing all the various parties who may have an interest in the child's future. These matters become clearer if we examine how the substantive and procedural rights of children operate in practice.

In essence, children's substantive rights may be summarized as (*a*) the right to be free from any conduct or situation likely to cause them harm and (*b*) the right of self-determination or autonomy—the power to make choices about their own lives. We have already seen how the enforcement of the first of these substantive rights will often be outside the powers of any court, depending instead on the availability of resources to meet the child's needs. Where the courts become involved, therefore, the issues are likely to be confined to harm caused by the parents or other adult care-takers. Courts may deal with harm caused by individuals, but they are relatively powerless when it comes to harm resulting from government policies or poor administration.

A similar problem arises in relation to the child's right to make choices. The child's choices will depend upon what is available. In the famous English case of *Gillick* [1985] 2WLR, 830, House of Lords), for example, the children's right to contraception and contraceptive advice, won through the courts, would be meaningless if there were no clinics available to offer this service to teenagers or if the only clinics offering the service charged fees which were far beyond what the Gillick children could afford. Similarly, a child in the care of a social services department cannot choose to be placed in a children's home rather than a foster family if the local council for the area closed all children's homes as an economy measure some five years previously.

A second problem for the promoters of children's autonomous rights through legal intervention is that what the child wants may not coincide with what the law wants. Parents may be prosecuted and imprisoned for child abuse without any consultation with the children, and the children may be removed from the home 'for their own safety', regardless of their wishes and at times without any attempt to find out their wishes. Where these matters are discussed with children, it is difficult to know how much influence on the course of events they have or should have and how much should be determined by the professionals involved.

Older children may be in a position to exercise some influence over the legal process, but it takes considerable courage and perseverance on the child's part to resist the relentless pressure from the legal machine. Take the example of a fifteen-year-old girl who had told a local authority social worker that her step-father had been sexually abusing her. She made it clear that, while she wanted the abuse to stop, she wished to remain at home and that she would refuse to repeat her allegations to the police or in court. The social services decided that, since she was old enough and sufficiently mature to have the right to make decisions for herself, they would offer her hostel accommodation and would not take legal proceedings. In this case it was paradoxically only by keeping the issue out of the legal arena that the substantive rights of the child could be protected.

A final problem can arise when children's rights are rigidly promoted and thus may actually cause harm to the children. An illustration comes from the case of an eleven-year-old girl who had been placed in a foster home after her mother, who was suffering from a psychotic illness, had failed to seek medical treatment when the child was dangerously ill. When she was interviewed at the Clinic the girl said that she wanted to return home, but at the same interview recalled how unhappy she had been living with her mother. Her drawings and play confirmed the ambivalence of the relationship with the mother and the child's anxieties about returning to live with her. While living in foster care her physical health and school performance had improved considerably. The mother, on the other hand, continued to suffer from psychotic episodes. If the law had given this child a substantive right of self-determination, a court would have had no option but to return the child home—a result that would in all probability have increased the child's suffering and the risk of long-term damage.

A law which gives children the right to choose imposes a burden of responsibility which many children, even some of those who have reached adolescence, are not ready to bear. For children to have to decide which parent they wish to live with after a divorce would in many cases cause severe conflicts of loyalty and feelings of guilt towards the 'deserted' parent. Perhaps, if children are to be given any substantive rights in this situation, it should be the right not to have responsibility for their parents thrust upon them.

Our concerns over the use of the courts and legal system to protect children's substantive rights may be summarized in the following way:

(a) The rights of children are not necessarily the same as the needs of children.

(b) In many instances the courts are unable to protect children's rights because they have no control over the resources on which those rights depend.

(c) In some cases the use of the legal system to force others to take account of children's rights may cause the child more harm than leaving matters as they are.

Procedural rights   These are rights which guarantee that children will be treated fairly in the decision-making process, but which do not in themselves directly affect decisions. They include the right to express an opinion on any matter which concerns their future welfare. In formal decision-making processes, such as courts and case conferences, they may require an adult (not necessarily a lawyer) to represent the child.

The concept of procedural rights may extend to any situation where adults have power over children's lives, such as schools, children's homes, and foster homes, and may require some complaints procedure to enable the child's grievances to be heard. Whether or not the existence of a complaints procedure should be extended to children in their own families is a controversial issue. In Sweden the Children's Ombudsman is available to listen to such complaints, and in France any child is entitled to write to the children's judge requesting an audience. These procedures are particularly valuable for older children whose parents will not grant them the freedoms that they feel are appropriate for their age. In most Anglo-Saxon countries, however, the only way in which children may challenge parental decisions is through the courts and even then they have to find a sympathetic adult to bring the case on their behalf.

It would be wrong to underestimate the importance of these procedural rights for children in influencing social attitudes towards children and the importance of the law in ensuring that these rights are respected. However, this is not the same thing as using the courts and the whole paraphernalia of the legal process each time that an important decision has to be made concerning the child's welfare or on each occasion that a child has a grievance to be aired. There is a world of difference between using the formal legal process to ensure that decisions about children are made according to procedures that are fair and just to the child and using that process regularly to determine what course of action would best promote the child's welfare or best interests.

The fact that some countries, such as France and Sweden, may appear to use their courts successfully to make substantive, welfare decisions about children may seem to contradict this distinction between the substantive and the procedural. However, if one examines more closely the actual decision-making process, one finds that the specialized procedures for child-welfare decisions in these countries' courts are both informal and conciliatory in their approach. They tend to be much closer to mediation sessions than to courtroom trials.

5. Establishing the facts

Many disputes that are brought to the legal system for resolution do not involve arguments about what the law says, but revolve rather around arguments over what happened. Much of the legal process, therefore, is concerned with discovering 'the truth' about past events. Were promises made? Was the car going too fast? Were any blows struck? Did the newspaper article lie about the private life of some celebrity? The legal system, therefore, holds itself out to be not just a resource for determining disputes about the interpretation of laws, but also an institution where 'the truth' can be established. The law provides in the courts a forum for establishing the truth where rules governing procedure, standards of proof, and admissibility of evidence ensure consistency and fairness. In Anglo-American systems these rules are strict and rigid in criminal trials, but in civil cases there is a growing tendency for the rules to be relaxed or dispensed with altogether.

This does not mean, however, that civil proceedings have ceased to be adversarial, but rather that there is much more scope than in criminal cases for the parties to negotiate between themselves as to what facts should be admitted without formal proof and what form the proof should take. Nor does it mean that civil proceedings, including child protection cases or parental disputes over children, are any less determinants of right and wrong. It is rare for these cases not to involve some argument over past events. Child protection case issues often revolve around the answers to these questions: 'Was the injury caused by the abuse?' 'Who was responsible for the abuse?' 'Who could have prevented it?' In inter-parental disputes there are different issues. 'Has the parent been loving, caring, responsible?' Courts will be asked to decide whose version of 'the truth' should prevail.

Establishing 'the facts' is not only a matter of courts finding cases proved or unproved or deciding for one party in preference to the other. In their decisions on the facts the courts in the Anglo-American system convey important messages to children and parents and to all those involved with the family. Even where court hearings take place in private in the absence of the press, all those concerned in the proceedings treat court decisions as authoritative statements of right and wrong, true and false.

This may be particularly important in those cases where the child has accused an adult of abuse. The official recognition of the fact that the child's allegations were well-founded may provide the child and those agencies trying to help the family with a solid foundation for their work. In the case of successful criminal prosecutions, the legal label in the form of a criminal record which is attached to the child abuser may in the future help to save other children from abuse.

However, there is a down side to the Anglo-American preoccupation with establishing 'the facts' in court. When the court fails to confirm the child's version of events, the result is often seen as a vindication of the alleged perpetrator. The implicit message that may emerge from the court is that the child should not be believed. Yet, as we have explained, the court's decision may be influenced by a number of different factors, including the inadmissibility of crucial evidence, the performance of witnesses in court and the selective perceptions of judges, magistrates, or juries. What the court decides to be 'the facts' may not, therefore, correspond with 'the truth' as recognized by others whose knowledge of the child and family is not confined by artificial rules or restricted to snapshot exposures. This version of the truth may see the child's allegations as well-founded and the court's refusal to accept them as an encouragement to the perpetrator to repeat the abuse.

Let us turn now from the functions of the law to examine to what extent these functions are compatible within the process of identifying and promoting children's needs.

Children's needs and the law

References to children's needs, the welfare of children, the child's best interests have proliferated in the statutes and law reports of all those countries where the Anglo-American system of justice applies. Some jurisdictions go as far as to list in detail the needs of children, while others leave matters very much to the interpretation of the courts in individual cases. The cumulative impression that they give is that the legal system is capable not only of resolving disputes between state and family, or between parents, or between parents and other child-carers but also of bringing the knowledge and wisdom of the law to bear upon complex issues concerning children's needs and even of promoting the needs of individual children.

We have little doubt that many judges, magistrates, and lawyers believe this to be true and that this belief acts as a strong motivation for their involvement in the emotionally draining work of the family courts. Yet, there is also a danger that lawyers, judges, magistrates, and others with a vested interest in keeping things much as they are at present, will tend to exaggerate the uniqueness and exclusiveness of the law's traditional roles and overemphasize the benefits to be gained through legal decisions and the legal process through such devices as the protection of individual rights, both procedural and substantive.

The criticisms that we have made concerning the use of legal intervention in child welfare cases are unlikely to please them. Nor are they likely to please those politicians who for ideological or economic reasons tend to see the passing of laws as an end in itself, with little concern to understand the limitations and dynamics of those institutions charged with putting laws into effect.

While we accept without hesitation that, as individuals, sympathetic and well-intentioned lawyers and judges may from time to time be able to improve the lives of children whose problems come before the courts, this is not, we would argue, because they are lawyers and judges, but because they are sympathetic and concerned individuals. By forcing good intentions to conform to very precise and correct forms (in order to protect rights and prevent the arbitrary use of power), the legal process may at times actually inhibit these good intentions or hem them in with conditions and provisos which detract from their benevolence. Nor should it be thought that tinkering with that process will in itself bring about changes in the fundamental nature of law and the social functions that the legal system serves. The legal process is not, for example, going to provide those material and emotional resources that give children security and allow them to blossom. Generally, all that law can do effectively is to manage the conflicts that arise between adults over the extent and nature of their relationships with children. Even here one may well question how effective the law is as a social institution for conflict management where the subject of the conflicts consists, not of material goods or property, but of relationships and emotional engagements.

Yet to leave these difficult emotional conflicts festering and unresolved may result in ambivalence and uncertainty in people's relationships with one another and to the children who are dependent on them. People may be reluctant to commit themselves to situations or relationships where their rights and responsibilities are unclear, where they cannot predict what the outcome will be if things go wrong. The most that can be said of law as a social institution performing essentially legal functions, as opposed to well-meaning judges and lawyers as individuals, is that it may on occasion help to influence adult's behaviour towards children in positive ways, but it is only one factor among many and often not a very important factor at that.

There is, unfortunately, the negative side of law to be taken into account. As we have seen, the operation of the legal process in children's cases may create more problems than it solves. Conflicts tend to be heightened; people tend to become more entrenched in their positions, rejecting any compromise as a loss of face and any concession as a defeat for their cause. Yet what appears like a major success of the lawyers in persuading the parties to a dispute to give up their excessive demands and recognize the importance of their children's welfare may, on closer examination, reveal itself as something less than a triumph for law. With adequate preventive measures and the availability of alternative, non-adversarial processes for resolving disputes, the conflict might never have reached such proportions. In other words, the legal process might in some (but not all) cases be doing no more than dealing with the problems that it itself has in part created.

Unfortunately, we can offer no magic remedy to these problems or dramatic revelations which are going to revolutionize child care or the legal system. Instead, we take a step backwards in two distinct senses. First, we go back to reconsider four case histories which we presented in earlier chapters. Secondly, we take a step backwards—to distance ourselves from the detailed problems of specific child-care and legal systems. From this detached vantage point we apply to these cases certain principles, derived from our previous discussions, which we believe to be important in promoting children's well-being. These principles relate to early preventive intervention, working with families to protect children and promote their welfare. They also concern limits to the effective use of the legal system and the potential harm to the child and family if these limits are infringed.

Each of the four cases that we have chosen for this detailed analysis presents different problems and calls out for different types of solution. The first concerns the 'yo-yo' child whose case is described in Chapter 3. The problem here was one of how to handle a parent–child relationship where a single parent suffered from recurrent bouts of serious mental illness. The second case involves a young child, whose parents were in the throes of a matrimonial dispute, telling her mother that her father had sexually abused her during access visits (Chapter 4). Next, we reconsider the plight of the young couple whose housing and financial problems combined with the stress of caring for difficult young children led to abuse (Chapter 2). Sexual abuse by a father is also at the centre of our fourth case (Chapter 5). Here, the parents had separated some years previously and the allegations of abuse were of a much more serious nature.

Case 1 (Chapter 3, pp. 49–50)

This was the case of a six-year-old boy with a young mother who suffered from a manic-depressive illness. The child's parents had met while both of them were undergoing treatment at a psychiatric hospital. On discharge from hospital, they had lived together in a pleasant council flat and it was during this period that their son was conceived. The birth and the baby's early weeks went smoothly enough, the couple receiving considerable support during this period from health and social services. As the baby grew and the support tailed off, however, the father found the demands made by a small child increasingly difficult. When the baby was nine months old, he left forever.

The mother felt abandoned both by her man and by the health and welfare services which had supported her so well during the early stages of the child's development. There followed repeated episodes of depression which resulted in her being admitted to hospital on several occasions. Each time the child was placed with a short-term foster family under a voluntary care agreement. After six such placements, the local authority decided to apply to court for a care order so that permanent arrangements could be made for the care of the child. The mother resisted the application. The magistrates refused the request for a care order, believing that a supervision order would be sufficient to protect the child. A second application to change the supervision order into a care order, when the mother had once again been admitted to hospital, was also turned down. However, when, after thirteen hospital admissions and periods of short-term fostering, the case came back to court for a third time, with an assessment from a psychiatrist from the Clinic that the child was suffering from these constant switches of home and caretaker, the court decided that a care order was the only answer. The child was placed immediately with long-term foster parents who were unwilling for the mother to maintain regular contact with her son until he had established a firm relationship with his 'new family'.

What could have been done?
First, there could have been much more support for the young couple early on, before the father left. With the benefit of hindsight, it is clear that two very young parents with a history of mental illness were extremely vulnerable. Was there no possibility at that stage, for example, of the whole family being admitted to a residential young family unit where they could have received help and guidance on how to care for their baby? If the risks of the relationship breaking down had been recognized early on, the family might have remained intact. If this had happened, some support from within the family might have been available during the mother's depressive bouts, so avoiding hospital admission and separation from her child.

Secondly, after the father had walked out, should not the young child have accompanied his mother to hospital instead of being put into care? Mother and baby units did exist in psychiatric hospitals at that time, but they were rapidly being closed down as a result of health service cuts and a national policy of care in the community for mental patients. If it had been possible to deal with the problem in this way, any transition to substitute care might have been much easier. Where the hospital staff had seen mother and child interacting over a long period, either clear indications might have become apparent that the relationship between mother and child was sufficiently good to warrant doing everything possible to provide support for the mother or there might have been an irrefutable case for concluding that the mother was quite unable to cope. In this case the staff might have been able to persuade her to have the child placed in long-term fostering without the need for three court applications and three contested care hearings.

Thirdly, even if this young mother had persistently refused to part with her child, it might still have been possible to avoid full-blown courtroom contests, the removal of parental rights, and the ending of parental visits. If there had existed some informal process (as in France or Holland) presided over by someone independent of the professional workers involved in the case, charged with attempting to secure parental agreement for measures to further the child's interests, it is possible that some arrangement could have been mutually accepted whereby the child would be placed with a long-term foster family, but the mother should have regular access. Of course, such an arrangement would have had to be carefully monitored and any problems referred back to the informal hearing or tribunal. There would have been no need for any formal court hearing unless the mother wished to appeal against the decisions of the informal hearing.

Case 2 (Chapter 4, pp. 62–4)

The bitter breakdown of a young couple's marriage formed the backdrop to this allegation by a four-year-old girl that her father had 'fondled her private parts'. This marriage breakdown had occurred over a year before the incident. It had been particularly painful because both parents had been involved in looking after the little girl and both were reluctant to 'give her up'. Their short marriage had been fraught with financial and housing problems. The stress these caused, together with those of meeting the needs and demands of a baby and then a toddler, with very little support either from their respective families or from the local community, in the end had overwhelmed them. They were in their twenties and were lacking in experience and insight into how to deal with relationship problems. They ended up by blaming each other for everything that had gone wrong.

Given this bitterness, it was perhaps not surprising that as soon as she heard about the 'fondling' the mother seized the opportunity to end all contact between her daughter and her former husband. She wanted him out of their life. Nor was it surprising that he should invoke the wardship procedure in order to bring the issue before the court. He thought she was an unfit mother and wanted to have his daughter living with him.

The 'fusional' relationship between mother and daughter made it impossible to untangle the truth about the fondling. It may have been true, but the child said many vicious things about her father. Even if she had not been rehearsed by her mother, it could well have been that she had been rewarded, consciously or unconsciously, for each verbal attack on her father.

What could have been done?
By the time the case came to court the warfare between the parents had reached such a pitch that it would have been very difficult to construct a truce which would have had any lasting effect. Any effective intervention would have had to have taken place well before the court case. Yet, how far back do you go? If the mother had not had such a deprived and unhappy childhood she might well have been more stable and better equipped to deal with the demands of a close relationship, a young child, and economic hardship. However, taking the early days of the marriage as the starting-point, decent housing conditions and some support with the care of the child might have reduced some of the stress. But what specific kinds of intervention might have avoided the bitter separation, unhealthy relationship between mother and daughter, the allegation of sexual abuse, whether true or false, and the inconclusive court hearing which did nothing to promote the little girl's welfare?

First, an effective conciliation service for families on the point of disintegration may not have saved the marriage, but it may have helped both parents to take a less selfish and destructive attitude towards the sharing of the little girl after separation. In addition, it could well have picked up the fact that the girl was being given very little space to develop separately from her mother. At this stage it might have been possible to refer mother and daughter to a mental health clinic without this being interpreted as an attack on the mother's parenting ability. The clinic may have been able to help the mother to see that such a fusional relationship could in the long term cause serious harm to the child.

Secondly, although, once the case had reached court, the parties had become so firmly entrenched in their positions that any movement was virtually impossible and the hearing developed into a ritualistic slanging match over the issue of the sexual abuse, a sensitive judge might have been able to keep the child's interests in the foreground. This might have led to an order for supervized access to give the welfare officer service a chance to work with the parents towards reducing their hostility to one another and their use of the child as ammunition in their warfare. Ideally, the welfare officer service should be equipped to take on this kind of long-term work.

Thirdly, as for the child sexual abuse, it would be foolish not to acknowledge the possibility that the abuse, albeit of a minor nature, may have occurred. Supervision of the father's access should have acted as a deterrent for any future abuse and the supervision could have been reduced and ultimately dispensed with when the risk of abuse seemed negligible.

Case 3 (Chapter 2, p. 29)

This case concerned a young couple with housing and financial problems which, combined with lack of sleep caused by their children's sleeping difficulties and the stress of living in a confined space, led to fights between the parents and subsequently to physical abuse of the children. The court decision was for the children to be taken into care, where they were placed with foster parents. Some time later the parents lapsed into depression and drinking and visits to the children became infrequent and erratic. Despite the mother's desire to have the children returned to her, the view of the court was that she would be unable to cope on her own and the children were freed for adoption.

One aspect of this case which we did not reveal in the original discussion is that the maternal grandmother and other close relatives were living close to this family. Unfortunately, this grandmother resented her daughter choosing to marry a husband whom she disliked and therefore had very little contact with her grandchildren. However, subsequently, when the children had been taken into care and the marriage had disintegrated, she offered to help look after the children, but by then it was too late.

What could have been done?

First, when the problems between the couple emerged, much more could have been done to try to involve the extended family and get them to help with the care of the children. For example, the maternal grandmother might well have been able to offer some respite by looking after the children at weekends. Had this case occurred after October 1991 this outcome might well have been more likely, as the Children Act specifically draws attention to the need to look to the extended family as possible carers for children.

Secondly, when the children were removed from their parents, arrangements could well have been made for the grandmother and close relatives to have access to the children and to have them to stay some weekends. Once again the Children Act may have helped here.

Thirdly, after the disintegration of the marriage, and the mother's attempt to assume care of the children, it might well have been possible at that stage to involve members of the extended family. By concentrating narrowly on the nuclear family, the welfare professionals seemed to have overlooked entirely the possibility of retaining the children in the wider family network. Although hostility and lack of contact between extended family members may initially make it appear that the parents and children exist as an isolated unit, and also make it difficult for the parents to involve their relatives in their problems, the prospect that the children will be damaged or lost often leads to co-operation and solidarity between family members and to help and support for the children and parents.

Case 4 (Chapter 5, pp. 82–4)

In this case of sexual abuse a child aged four was referred by a High Court judge to the Clinic for assessment. The child had told her playgroup leader of various kinds of penetrative abuse she had experienced when visiting her father.

The girl's mother had suffered a deprived and disrupted childhood, having been brought up by a series of foster parents from the age of eight. She had married a man considerably older than herself and they had had one child. When the marriage broke down the father had continued to play an active part in looking after the girl. She used to spend long periods alone with him. For the mother this represented a relief from looking after her child who had become extremely difficult to handle, believing herself to be all-powerful and attempting to domineer and control every adult with whom she came into contact. She also wet and soiled herself and was aggressive towards other children. Her mother saw her in an entirely negative light. The child was driving her to despair, but at no time had she sought any help and none had been offered to her.

Once the sexual abuse had been alleged, the concern of social services and subsequently the court centred around this issue. Was there sufficient evidence or was it a figment of the child's fantasy? When the abuse could not be proved to the satisfaction of the judge, the court case simply fell apart. Mother and daughter were left to carry on their lives much as before with no additional help or support. The father had disappeared from the scene by this time, so access visits abruptly ceased. It was only six months later, when the little girl's behaviour became so bizarre that social services and the judge finally recognized that she needed urgent help, that a place was found for her in a residential home.

What could have been done?
Above all, this case provides a graphic illustration of the effects of myopic social policies towards child care which transform social workers into a sort of family police force whose primary task is to react to specific acts of abuse by protecting the child against the suspected adult. Long before she told the playgroup leader of the sexual abuse this child's behaviour must have exhibited tell-tale signs of disturbance which either passed unnoticed or were noticed but considered not a sufficient cause for intervention.

First, the sight of an isolated, single mother struggling to cope with an extremely difficult child should have alerted someone among the professionals with whom the family came into contact that all was not well. If the child had attended nursery school, instead of going to a playgroup for only two and a half hours a day for little more than half the weeks of the year, it may well have been that the family's problems would have been detected earlier and support offered.

Secondly, if someone had acted, mother and child could have been referred to a child mental health clinic. At that stage, work with mother and child would have stood some chance of success, whereas, as in the previous case, once court proceedings had been taken any chance of dealing with the problem in a non-combative way was effectively sabotaged. This work could have taken the form of a residential placement in a mother and child unit.

Thirdly, assuming that the sexual abuse had in fact occurred, the Clinic would have been well placed to address the issue in the context of therapeutic intervention rather than in the highly charged atmosphere generated by legal proceedings. It is much more likely that clear evidence of the abuse would have come out of this situation than from the narrow investigation that the Clinic was asked to conduct by the court.

Next, if the mother had rejected the need for any help for her child and continued to ignore the child's obvious problems, the matter could have been referred to an independent, informal hearing, along the lines that we discussed in Case 1. The object of this hearing would have been to obtain the mother's consent to and involvement in a programme of support for the child. If the mother still withheld her agreement, the panel or tribunal would have the power to implement such measures as were needed for the child's protection and the mother would have a right of appeal to a formal court.

Finally, since the father had disappeared from the scene by the time the court case was over, there was no question of access continuing. If he had remained, there would have been a major risk to the child in continuing her visits to her father, given the serious nature of the alleged abuse. Only if the father agreed to supervized access should he have been allowed to remain in contact with his daughter. Once again this could have been handled by an informal hearing with the possibility of the father applying to a formal court if he was aggrieved by the decision. It would probably have been to the little girl's long-term benefit to continue to see her father rather than all visits suddenly ending, but under no circumstances should she have been left alone with him in a situation where the alleged abuse could have recurred.

Discussion

We have set out our belief that the legal process, particularly where it takes the form of an adversarial contest fought out at an oral hearing, often proves to be incompatible with a child-centred approach to issues of abuse and family conflict. This belief is based on our experience of family cases which pass between court and clinic. The preceding chapters have concerned a detailed examination of the effects of legal intervention upon children, parents, social work practice, and the therapy conducted by clinic staff.

Our re-examination of four of the case histories from earlier chapters reveals a further dimension to the protection of children and the management of child welfare which takes us back to the discussion of social policy issues in Chapter 2. The controversies which we have described over the most effective way to intervene to promote children's welfare are not merely local demarcation disputes between legal and clinical ways of doing things. They are also part of a much broader political debate concerning the allocation and control of wealth and resources over a wide range of activities.

What we have experienced in recent years is the emergence of law as the dominant institution for the ordering of any intervention in relations between parents and children, and the extension, through Rules, Regulations, and Guidelines, of legal concepts and procedures to cover every aspect of child welfare and protection.

This is not, as some legal commentators would have us believe, the inevitable consequence of the progress from disorder to order. They are rather the result of clear political choices. Once these choices have been made and child welfare issues start to become legal issues, *child law* comes to exist as part of the legal discourse, taking on a momentum of its own, generating a new brand of specialist lawyers, court social workers, and guardians *ad litem*. Specialized family courts and children's courts spring up creating new jobs, new vested interests to be sustained by a continual flow of legal cases. In England and Wales this process has culminated in the introduction of the Children Act 1989.

The collection of images that we have presented give some idea of the complexity of child welfare issues and of the enormous problems involved in understanding the way that families operate so as to identify how the child's best interests might be secured. They have also provided some evidence of the disruptive and destructive effects that the rigid and insensitive operation of legal process may have in practice. These images are a far cry from the simplified and idealized views of families, children, and the legal and child welfare systems implicit in the Children Act and presented in the parliamentary debates, and in articles in legal and social work journals about the Act. Above all else is the assumption in the legal discourse that, once a child has been identified at risk of 'significant harm' or suffering as the result of hostility between its parents, people's behaviour will by and large become rational and sensible in their search for ways of meeting the child's needs. This assumption, however, is not borne out by the evidence that we have presented. On the contrary, when presented with highly emotive situations people, even lawyers and judges, tend to behave in irrational ways. Furthermore, the 'rationality' of child welfare may not, as we have seen, be the same as 'legal rationality' or 'economic rationality' when it comes to making decisions about children and their families. For reasons already explained, it is necessary for the law to maintain the myth of rationality even if it conflicts with people's actual experience of the way that families, social services departments, the police, and the courts operate in practice, but the maintenance of the myth is not necessarily beneficial to children's interests.

The lesson for the future which we believe emerges from the evidence set out here is that, contrary to current beliefs in both legal and social work spheres, an effective child welfare or child protection policy does not depend primarily on the quality of the justice dispensed by the courts and legal system. Indeed, justice in the narrow legal sense may be counter-productive to the promotion of child welfare. Similarly, it does not depend upon the efficient and comprehensive codification of child care. Yet with the passing of the Children Act the point has been reached that, whenever a decision is required, social workers and mental health workers either have to consult lawyers or refer to an endless stream of Rules, Regulations, Guidelines, and Directives designed to regulate their relations with children and their families. The sweeping juridification of a whole area of social activity which has taken place over the past ten or so years is reminiscent of the way in which law and the fear of legal repercussions had far-reaching effects on medical practice in the United States. The play-safe policies and decisions which such legal pressures provoke may in some cases benefit children. In other cases they may well have the opposite effect. Perhaps their most pernicious result, however, is that by transforming social problems into individualized legal problems, they mask the damage caused by lack of investment in those social areas essential for the healthy development of children—housing, education, and health—lack of resources in the provision of substitute and relief care and lack of general preventive work with parents and children.

Principles for defining the limits of law

We end this chapter on a more positive note by setting out a series of principles which, like the principles of the Children Act referred to in Chapter 2, we would wish to see adopted by policy-makers. These are principles which in the first place restrict the negative impact of imposing legalistic interpretations and solutions on social and interpersonal problems, and, secondly, which provide clear and positive policy- and decision-making criteria.

1. Avoiding the dominance of legal 'truth'

As we have seen throughout the cases presented, the version of the historical truth set out in the legal decision may be rather different from that contained in a clinic's files or discussed at case conferences, because the assessment of people and past events are likely to have undergone very different selection and interpretation processes. These differences in processing serve the different objectives of courts and clinics and social work (see Table 1). For law, as we have illustrated, the objectives for which the establishment of truth is an essential element are concerned with managing conflict, conveying moral messages to the outside world about the way that adults should behave towards children, and about the intrinsic fairness of the legal process itself and its ability to determine what is right for children.

The law's version of 'the truth' typically serves a process of coding the issues surrounding the child's welfare into a series of choices which the court is able or appears to be able to determine. This may take the form of a choice between two principles, for example, giving preference to the mother as opposed to not interfering with the children's present situation, where they are being cared for by their father and grandmother; or it may involve a choice between people or situations in identifying, for instance, which of the two parents is the *psychological parent*. Either way, the complexities and ambiguities, which characterize the clinic's versions of truth, are reduced to their simple proportions.

It is not sufficient, therefore, to explain away all the problems between court and clinic that we have recounted as mere misunderstandings, failure of communication, or resulting from ignorance or prejudice on the part of the clinic or the judiciary. They arise, rather, wholly or in part from profound differences in the very nature of the different processes involved and the different objectives that those processes are serving. Table 1 contrasts some of these differences.

A major problem faced by both clinics and child welfare agencies at the present time arises directly from the need for the law to establish 'the facts' in order that legal determinations may be made upon those facts. The result is that much of the time and energy of social workers and clinical staff in England and Wales is devoted to investigative work to the obvious detriment of therapeutic and family support work. Furthermore, as we have demonstrated through several case illustrations, the role of investigator is largely incompatible with that of helper. In some cases the two roles conflict to such an extent that the chances of securing parental cooperation are totally jeopardized by the need to collect and present 'facts' in court.

Yet it does not have to be like this. Other countries have succeeded in separating the investigative role from the therapeutic role. In France, for example, investigations into child abuse are carried out mainly by prosecutors, court social workers (*éducation surveillée*), and by specialized sections of the police (*brigade des mineurs*), leaving social workers from social services and the voluntary sector free to work with the family. In Holland, confidential doctors, investigative social workers, lawyers of the

TABLE 1 *Differences of process and objective between court and clinic*

Court	Clinic
Objectives	
Ensuring justice and equality between participants.	Defining children's needs.
Providing a stable, morally acceptable account of adult–child relationships.	Finding a solution which will provide security and stability for the child.
Promoting the legal process as capable of determining what is best children.	Promoting the clinic as capable of determining what is best for for children.
Procedures	
Formal rules designed to ensure fairness between the parties.	Ad hoc or semi-formal arrangements designed to investigate issues and define child's needs/problems.
Issues defined according to legal categories.	Issues defined according to professional areas of responsibility.
Preliminary process to reveal information and arguments in advance and encourage settlement.	Informal discussions with those involved in child's life.
Evidence	
Exclusionary rules to ensure admissible reliability of information, e.g. hearsay, previous convictions.	All relevant information.
Designation of experts—those permitted to give opinions.	All opinions admissible, but some given more weight than others.
Issues presented by oral evidence and tested for truthfulness by cross-examination. Once established, version of truth may be modified only by appeal.	Written or oral evidence accepted. Shared view emerges from combining information from different sources. Not definitive, the view may be modified as new information emerges.
After decision	
Matter returns to court only by demand of one of the parties.	Monitoring of plans to promote child's welfare. Plans adjusted according to results.

Child Protection Council, and the police are responsible for conducting enquiries into child abuse.

Some jurisdictions also succeed in avoiding the conflict of objectives arising from the dual role of courts to determine 'the facts' and assist in promoting the welfare of the child. In Scotland, for example, any disagreement by the parents or the child over allegations of child abuse are heard in the Sheriff's court, where disputed facts are subjected to a legal process of fact-finding. If proved, the matter is then transferred to the Children's Hearing where lawyers are rarely present. Most jurisdictions on the continent are sparing in their use of court hearings for fact-finding purposes. In Holland, the evidence presented to the juvenile court judge takes the form of a report from the Child Protection Council. Although lawyers may be present to represent children and parents, the facts set out in the report only rarely become an issue.

2. *Engaging the family*

If one were to start from scratch and try to design an institution which was to concentrate exclusively on promoting children's needs, either directly or indirectly through education and persuasion of significant adults in the child's life, what would be likely to emerge would be very different from those family courts existing in most Anglo-Saxon legal systems. Perhaps the most important features that we would wish to see would be directed at involving rather than alienating the family.

This engagement of the family appears to us an essential element in any process which aims to respond to children's needs. Where the court's function is essentially that of resolving disputes, by the time the parties reach the courtroom door, they—whether they be the two parents or the social services department and the family—are likely to be very much at odds with one another. Engagement of the family, whether through cooperation between warring parents, or the willing involvement of parents who are resisting state intervention to protect their child, is often out of the question. Where it does occur, it takes place either at an informal level thanks to the efforts of conciliators or lawyers negotiating outside the courtroom or through the dogged efforts of individual judges who persuade the contestants to lay down their arms and try to work together in the interests of the children. Whether these attempts at engaging the family occur is a matter of chance rather than their being guaranteed by the legal system.

The Children Act, its Regulations, and the Guidances published by the Department of Health on the operation of the Act, do go some way in the direction that we are proposing. These draw to the attention of social services departments the need to maintain family links by, for example, placing the child near the family home. Secondly, they require social services to consider the extended family as a potential resource for meeting the child's needs. However, the effectiveness of such exhortations in engaging the family will, as we have indicated, depend upon their taking place at an early stage, that is, before the legal process has polarised positions and made any cooperation extremely difficult. It will also depend upon there being resources available to allow, for example, children to be placed close to the family home.

The other set of requirements relates to joint planning between parents and local authorities for the child's future. The Children Act, according to the Health Department's Guidance 'assumes a high degree of co-operation between parents and local authorities in negotiating and agreeing what form of accommodation can be offered and the use to be made of it'. Parents, therefore, according to the Guidance, should be invited to attend reviews and should be consulted before any decisions are made concerning the child's future.

Admirable as such attempts to involve parents in the formal decision-making process may be, they need to be seen against a background of reinforcement through the law. Families and social services are not equal parties, so that any idea of partnership between them is to misrepresent the reality of the situation. The only power that aggrieved parents have is to invoke the law, and the Children Act with its codification of social welfare gives them ample opportunity to do so. Invoking the law in the English context, however, involves a move from co-operation to confrontation. If the case goes to court, it entails the making of a right/wrong decision, the creation of winners and losers and, so far as future prospects for co-operation are concerned, a much worse situation than existed previously. If the matter is settled through negotiation between the parties or their lawyers, the result will be a compromise between their respective interests and not necessarily the best solution from the child's point of view. We should add that the child is powerless in this negotiation process. The child has a right to be consulted as to his or her views, but that is all.

Such co-operation, reinforced by the threat of legal proceedings, is far removed from the notion of engaging the family that we would wish to see. To engage the family involves a process of understanding the family situation in all its complexity, and setting about the long and difficult process of changing the family dynamics through education and persuasion in ways which promote the child's interests and meet the child's needs. Often it will need the intervention of an independent authority figure to arbitrate where there is disagreement in ways that minimize the conflict and ensure that the child's needs are not forgotten in the quest for compromise.

3. Effective control over resources

A decision-making process which concentrates on children's needs presupposes that there are the resources available to meet those needs and that these resources are at the disposition of the decision-making body. It would be a rather pointless exercise if this were not the case. Say, for example, that it was decided that a child needed a daily period of nursery education in order to relieve the mother's stress, monitor the child's progress, and improve his or her social skills. What would be the point of making such a decision if there were no places available in any of the state-run nursery schools and no funds which could be applied to pay for the child to attend a private school. Yet this is precisely the paradoxical position of the courts in relation to child welfare resources and services. Courts in most jurisdictions may shuffle the pack of parents, children, and substitute carers by making orders as to who will live with whom and who will have contact with whom, but they cannot usually control resources. If there are no places in foster families, nurseries, or children's homes close to where the child's family lives, the courts cannot create places. If financial stringencies have led to the social services' home-help facility being cut, the courts cannot decide on the provision of such assistance to a family where the mother cannot cope alone with the demands of child-rearing. The options open to the courts are determined, not by the law, but by the availability of services and resources for children and families.

The question then arises as to whether we would want the courts to be used to direct how and where child-care resources should be deployed. Are court-driven social services departments, where resources are deployed according to what judges and magistrates identify as children's needs, really a good idea? Should not child care policy be decided by elected representatives in local and central government according to the broad needs of children and families as identified by professionals working in a particular geographical area? Many people find it repellent for decisions over hospital treatment to be made according to financial criteria rather than patient needs. Is it not equally unacceptable for child welfare decisions to be left to the lottery of the legal process?

This is not to question the appropriateness of any legal intervention where resource implications stem from the court's decision. Clearly, in some cases the quality and appropriateness of the substitute care offered by social services may be an important factor in the legal decision as to whether the child should remain in care or return to the family home. However, it does raise serious questions over the kind of situations that we described in Chapter 3 where legal proceedings were being used with the express intention of obtaining a court order to put pressure on the social services administration to find the resources necessary to help a particular child or family. Why should that child or family be favoured above others whose need may be as great, but whose problems are not amenable to legal proceedings? To allow judges in their judicial capacity to interfere with the policies of social services departments risks distorting those policies in ways that lead eventually to a court-driven child care system. For these reasons we would strongly oppose such a system, preferring the fight for adequate provision for children to take place in the political arena rather than in the courts. Decisions concerning resources to meet children's needs should be taken within the system that provides those resources.

4. Promoting continuity in child welfare

Throughout, we have drawn attention to the episodic way in which the law tends to intervene in the lives of children. This we have compared with the way in which institutions such as families, child welfare clinics, and mental health clinics decide upon what is best for a child as a continuous process—a process which allows for adjustments whenever circumstances change and as the child develops.

Some countries have tried within the legal process to replicate this continual surveillance of the child's changing needs and fine-tuning in response to them. The French children's judges, for example, take upon their shoulders the personal responsibility (*suivi*) for the welfare of children who become the subject of a child protection *dossier*. Other countries, such as Holland, impose that responsibility only in a secondary capacity—the judge as super-supervisor. In both these cases the judge acts more in an administrative than in a judicial capacity.

In most Anglo-Saxon common law jurisdictions, law is kept separate and distinct from administration, so that matters generally come before the judge or magistrate for adjudication only where there is some dispute or where leave of the court is required to exercise some statutory power in relation to the child. An effective needs-related system of decision-making would clearly require continuity so that the people who make the decisions are ideally involved in the family, its problems, as they evolve and affect the child over a long period. Such continuity also enables decision-makers to act in a 'scientific' manner, their decisions reflecting the rapidly changing nature of childhood and the results of previous measures which have been tried in relation to the child and family. The law as it is practised in most Anglo-Saxon countries seems quite inappropriate for this kind of exercise. Rather it allows decisions to be made about children's welfare by people who see no more than shapshots of the child's life.

So, to summarize, the basic requirements of a system designed to concentrate upon the needs of children are:

• The limited use of the legal system as the appropriate mechanism for determining issues concerning children's welfare.
• The capacity to engage the family in the child's future welfare.
• The ability to control resources or provide authoritative directives to those controlling resources.
• Continuity in the involvement with the child and family.

Further reading

The theory of law as an autopoetic system

Autopoietic Law: A New Approach to Law and Society edited by Gunther Teubner (De Gruyter: 1988).
How the Law Thinks about Children, by Michael King and Christine Piper (Gower: 1990).
'Law as a Social System' by Niklas Luhmann, *Northwestern University Law Review* (1989) 83, nos. 1 and 2, 136–50.

Children's rights

Gillick v. *West Norfolk and Wisbech Area Health Authority*, [1985] 2 Weekly Law Reports, p. 830, House of Lords.
The Rights and Wrongs of Children, by Michael Freemen (Frances Pinter: 1983).

Proof and evidence in children's cases

The Evidence of Children: The Law and the Psychology, by J. R. Spencer and Rhona Flin (Blackstone Press: 1990).
The Protection of Children, by R. Dingwall, J. Eekelaar, and T. Murray (Blackwell: 1983).
Report on the Evidence of Children and other Potentially Vulnerable Witnesses, by the Scottish Law Commission (SLC no. 125, 1990).

The Report of the Pigot Committee, Home Office (HMSO: 1989).

'There Is a Book Out . . . : An analysis of Judicial Absorption of Legislative Facts' by P. Davies, *Harvard Law Review* (1987) 100, 1539–603.

Analyses of the Children Act 1989

Governing the Family. Child Care, Child Protection and the State, by Nigel Parton (Macmillan: 1991).

The Reform of Child Care Law: A Practical Guide to the Children Act 1989, by John Eekelaar and Robert Dingwall (Routledge: 1990).

Part three

Professions and procedures

6. The legal process in family disputes and the alternatives*

6.1. Solicitors and clients

RICHARD INGLEBY

This reading discusses the implications of the data about the relationships between solicitors and their clients. Five issues are considered: translation, empowerment, advice as to legal entitlements and the importance of the formal law, solicitor–client negotiation and the litigotiation scale, and the validity of the conclusions.

Translation

Chapter 2 introduced one of the key issues in solicitors out-of-court activity as the translation question, whether solicitors or clients controlled the outcomes of their interactions. This has serious implications for the legal profession. It will be argued here that the question of whether clients' or solicitors' desired outcomes prevailed is one which cannot be taken of itself to be a measure of professional competence. Whether solicitors control their clients cannot be considered without reference to controls on solicitors themselves. There are four reasons for this conclusion: (1) problems of quantification; (2) the legality of desired outcomes; (3) requirements of professional competence; and (4) third-party interests.

First, the problem of quantification. In any situation where people talk to each other and influence each other's decisions it is difficult to separate their inputs (Ellmann 1987: 717). It is also possible to argue that any professional contact necessarily involves modification of the client's expectations (Greenbaum 1987: 554). Indeed, this would seem to be one reason why clients seek professional advice in the first place.

These indeterminacies suggest that a clear answer will rarely be

---

* NB. Cross references to chapters shown here refer to the original text from which this chapter was taken.

available as to whose input is represented by the outcome. Cain herself classifies as 'doubtful' a case where 'the opinion of each party appeared to carry equal weight' (1979: 346). The data in this study suggest that the phenomenon of 'equal weight' needs to be joined by other gradations. This makes it preferable to discuss translation in terms of a continuum, representing the varying contributions of solicitor and client to the final outcome (Galanter 1983: 119; Sarat and Felstiner 1986: 125). Fig. 1 illustrates the difficulties of quantification, and I would not want to suggest that the solicitor and the client are the only influences involved.

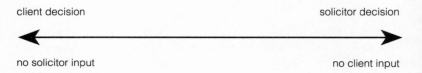

Fig. 1 Solicitor-client input continuum

There are other reasons why attempts to quantify inputs are not straightforward. The idea that clients have one desired outcome needs to be challenged. Matrimonial disputes comprise a number of elements: finance, housing, child care, status, etc. And each of these issues is capable of further subdivision: finance includes property and support; child care includes custody and access. A second reason why the concept of a desired outcome is difficult to sustain is that clients' attitudes are not constants. Needs and perceptions of needs change over the processing of a dispute (Sarat 1988: 708–9).

The second set of difficulties in using the translation concept as a measure of professional competence concerns the legality of the client's desired outcome. The discussion of whether the client's outcome is chosen must take into account whether the client's desired outcome *can* be chosen. One possible explanation for the feelings of alienation and loss of control which clients are alleged to experience at the hands of their solicitors is the conflict between what the client wants, and what the client is entitled to. These may not necessarily be one and the same, if one accepts that rules do not have a completely open texture (Cain 1979: 374; Sarat and Felstiner 1986: 131; see also Parsons 1954: 378, 381). The cases in this study which illustrate this most clearly are those where the issue of quantification is easiest. In the 'all-or-nothing' situations where custodial parents sought to deny access because of the non-custodial parents' new partner, one attitude to an issue was consistently maintained despite advice to the contrary from the solicitor. A further point is the need to consider whether the control should be seen in the rules of the legal system, rather than in the professional whose role is to communicate those rules. A parent's desire that their children have no contact with the non-custodial parent cannot be fulfilled in a legal system which contains a strong presumption in favour of continued contact between non-custodial parents and their children.

The relevance of this to the use of translation as a measure of professional competence is clear. The cases above reveal two important points: (1) that the solicitors tried to dissuade custodial parents from pursuing such a claim, (2) with varying degrees of success. Is it good or bad practice successfully to persuade a client not to pursue a course of action which is doomed to failure? Although the boundary between advice and persuasion is unclear, should a good solicitor accept the client's instructions uncritically and pursue them vigorously? Cain discusses the non-translation of the desired outcome of a husband who 'wanted either custody or to see his child every day' (1979: 347). From the facts which Cain provides, both these desired outcomes would seem unattainable. Cain's other exceptions to the general pattern of translation in matrimonial matters involved further similarities with the situations which arose in this study of a clash between the expectations of some clients and the rules of the formal law. The husband who was 'dissatisfied with the amount of maintenance he would have to pay' had no shortage of counterparts in this sample, nor, one presumes, elsewhere (Cain 1979: 347). But if Cain's research had involved the wife of this client, it is likely that she would also have been dissatisfied with the amount of maintenance. Using the translation test as a measure of professional competence would lead to at least one, and probably both, lawyers being categorized as incompetent.

The discussion of whether clients' desired outcomes are attainable is even more complicated where the rules of the law coincide with the client's desired outcome but the practice of the law does not. One example of this is the coincidence between the desire of some clients for vindication and the fault grounds in section 1(2) of the Matrimonial Causes Act. But the practice of the courts is essentially no-fault, as there are insufficient judicial resources to scrutinize the reasons for the breakdown of marriages, and the supervision which is present relates more to procedural than substantive matters (Ingleby 1989*b*). Therefore the fault-based system 'helps to create a set of expectations which cannot be fulfilled' (Davis and Murch 1988: 86). The importance of this is that studies of clients' expectations of the legal system have concluded that 'erroneous expectations contribute to their ultimate dissatisfaction with the process' (O'Barr and Conley 1988: 151). Matrimonial clients' expectations are incapable of being fulfilled and the solicitor has to preserve the client's faith in the system to resolve the issues arising from the breakdown. The client's cynicism is understandable as is its direction to the person or bodies responsible for the communication of the system's rules.

A third problem with the use of translation as a measure of professional competence is that the profession is subject to its own competence test, the rules of professional negligence. In the discussion of registration in Chapter 3 it was seen that the solicitor was anxious to secure the client's signature to a statement that they had been advised against that course of action. Whether the client should have signed a further statement, that they were aware of the effect of the disclaimer, is another question. This situation has obvious similarities with Cain's criticism of a solicitor's reluctance to accept a client's desire 'that no provision for maintenance by her ex-husband should be made' (1979: 317). In such a situation the solicitor has to guard against future allegations of negligence if the client regrets the dismissal of the claim at a later date. A further aspect of a solicitor's professional duty to the client is advice as to the costs of pursuing particular courses of action. At what point does such advice become threats about the costs of a contested hearing?

A fourth problem is of particular relevance in the area of matrimonial law, the issue of third-party interests. Should a solicitor advise about the possible impact of litigation on children? The possible third party benefits from the compromise of claims raise questions more easily than they provide answers. They have the potential to legitimize a considerable degree of coercion. Solicitors' advice of the probable failure of a course of action, and the benefits to third parties of the recommended alternative can also be seen as an attempt to impose on the client the solicitors' idea of the most satisfactory way of resolving the dispute (Weitzman 1985: 237).

To summarize this discussion, there may be very good reasons why solicitors cannot translate their clients' chosen outcomes. These reasons lie in the content of the applicable legal rules. For the client, the rules are personified in the solicitor and it is the solicitor, rather than the rules, who has failed to meet the demand.

Empowerment

The notion that divorcing parties necessarily lose control over their dispute when they seek legal representation has just been questioned.

Rather than taking the dispute out of the client's hands, it could be argued that there are three ways in which solicitors 'empower' divorcing parties by increasing their capacity to resolve disputes themselves: (1) providing a forum which enables claims to be made more effectively than if the parties were not represented (Folberg and Taylor 1981: 12); (2) making clients aware of their rights against each other; and (3) making clients aware of their rights against the state (Ingleby 1988b: 17).

One case where empowerment in terms of forum-provision was particularly apparent was discussed in a preliminary report of this study (Ingleby 1988b). The spouse's solicitor was attempting to secure more access to the child of the observed client. When the solicitor received the letter asking for more access, her client instructed her to write that a longer time would be permitted. A later response to this letter acknowledged the increase and requested 'a modest extension . . . on other occasions'. Having taken instructions, the solicitor replied that her client was already extending the amount of access, as the child, with the client's consent, had been staying for longer than the time negotiated between the solicitors. A later letter from the spouse's solicitors wrote that, 'we are of the impression that your client may be agreeable to overnight access . . . please let us know if this is the case'. This led to an arrangement for overnight access. The spouse's solicitors then wrote that 'we understand access is proceeding very satisfactorily . . . our client is most grateful, in particular for the additional access . . . in view of the success, would your client consider some limited holiday access?' The note of the conference following the receipt of this letter states: 'she agreed to holiday access but would prefer him to ask her rather than us'. The solicitor then wrote to say that her client was 'happy for access during . . . holidays, amenable to any reasonable proposals your client puts forward and happy to speak to him direct'.

These exchanges, which show the dynamic nature of the parties' preferences and therefore the dispute itself (Sarat 1988), might be interpreted in terms of the client's increasing confidence in dealing with the issues concerning her child without the solicitor. On one level this might be explicable in terms of the general transition from marriage (Hart 1976; Wallerstein and Kelly 1980). The negotiations may also have reflected the client's growing awareness that her position as custodial parent was not under threat. But the data also permit the conclusion that the formal, arm's-length, legally represented negotiations contributed to the eventual solution by enabling concessions to be made without the fear that advantage would be taken of them.

Two further points can be made. First, the solicitor demonstrated no reluctance to let go when she was confident that the client wanted this. Second, despite the fact of legal representation, it is clear from the correspondence that negotiations were taking place between them simultaneously. The solicitors' task was to ratify and monitor those negotiations rather than to dictate their content. (In the context of financial issues, the phenomenon of 'parallel' negotiations raises the question whether clients who relied on social security for their financial support concealed financial arrangements between them from their solicitor (Davis 1988: 122). They might have feared that their disclosure would disadvantage them, given the absence of disregards in relation to social security entitlements.)

The second way that solicitors can be seen to empower divorcing parties is by providing them with knowledge of their rights against each other. Some clients derived from their solicitors, rather than from other sources, the knowledge that rights to the equity in the home could be gained other than by direct contribution to the purchase price, or that injunctive relief was available to protect against violence. Such advice might be regarded as a non-controversial and necessary part of solicitors' professional identity. But two points need to be made in relation to it.

The first is that this sort of empowerment may provide an explanation for the myth of solicitors' adversariality. Clearly, some parties resented the fact that, on divorce, their partners had a claim to property which they regarded as their own. One spouse was reported to have left the matrimonial home saying there was 'no way' that his wife could have the house. The client was advised that she did have an interest in the house. Her husband's conception of her entitlement was different to the legislature's. There were therefore conflicts on two levels. One was between the expectations of the parties to the marriage; the other was between the expectations of one of the parties to the marriage and the relevant legal norms. While the marriage subsisted, the existence of these conflicts was concealed. But the uncovering of the conflicts on the breakdown of the relationship (Delphy 1984: 94) might go some way to explaining the conventional wisdom that solicitors 'stir up trouble'. The trouble is the frustration of the expectations of the party who has previously relied on the disempowered party's subservience.

A second point which must be made in relation to this discussion of empowerment is the contrast between the solicitor's conception of the client whose interests are to be protected and the mediator's conception of the clients' situation as a 'problem' which is to be treated. The conception of the individual which underlies each profession's approach is a fundamental issue. Levy cites Trilling's comment that 'Some paradox of our nature leads us, when once we have made our fellow men the object of our enlightened interest, to go on to make them the objects of our pity, then our wisdom, ultimately our coercion' (1984: 533). The position of a client instructing a solicitor would seem to provide better protection against such coercion than the position of a party to a problem which requires treatment. In a situation of inequality, each party has different control. To talk of 'the parties" control is as inaccurate as discussion in terms of 'the' marriage or 'the' divorce. The analogy between the treatment of a disease and the treatment of a dispute which is implicit in some of the mediation literature is imprecise. A dispute necessarily has at least two parties involved. It is not appendicitis.

The third type of empowerment is the aiding of access to the benefits of the welfare state. The importance of the public sector to the distribution of housing and financial support for large numbers of divorcing people has never been in doubt. The data illustrate that solicitors perform the function of aiding their clients' access to such benefits. They advise clients about their rights from, and obligations to the DSS, the fiscal implications of divorce, and the application of public housing legislation to the context of divorce. Clients who needed this advice obviously valued it if they had not received it from other directions (Pahl 1985: 87). It may be that solicitors are particularly well placed to provide information about the resources available from the welfare state, as they can do so without the stigmatizing associations which might apply to 'welfare' workers (Borkowski *et al.* 1983: 111; Davis 1988: 139–40; Murch 1980: 35). Again, the conception of the individual as a source of rights rather than as a problem to be treated is an important one.

The amount of time involved in advising clients about their relationship with the welfare state did not receive much prominence in Mnookin and Kornhauser's framework, which was mainly concerned with the legal relationship between the divorcing parties. To this extent the framework is not directly applicable to England, and other jurisdictions where there is an established welfare state (Griffiths 1986: 140; Melli *et al.* 1988). The laws which provide the shadows for solicitors' activity must be taken to include the laws of state agencies such as the DSS and the local authority housing departments. There are obviously disparities between the law and lore of these bodies.

Advice as to legal entitlements and the importance of the formal law

The previous two sections of this chapter have looked at solicitors' advice to clients in terms of translation and empowerment. This section discusses the impact, if any, of the formal law on this advice. Mnookin and Kornhauser posited that one determinant of out-of-court bargaining, and presumably of solicitors' advice to clients, would be the bargaining endowments created by the norms which would be applied if the dispute was resolved by the court (1979: 985). The data revealed that there are practical problems with the application of this point to any particular negotiation. The discretionary nature of many areas of the law makes the extent of these endowments uncertain (*Sharpe* (1981) 11 *Family Law* 121 per Ormrod LJ; Baker *et al.* 1977: para. 2. 5; Mnookin and Kornhauser 1979: 972). This imprecision was illustrated by the absence of any clear legislative or judicial guidance as to what is 'reasonable' in the discussion of access. The situation is little clearer where, as in section 25(2) of the Matrimonial Causes Act 1973, the statute prescribes factors which the court should consider, but gives little indication as to their relative importance. The imprecision is increased by the fact that the 'value' of the client's case in court cannot be determined until the court itself has determined which of the parties' interpretations of the law and the facts is the more compelling. An endowment is not so much created as suggested by the content of the law.

The imprecision in the nature of the legal endowments is further increased by the fact that there are endowments from other aspects of the dispute. It is possible to conceptualize one partner's level of guilt as the partner's bargaining endowment. Erlanger *et al.* write that 'the same flexibility that allows generosity and creative arrangements also allows emotional intimidation, asset-hiding, and the exertion of financial leverage . . . the "flexibility" of the informal setting invites the intrusion of nonlegal considerations into what are ostensibly legal decisions' (1987: 597). We can go further, and argue that the flexibility of the informal setting compels, rather than invites, the non-legal considerations. Discretionary rules from the legislature increase the relevance of the parties' preferences, strategic behaviour, and transaction costs in relation to the bargaining endowments conferred by the formal law. The strength of the informally created norms is such that they can even override apparently inflexible law (Carson 1970).

One consequence of the imprecision is to increase the power of professional advisers *vis-à-vis* their clients because there is no benchmark against which clients can test the advice. The client can only rely on the solicitor's inside knowledge of the system. Discretion puts legal advisers in the same proverbial position as the press barons. They have the power to sell their expert advice, but their responsibility is diminished by the difficulties of proving that such advice is wrong.

Another consequence of the imprecision is the potential for mistrust on the part of clients. If a solicitor can only advise of a wide bracket of possible outcomes, the client may feel a certain degree of cynicism as to what they are actually paying for. The client may also not take the advice in the spirit with which it is offered. Rather than seeing the bracket as defining the range of legitimate expectations, the client might take the top of the bracket as their entitlement. In a time of uncertainty, clients accord more certainty to the professional's statement than the professional intended (Roth 1963). This may create a sense of injustice if the expectation is not fulfilled, and the non-fulfilment is rendered more likely by the fact that the solicitor's advice, however loosely framed, will have been based on the client's instructions. The client will present their own (probably self-serving) side of the story and the spouse's solicitor's bracket of possible outcomes is likely to reflect equivalent, but probably contrary, considerations. The paradox is that only the client knows the extent to which their instructions are an accurate reflection of the entirety of the dispute. So the client may be better placed to evaluate the solicitor's advice than the solicitor.

Another dynamic in the relationship is that solicitors' advice is influenced by their desire to secure the support of their clients. If this leads to the solicitor's reluctance to provide a 'worst-case scenario' to the client there is the further paradox of the solicitor's dependency on the client endangering the extent to which the client can rely on the solicitor.

It is difficult to see how these tensions can be resolved. If the solicitor provides indefinite, 'well it all depends' advice or no advice at all, this will lead to complaints about uncertainty and incompetence (Davis 1988: 95). If the solicitor provides optimistic advice, problems are being stored up for the later stage when what is offered in settlement might have to be sold to the client as being the best available. A third option is to provide realistic or pessimistic advice, lowering the client's expectations so as to increase the possibility of satisfaction with the outcome. This may lead the client to seek representation from a 'better' solicitor, who can advise more favourable outcomes. It may also violate the solicitor's duty to represent the client to the best of their ability. The solicitor's pursuit of the client's interests might be less enthusiastic if the aims are limited to what can be assured at the early stages of the representation.

Matrimonial law is therefore an example of the phenomenon of uncertain rules devolving decision-making from the legislature to solicitors and their clients (Galanter 1974; Ingleby 1991; Rein 1976: 22; Smart 1981: 160). The reluctance of solicitors to overturn agreements which clients have made may reflect the lack of any grounds on which to do so rather than, or in addition to, a preference for client self-determination.

Another problem in quantifying the nature of the bargaining endowments created by the formal law is that the existence of a bargaining chip does not contain an unequivocal indication of its origin. For example, the negotiation of financial agreements in terms of needs and resources reflects factors which are referred to in sections 25(2)(a) and (b) of the Matrimonial Causes Act. But needs and resources are also important determinants of clients' need for legal advice, and willingness to accept or propose offers of settlement. This is just one of the 'continuities between informal and formal, between legal and everyday life' (Galanter 1985: 652). It would be difficult to argue that the relevance of needs and resources arises solely because of section 25. In other cases, the content of the norm provides a clearer indication of its source. The parties' attitude to the breakdown of the marriage, which is one determinant of the readiness to accept any particular outcome of the bargaining process, is not in section 25.

These points go beyond the discussion of how precisely the particular elements in Mnookin and Kornhauser's framework can be applied to the negotiation of out-of-court settlements. The importance of which norms in the client culture are reinforced by the legal rules is emphasized by Cotterrell, who discusses the selective way in which legal ideology reinforces assumptions about the nature of society. He argues that 'the ideology of law's incompatibility with substantial egalitarian policies . . . is grounded . . . fundamentally in what may be termed "supporting ideologies" of property, liberty, the minimal state, and the rule of law' (Cotterrell 1988: 8). Trubek also makes the point that 'Legal discourse includes subtle methods of valuing certain kinds of behaviour, such as instrumental striving for material goods, and disvaluing others' (1988: 121).

All this is illustrated by the discussion of financial negotiations in Chapter 7. The 'property law' norm of separate ownership of property is reinforced during the marital relationship, where the parties retain title to their separate property. It is only on breakdown that all the property is divisible. The 'egalitarian' norm of joint, or at least adjustable, ownership in the Matrimonial Causes Act represents the expectation of the economically weaker party. The Act thus legislates a morality of community not present in other areas of the law (Felstiner *et al.* 1981: 613). In this way the law creates a distinction between potential power and persuasive strength (Gulliver 1979: 189–91). The weaker party is empowered by the opportunity to reinforce their claims by appealing to the normative statements in the legislation. This is because the Matrimonial Causes Act provides 'the possibility . . . of gaining and using negotiating strength through claims to conformity with normative rules and values that are taken to be axiomatic and/or to represent the acknowledged social order' (Gulliver 1979: 192).

The claim to conformity depends on the content of the law. An attempt to deny access because of disapproval of a new partner is illegitimate; an attempt to keep the home as shelter for children is not. Although the law can legitimize and delegitimize certain claims, the existence of an equality-oriented law is not enough to create equality. 'Law' is not a single rule, but a complex of many levels of ordering. In the context of financial settlements, the effect of breakdown is often to heighten notions of 'what's mine and what's yours' (Davis 1988: 202). Such notions are supported by the law's concentration on 'the "sanctity" of private property rights . . . [and] freedom from interference with the person or property' (Cotterrell 1988: 9–10). The equality law therefore has to fight for its place in the context of other norms which are in conflict with it, and whose influence on the parties predates it. Further, the equality law has to displace norms which have been reinforced during earlier stages of the parties' relationship. The party who asserts it has to 'claim victimhood' because the basis of a claim in terms of need means that the claimant has to declare that they have been disadvantaged (Trubek 1988: 127).

Law reform therefore needs to be seen in terms of its impact on the expectations which parties bring to the legal process and not only in terms of its effect on courts and legal practitioners. On this analysis one way that legislation reforms is the imperceptible changing of the climate of opinion, or, more precisely, some aspects of the various climates of opinion, so that notions of right and wrong are altered. A reform such as the Matrimonial and Family Proceedings Act, which is based on the presumption that there is an alimony-drone problem, decreases expectations of post-divorce available on the basis of a period of time having elapsed from a declaration will, in addition to removing courts from their supervisory jurisdiction and solicitors from their peg-hanging activities, contribute to a climate of divorce being thought to be easier (1990). Married people are more likely to see divorce as a remedy for their situation, since the reforms will remove the possible barrier to divorce which was provided by the image of protection in the fault grounds.

Solicitor–client negotiation and litigotiation scale

In Chapter 2, the litigotiation scale was introduced as an indicator of solicitors' litigiousness. The scale can also be used as an indicator of the solicitor–client relationship, in terms of how much the court has to be invoked before advice is accepted. Some reasons for settlement might be classified thus, in terms of the level to which the court is invoked:

9 Incarceration
8 Contempt proceedings
7 Judicial determination
6 Barrister at door of court
5 Court proceedings imminent
4 Court proceedings threatened
3 Advice on consequences of no agreement
2 Encouragement to settle by solicitor
1 Desire for agreement with spouse

The data in the previous chapters indicate the varying levels of persuasion which solicitors can bring to bear on their clients to 'advise' them of the legalities of their situation. The negotiation between solicitors and clients is an often underrated feature of out-of-court processes (Lempert and Sanders 1986: 177). Some clients arrive at their solicitors already willing to carry out their obligations to their spouses. Others become willing as soon as they are advised. Further up the scale, some need the threat, or even the imminence of court proceedings, to persuade them to come to some settlement. A few clients reached the door of the court and, particularly in the domestic violence cases, there were situations where a hearing was necessary. If a hearing is necessary it is possible that proceedings will have to be taken to enforce the decision in that hearing. It may even be that incarceration is necessary.

The validity of the conclusions

In Chapter 2 it was stressed that the aims, assumptions, and methods of a research project must be taken into account in considering the validity of its conclusions. This must include the way the solicitors were selected in this study. The initial contact with two of the five solicitors was made during the pilot study in January 1985, and with the other three in April 1985. The first solicitor had a reputation as an experienced matrimonial solicitor and subsequent contacts flowed from her, presumably 'in line with existing networks of friendship and enmity, territory and equivalent "boundaries"' (Hammersley and Atkinson 1983: 73). The fact that the solicitors were selected in terms of their perceived amenability to the project made it likely that they would be more specialized than the profession as a whole, would take greater care of their client's emotional state, and might be more careful to consider every possible avenue for aiding their clients' access to the benefits available from the welfare state. It may also be that such solicitors would have taken particular care to explain the need for translation to their clients and been more reluctant to pressurize their clients into certain courses of action. Of course, no conclusive view can be offered on these points because there was no control group of unamenable solicitors.

The characteristics of the clients could be examined by reference to the way they were chosen and by reference to a baseline. The clients were selected by the solicitors, because the solicitors had to secure their clients' consent to the research. The only directions given the solicitors were for variations in the gender, wealth, and child-care responsibilities of the clients. I deliberately asked not to be given 'special' or 'difficult' cases. When the field-work started, about three months after the solicitors' consent to the project had been secured, the solicitors gave me either particular files, or a list of names of files which I could request from the secretaries.

Could it be that I was only given cases which the solicitors felt proud of? If concealment had been their aim they would hardly have granted me access in the first place. There was no shortage of reasons for declining to participate in the project. The notion that I was deliberately deceived seems unlikely, given the level of co-operation and the nature of the cases to which I was allowed access. Of course, it could be argued that I was the victim of an elaborate dupe, a point which it would be impossible to refute as in any conspiracy theory. But there comes a stage in such discussions when the explanation is intuitively implausible, when the response is no longer 'They would, wouldn't they' but a more direct 'Come off it!'

If the sample is analysed in terms of a baseline, it is clear that the clients were not selected in a manner calculated to provide a nationally representative sample of divorcing parties (Griffiths 1983: 168). No such sample could have been obtained through lawyers in any case, as many members of the divorcing population are not legally represented for the proceedings. The figures in Tables 1 to 3 are all taken from a study carried out during the period when the field-work took place (Haskey 1986). Three variables are set out in Tables 1 to 3.

TABLE 1   *Duration of marriages ending in divorce in England and Wales*

Length of marriage (years)	% of divorcing population, 1985, as in Haskey (1986)	% of sample of 46 couples
0–4	35	19.6
5–9	24	23.9
10–19	26	30.4
20+	15	26.1

TABLE 2   *Number of dependent children of divorcing couples in England and Wales*

Number of dependent children at divorce	% of divorcing population, 1985, as in Haskey (1986)	% of sample of 46 couples
0	44.5	23.9
1	24.4	19.6
2	22.8	41.3
3	6.4	10.9
4+	1.9	4.3

Table 1 sets out the data relating to the marriage duration of divorced couples. The sample is more weighted in favour of longer marriages than the national statistics. A possible explanation for this is provided by Table 2, which indicates a more striking way that the sample varies from the divorcing population as a whole. It compares the sample with the national statistics of the number of divorcing parties' children. The proportion of cases in the sample where there are no dependent children is about half of that in the divorcing population as a whole. Eekelaar and

TABLE 3   Grounds used for divorce in England and Wales

Ground used for divorce	% of divorcing population, 1985, as in Haskey (1986)	% of sample of 48 couples
Adultery	31.1	33.3
Unreasonable behaviour	37.4	39.6
Desertion	1.1	2.1
2-year separation	24.7	12.5
5-year separation	5.7	12.5

Maclean concluded that divorcing parties without children were less likely to seek legal representation than those who did have children (1984: 219). Divorces without children are less likely to lead to a continuing financial relationship between the parties and so the issues are more easily resolved without legal representatives. Tables 1 and 2 are also related in that marriages of longer duration may be more likely to have had children, and are more likely to lead to situations where there is a need which leads to the invocation of the legal process. It seems fair to conclude that the variations between the sample and the national statistics can be explained on the grounds that the sample is not representative of all divorcing parties because it was only taken from divorcing parties who visited a solicitor.

Table 3 sets out the percentage of the divorcing population who proceeded on the various grounds in the national statistics and in the sample. The number of divorces in the sample is expressed as forty-eight because the two cross-petitions are each treated as being two divorces. There are only two significant differences between the two columns. The first is that the sample contains an underrepresentation of parties proceeding on the two-year-separation ground. It was noted in Chapter 8 that the petitions where ground (d) was used could hardly be said to represent consent. In the only case where the use of this ground did correspond with consent, the file was closed when the client decided to deal with the issue of status on their own. If the only case where the parties were agreed was the only case where representation was not regarded as necessary for the petition, this would explain the data in Table 3. Petitions on ground (d) are most likely to be those where the parties are not legally represented.

The second variation in Table 3 is the overrepresentation of petitions on the five-year-separation ground. Such petitions are those where the parties are most likely to be represented because the use of the ground characteristically indicates an absence of consent to the divorce itself. The differences between the sample and the national statistics seem to stem from the fact that this sample was selected via solicitors and so excludes those divorcing parties who are not legally represented.

The question of representativeness can also be put in terms of the remarkable similarities between the facts of the cases in this sample and those of other studies (Eekelaar and Maclean 1990: 624). The decisions made with regard to the disposal of the matrimonial home were similar in substance and process to those found by Southwell (1985) and by Eekelaar and Maclean (1986). The relationship between unemployment and divorce was also consistent with previous studies. The child-care issues were the same as those found by Mitchell (1984), the access orders were similar to those found by Maidment (1976), and the custody orders were consistent with the national variations detected by Priest and Whybrow (1986). There does not appear to be any situation where the data were in serious conflict with those found by other researchers. The similarities and explicable differences between the sample and the national divorcing population provide some reassurance for the validity of the conclusions which have been offered in this chapter.

References

BAKER, W. B., EEKELAAR, J. M., GIBSON, C., and RAIKES, S. (1977), *The Matrimonial Jurisdiction of Registrars* (Oxford, Centre for Socio-Legal Studies).

BORKOWSKI, M., MURCH, M., and WALKER, V. (1983), *Marital Violence: The Community Response* (London, Tavistock).

CAIN, M. E. (1979), 'The General Practice Lawyer and the Client: Towards a Radical Conception', 7 *International Journal of the Sociology of Law*, 331–54.

CARSON, W. G. (1970), 'Some Sociological Aspects of Strict Liability and the Enforcement of Factory Legislation', 33 *Modern Law Review*, 396–412.

COTTERRELL, R. (1988), 'Feasible Regulation for Democracy and Social Justice', 15 *Journal of Law and Society*, 5–21.

DAVIS, G. (1988), *Partisans and Mediators* (Oxford, OUP).

—— and MURCH, M. (1988), *Grounds for Divorce* (Oxford, OUP).

DELPHY, C. (1984), *Close to Home: A Materialist Analysis of Women's Oppression* (London, Hutchinson).

EEKELAAR, J. M., and MACLEAN, M. (1984), 'Financial Provision on Divorce: A Reapppraisal' in Freeman, M. D. A. (ed.), *The State, the Law and the Family: Critical Perspectives* (London, Tavistock).

—— —— (1986), *Maintenance after Divorce* (Oxford, OUP).

—— —— (1990), 'Divorce Law and Empirical Studies—A Reply', 106 *Law Quarterly Review*, 621–31.

ELLMANN, S. (1987), 'Lawyers and Clients', 34 *UCLA Law Review*, 717–79.

ERLANGER, H. S., CHAMBLISS, E., and MELLI, M. S. (1987), 'Participation and Flexibility in Informal Processes: Cautions from the Divorce Context', 21 *Law and Society Review*, 585–604.

FELSTINER, W. L. F., ABEL, R. L., and SARAT, A. (1981), 'The Emergence and Transformation of Disputes: Naming, Blaming, Claiming . . .', 15 *Law and Society Review*, 631–54.

FOLBERG, J., and TAYLOR, A. (1984), *Mediation: A Comprehensive Guide to Resolving Conflicts Without Litigation* (San Francisco, Jossey Bass).

GALANTER, M. (1974), 'Why the "Haves" Come Out Ahead: Speculations on the Limits of Legal Change', 9 *Law and Society Review*, 95–160.

—— (1983), 'Reading the Landscape of Disputes: What We Know and Don't Know (and Think We Know) about Our Allegedly Contentious Society', 31 *UCLA Law Review*, 4–71.

—— (1985), 'Vision and Revision: A Comment on Yngvesson', *Wisconsin Law Review*, 647–54.

GREENBAUM, E. H. (1987), 'How Professionals (Including Legal Educators) "Treat" their Client's, *Journal of Legal Education*, 554–75.

GRIFFITHS, J. (1983), *The General Theory of Litigation: A First Step* (Madison, Institute for Legal Studies).

—— (1986), 'What Do Dutch Lawyers Actually Do in Divorce Cases?' 20 *Law and Society Review*, 135–75.

GULLIVER, P. H. (1979), *Disputes and Negotiations: A Cross-Cultural Perspective* (New York, Academic Press).

HAMMERSLEY, M., and ATKINSON, P. (1983), *Ethnography: Principles in Practice* (London, Tavistock).

HART, N. (1976), *When Marriage Ends: A Study in Status Passage* (London, Tavistock).

HASKEY, J. C. (1986), *Recent Trends in England and Wales: The Effect of Legislative Changes* (London, HMSO).

INGLEBY, R. S. (1988b), 'The Solicitor as Intermediary', in R. W. J. Dingwall and J. M. Eekelaar (eds.), *Divorce Mediation and the Legal Process* (Oxford, OUP).

—— (1989b), 'Rhetoric and Reality: Regulation of Out-of-Court Activity in Matrimonial Proceedings', 9 *Oxford Journal of Legal Studies,*m 230–50.

—— (1991), 'Financial Provision on Divorce in Australia: Discretion Discredited?' in L. J. Weitzman and M. Maclean (eds.), *Economic Consequences of Divorce* (Oxford, OUP).

Law Commission (1990), *Report No. 192: Family Law: The Ground for Divorce* (London, HMSO).

LEMPERT, R. O., and SANDERS, J. (1986), *An Invitation to Law and Social Science* (New York, Longman).

LEVY, R. J. (1984), 'Comment on the Pearson-Thoennes Study and on Mediation', 17 *Family Law Quarterly*, 525–33.

MAIDMENT, S. (1976), 'A Study in Child Custody', 6 *Family Law*, 196–201, 236–8.

MELLI, M. S., ERLANGER, H. S., and CHAMBLISS, E. (1988), 'The Process of Negotiation: An Exploratory Investigation in the Context of No-Fault Divorce', 40 *Rutgers Law Review*, 1133–72.

MITCHELL, A. K. (1984), *Children in the Middle: Living Through Divorce* (London, Tavistock).

MNOOKIN, R. H. and KORNHAUSER, L. (1979), 'Bargaining in the Shadow of the Law: The Case of Divorce', 88 *Yale Law Journal*, 950–97.

MURCH, M. (19890), *Justice and Welfare in Divorce* (London, Sweet and Maxwell).

O'BARR, W. M., and CONLEY, J. M. (1988), 'Law Expectations of the Civil Justice System', 22 *Law and Society Review*, 137–61.

PAHL, J. (ed.) (1985), *Private Violence and Public Policy: The Needs of Battered Women and the Response of the Public Services* (London, Routledge and Kegan Paul).

PARSONS, T. (1954), *Essays in Sociological Theory* (New York, Free Press).

PRIEST, J. A., and WHYBROW, J. C. (1986), *Custody Law in Practice in the Divorce and Domestic Courts: Supplement to Law Commission Working Paper No. 96* (London, HMSO).

REIN, M. (1976), *Social Science and Public Policy* (Harmondsworth, Penguin).

ROTH, J. A. (1963), *Timetables: Structuring the Passage of Time in Hospital and Other Careers* (Indianapolis, Bobbs-Merrill).

SARAT, A. (1988), 'The "New Formalism" in Disputing and Dispute Processing', 21 *Law and Society Review*, 695–715.

—— and FELSTINER, W. L. F. (1986), 'Law and Strategy in the Divorce Lawyers' Office', 20 *Law and Society Review*, 93–134.

SMART, C. (1984), *The Ties that Bind: Law, Marriage and the Reproduction of Patriarchal Relations* (London, Routledge and Kegan Paul).

SOUTHWELL, M. (1985), 'Children, Divorce and the Disposal of the Matrimonial Home', 15 *Family Law*, 184–6.

TRUBEK, D. M. (1988), 'The Handmaiden's Revenge: On Reading and Using the Newer Sociology of Civil Procedure', 51 *Law and Contemporary Problems*, 111–34.

WALLERSTEIN, J. S., and KELLY, J. B. (1980), *Surviving the Breakup: How Parents and Children Cope with Divorce* (London, Grant McIntyre).

WEITZMAN, L. J. (1985), *The Divorce Revolution: The Unexpected Social and Economic Consequences for Women and Children in America* (New York, Free Press).

6.2. Alternative dispute resolution and divorce: natural experimentation in family law

LEE E. TEITELBAUM
LAURA DUPAIX

Experimentation in divorce procedure

To a considerable extent, the movement towards mediation and other methods of dispute resolution in divorce cases seeks to address the conditions of modern divorce just outlined. Perhaps its greatest appeal lies in the frank recognition that, formal divorce theory notwithstanding, a dissolution decree does not end familial relations. Moreover, Alternative Dispute Resolution ('ADR') proponents accept that, while children may be harmed less by divorce than by continuation of an unsatisfactory relation between their parents, they none the less may suffer greatly when their families are formally disrupted. Accordingly, it is important to examine the movement towards procedural reform for what it is: a significant experiment in the manner of social and legal response to marital breakdown. Such an inquiry requires an examination of the reasons for asserting that a non-contentious methodology will achieve at least some of the goals that the current adjudicative approach fails to accomplish.

A. The reasons for change

In most legal reform movements, proponents point to specific failures of existing legal strategies to accomplish some express or implicit purpose and offer a new way of achieving that purpose. Alternatively, proponents identify some value that is not achieved by existing law because it was not adequately considered in the formulation of the current scheme, and urge a reform that will advance that value in addition to, or in place of, previously accepted values. This is not to say, of course, that such reforms are value-free; on the contrary, they quite plainly continue in force the express and implicit values on which the original scheme was founded. However, those values are accepted as non-controversial. The second kind of reform, however, requires express discussion not only of empirical questions but also of the new value to be pursued in a reformed legal regime. Indeed, efficiency may not be in issue at all; it may well be that what is wrong with the former system is precisely its efficiency, achieved at a cost to values other than efficiency (such as openness or substantive fairness).

Very often, however, it is not obvious which of these provides the real ground for reform, and this is true of divorce reform as well. It is difficult to be clear about the extent to which the ADR movement rests on relatively simple instrumental claims and the extent to which it either seeks or assumes different values in the resolution of marital disputes. As a way of approaching this question, it may be useful to describe some of the commonly identified advantages associated with mediation.

1. Adjudicative dispute resolution works best when the object is to determine past conduct and to make a judgment that is only concerned with the consequences of past behaviour. It works less well when the focus is on complex relationships which will continue in some significant form after this particular dispute is resolved. Adjustment of the incidents of the divorce implies ongoing and often complex financial and social relationships.[1]

2 Adjudicative dispute resolution is characterized by formal rationality. The rules governing its operation are intended to govern all disputes falling under them and are therefore insensitive to the particular circumstances of individual disputes. Mediated settlement allows fuller exploration of facts and positions and therefore offers a more satisfying and more accurate evaluation of particular situations.[2]

3 Adjudication is ill-suited to the interests of children in custody matters. A mediated agreement is more likely than a judicial decision to match the parents' capacity and desires with the child's needs; on the other hand, the litigative process itself is likely to create adjustment problems for the children and their parents.[3]

4 Compliance with adjudication is based simply on force or its threat. Neither is routinely effective, as our experience with child support awards and the frequency of relitigation concerning custodial issues make clear. Mediated results, by contrast, are the result of participatory activity and the disputants are likely to have a strong commitment to the result reached.[4]

5 Adjudication is a costly enterprise, from the perspectives of the court and the parties. Domestic relations cases now occupy a great deal of

scarce judicial time and resources. Moreover, they consume a substantial part of the wealth available to the parties, in some cases even reducing the standard of living available to them after divorce. Mediation is a less costly method of dispute resolution on both counts.[5]

6   As a result of the financial and emotional costs associated with litigation, family disputants are frequently dissatisfied with their awards. Dissatisfaction impeaches the legitimacy of the process itself and indicates a risk of future disputes. The participatory character of mediation mitigates the risks of dissatisfaction and, accordingly, of future difficulty.[6]

These are, on their face, plausible claims, and accord with both popular and, particularly, professional assessments of domestic relations matters.[7] Moreover, they are framed in apparently instrumental terms: mediation will carry out generally accepted goals of divorce settlement and avoid undesirable side-effects better than litigated settlement.[8]

Indeed, some of the arguments listed above are relatively modest claims of greater efficiency or accuracy. This is plainly true of the assertion that mediation will save court time and client expense. A procedure which is less time-consuming and costly is, *ceteris paribus*, preferable to one which is more so.

Another argument in favour of non-adjudicative resolution of custody disputes also seems purely instrumental in character. When it is argued that decisions reached through mediation are more likely in fact to advance the child's interests than are litigated results,[9] the apparent concern is simply with accurate fact determinations. These are claims about efficient procedure, no different from arguments about six or twelve person juries or the utility of science masters in complex litigation. The issue is to be understood as empirical: which approach will resolve typical adjudicative issues most efficiently and accurately?

These modest claims are not, however, the backbone of the argument for alternative dispute resolution in the family law area. The major claims are instrumental in form, but incorporate elements that are not merely matters of efficiency or accuracy, at least in an ordinary sense. Take, for example, the contention that the child's interest will be served by reliance on mediation: that parents who have decided on some custodial scheme through a participatory process will be more committed to that scheme and thus more likely to abide by it. In an important sense, this is an instrumental claim. Judicial determination of custody has traditionally turned on an assessment of the child's 'best interests', and ADR proponents argue that this ultimate end is more likely to be realized through non-contentious than through litigative methods. However, taken as a basis for substituting mediation for judicial review, this is more than merely an efficiency or accuracy claim. Courts have traditionally deferred to parental determinations regarding custody, and it is rare in practice for a court not to accept their views on custody.[10] None the less, a number of legislatures and courts have also declined to grant unconditional acceptance to parental agreement, secured with or without negotiation, because of the complexity of interests and considerations that may operate.[11] To accept a mediated settlement on the basis of the parents' greater expertise may entail, therefore, a change of substance.

A less obvious shift, but one with greater substantive implications, is associated with the forward-looking nature of mediation itself. The argument that the child's interests will be better served by mediated rather than adjudicated solutions redirects attention from the customary formulation of the issue—which parent is better able to care for the child—to an inquiry into how the parents (and perhaps the child) will view whatever arrangement is adopted and how strong their commitments to that relationship will be. The child's 'best interests' thus is understood more as a function of the relationship that follows placement than of the placement itself.

This redirection of attention is plainly at odds with certain substantive assumptions underlying modern divorce reform, particularly the belief that dissolution terminates the prior relationship. A standard work on divorce mediation urges viewing the family as an 'interacting communications network',[12] a systems view that applies not only to achievement of an agreement but forms the basic premise for the terms of that agreement.[13]

A more specific but perhaps equally important substantive implication of this redirection of attention concerns the nature of custodial arrangements. Mediation research projects have found that joint custody was far more commonly adopted, at least in successful mediations, than is generally the case. One study reports that nearly 70% of those who reached agreements through mediation chose joint custody, whereas joint custody occurred in less than 30% of non-mediated outcomes.[14] It is, of course, difficult to be sure about the meaning of these data. All mediation studies incorporate substantial selection procedures. At times selection was done by courts, which screened mediation participants to assure that only 'suitable' cases were assigned to this form of treatment;[15] in other studies the couples themselves decided whether they would participate.[16] The authors of the Denver Custody Mediation Project and the Custody

Mediation Project themselves recognize the likelihood that the couples who chose, or were chosen, to mediate were initially inclined towards participatory settlement and might have been disproportionately inclined towards joint custody as well.[17]

These circumstances make it impossible to say that the use of mediation itself results in a higher incidence of joint custody. However, mediators often hold values which lead them to encourage this form of resolution. To the extent that mediators believe that joint participation in family affairs is itself a valuable thing and that, even after divorce, the family remains an interacting communications network, they may prefer joint legal custody and the concomitant sense of preserving all of the parent–child relations that mark a stable family. Indeed, some mediators are quite explicit about their preference for this arrangement, believing that 'parents should be encouraged to share in joint legal custody'.[18]

If, as both proponents of mediation and commentators seem to think likely,[19] an emphasis on cooperation and compromise will produce either a formal or informal preference for (and perhaps pressure towards) joint custody, this preference is a change of substantial significance in most jurisdictions. It may also be a substantial change for the parties involved. While it is true that there is a degree of current enthusiasm for joint custodial arrangements, it is also true that we know very little about its meaning for children. What research has been done usually has the following characteristics: very small samples,[20] self-selected couples,[21] and very little reliable information concerning the effects of joint custody.[22] That arrangement may, as proponents have claimed, provide a stronger sense of relationship between the child and both parents in at least some cases;[23] it may also create the further occasions for parental conflict and inconsistency of rules which opponents have traditionally feared.[24]

Whatever its effects on families after divorce, however, a preference for joint custody employed by mediators or implied by mediation will affect the bargaining positions of spouses. It is significant in this respect that the principal support for joint custody, particularly as a preferred arrangement, comes from fathers' rights groups and that it is often opposed by groups which espouse the interests of women.[25] To the extent that mediators regard joint custody as desirable, and perhaps regard its serious consideration as a sign of good faith mediation, women may find as a practical matter that their bargaining position is significantly weakened. An impetus toward joint custody may provide a useful bargaining device for husbands, who may use it as a threat in connection with settlement of property, alimony, or child support levels before the

dissolution order is entered.[26] The threat of joint custody may also be uti-
lized to counter petitions for upward modification of child support even
after dissolution.

The emphasis on 'satisfactory' post-divorce relations expressed by proponents of mediation may also affect the resolution of non-custodial
issues. It is at least reasonable to suppose that child support may be heavily influenced by assessments of the father's commitment to support
rather than by the family's station of life. Much the same could be said
about spousal maintenance. An order that is unsatisfactory to the mother
will never place her in a position to begin life anew; an order that is
unsatisfactory to the obligor invites partial, delayed, or even non-payment. This shift of focus is not merely a question of process; it plainly
shifts to some degree the substantive concern from identifying a level of
support that seems to be appropriate in view of the prior history of the
family to a prediction regarding the post-divorce conduct of members of
the theoretically-terminated family.

The movement towards alternative dispute resolution in connection
with marital dissolution is not, therefore, a simple experiment in procedure. It supposes in many instances a substantial reformulation of the
issues, away from enucleated judgments about which of two parents
seems best able to care for a child, what support level will maintain a certain standard of living, or how property might be equitably distributed,
and toward the creation of a set of post-marital relationships that will be
relatively acceptable to the disputants initially and in the long run.

B. Considering the experiment

The various aspects of procedural reform in connection with marital dissolution require consideration of both empirical and value questions. It is
too facile to say that some elements raise empirical issues and others present questions of value. As we have already observed, even claims which
seem to rest on simple empirical bases—that alternative dispute resolution methods will reach more accurate or more efficient or less costly
results than adjudicative procedures—incorporate assumptions about the
values of efficiency or a particular kind of accuracy. At the same time,
claims which expressly or implicitly embody substantive reformulations
contain empirical propositions as well.

C. The question of efficiency

Take, for example, the questions of cost and efficiency. There is, on the
one hand, a fact question: whether litigated resolution of issues associ-

ated with marital dissolutions is 'too costly'. The implicit sub-issues are, of course, whether the traditional approach *is* costly and whether mediated resolution, for example, would be less costly.

Relatively little information on these questions exists. It is certainly true that divorce and related matters have made up a steadily increasing proportion of judicial dockets and now constitute about one-half of all cases filed in state courts.[237] This increase itself has prompted concern that courts have been overwhelmed by matrimonial actions,[28] and that the costs of litigation overwhelm the divorcing parties. On these latter issues, however, our information is less clear.

Unlike almost any other area of law, all cases of divorce must go to court, regardless of the existence of genuine dispute. Accordingly, increases in divorce filings indicate nothing more than an increase in formally-recognized marital breakdown; they do not say anything directly about the frequency of actual disputes, the costs of such disputes or the consumption of judicial resources. Indeed, it appears that most matrimonial cases are uncontested, at least by the time they come to court,[29] and that the rate of uncontested cases has actually increased over time.[30] Moreover, these uncontested matters are frequently heard in what can only be considered an efficient if not perfunctory fashion: average times in urban courts may run as low as seven and one-half minutes.[31]

It is thus difficult to assess the overall cost of marital dissolution simply from case-load statistics. Empirical evidence concerning the absolute and relative costs of traditional divorce procedures is rare and difficult to interpret. The Custody Mediation Project is the best-known study to include a calculation of relative costs. In the Denver aspect of this study, the authors, who generally favour mediation on cost as well as other grounds, found at best 'some evidence of modest savings in private attorneys' fees . . . among successful mediation clients'.[32]

In this experiment, cases where custody disputes appeared likely were randomly assigned to a mediation or control-group status. The mediation group were offered, but not required to accept, free mediation services. Those who chose to participate were assigned to male–female teams comprised of lawyers and mental health professionals trained in mediation techniques; spouses in the control group and those in the experimental group who chose not to participate pursued the usual method of custody resolution. The authors classified mediation, for those who chose it, as 'successful' and 'unsuccessful' according to whether they reached an agreement in mediation. In fact, the mediation group included 123 individuals who were equally divided between success and failure. The average fee paid to attorneys by the successful mediation group was $1,325. Those who were unsuccessful paid an average of $1,544 to attorneys, and control group members paid an average of $1,536.[33] Only successful mediation produced an average saving in private costs, and the difference is not dramatic. Moreover, the group of 95 persons that was selected for but declined participation in the mediation project had lower attorneys' fees than even the successful mediation group: they paid an average of less than $1,300. The same general pattern appears in connection with the large sample included the Custody Mediation Project, although unsuccessful mediation group respondents paid somewhat less than those who were in the 'adversarial' group $2,010 and $2,350, respectively).[34]

It is hard to interpret these data confidently, but they do make clear the difficulty of maintaining that one method of dispute resolution is systematically and significantly less expensive to the lay public than another. Certainly there is no reason to believe that mandatory mediation will produce lower costs given the equivalent expenses incurred by unsuccessful and control group members.

These data deal, of course, with expense to the private actors in divorce rather than with the public cost of adjudicating contested custody matters. The difference in public cost, as estimated in the Denver project, does not seem to be significant. The total cost of a sample of mediated cases amounted to about $40,000, based on an assumption of 4.0 hours of bench time per hearing; the public cost for non-mediated cases was about $45,500.[35] However, the calculation of expense assumes a greater use of custody investigations in non-mediated cases than mediated cases, which in turn supposes some systematic reason for believing that mediation mitigates the need for such investigations. In addition, the cost of mediation services was based on the costs of the Custody Mediation Project, *excluding* programme overhead.

Other confounding factors may also be involved. The self-selection of couples for mediation in the Denver Project strongly suggests that the mediating group was more disposed towards settlement than either the control group or the group that rejected the offer of mediation, and this by itself may have reduced time and therefore cost. Any assumption about significant savings in the cost of processing custody cases through mediation has therefore yet to be satisfactorily substantiated.

A second measure of efficiency is time consumption. Here again the case for preferring mediation is at best unclear, even from the perspective of its advocates. The Denver Custody Mediation Project found that the average successful mediation respondent moved from 'initiation of proceedings' to 'final order' in 9.7 months.[36] The control and rejecting groups averaged 11.9 and 11.1 months, respectively, between *filing* and final orders.[37] It is not clear whether 'filing' and 'initiation' dates are the same and thus whether the comparison is founded on a common measure. Even assuming comparability, the significance of a six-week difference in resolution time does not seem very great. Moreover, the longest period of time (13.4 months, on the average) was required, as one might expect, for cases in which mediation was attempted but did not result in agreement.

If, however, research did reveal that alternative methods of resolution were less expensive or consumed less time, it would not necessarily follow that they should be adopted. Consumption of judicial time and resources, or even private expense, do not themselves demonstrate the desirability of substituting alternative for traditional methods of dispute resolution. With respect to the consumption of time, the slight increase observed—even if we accept its existence, methodological questions notwithstanding—may well be attributable to (generally) successful efforts by counsel to resolve custodial disputes through negotiation. As Professor Levy has observed, there is nothing more common in domestic relations practice 'than an attorney's "cooling out" an angry client by delay—to make negotiations easier and more likely to succeed'.[38] As he also points out, that 'cooling period' seems to yield results: 85 to 90 per cent of all divorce cases are settled by spouses and their lawyers prior to trial.[39]

As to the issue of public cost, it may well be thought that the allocation of legal resources to marital dissolution is a peculiarly appropriate distributive choice. Divorce and its incidents are, for most disputants, the only occasion on which they will come into contact with law in its formal sense. Moreover, it is for most disputants a very important matter. As an economic proposition, the outcome of divorce cases determines the level of comfort and the range of opportunity available to the formal parties and to their children. As a social matter, these proceedings define, at least initially, crucially important relationships between parents and their children. From the parents' point of view, the divorce decree will determine the location and extent of custodial and visitation rights; from the children's perspective, that order says much about both their immediate and long-range relationships with their parents.

Domestic relations matters may also carry symbolic significance for the parties. They provide an occasion on which one party may declare her effort to maintain the family, or the strength of his bond with his children. While divorces may be 'routine' from an institutional perspective, they are often not routine from the viewpoint of those whose careers and lives are profoundly influenced by the results. It maybe that these cases do not squander but are especially deserving of public resources and concern.

D. Structural claims

When legal reform moves beyond simple claims of enhanced efficiency and accuracy, inquiry in turn becomes more complex. This is particularly true in connection with procedural reform in the domestic relations area. The value questions are, to a considerable extent, implicit rather than explicit. Moreover, the value questions are joined with claimed regarding the capacity of alternative dispute resolution strategies to achieve 'better' solutions, creating a form of mixed statement that might be called a 'structural assumption'. The form of these assumptions is: 'Mediation has characteristics which are better suited to achievement of some ultimate goal.' Two propositions are imbedded in this statement: first, that adjudication, because it has other characteristics, will not be able to achieve these desirable goals, and, second, that mediation, because it is better suited structurally to achievement of those goals, will be successful. The claims made by ADR proponents include a number of propositions of this sort. One is that the continuing-relationship aspect of family controversies requires a 'person-oriented' and forward-looking rather than an 'act-oriented' and backward-looking form of procedure. A second such proposition is that the adversarial system produces or assures conflict after divorce, whereas non-contentious methods will not. A third is that participatory methods will enhance 'satisfaction' and thus desirable post-divorce relations.

Consider, for example, the series of claims that centre around party satisfaction. It is said that divorcing parties are often dissatisfied with the outcomes reached through the traditional process. A preference for alternative methods supposes two things: that it is the judicial processing of divorce that produces dissatisfaction and that alternative methods will reduce the level of dissatisfaction.

Initially, one would want to specify the meaning of a high rate of dissatisfaction. It may mean that divorcing parties are more dissatisfied with the results of their legal encounters than are other litigants. It may also mean that, as an absolute matter, the level of dissatisfaction is too high. It bears notice, however, that marital dissolution may be a special type of litigation: that we would expect high rates of unhappiness or dissatisfaction, both generally and compared with other kinds of disputes.

This may be the case for several reasons. In the first place, the dissolution of a marriage is often the first and only significant encounter these parties have with legal proceedings. Secondly, the results of dissolution proceedings are very important to the parties. We have already seen that they define both the economic and social careers of the spouses and their children, and that they often carry in addition to their practical significance a considerable symbolic freight.

Moreover, outcomes in divorce cases reflect special kinds of trade-offs not routinely found in ordinary litigation. In the usual contract or tort case, the value of the outcome, and the values on which the parties negotiate or litigate, are roughly symmetrical: it is $5,000 out of one pocket and into another. The importance and the meaning of the case is approximately the same for both plaintiff and defendant. These conditions are rarely found, however, in marital dissolutions.

As we saw earlier, divorce settlement includes a number of financial and social issues which are typically resolved interdependently. For a wife who has followed a traditional spousal role, custody of children may be crucially important to her definition of her identity and far more important than the level of alimony or division of property. For a husband who deeply regrets the collapse of the marriage, continued custody or generous visitation may be similarly crucial, and obtaining such rights by conceding a greater alimony or property award may seem worthwhile. In addition, changes in substantive law regarding divorce and its incidents have affected the positions of divorcing parties and particularly of women. Wives without children face considerable uncertainty regarding the likelihood, amount, and terms of a support award; wives with children face uncertainties with respect to custody, child support, and spousal maintenance. It may well be that wives will be happy with neither a negotiated nor a litigated result under these substantive conditions. It is not the *process* of dispute resolution which accounts for this dissatisfaction, but rather the asymmetrical power relations of the spouses combined with a substantive law which permits the husband to force the wife to assume what seems to be an unacceptable risk.

Moreover, dissolution—whether achieved by negotiation, litigation, or mediation—does not and cannot finally resolve the relations of the parties. A contract or tort action comes to an end. The parties know where they are, and what their futures will look like. A divorce ends one aspect of the legal and social relations between spouses, but leaves some of those relations in place and creates new and additional relations which may not end for many years, if at all. There is not that satisfaction that may come with new beginnings.

It is of course true that alternative dispute resolution theory recognizes these circumstances more fully than traditional dispute resolution, but to recognize a circumstance is not to relieve it. If, as is plausible, high levels of dissatisfaction among divorce litigants result from the substantive law and from the non-conclusive nature of marital dissolutions, procedural change may not significantly reduce those levels.

Nor is there currently satisfactory empirical evidence on this point. The Denver Mediation Project study discussed earlier is one of the few to gather data on client satisfaction. As one might expect, satisfaction levels differed greatly between those for whom mediation was successful and those for whom it was not. While 70% of the successful mediation group reported that they were 'highly satisfied' with mediation, only 22% of the unsuccessful group did so.[40] The larger Custody Mediation Project reported even higher levels of satisfaction for both successful and unsuccessful mediation (90% and 59%, respectively).[41]

However, there are significant problems with accepting these results. For one, what the respondents had in mind by 'satisfaction' is not explored. It could mean that they were objectively satisfied, or that they were 'satisfied' as compared with their expectations of a litigated settlement. Moreover, some projects (including the Denver Project) provided mediation services without charge, while the traditional litigation approach is believed to be expensive: that economy itself might be considered satisfying. In addition, the fact of participation in an 'experiment' alone may tend to affect attitudinal measures.[42]

Finally, the self-selection in some studies and judicial prescreening in others may have produced a mediation group that was especially likely to be satisfied with a cooperative procedure. Indeed, strong evidence for this inference emerges from comparing the results of the Denver and larger projects. While the level of satisfaction in the later study was higher than for the earlier Denver study, the authors quite rightly recognize that the mediating groups differed in these studies and that group characteristics may have had something to do with defining satisfaction levels. In particular, the sample reporting the highest satisfaction levels included more younger couples with shorter marriages and younger children,[43] a constituency that might well find relatively informal settlement congenial.

Similar questions arise with respect to judgements of 'fairness'. It is interesting in this connection that belief in the fairness of outcomes does not match levels of satisfaction. Only about one-half of even the successful Denver Project mediation group described the process as 'perfectly fair' or believed that both parties had 'equal influence' in the decision. Less than 20% of the unsuccessful group believed the process to be 'perfectly fair' and barely more than one-third believed the parties equally situated.[44] Again, somewhat higher figures regarding the perception of fairness are found for the later study[45] but the methodological problems discussed in connection with satisfaction apply here as well. Moreover, there were significant levels of reported 'anger' and sense of 'unpleasantness' at every site.[46]

In view of the reasons for thinking that substantive law affects the reality and perceptions of power held by spouses when a marriage ends, it is particularly important to know whether the sense of fairness was equally distributed between husbands and wives. Feminist critics of mediation in this context have often suggested that divorce and custody mediation tend to disempower women.[47] Although a complete analysis is not available, there is reason to think that women are significantly more likely to regard mediation as threatening and balanced against them than are men. While women did report that mediation helped them in understanding themselves and their spouses, they were also far more likely than men to report a sense of being pressured into agreement, a lack of comfort in expressing their feelings, anger during mediation sessions, and a sense that mediators essentially dictated the terms of the agreement.[48]

Finally, it is important to remember that experimental enterprises may be conducted under conditions that would not prevail in large-scale implementation. Much of our experience with alternative dispute resolution and particularly with mediation in the divorce context has involved relatively small experimental settings in which there has been an interest in reaching favourable results and devotion of a relatively great amount of time and resources to intervention. These are luxuries which may only be available when small numbers of divorces are sought to be resolved over the course of a year. It is far less clear that levels of satisfaction and perceived fairness achieved under these conditions could be replicated if *all*, or even very many, dissolutions were treated over the same time period. An intensive boutique practice may not tell us much about wholesale dispute resolution.

A second structural assumption often is urged in connection with resolution of custodial issues in particular. The distress experienced by children of divorce will be mitigated, it is said, by non-contentious resolution of custodial and visitation matters. A common form of this argument was adopted by the New York Law Revision Commission:

The available evidence points almost without equivocation to the conclusion that children are better off it both parents are meaningfully involved in their lives after their separation. . . . Therefore, the challenge for the custody dispute resolution system is how to organize itself so as to maximize the number of families in which both parents are involved in the child's post-separation life. Available evidence suggests that reliance on adversary litigation controlled by the parents and their lawyers as a primary technique for dispute resolution does not further this goal and, indeed, works against it.[49]

It may or may not be true, as the Commission claims, that the adversarial process 'exacerbates the harmful effects of divorce on children'.[50] However, that claim is entirely structural. Although the Commission refers to 'available evidence' supporting that conclusion, it cites nothing which would normally be regarded as 'evidence' to support its point. Indeed, in the entire discussion of this point under the heading 'Custody Litigation Increases the Child's Distress', reference is made only to a 1954 non-experimental study,[51] to legal authority concerning the weight given to the child's preference in custody battles,[52] and to an article on the effects of divorce on fathers.[53]

Moreover, much of the literature regarding the effects of divorce on children cited by the Commission suggests an alternative interpretation: that it is the divorce itself, and the effects of divorce on parents, which largely account for the distress of children. Parents are often preoccupied with bitterness towards each other and with the adjustments they must make in their own lives. They must adjust their financial and social lives to new conditions. This preoccupation results in diminished parenting, whether physically (through greater absence from the home) or emotionally (through decreased pleasure in the parent–child relationship, reduced interaction, and inattentiveness to the child's needs and wishes). Indeed, parents may often at some level view the child's presence as a troublesome reminder of the failed marital relationship and as an impediment to his or her complete independence upon termination of the marriage.[54]

It is unclear to what extent these circumstances might be relieved through a non-litigative divorce procedure. However, it would be unduly optimistic to assume that such conditions are largely the result of procedure rather than the conditions associated with divorce itself and that innovation of this sort can markedly relieve the distress of children whose parents can no longer live together.

A third structural assumption implicit in ADR proposals is that the outcomes will be in some sense fairer and more accurate because their procedure is less narrowly focused on the questions put by traditional legal categories and focused upon by judges.[55] The fairness issue is a difficult thing to evaluate, because we do not have some universal or objective standard of fairness against which we could compare results.[56] However, one way of looking at fairness in the legal system is to say that it requires that people be treated as equals and that, particularly, imbalances in power that occur through prestige, wealth, and the like not be allowed to determine the outcome of disputes.

It is, of course, the principal claim of the current legal system that it seeks, as far as possible, to place litigants on an equal footing before the law. It is also a principal criticism of the current legal system that it fails to do so and, indeed, cannot do so within an economic and political system that maldistributes power as pervasively as ours does. Accepting the latter argument, however, it hardly follows that alternative *procedural* remedies will solve the problem. Any procedure remains imbedded not only in a body of substantive law but also in our existing political and economic arrangement. It is also possible that in some instances mediation not only fails to remedy the problem of maldistributed power but may create special risks of unfairness.

Most current alternative strategies rely on a neutral mediator: a lawyer or other professional who represents neither side but is, perhaps, 'counsel to the situation', in Brandeis's phrase.[57] When Brandeis used that phrase, however, he was talking about mediating disputes among corporate actors who, one may suppose, were approximately equal in power, in resources, and in their stake in the outcome. As we have seen, this is often not the case with divorcing couples. Particularly in families which have followed traditional role allocations, one party has most of the money. And, as we have also seen, a variety of non-financial considerations may affect the value placed on disputed issues. A traditional mother may have an immense investment in the custody of her children: an investment so great and so important to her definition of herself that she will concede almost everything else to assure that she does not lose on this issue. A husband, on the other hand, may be inclined to claim a desire for joint custody, or even sole custody. He may do so as a negotiating item. He may do so because the custody claim has symbolic significance to him; he cannot bear to be perceived as unconcerned with his children. Finally, the father may make a custody claim because he quite simply wishes custody himself. Whatever the basis, that claim by itself may change the mother's position regarding property, alimony, and even child support. It may also deter her from considering, or at least uttering, a desire to go to school or pursue some career opportunity because doing so might imply that her commitment to her children is less than complete.

Of course, these things may and do happen in litigative settings, especially when the issues are finally resolved through negotiation (as most are); they are a product of the substantive law and social role allocations rather than of the procedure used for marital dissolution. However, it is worth considering the hypothesis that the position of the more vulnerable spouse will be even weaker without partisan assistance than it would be with such help. An advocate is freer than a neutral intermediary to advise the mother that, for example, local judges in practice rarely grant custody to fathers, or of prevailing trends in alimony or property division. Similarly, an a advocate may more readily advise a vulnerable husband about the possibility of joint custody and the potential costs of open-ended spousal support or wholesale property transfers.

Questions of fairness also arise with the implication that non-judicial strategies allow for the incorporation of factors that are relevant, and indeed often crucial, to the collapse of social interchange but are routinely ignored by courts engaged in dispensing formally rational justice. The insistence on evidentiary rules, the limitations of proof to matters that are of formal legal consequence, and other 'legalistic' rules produce a sense of unreality in divorce adjudications. Trials only seek to capture a limited version of what happens in the world, and their insistence on those limits excludes information that is important to understanding what is really in dispute.

There is indeed something appealing to a rejection of legal formalism, particularly for lawyers who see the extent to which adjudication narrowly defines disputes that are far more deeply textured in their concrete settings. Nonetheless, two points should be considered before adopting the ADR view. One is that it may not be possible, in a post-Industrial world, to identify generally-shared principles regarding both marriage and post-marital life. The second is that the values to be employed—even community values, for example,—ought to be examined.

We can be sure that some values will be on mediated settlements. Neutrality implies non-partisanship, but even a neutral actor must bring some ideas of better and worse to bear as he or she interprets or conveys positions and urges settlement. Inevitably, a mediator or other non-judicial agent will rely on values derived from his or her professional training, or on community values, or perhaps on some combination of these, often without disclosing or perhaps even recognizing that reliance or the nature of those values.[58]

It is also possible to inquire as to the existence of generally shared values in modern urban communities. But even if we suppose the existence of community values, it does not follow that they are, because of their popular acceptance alone, appropriate for legal purposes. One need only imagine a dispute between a black man and a white man in the South in the 1950s or remember the lengthy history of national efforts to extinguish Southern community values as a determinant of the operation of law. Domestic relations disputes, because they are so much a matter of community interest and deal with relations which engage every member of the community, may be especially likely to call forth deeply held local values which vary sharply from legal norms regarding divorce and familial relations. In one community, it may be thought that husbands still possess a right of reasonable correction over their wives: conduct that, from the perspective of judicial and legislative agencies, might be considered spouse abuse. The same community may conceive that a woman's proper role is child-care; from this it might follow that women who wished joint rather than sole custody should not be seriously heard or, worse, are properly regarded as unfit for custody themselves. It might likewise follow that joint custody sought by a husband would receive little serious attention if the wife opposed it. Community values may further hold that women should not enter the workplace, and even a neutral actor imbued with that norm would find it hard to accept the position of a wife who sought rehabilitative alimony or sought custody while also intending to work. Indeed, these dangers seem peculiarly great in precisely those settings where one could identify common values most readily: communities which are relatively homogeneous or where those with social authority share a single, strongly-held set of religious or other values.

The risk that community values will supersede judgements reached as a matter of legislative or even constitutional policy is not to be accepted lightly. And, of course, a similar risk may arise with respect to values that affect mediators drawn from professional ranks, including the legal profession.[59]

Apart from considerations related to outcomes, fairness may also have a structural and symbolic aspect. To the extent that mediation is seen as an alternative to adjudication rather than as an effort to avoid its necessity, it is important to ask whether it is right to exclude divorcing persons from access to courts. Proponents of mandatory non-judicial dispute resolution suppose that, for the most part, disputants do not really want to go to court or, if they do, it is because they have not really thought about matters in a rational and sensible way.[60] This is no doubt true in some cases. But there are other situations in which it is important to examine whether disputants should have access to the forum which is, rightly or wrongly, associated with the public vindication of rights.

There are surely occasions when people want to go to court because they seek a public audience for some purpose. This is often true of defamation suits, and may be true in some domestic relations disputes as well. A spouse who cares deeply about the institution of marriage may want to declare publicly that he or she has done the best that could be done; a claim that may be made, often enough, under the guise of denying incompatibility.[61] A wife who has been beaten, abandoned, or the victim of adultery may wish to make some public authority aware of the fact. A husband who wants to share custody of a child may wish a public declaration of his desire for that relationship, even if it is unlikely that joint custody will be ordered.

It may be tempting to dismiss these desires as exactly the kind of abuse of law that ADR is meant to address. However, that view assumes that efficiency is the primary or even the sole value in dispute resolution. But judicial proceedings can serve symbolic and ceremonial functions which ought not be denied without reflection. This suggestion is not a new one;[62] none the less, it may be worthwhile to further illustrate the point by an anecdote concerning a family dispute (although not a marital dissolution) which reveals just these functions.

The details of this case come from a colleague who is a clinical law teacher and is, as it happens, very much interested in alternative dispute resolution. This colleague represented several members of the family of an elderly Hispanic woman who had recently died. The testator had left her entire estate, which was modest, to a niece who had spent time with her during the last years of her life. The descendant's daughters and grandchildren sought to set aside the will on the ground of undue influence. The lawyer for the contestants saw this as the kind of case which should be settled informally. The estate was small, the prospects for demonstrating undue influence were slight (as they usually are), and the hearing would be relatively complex. Moreover, it would be necessary for relatives on both sides to testify regarding their personal feelings, relations, and conduct. Accordingly, the attorney proposed various alternatives to litigation, including settlement or the services of a mediator to try to resolve the dispute.

Eventually, the clients rejected counsel's advice and the case went to court. Testimony was given and, at the end of the hearing, all of the contestants met and embraced each other. What became clear only after the trial was that the immediate relatives wanted very much to declare, out loud and in public, their love for and loyalty to their mother or grandmother. Their suit was not so much to overturn the will as to rebut an inference that the community might draw from it: that the daughters and granddaughters had abandoned this elderly and widely loved matriarch, coldly leaving her to the care of a more remote relative. The court proceeding provided them an opportunity for demonstrating to each other and to the community at large their compliance with familial obligation: an opportunity that would not have existed through informal settlement.

The most obvious point of this story is that trials serve purposes other than the efficient resolution of disputes. The story has another point as well. The contestants' attorney did not see the reason for the suit, although that lawyer is an extremely intelligent and sensitive clinical teacher and, moreover, a Hispanic from the kind of community in which this family lived. It is unlikely that any lawyer or mediator would have accurately interpreted the situation of these clients if this lawyer did not, and it is also unlikely that the clients themselves would be clear about what they sought. A due sense of modesty may require, therefore, that we not prohibit clients' access to courts, even if their conduct seems irrational, without greater confidence than we can claim about our capacity to understand the purposes that formal and public audience may serve for laymen.

Caveat and conclusion

The discussion to this point has focused on the questions of law and fact that we should seriously entertain before seeking to solve problems associated with out ongoing natural experiment in the law of marital dissolution by a second experiment in procedure. What has been said should not be taken as an indictment either of procedural reform in connection with domestic relations law or, most especially, of experimental approaches to legal reform. On the contrary, the principal concern is that both reform and experimentation be taken seriously and considered broadly.

With respect to the question of experimentation, we face an odd but none the less common situation in law: proposals for or even introduction of a potentially far-reaching programme which we choose not to regard as an experiment. By focusing on instrumental claims and seemingly adhering to conventional goals, the meaning and implications of reform are obscured rather than made the centre of attention. This strategy leaves us unable to adequately assess what we have undertaken.

It is true that some research on mediation has been done, but enough has been said here and elsewhere[63] to show its weaknesses. The few genuine experimental studies that have been attempted were seriously compromised by their essentially private character. As long as the experimental group is limited to persons who choose or are chosen to participate, it will be impossible to assume that they are representative of any larger population. Post-hoc studies suffer from the same problems of selection, and are complicated further by variations in all respects, from record-keeping to kinds of services delivered. Moreover, none of the research has frankly confronted either the substantive context in which divorce takes place or the questions of values associated with the proposed reforms.

Criticism of this kind is readily offered; solutions are more difficult to formulate. It may, however, be worth recalling an idea that Professor Donald Campbell floated (generally unsuccessfully) some years ago. He suggested that, as the Great Society moved ahead with its programs, it should be coupled with an 'experimenting society', on which

tries out proposed solutions to recurrent problems, which makes hard-headed multi-dimensional evaluations of the outcomes, and where the remedial efforts seems ineffective, goes on to other possible solutions. The focus will be on reality testing and persistence in seeking solutions to problems. The justifications of new programs will be in terms of the seriousness of the problem, not in the claims that we can know for certain in advance what therapy will work.[64]

From time to time, such notions have been adopted in connection with enterprises that are plainly recognized as major social experimentation[65] or where experimentation is explicitly foreseen.[66] Explicit and state-authorized experimentation is, of course, subject to constitutional and other limitations.[67] None the less, incorporating a rigorous experimental program for mediated or other methods of dispute resolution within marital dissolution procedures is neither clearly unethical nor clearly unconstitutional,[68] and is well worth serious examination.

Plainly, any research programme of this sort must attend to the kinds of issues raised above. Existing research has very usefully presented, even if it has not resolved, a number of these issues. It has also served the eminently valuable purpose of providing a target for criticism through which the existence of other issues, a number of which are suggested above, might be identified.

However, research by itself is not the only approach we should take to a serious social issue. For reasons suggested above, it is far from clear that any one procedural strategy will successfully resolve the problems inherent in family disputes. Interest in this approach should not, therefore, deflect inquiry from other issues that might also warrant pursuit. If, for example, we are committed to the belief that change in the procedures used for dissolutions will relieve the anger of spouses and the distress of children, that conviction might incline us not to review effects of the substantive divorce experiments presently in force. Such a failure would ignore the profound ways in which substantive revisions have affected the meaning of dissolution both during and after the divorce itself.

The same belief might lead us to avoid close examination of the procedure currently used for marital dissolutions. There is a tendency, particularly among some ADR advocates, to picture a world with two possibilities. In one corner, there is the traditional, contentious legal proceeding in which lawyers force their clients into the most adversarial position imaginable and then batter each other to the profit of nobody except the advocates themselves. This is the Dickensian view, whose pale reflection might perhaps be found in *L.A. Law*. In the other corner, we have the sensitive, non-contentious mediator who discovers the common ground between two parties who do not really hate each other and do not really want to fight the matter out. This is the ADR model.

The world is more complicated than this dichotomy suggests. As an empirical matter, the Dickensian view draws largely on stereotype and anecdotal experience. In fact, we know relatively little about how lawyers advise their clients.[69] A recent study of divorce lawyer–client interaction indicates that most divorce lawyers advised their clients to try to settle the full range of issues in the case and, indeed, sought to interpret the formally contentious aspect of legal proceedings in a way that encouraged them to accept settlement.[70] Indeed, it may be that divorce lawyers—far from promoting contention—are readier than their clients to define the ultimate goal of representation as the resolution of property and monetary issues and to exclude the emotional focus that clients bring to their marital dissolutions.[71]

Nor do current legal ethics require that divorce proceedings be waged as a war of annihilation. Ethical rules permit and perhaps encourage lawyers to raise with their clients questions and fairness and decency as well as questions of long-run economic consequences.[72] In no sense does professional responsibility demand that lawyers employ every imaginable discovery device or abuse opposing counsel and his or her client.

Although tactical delay may well serve the purposes of a client who is more powerful than his or her opponent, attorneys are not privileged to employ this strategy even if a client wishes it.[73]

It is also true that some lawyers will not accept these limitations and take the easier path: do what you think your client wants or what will best insulate you from subsequent criticism or even suit. But it is not necessary to follow this path; nor is it required as a normative matter.

Our current approach to marital dissolution is a remarkable social experiment with yet unknown meanings and consequences. Because of its importance, we should take this and other experiments associated with the breakup or, perhaps, the reformulation of families very seriously. We cannot assume that some relatively simple procedural solution to the economic and social consequences of dissolution waits only to be recognized; rather, the implications of this experiment need to be evaluated from a variety of perspectives and with as much clarity and imagination as we can muster.

Notes

1. See, e.g., S. Goldberg, E. Green, & F. Sander, *Dispute Resolution* (1985) at 314; Silberman & Schepard, 'Consultants' Comments on the New York State Law Revision Commission Recommendation on the Child Dispute Resolution Process', 19 Column. J.L. & Soc. Probs. 399, 400 (1985).

2. See, e.g., S. Goldberg, E. Green, & F. Sander, *supra* at 314.

3. See, e.g., Folberg, 'Divorce Mediation—Promises and Problems', in S. Goldberg, E. Green, & F. Sander,*supra*, at 317–18; 'Recommendation', *supra*, at 123–24. *Recommendation of the Law Revision Commission to the 1985 Legislature Relating to the Child-Custody Decision-Making Process*, 20 Colum. J.L. & Soc. Probs. 05 (1985).

4. See, e.g., S. Goldberg, E. Green, & F. Sander, *supra*; 'Recommendation', *supra* 124; Silberman & Schepard, *supra* at 400–02.

5. Pearson & Thoennes, 'Divorce Mediation: An Overview of Research Results', 19 Colum. J.L. & Soc. Probs. 451, 477–9 (1985); 'Recommendation', *supra*, at 126–27.

6. Pearson, Thoennes & VanderKooi, 'Mediation of Contested Child Custody Disputes', 11 Colo. Law. 336 (1982).

7. For a discussion of the relationship between the claims of helping professionals and the movement toward mediation, see Fineman, 'Dominant Discourse, Professional Language, and Legal Change in Child Custody Decisionmaking', 101 Harv. L. Rev. 727 (1988).

8. See, e.g., Pearson & Thoennes, 'Mediating and Litigating Custody Disputes:

A Longitudinal Evaluation', 17 Fam. L.Q. 497 (1984); O. J. Coogler, *Structured Mediation in Divorce Settlement*, 7–8 (1978).

9. See *supra* text accompanying note 3.

10. Mnookin & Kornhauser, 'Bargaining in the Shadow of the Law: The Case of Divorce', 88 Yale L.J. 950, 954–6 (1979); Hansen, 'The Role and Rights of Children in Divorce Actions', 6 J. Fam. L. 1, 2 (1966).

11. See, e.g., Uniform Marriage and Divorce Act § 306(b): 'In a proceeding for dissolution of marriage or for legal separation, the terms of the separation agreement, *except those providing for the support, custody, and visitation of children*, are binding upon the court . . .' (emphasis supplied). Similarly, a number of courts have refused to enforce provisions in separation agreements calling for arbitration of custodial issues. See Wertlake v. Wertlake, 127 N.J. Super. 595, 318 A.2d 446 (Ch. Div. 1974), *rev'd on other grounds*, 137 N.J. Super. 476, 349 A.2d 552 (App. Div. 1975); Holman & Noland, 'Agreement and Arbitration: Relief to Over-Litigation in Domestic Relations Disputes in Washington', 12 Willamette L.J. 527 (1976). But see Sheets v. Sheets, 22 A.D.2d 176, 254 N.Y.S.2d 320 (1964) (no clear reason for refusing to accept arbitration awards regarding custody); Comment, 'The Enforceability of Arbitration Clauses in North Carolina Separation Agreements', 15 Wake Forest L. Rev. 487 (1979).

12. Lederer & Jackson, 'The Mirages of Marriage', 14 (1969), quoted in H. Irving, *Divorce Mediation: A Rational Alternative to the Adversary System*, 24 (1981).

13. In a recent article, Professor Fineman contrasts this shift of focus with traditional family law policy. Fineman, *supra* note 7 at 732. It is worth adding that an approach which seeks to reconstruct the family upon divorce also contradicts central assumptions of modern divorce policy in areas other than custody. Certainly the principal thrust of current theories of property division and spousal maintenance, and especially the modern animus against alimony as a form of pension, is to terminate the family relationship upon divorce as sharply as possible.

We are not, however, entirely convinced that a shift of this sort is undesirable or that it entails a commitment to joint custody or any other custodial arrangement. Even on a conventional concern for the child's best interests, it would still be necessary to believe that joint custody typically best serves those interests: a position far from adequately demonstrated. See *infra* text accompanying notes 20–24. But it might also be possible to conclude that the position of the mother after divorce should reflect her commitment during the marriage, just because divorce itself should not be regarded as creating an entirely new set of relationships. Accordingly, and without need for a new inquiry into the child's best interests, a mother who (with the father's explicit or implicit agreement) has defined herself *during* marriage in terms of child care should be entitled to carry out that construction of her identity after the marriage has ended.

14. Pearson & Thoennes, 'Mediating and Litigating Custody Disputes: A

Longitudinal Evaluation', 17 Fam. L.Q. 497, 506 (1984). See also Pearson & Thoennes, 'Divorce Mediation: An Overview of Research Results', 19 Colum. J.L. & Soc. Probs. 451, 462 (1985); Pearson, Thoennes & VanderKooi, *supra* note 6, at 3242.

15. See K. Kressel, *The Process of Divorce*, 186 (1985).

16. This was true of the Denver Custody Mediation Project and of a number of non-experimental projects whose data have been incorporated into analyses of mediation. The attrition rate has been very high: about 50% of those offered such services have declined them. See Pearson & Thoennes, *supra* note 14, at 500–02.

17. Id. at 507.

18. J. Haynes, *Divorce Mediation*, 34 (1981); see also Coombs, 'Noncourt-Connected Mediation and Counseling in Child-Custody Disputes', 17 Fam. L.Q. 469, 479–80 (1984).

19. Whether they approve or not. Cf. Pearson & Thoennes, *supra* note 5, at 462–63 (favourable) and Johnson, 'Custody Mediation Is Proposed', *N.Y. Times*, 25 Apr. 1985, at C12, col. 3 (expressing concern about preference for joint custody).

20. See, e.g., Abarbanel, 'Shared Parenting After Separation and Divorce: A Study of Joint Custody', 49: 2 *Am. J. Orthopsychiatry*, 320 (1979) (four families); Steinman, 'The Experience of Children in a Joint-Custody Arrangement: A Report of a Study', 51 *Am. J. Orthopsychiatry*, 403 (1981) (thirty-two children in 24 families); D. Luepnitz, *Child Custody: A Study of Families After Divorce* (1982) (eighteen joint custodial parents in eleven arrangements).

21. The families studied by Abarbanel and Steinman, *supra* note 20, were voluntary joint custody arrangements. The families studied by Luepnitz, *supra* note 20, did include instances of court-ordered joint custody. It seems fair to say that, to this point, most research involves 'almost exclusively middle class parents who were early joint custody enthusiasts and whose agreements were self-initiated'. Scott & Derdyn, 'Rethinking Joint Custody', 45 Ohio St. L.J. 455, 484 (1984).

22. In most studies, the effects of joint custody are determined entirely by parent interviews. For a review, see Scott & Derdyn, *supra* note 21, at 485–86.

23. Comment, 'Joint Custody: An Alternative for Divorced Parents', 26 UCLA L. Rev. 1084, 1116–17 (1979); Kelly, 'Further Observations on Joint Custody', 16 U.C.D. L. Rev. 762, 763 (1983); Trombetta, 'Joint Custody: Recent Research and Overloaded Courtrooms Inspire New Solutions to Custody Disputes', 19 J. Fam. L. 213, 231–2 (1981).

24. See, e.g., Skoloff, 'Joint Custody: A Jaundiced View', Trial 52, 53, (Mar. 1984).

25. See Scott & Derdyn, *supra* note 21, at 462, and sources cited therein.

26. See *supra* text accompanying note 21; *A/B.A. Report on Child Support, Custody and Visitation* (1985) (suggesting that 'graymailing' is common in states where joint custody is in effect).

27. State court caseload studies clearly reveal the increase in divorce and other family cases over time. A study of dockets in two counties in California between 1890 and 1970 indicates that family cases made up 18% of the docket in one county and 19% in the other during 1890. By 1970, these proportions had risen to 52% and 62% respectively. Friedman & Percival, 'A Tale of Two Courts: Litigation in Alameda and San Benito Counties', 10 Law & Soc'y Rev. 267, 281–2 (Tables 3 and 4) (1976). By contrast, property cases fell from about one-quarter of court business in these counties to less than 4% over the same time period. Id. A similar pattern appears in a study of the civil docket of the St. Louis Circuit Court between 1820 and 1970. Family law and estate cases made up none of the docket in 1820, about 14% in 1865, and 46% of the docket in 1970. McIntosh, '150 Years of Litigation and Dispute Settlement: A Court Tale', 15 Law & Soc. Rev. 823, 829 (Table 2) (1980–1).
28. See, e.g., Pearson & Thoennes, 'Mediating and Litigating Custody Disputes: A Longitudinal Evaluation', 17 Fam. L.Q. 497 (1984).
29. Current estimates place the contest rate at about 10%. E.g., Foster & Freed, 'Divorce in the Fifty States: An Overview', 14 Fam. L.Q. 4, 229 (1980); Levy, 'Comment on the Pearson–Thoennes Study and on Mediation', 17 Fam. L.Q. 525, 530 (1984).
30. The St. Louis caseload study indicates that about two-thirds of divorce cases were resolved by contested judgment during the period studied. McIntosh, *supra* note 27, at 843, Figure 3.
31. Frank, Berman, & Mazur-Hart, 'No Fault Divorce and the Divorce Rate: The Nebraska Experience—An Interrupted Time Series Analysis and Commentary', 58 Neb. L. Rev. 1, 55 (1978). The average length of hearings statewide was only 16 minutes. Similar lengths were found for a study of Iowa dissolution proceedings (15–20 minutes). Sass, 'The Iowa No Fault Dissolution of Marriage Law in Action', 18 S.D.L. Rev. 629, 650 (1973).
32. Pearson & Thoennes, 'Mediation and Divorce: The Benefits Outweigh the Costs', 4 Fam. Advoc. 26, 32 (1982) [hereinafter 'Benefits'].
33. Id. at 31.
34. See Pearson & Thoennes, *supra* note 5, at 477.
35. 'Benefits', *supra* note 32, at 29.
36. Pearson & Thoennes, 'Mediating and Litigating Custody Disputes: A Longitudinal Evaluation', 497, 507 (1984).
37. Id.
38. Levy, 'Comment on the Pearson–Thoennes Study and on Mediation', 17 Fam. L.W. 525, 530 (1984).
39. Id.
40. The authors describe the latter group as only 'slightly less enthusiastic' because most members of that group also indicated that they would recommend mediation to a friend (81%) and would mediate again (64%). It is a matter of judgement whether these are as important indicators of 'satisfaction'

with mediation as are the results of the question directly addressing that issue.

41. See Pearson & Thoennes, *supra* note 28, at 519, Table II.

42. 'The problem [of validity] is compounded in some studies (such as the DCMP) by providing mediation gratis, while the traditional approach employing lawyers is expensive. The placebo effect is especially likely to contaminate attitudinal measures, such as general satisfaction, which are precisely the ones which have yielded some of the most impressive evidence in mediation's favor.' See K. Kressel, *supra* note 15, at 191.

43. Id. at 187.

44. Id.

45. See Pearson & Thoennes, *supra* note 28, at 505.

46. Id. at 466.

47. See, e.g., Lerman, 'Mediation of Wife Abuse Cases: The Adverse Impact of Informal Dispute Resolution on Women', 7 Harv. Women's L.J. 57 (1984); J. Avner & S. Heiman, *Divorce Mediation: A Guide for Women* (NOW Legal Defense and Education Fund, Inc., 1984).

48. See Pearson & Thoennes, *supra* note 5, at 468.

49. See 'Recommendation', *supra* note 3, at 119. This is a common enough claim among proponents of the mediation. O. J. Coogler, in the dedication to his book, *Structured Mediation in Divorce Settlement* (1978), at v, says: 'I am indebted to my former wife and the two attorneys who represented us in our divorce for making me aware of the critical need for a more rational, more civilized way of arranging a parting of the ways. Her life, my life, and our children's lives were unnecessarily embittered by that experience.'

50. 'Recommendation', *supra* note 3, at 119.

51. W. Gellhorn, *Children and Families int he Courts of New York City*, 308 (1954).

52. See 'Recommendation', *supra* note 3, at 120 n.51.

53. Jacobs, 'The Effect of Divorce on Fathers: An Overview of the Literature', 139 *Am. J. Orthopsychiatry*, 1235 (1982).

54. See Wallerstein, *The Overburdened Child: Some Long-Term Consequences of Divorce*, 19 Colum. J.L. & Soc. Probs. 165 (1985).

55. See *supra* text accompanying note 48.

56. The data on fairness reported in mediation studies deals only with *perceptions* of fairness and, moreover, with perceptions concerning the process.

57. Neutrality is the crucial aspect of the mediator's role. See, e.g. 'Recommendation', *supra* note 3, at 123: 'Mediation injects into a dispute a neutral third party whose role is to work with the parties to develop a mutually agreeable settlement. . . .'

   The role of 'the lawyer to the situation', which had some of the characteristics of mediation, was advocated by Brandeis; it was, ultimately, one of the charges of impropriety raised against him at his confirmation hearing. For an evaluation of the difficulties of that role, see Frank, 'The Legal Ethics of Louis D. Brandeis', 17 Stan. L. Rev. 683 (1965).

58. For one clear example of the presence of values that are not necessarily associated with partisanship, recall the preference for continuing relationships and joint custody in particular held by a number of proponents of mediation. See *supra* text accompanying note 9.

59. A set of standards for practice by lawyers acting as mediators has recently been approved by the House of Delegates of the American Bar Association. 'Standards of Practice for Lawyer Mediators in Family Disputes', 18 Fam. L.Q. 363 (1984). These standards emphasize requirements of training, experience, and temperament, respect for voluntariness, and maintenance of a neutral role by the lawyer-mediator. They appear to assume, however, that neutrality in the sense of non-alignment is the same thing as value-neutrality, and the latter issue never receives mention.

60. See *supra* note 8 and sources cited therein.

61. In many jurisdictions, even a divorce action founded on allegations of incompatibility may be resisted by a spouse who wishes to preserve the marriage. See *In re* Marriage of Mitchell, 545 S.W.2d 313, 314 (Mo. Ct. App. 1976).

62. See, e.g., Abel, 'Redirecting Social Studies of Law', 14 Law & Soc'y Rev. 804, 821 (1980).

63. See, e.g., K. Kressel, *The Process of Divorce*, ch. 9 (1985); Levy, 'Comment on the Pearson–Thoennes Study and on Mediation', 17 Fam. L.Q. 525 (1984).

64. D. Campbell, 'Application for a Grant to Support Research on Methods for the Experimenting Society', submitted to the Russell Sage Foundation, 1970. See Campbell, 'Reforms as Experiments', 24 Am. Psychologist 409 (1969).

65. The New Jersey negative income tax experiment, for example. See Kershaw & Small, 'Data Confidentiality and Privacy: Lessons from the New Jersey Negative Income Tax Experiment', 20 Pub. Pol'y 257 (1972).

66. For example, the 'demonstration projects' provision of the Social Security Act gives broad power to the secretary of the Department of Health and Human Services to authorize state agencies to carry out projects at variance with ordinary requirements. The relevant provision is 42 U.S.C. §1315 (1982). Any experimental, pilot, or demonstration project conducted under this authority must be 'likely to assist in promoting the objectives [of the Social Security Act plan which is the subject of the experiment]'. Id. Pursuant to this provision, experiments requiring co-payment by groups of Medicaid recipients and registration for training and employment for certain families receiving Aid for Families with Dependent Children have been undertaken and upheld against legal attack by lower federal courts. California Welfare Rights Organization *v.* Richardson, 348 F. Supp. 491 (N.D. Cal. 1972) (co-payment plan); Aguayo *v.* Richardson, 352 F. Supp. 462 (S.D.N.Y. 1972), *aff'd as modified*, 473 F.2d 1090 (2d Cir. 1973) (employment plan).

67. See generally Teitelbaum, 'Spurious, Tractable, and Intractable Legal Problems: A Positivist Approach to Law and Social Science Research', in

Solutions to Ethical and Legal Problems in Social Research, 11 (R. Boruch & J. Cecil (eds.), 1983).

68. See id. at 36–45 for a review of some of the legal and ethical issues.
69. Sarat & Felstiner, 'Law and Strategy in the Divorce Lawyer's Office', 20 Law & Soc'y Rev. 93, 94 (1986).
70. Id. at 109.
71. Id. at 132. Obviously this observation is not restricted to divorce lawyers. The impetus towards settlement has been routinely observed in connection with public defender practice as well. See, e.g., Blumberg, 'The Practice of Law as a Confidence Game', 1 Law & Soc'y Rev. 15 (1967).
72. See, e.g., *American Bar Association, Model Rules of Professional Conduct* Rule 2.1 (1983): 'In representing a client, a lawyer shall exercise independent professional judgment and render candid advice. In rendering advice, a lawyer may refer not only to law but to other considerations such as moral, economic, social and political factors, that may be relevant to the client's situation.' The Comment to that rule observes that 'Advice couched in narrowly legal terms may be of little value to a client, especially where practical considerations, such as cost or effects on other people, are predominant. . . . It is proper for a lawyer to refer to relevant moral and ethical considerations in giving advice.' Ethical Consideration 7–8 of the *American Bar Association, Model Code of Professional Responsibility* takes the same position.
73. See *American Bar Association, Model Rules of Professional Conduct* Rule 3.2 and Commentary (1983); C. Wolfram, *Modern Legal Ethics*, 600 (1986). It is, of course, true that the line between legitimate and illegitimate advantage is sometimes hard to draw and that compliance with the rule depends greatly on the integrity of individual lawyers. None the less, some efforts to control harassment have been undertaken. Perhaps the most familiar is the relatively strict standard of diligence and good faith required by the 1983 amendment to Federal Rule of Civil Procedure 11 (concerning pleadings, 16(f) (pretrial conferences), and 26 (discovery). These rules also direct trial courts to impose sanctions on an offending party, that party's lawyer, or both in case of violation.

6.3 Divorce Mediation—The Virtues of Formality?*

ROBERT DINGWALL
AND DAVID GREATBATCH

This is not an essay about findings so much as about issues and policy in mediation, particularly in the context of divorce. It grows out of a programme of work which now reaches back almost ten years and which has been described in a number of published accounts (see Bibliography). A recurrent finding has been the extent to which mediators' control of the process gives them great resources to influence outcomes. It has led us to question the common claim of mediators to offer clients a service which gives them more scope for self-determination and is more empowering than traditional adversarial methods of resolving disputes. Recently, we have been trying to test our own claims by looking specifically for points in our corpus, of about 140 hours of material from 10 very different sites, where clients successfully influence mediators. We have not been able to locate more than a handful of these. Where they do occur, what is striking is the ability of mediators to change the direction of their talk in full flight and to incorporate client interventions into their own preferred strategy for the session. We must emphasize that our comments are not directed at any lack of skill on the part of mediators: indeed we are frequently consumed with admiration for the subtlety and sophistication of their interactional competence. Nevertheless, we continue to be concerned about the lack of accountability and regulation evident in mediation practice. In traditional sociological language, what we are seeing is an exercise of power. The question is how that might be turned into authority, the legitimate and legitimated use of power (Weber 1947).

There are clearly some powerful forces promoting mediation and some important arguments in its favour. In particular, it seems to be

*An earlier version of this paper was presented at the Annual Meeting of the UK Socio-Legal Studies Association, Exeter, March 1993. We are grateful to Mavis Maclean for organizing the panel and to the audience on that occasion, particularly Carol Smart and Fran Wasoff, for their helpful suggestions.

potentially a less costly way of dealing with the rising volume of divorce cases in all Western societies, although, as a number of commentators have pointed out, it may also indicate the priority attached to family matters that governments see this jurisdiction as a particular target for cuts in public expenditure. We also have some sympathy with the idea that families are likely to be better informed about their own circumstances than any external agency and that it is desirable that they should be given every opportunity to make use of this in trying to produce a privately-ordered settlement. We recognize, though, that unregulated private ordering is likely to result in the systematic disadvantaging of parties with limited private or public resources, normally women and children. Again, it is perhaps worth emphasizing that, although we have been and continue to be critical of significant aspects of mediation *practice*, we do not reject the *principles*. We too would like to see a low-cost, accessible dispute resolution service which helps families to produce agreements that respect their individual needs and circumstances. However, the problems of professional power do not disappear merely because the professionals involved are psychosocial specialists rather than lawyers or judges.

We are, however, increasingly conscious that to be critical is not enough. How can research on the social interaction between mediators and their clients lead to positive proposals for practice that will strengthen its accountability?

In thinking about this question, we have been strongly influenced by an important but rather neglected paper by Max Atkinson (1982) in which he tries to understand what is accomplished by formality in social interaction. His argument starts from the importance of the formal/informal distinction in sociological writings. It is one of the commonest rhetorical contrasts employed in the literature. In fact, he suggests, this is a borrowing from lay discourses, from a distinction made by ordinary people in their everyday analyses of the social worlds through which they are moving. The distinction has become increasingly evident in recent years. To describe something as formal is often to express a criticism, while the description of an encounter or an institution as informal carries a positive connotation. These are not objective qualities—we may equate formality with good order and informality with chaos in some contexts, but these tend to be exceptional.

From this observation, Atkinson is led to propose two questions:

- What is it that leads actions to be recognized as formal?
- What are these features actually doing interactionally?

Formal interaction is distinguished from everyday conversation by a set of detailed variations in its production which allow participants and observers to recognize that they are involved a special kind of occasion. These may include variations in elements like turntaking rules, topical and thematic management, opening and closing sequences. Atkinson argues, however, that these differences are neither arbitrary nor accidental. They have been produced by the participants in attempting to solve particular kinds of interactional problem. They are not simply ceremonial or rhetorical, but deeply functional for the accomplishment of certain social tasks. The sociologist's objective must be to understand these functions, rather than simply to parrot lay criticisms in more arcane language.

Atkinson's particular target is the kind of courtroom ethnography which asserts that all variations from everyday conversational behaviour are designed to confuse, bewilder, harass, or oppress the unfortunate victims of the trial process. He argues that many features of courtroom interaction, and by implication other symbolic communication in this site, can be better and more economically understood as practical solutions to an interactional problem, namely the maintenance of shared attentiveness in a multi-party setting. In ordinary conversation, turntaking provides a motive for attentiveness. The fact that we may be required to speak, in a way which articulates sensibly with what has gone before, leads us to listen. We are likely to be able to trade on some kind of background knowledge of the other party or to have ready access to ways of checking our understanding of their talk, or their of ours, without disturbing the general flow of the interaction or the accomplishment of whatever objective we may be trying to achieve. In a multi-party setting, many of these assumptions break down. The likelihood of being required to take the next turn is so remote that the order may be undermined by the development of side involvements, the diversion of attention from the main business, or the break-out of other talk and activities. Many of the allegedly oppressive features of courtroom design and behaviour function as solutions to this problem.

To give just three specific examples:

- Turn allocation. Courts use a mixture of pre-allocation and orchestration (Dingwall 1981) to order talk. This solves problems like the invisibility of pre-vocal beginning markers, such as an exchange of glances or a clearing of the throat, which catch another's attention as a prelude to engaging them in conversation. In English courts, the command to rise

terminates the various side-involvements and focuses attention on the bench area from whence the business will be initiated.
- Speaker identification and visibility. Courts are loaded with identification details—location of participants, dress, wigs, etc.—which serve to identify the roles being taken, even if the individuals have never been in that particular court before.
- Pace variation. Courtroom talk is slowed by the judge's notetaking, which facilitates everyone's access to its content. The judge monitors the intelligibility of the talk, which can occasionally give rise to comic results!

There is a problem of teleology about all functionalist arguments: just because something has evolved in a particular way, this does not mean it was intended to serve its current function or that it is the best of all possible solutions to the problem it is assumed to solve. Atkinson is certainly at pains to stress that his analysis does not exclude the possibility of other solutions to the problem of shared attentiveness. Some aspects of the ceremonial order of the British courtroom are almost certainly communicatively redundant, although they may have been important at a time when the client population was less literate or familiar with the scenes through media depictions. However, this analysis does open up an interesting line of thought in challenging us to consider whether formal features of talk and social organization have a positive role to play in making certain sorts of activity possible at all before we move to condemn them as mystifications.

The analysis is particularly relevant to mediation because of the way this is treated as a paradigm of informal justice. To listen to mediation practitioners talk, it is often as if the ideal session is experienced by clients as if it were a round-table conversation in their own home. The mediator merely acts as a facilitator to encourage this conversation, providing an environment where people can work out their own problems in their own way.

As the evidence accumulates, from our own research and from people like Rifkin and Cobb and Forester on the use of mediation in other settings, this view is becoming harder to defend. Another picture is being painted, of the insidious and unaccountable power of mediators in the way that they *frame* and *orchestrate* the interaction.

Our proposal, then, is that one way to approach this as a policy issue may be through a more careful consideration of what formality achieves in courts. If we abandon the negative stereotypes of court processes which have often been erected by advocates of mediation, we may be able to identify interactional solutions to organizational problems which suggest possible models for mediation practice. What might these be?

Reflecting his background in the development of conversation analysis, Atkinson's stress is on formality as a solution to an important interactional problem, sustaining a single focus of attention in a large and disparate group over a lengthy period of time. We would extend this argument, though, to suggest that formality is not just about co-ordinating talk but, in the courtroom setting, is also constitutive of the process of doing justice through talk. It is, in other words, strongly implicated in the court being seen, or perhaps better, being *heard* to do justice. The formal structures do not just provide for the co-ordination of talk but also provide for the work that gets done through the talk.

Mediation is not a pure example of the multi-party settings described by Atkinson. In some respects, particularly in the identities ascribed to the participants and the ecology of the settings under which it occurs, it is much closer to the dyadic settings of mundane conversation. This, in a way, is what makes it so dangerous. The people involved, whether as parties or mediators, assume that the consensual, self-regulatory procedures of ordinary conversation will be sufficient to ensure a just and equitable process and outcome. As sociologists have recognized for most of this century, though, triads, like most mediation sessions, represent a step change from dyads. They are far more like n-party encounters in terms of the problems of turn allocation, topic control, and thematic unity and checking out. That is why orchestration and framing take on such importance.

In the adversarial process, turn allocation is not just a motivator of attention. It is also a move within a moral economy of talk. This aspect of conversational analysis is not commonly highlighted but is one of the most significant elements of its approach. The production of the right sort of talk at the right sort of place is not simply a matter of skill but can also be a matter of obligation. To fail to produce an appropriate next turn can call into question one's competence as a human actor. Goffman puts it more sharply when he talks of Felicity's Condition, the production of an utterance which is so appropriately linked to its total environment that it does not disconfirm the hearer's assumptions about our sanity. In this case the distribution of turns is not just a distribution of rights to talk but also of duties to listen. In the environment of a court the duty to listen is rigorously enforced by the prohibition of side-interactions and the placement of the judge in such a way as to be able to observe and admonish any breaches of this duty. There is an elaborate and visible turn taking system which provides a public display of the assignment of rights and duties at particular times and a basis for sanctioning severe or persistent breaches of the focus on the task in hand.

The content of the talk is similarly circumscribed by an elaborate body of rules, called the rules of evidence, which can be invoked to define what may legitimately be talked about by whom. These function as what sociologists of language would describe as rules of relevance, the participants' understanding of what it takes for talk to be seen as coherent and connected. In many contexts, for example, participants in a conversation will jointly adopt recognizable patterns of interaction to manage changes in the immediate topic or in the overall theme of the conversation so that the transition can be made to appear more or less seamless. Sudden changes in topic or theme can lead to demands for special justification. In courts, however, the production of coherence in the examination of a witness, for example, is not a co-production between the witness and the examining counsel, but between the counsel for each side. A witness who challenges an abrupt shift of topic is likely to be directed simply to answer the question. It is only the other counsel or possibly the judge who can ask for an explanation of the way in which one question might be connected to its predecessor or the reason why the examination has now taken up a different line.

Rules of relevance also characteristically provide for the moral tenor of an encounter, the characters and motives that can properly be ascribed to each other by the participants. An important element of courtroom interaction is its strong commitment to surface courtesy among the regular participants. 'M'learned friend' is never called a fool and a scoundrel in public. No judge, even one who is present only through the pages of the Law Reports, makes a mistake as opposed to misdirecting himself. The enforcement of this moral order is another aspect of the judge's management of the interaction in the courtroom, backed up by the law of contempt and the professional codes of the various occupations represented in the setting.

The point is that in a court hearing the framing of the talk and its orchestration are made visible. In a sense this is precisely what formality *is*, the availability of an explicit body of rules and procedures for the management of the event and for the definition of an arbiter or enforcer to interpret and apply the rules in the particular circumstances of *that* occasion. The source of power is clearly evident, as is its transmutation into authority by the disciplining force of the body of rules and procedures.

All the participants can see the flow of power and develop their strategies accordingly, whether in alignment or in opposition to it. In mediation, by contrast, these are precisely the things which the neo-conversational style tends to blur and conceal. Informality creates an opportunity for abusive and oppressive interventions by denying the sources of the mediators' power. Indeed its regulation becomes a non-issue. It is reduced to a matter of the individual ethics of the mediator, the claim to 'trust us' which has come to be treated with increasing and deserved scepticism when made by other professionals. Leaving things to professional ethics risks becoming little more than a warrant for allowing the covert imposition of one group's values where *caveat emptor* does not apply.

An understanding of the functions of formality, however, may provide us with a basis for the regulation of practice through specific requirements of the forms of talk used. This is not, it must be stressed, an argument *for* the adversarial process. It is an argument for learning *from* the adversarial process. What specific recommendations might emerge? At this time, we have only just begun to think through our data in these terms. However, a few things stand out immediately.

- Make the framing of the session more visible. This involves giving particular attention to the design of any preparatory literature which is given to clients and to the establishment of a practice of opening sessions with a 'mediator monologue' which explains the framing rules, particular those relating to legitimate topics, ascriptions of character, turntaking, and so on and which sets out the role of the mediator in enforcing these: 'If anybody starts doing X, I shall do Y'.
- Adopt and implement special turntaking rules. The literature has drawn attention to the problem of the person who gets to tell their story of the conflict in second place.[1] He or she often feels constrained to construct a reply to the first story-teller, which may undercut the integrity of the case that could be made. This problem needs to be confronted so that each party has an opportunity to make an opening statement uninterrupted by the other and the second party has their attention drawn to their structurally disadvantaged position and is helped to present the story they would have told had they gone first. Only then should the mediator allow the parties to explore the ways in which they can influence each other's views in the hope of producing a jointly acceptable story.
- No invisible knowledge. If a mediator is aware that a proposed agreement is likely to be unacceptable to a court or cuts across the legal

interests of a party, then the mediator should state this explicitly rather than using the procedures we have described to derail or steer negotiations in particular directions without acknowledging the basis for this intervention. Similarly, if a mediator is relying on expert knowledge of child welfare to encourage particular arrangements for custody or visitation (residence and contact in England), the parties should be told in so many words.

- At the conclusion of the session, there should be no 'invisible ending'. If letters are to be written about an agreement, they should be written by the parties, with the mediator ready to advise on drafting.

None of these are remarkable innovations and you will find some mediators in some places doing most of them. What we are arguing is that all mediators, or certainly those operating under public sponsorship, should be expected to do all of them. The result will undoubtedly be more formal: it should, however, provide the basis of a more uniform service, which is an important concern in any publicly sponsored programme. It will certainly be a service which offers fewer opportunities for clients to be treated in oppressive ways, without recognizing that this is occurring and what, if anything, they can do about it.

Note

1. I should perhaps explain that I am using the word 'story' in a technical sense here as a generic way of describing the participants' various versions of what might be said about the past, present, and future of the dispute. I do not mean to imply that it is either true or false, although it is certainly carefully fabricated, or that it has to be concerned with the past.

Bibliography

As a result of ill-health, I have had to write this more quickly than I planned so that the usual scholarly apparatus is rather truncated. The main reference is to Atkinson, J. M. (1982) 'Understanding Formality', *British Journal of Sociology*, 33, 86–117. The approach draws fairly generally on Goffman and on conversation analysis and the sources should be fairly obvious to anyone who knows the tradition and our previous work. The essay does not, however, presume a detailed knowledge of this literature. A full bibliography of our own work follows for anyone who is interested in following up the evidential basis of the findings stated in here.

ROBERT DINGWALL, 'Some Observations on Divorce Mediation in Britain and the United States', *Mediation Quarterly* 11 (March 1986), 5–24.

ROBERT DINGWALL and JOHN EEKELAAR (eds.), *Divorce Mediation and the Legal Process: British Practice and International Experience* (Oxford University Press, Oxford, 1988).

includes

ROBERT DINGWALL, 'Empowerment or Enforcement? Some questions about Power and Control in Divorce Mediation'.

JOHN EEKELAAR and ROBERT DINGWALL, 'The Development of Conciliation in England'.

ROBERT DINGWALL and JOHN EEKELAAR, 'Divorce Procedure: A wider vision?'.

ROBERT DINGWALL and ADRIAN JAMES, 'Family Law and the Psycho-social Professions: Welfare Officers in the English County Courts', *Law in Context* 6, 1 (1988), 61–73.

ROBERT DINGWALL, 'Research in the UK', in *Proceedings of the Transatlantic Conference on Family Conciliation, 27–28 May 1986, London* (National Family Conciliation Council, Swindon, 1987).

ADRIAN JAMES and ROBERT DINGWALL, 'Social Work Ideologies in the Probation Service: The Case of Civil Work', *Journal of Social Welfare Law* (1989), 323–38.

DAVID GREATBATCH and ROBERT DINGWALL, 'Selective Facilitation: Some Preliminary Observations on a Strategy Used by Divorce Mediators', *Law and Society Review*, 23, 4 (1989), 613–41. Reprinted in an edited and abridged form in *Family and Conciliation Courts Review*, 28, 1 (1990), 53–64.

ROBERT DINGWALL, 'Divorce Mediation: A Case Study in the Application of Frame Analysis', in Kurczewski, J., and Czynczyk, A. A., *Family, Gender and Body in Law and Society Today* (Sociology of Custom and Law Department, Institute of Applied Social Sciences, University of Warsaw, 1990).

ROBERT DINGWALL and DAVID GREATBACH, 'Behind Closed Doors: A Preliminary Report on Mediator/Client Interaction in England', *Family and Conciliation Courts Review*, 29, 3 (1991), 291–303.

DAVID GREATBACH and ROBERT DINGWALL, 'The Interactive Construction of Interventions by Divorce Mediators', in Folger, J. P., and Jones, T. S. (eds.), *Third Parties and Conflict: Communication Research and Perspectives* (Sage, Newbury Park, CA).